*Praise for Victor Sebestyen's*

# 1946

"Sebestyen is a witty storyteller with a wide-ranging intellect. . . . [*1946*] is liberally peppered with fascinating asides and anecdotes that humanize its subjects. . . . An appealing introduction, aimed at a wide audience, to events that continue to shape global affairs."  —*Kirkus Reviews*

"[An] informed, engaging, and accessible history of the year that U.S. president Harry Truman called the year of decisions. . . . With mesmerizing detail and riveting vignettes scattered throughout, Sebestyen explores virtually every major postwar theme and event."  —*Publishers Weekly*

"Sebestyen chronicles crucial events of 1946 in this outstanding work. The author does not shy away from the explicit and heartbreaking details in creating a powerful and readable account of this challenging year. Highly recommended for anyone interested in world history or for those seeking to understand why the world is as it is today."  —*Library Journal*

"Cogently argued and gripping, global in scale . . . this is a groundbreaking book, as well as a thoroughly good read."  —Andrew Roberts, *The Mail on Sunday* (London)

"An exceptionally involving and horrifying book. . . . Grindingly awful detail."  —Sam Leith, *The Spectator* (London)

# VICTOR SEBESTYEN

# 1946

Victor Sebestyen was born in Budapest. Newspapers he has worked for include *The Times* (London), the *Daily Mail*, and the *London Evening Standard*. Sebestyen has written for many American publications, including *The New York Times*. He was an associate editor at *Newsweek*.

www.victorsebestyen.com

## ALSO BY VICTOR SEBESTYEN

*Revolution 1989: The Fall of the Soviet Empire*
*Twelve Days: The Story of the 1956 Hungarian Revolution*

# 1946

The Making of the Modern World

VICTOR SEBESTYEN

VINTAGE BOOKS
A Division of Penguin Random House LLC
New York

FIRST VINTAGE BOOKS EDITION, NOVEMBER 2016

*Copyright © 2014 by Victor Sebestyen*

Grateful acknowledgment is made for permission to reprint lyrics from "Don't Let's Be Beastly to the Germans" by Noël Coward, copyright © 1943 by NC Aventales AG. Reprinted by permission of Alan Brodie Representation Ltd. and Bloomsbury Methuen Drama, an imprint of Bloomsbury Publishing Plc.

The Library of Congress has cataloged the Pantheon edition as follows:
Sebestyen, Victor.
1946 : the making of the modern world / Victor Sebestyen.
pages ; cm
Includes bibliographical references and index.
1. World politics—1945–1955.  2. Nineteen forty-six, A.D.  I. Title.
D843.S365 2015  909.82'4—dc23  2015014902

**Vintage Books Trade Paperback ISBN: 978-1-101-91028-3**
**eBook ISBN: 978-1-101-87043-3**

*Author photograph © Stacey Mutkin*

www.vintagebooks.com

Printed in the United States of America

*To Paul Diggory and Wendy Franks*

# Contents

# Illustrations

Tokyo: people queue to collect their cigarette ration (© The LIFE
Picture Collection / Getty Images)

MacArthur returns to Manila (© Getty Images)

The Bikini Atoll bomb: the Atomic Age (© SuperStock)

Insert following page 280

General George Marshall and Zhou Enlai (© Gamma-Keystone /
Getty Images)

Mao Zedong (© Underwood Photo Archives / SuperStock)

General Marshall with Chiang Kai-shek and his wife, Mei-ling
(© The LIFE Picture Collection / Getty Images)

Poverty and starvation in China (© Image Asset Management Ltd. /
SuperStock)

Jawaharlal Nehru and Mohandas 'Mahatma' Gandhi (© The LIFE
Picture Collection / Getty Images)

Mohammed Ali Jinnah (© AFP / Getty Images)

Communist partisans in Athens during the Greek Civil War
(© Getty Images)

Greek partisans line up for battle (© Heritage Images / Getty Images)

Marshal Josef Broz Tito (© Getty Images)

Pro-Tito graffiti in Yugoslavia (© The LIFE Picture Collection / Getty
Images)

David Ben Gurion (© Mary Evans / Epic / Tallandier) and Menachem
Begin (© Getty Images)

The King David Hotel in Jerusalem after it was blown up by the Irgun
(© The LIFE Picture Collection / Getty Images)

Some rare good news in gloom-laden Britain, mid-1946 (© The LIFE
Picture Collection / Getty Images)

A postcard to mark the first anniversary of the liberation of the
Dachau concentration camp (© Interfoto / Friedrich / Mary Evans)

*Maps*

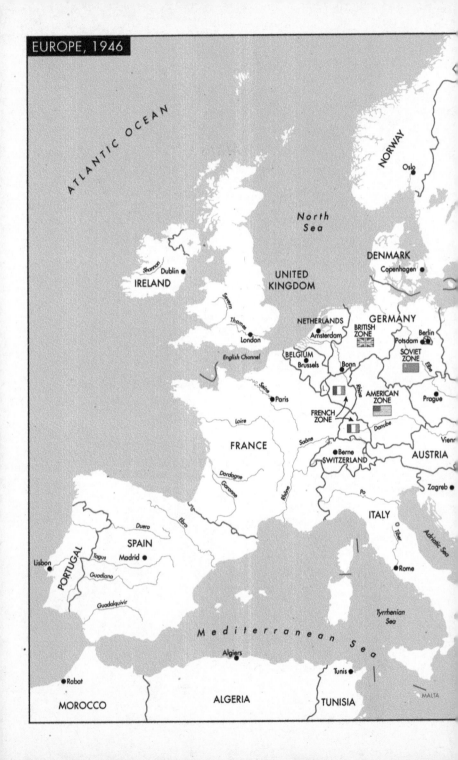

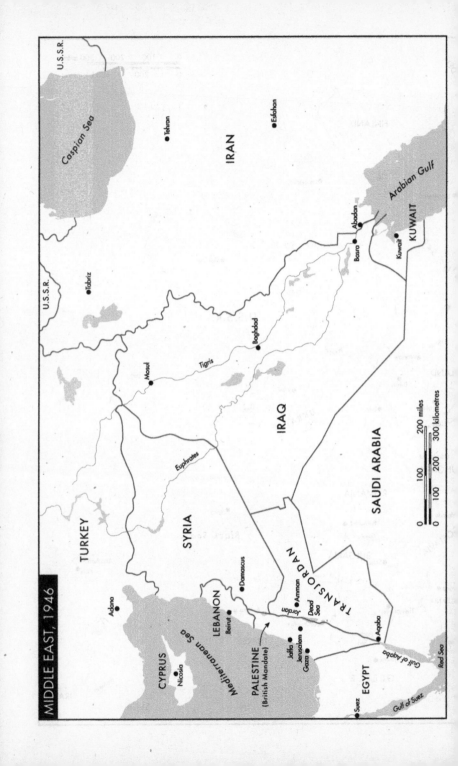

MIDDLE EAST, 1946

U.S.S.R.

Caspian Sea

IRAN

● Tehran

● Esfahan

Arabian Gulf

U.S.S.R.

● Tabriz

● Abadan

● Basra

KUWAIT

● Kuwait

● Baghdad

● Mosul

Tigris

IRAQ

SAUDI ARABIA

TURKEY

Euphrates

● Adana

SYRIA

● Damascus

CYPRUS

● Nicosia

LEBANON

● Beirut

Mediterranean Sea

PALESTINE
(British Mandate)

● Jaffa
● Jerusalem
● Gaza

Jordan

● Amman

Dead
Sea

TRANSJORDAN

● Aqaba

Gulf of Aqaba

Red Sea

EGYPT

● Suez

Gulf of Suez

0        100        200 miles
0    100    200    300 kilometres

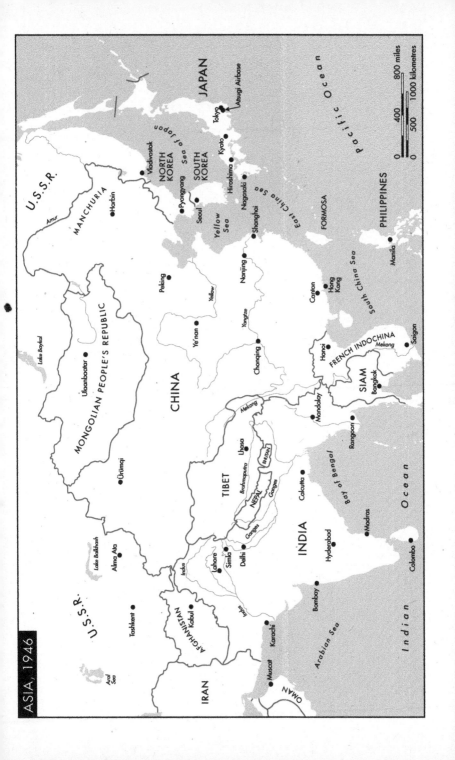

ASIA, 1946

# Introduction

As a journalist, I have covered events ranging from the fall of the Berlin Wall and the collapse of the former Soviet Union to the cycle of violence and counter-violence in the Middle East over the existence of Israel and Palestine. Throughout, America has dominated as the world's superpower. During many visits to India I have seen a desperately poor country, once stuck in the past, transform itself into a vibrant society, looking to the future, while China, still run by people calling themselves communists, moved from permanent revolution to a form of rampant capitalism. When, as an historian, I tried to trace the roots of all these events and stories I found myself returning always to one reference point: 1946.

This was the year that laid the foundations of the modern world. It was the start of the Cold War, of a global fragmentation along ideological lines, and of Europe being split on either side of an Iron Curtain. Israel would not come into being for two years, but 1946 was the year the decisions were made to create a Jewish homeland, with consequences that have remained so fateful since. It was the year independent India was born as the world's most populous democracy, that old Britain as a great imperial power began to die. All the old European empires were fading, though imperialism has lived on in a different non-dynastic form. It was the year the Chinese communists launched their final push for victory in a civil war that led to the re-emergence of China as a great power. With this book I hope to show how decisions made in 1946 have shaped the world we live in today.

In 1946 there was little optimism anywhere. At the start of the year a senior American official who had just returned from a visit to Europe went to the White House and reported to President Harry Truman in apocalyptic terms: 'The very foundations, the whole fabric of world organization which we have known in our lifetime and which our fathers and grandfathers knew' was threatened. He was not exaggerating. As so often happened, Winston Churchill found the most eloquent words with which to express the feelings of millions. In September 1946 he described the continuing aftermath of World War Two: 'What is the plight to which Europe has been reduced? Over wide areas, a vast quivering mass of tormented, hungry, careworn and bewildered human beings gape at the ruins of their cities and homes and scan the dark horizons for the approach of some new peril, tyranny or terror. Among the "victors", there is a Babel of jarring voices. Among the vanquished, a sullen silence of despair.'[1]

Churchill was speaking of Europe, but he could also have been talking about large tracts of Asia. He feared, as many rational people did, the arrival of 'a new dark age – with all its cruelty and squalor'. In no other war had so many people been killed in such a short space of time – around sixty million in six years. Now the World War had stopped, but the dying had not. The moment of 'liberation' the previous year had been exhilarating, but soon reality set in: civil wars would continue for the next four years in China and Greece; there were rebellions against the Soviets in Ukraine, where nationalists also fought Poles in a brutal conflict that cost more than fifty thousand lives; wars of independence flared up in various parts of Asia; despite the Holocaust, after the war, outbreaks of anti-Semitism in Eastern Europe claimed the lives of around fifteen hundred Jews who had somehow managed to escape the Nazis.

In much of Europe there were no schools, no transport links, no libraries, no shops – there was nothing to sell or buy – and almost nothing was manufactured any longer. There were virtually no banks, which didn't matter all that much as money was worthless. There was no law and order; men and children roamed the streets with weapons, either to protect what they possessed or to threaten the possessions of others. Women of all ages and backgrounds prostituted themselves for food and protection. Morality and traditional ideas of ownership had changed utterly; now the imperative was usually survival. This was how millions of Europeans lived in 1946.

Berlin and Hiroshima provided the most powerful images of the war: in both cities around three-quarters of the buildings had been destroyed by Allied bombing. But from the Seine to the Danube delta the heartland of Europe had been ravaged. In China, the Japanese, before their defeat, blew up all the dykes along the Yellow River, flooding three million acres of good farmland that took three decades to recover and caused enduring hunger for millions.

There was mass starvation and economic collapse. In the Eastern half of Germany, Ukraine and Moldova, around three million people died from hunger in the eighteen months after the war. In the Polish town of Lwów, the story that a mother driven mad with hunger killed and ate her two children barely made the newspapers. In Hungary inflation reached an unenviable world record of 14 quadrillion per cent (that's 15 noughts). Worthless currencies throughout Europe were replaced by bartering in cigarettes or scrounging from foreign armies. The northern hemisphere was swamped with refugees, particularly in Central Europe where prisoners of war, forced labourers and emaciated survivors of Nazi concentration camps were all grouped by the victorious Allies as 'displaced persons'.

After the First World War, borders were shifted and new countries were invented, but people were left in place. In 1946 the opposite happened. The Red Army's sweep to victory was accompanied by a massive programme of ethnic cleansing as nearly 12 million Germans were expelled westwards. Two and a half million people in Western Europe were forced to return back east to the tender mercies of Stalin and his henchmen, mostly against their will, and some at gunpoint by the troops from the Western Allies.

This book takes a global view, written as a chronological narrative, that the world was transformed more profoundly after the Second World War than after the First. That war destroyed empires which had lasted for centuries – the Ottoman, the Romanov and the Habsburg. From 1945 on, the remaining old European empires, such as the British, were no longer sustainable, despite some doomed efforts by fading powers to cling on to former glories. Imperialism was no longer dynastic but ideological – loyalty was demanded less to a king or emperor than to an idea, say Marxism–Leninism. Some readers may be surprised that much of the story I tell here is centred on Europe. But that is where the Cold War, the clash of civilisations which continued for the following four decades, was sharpest, at least when it began. What happened in Germany and Eastern Europe, Britain and France, in 1946 was considered by the major players at the time to be of the utmost importance. If there were to be a new armed conflict – and in 1946 it very much looked as though there might be – the battleground was likely once again to be in the heartland of Europe. It seemed to me sensible, therefore, to focus the book in Europe, at the same time showing how events in 1946 were dramatically shaping the future of Asia and the Middle East.

One country emerged from the war much stronger. Alone among the chief protagonists in the conflict, mainland America was physically untouched. The overwhelming dominance of the US as the world's economic, financial and military powerhouse dates from 1946. The war lifted America out of the Depression. The contrast between America's new wealth and the poverty of its enemies and allies was of profound importance in the aftermath of the war.

In much of Asia 'liberation' is not exactly the right word for events following the surrender of Japan. The European empires attempted to reassert their dominion over their old colonies: the French in Indo-china, the Dutch in the East Indies, the British in Malaya and Singapore, but they couldn't sustain traditional-style colonial rule for long. The agony of withdrawal was worse and more bloody for some than others – humiliatingly for France in Vietnam for example. In the sub-continent, the British were desperate to leave as soon as they could; with indecent haste according to many critics, who argue that the British 'scuttled' and caused the violence that accompanied the partition of India and Pakistan. It seems to me folly to imagine that the British could have prevented the massacres, short of despatching hundreds of thousands of troops. Almost the only thing the Hindus and Muslims in India agreed on was that the British were the problem, not the solution.

Arthur Schlesinger Jr., the historian and one-time aide to President Kennedy, described peace-making after the war as 'not so much a tapestry as . . . a hopelessly raveled and knotted mess of yarn'. A war that had been fought to prevent Germany dominating and despoiling Europe ended with the danger that the USSR would take Germany's place. For the last quarter of a century the conventional view among politicians and historians has been that the West 'sold out' Central and Eastern Europe to the Soviets, a deed done principally by President Franklin D. Roosevelt, with a helping hand from Churchill, at the Yalta Conference in February 1945. The argument has gone that Roosevelt, who had just a few weeks to live, was too ill and weak to stand up to Stalin, and the West had naïvely given away Eastern Europe for nothing in a settlement that amounted to 'appeasement' of communism. This has become orthodoxy, even though the narrative was formed before Soviet archives began to open after 1991, revealing how determined the Soviets were to keep what they had already gained by force of arms.

Eastern Europe was not America's or Britain's to 'give away'.

Soviet troops had already gained possession of most of the region. There was nothing the West could have done about it at the time of Yalta, which took place before the defeat of Germany, or afterwards. At Yalta, five months before the atom bomb was even tested, the Americans believed that they would need the Soviets' help to invade Japan.

Far from being naïve, the Western Allies were cynical. They kept the Russians fighting and dying on the Eastern Front so that fewer American and British soldiers would be killed when, eventually, D-Day came. The longer Roosevelt and Churchill delayed invading France, the more territory the Soviets would gain in the East. It was a straightforward and deliberate calculation: more dead Russians meant fewer dead Americans and British. Who is to say they were wrong. In 1946, and for years afterwards, the general feeling among politicians and historians was that Western leaders were being realistic and practical. The post-war settlement was the best they were likely to achieve and a price worth paying to defeat Hitler. Critics of the Western Allies have never been able to show how they could have got a better deal, what they would have done to prevent Soviet domination of Eastern Europe.

\*

A word on geography and terminology. Throughout this narrative (as above) I have taken the liberty of using the terms Central Europe and Eastern Europe interchangeably. I do not wish to tread on toes. Entire books have been written about the 'meaning' of Central Europe as an idea, where it ends and Eastern Europe begins. I intend them to mean the same thing, purely to avoid repetition as far as I can. Similarly with the Soviet Union, the USSR and Russia. Obviously I know that 'Russian' is not the same as 'Soviet'. I use them loosely solely in the interests of style.

The Cold War began within months of the end of the most destructive war in history. Along with the fear of hunger and disease, in 1946 the biggest terror for most people was of renewed global warfare, this time between the Allies who had defeated Germany. There was nothing inevitable about the Cold War, though the differences between the West and a dictatorship controlled by a man such as Stalin were so great that enduring trust and cooperation were never a serious possibility. As I show, the leaders and their people stumbled through misunderstandings and, occasionally, deliberate policy into a conflict of ideas, clashing interests and aspirations that had terrible consequences for millions of people over two generations – including, in a minor way, for myself, a refugee from tyranny behind the Iron Curtain. This has been more than a story for me. It has been part of a search for my roots.

Victor Sebestyen
*London, February 2014*

# 1

## 'I'm Tired of Babying the Soviets'

The coup had been almost bloodless. On 15 December 1945, the new Prime Minister of the People's Government of Azerbaijan had just announced his first proclamation to a bemused people, from his capital, Tabriz, in north-west Iran. Henceforth, he declared, his fledgling nation would cease to be a province of Iran, ruled by a distant and 'alien' shah in Tehran. It would become an autonomous republic. Rather than Farsi, the Turkic dialect spoken by most Azeris would now be the official state language. A new constitution would guarantee freedoms long suppressed by Iran's autocratic rulers. The banks would be nationalised. There would be 'a job for everybody who wants one'. Peasants would be given land expropriated from big absentee landlords in a far-reaching socialist revolution.[1]

Ja'far Pishevari was an unlikely nationalist firebrand much less communist dictator. At fifty-two, this stocky, good-natured PM had been a journalist most of his life, and a low-level Comintern agent, apart from the nine years he had spent in an Iranian prison for 'subversion'. Most of his family had lived in the USSR for years; one of his brothers was a doctor in the Red Army. Pishevari had been relatively unknown until 1944, except as the author of a few fiery articles promoting Azeri nationalism. His story became a brief cause célèbre among the left/liberal intelligentsia in Tehran when he won election to the Majlis, the Iranian Parliament, but was barred from taking his seat by the Shah's government. He returned to obscurity, then to his own amazement, let alone that of anyone else, he was handpicked by Joseph Stalin, the Soviet leader in the Kremlin, to be front man for the new order in a strategic part of central Asia, bordering the Soviet Republic of Azerbaijan.

In Marco Polo's time Tabriz had been one of the largest cities in the world, the principal gateway to the Orient – 'a great city of beautiful gardens ... exceptionally positioned for merchants,' as the Venetian traveller described it. After Tamerlane sacked it in 1392, history and other potential conquerors passed by Tabriz for several hundred years. In the middle of the twentieth century it was a dusty, sleepy town of some 110,000 mostly poor artisans, traders and subsistence farmers. The gardens were long gone. A few grand buildings stood amidst the mud huts and general squalor. Now this backwater was centre stage again. If the Cold War can be said to have started anywhere, Tabriz is the place. Over the next few weeks, only a few people at the highest levels in Washington, London and Moscow knew how very close the world came to the start of a new war.

Pishevari established himself in the biggest and grandest of the remaining buildings – an enormous, if ugly, palace that had once belonged to an Iranian provincial governor. He held court in a vast reception room decorated in gilded eighteenth-century French style. Soviet troops stood guard outside the door. 'He looked deceptively unlike a ruthless communist gauleiter,' a visitor recorded. 'He stood about five feet five inches, had steely grey hair and a small brush moustache under a sharp hook nose ... [he wore] a shiny blue serge suit and a collared shirt frayed at the cuffs and noticeably soiled at the collar, which was buttoned but tieless. His hands were the rough hands of the peasant and the fingernails were dirty.'[2]

Western diplomats agreed that the real power in the new state belonged to the diminutive, smartly dressed Mohammed Biriya, a sinister figure in his mid-forties who had done much to foment revolution as head of the Society of Friends of the USSR. Formerly, Biriya had been a talented professional flautist and leader of the

Tabriz street cleaners' union. Officially, his title was Minister of Propaganda but, more importantly, he ran the secret police, whose members were trained by Russian advisors from the NKVD. They had been arresting opponents for the last few days, roughing up well-known anti-communists and other potential opponents.

Three days earlier, members of Pishevari's ragbag People's Army had taken over the police stations in Tabriz and the surrounding area, the central post office and the radio station, the classic revolutionary targets, and blocked all principal roads into the city. But the coup could not have succeeded without help from outside. There were between thirty and fifty thousand Soviet troops in or near Tabriz. Without firing a shot, one Russian detachment surrounded the Iranian army headquarters on the outskirts of the city and disarmed the garrison. The central government in Tehran despatched a small relief column, but it was halted on the main road between the two cities when confronted by a far stronger Soviet force as it reached the border of the 'rebel' province. The commander turned his soldiers back.

The Soviets claimed they were aiding freedom-loving Azeris, many of whom had family connections in the USSR, and had intervened 'to avoid unnecessary bloodshed.' But it was a lie. Amidst the strictest secrecy in order to maintain plausible deniability, the Russians had begun planning the takeover in the summer of 1945. The proof emerged only five decades later, after the USSR fell apart. Officials from Baku, the capital of the Soviet Republic of Azerbaijan, and in Moscow, organised the coup meticulously and financed it. Stalin personally gave the go-ahead and later was made aware of every significant detail. The Soviet spy chief, Lavrenti Beria, was in nominal charge of the operation from Moscow, but the nuts and bolts would be the responsibility of the local Communist Party boss in Baku, Mir Bagirov.

The strategy had been decided in Moscow on 6 July, at a meeting of senior Soviet magnates who authorised Bagirov to 'organise a separatist movement . . . which would agitate for an autonomous Azerbaijani province'. It named Pishevari as leader of the new organisation, which Kremlin officials insisted should be called the Azerbaijan Democratic Party, the ADP, in a crude and pointless effort to make it look different from the Communist Party, the Tudeh. Funds were provided, reasonably generous sums given the dire condition of the post-war Soviet economy. The ADP launched a newspaper that avoided socialist agitprop but was designed to fuel ethnic tensions.[3]

The ADP was supplied with weapons to arm a partisan group of around 3,000 fighters, which would later form the core of a People's Army. But Kremlin officials insisted that 'the equipment must be of foreign make' to hide its origins. Pishevari was given a million US dollars in convertible currency, a large sum for Moscow at the time. By the end of November, the ADP proudly reported to the Kremlin that it had assembled thirty units of a hundred men each, supplied with 11,000 rifles, 1,000 pistols, 400 machine guns, 2,000 grenades and more than a million rounds of ammunition 'ready to fight whoever stood in the way of . . . autonomy for Azerbaijan.'[4]

The takeover mystified Iranian Azeris, most of whom were unconcerned with nationalism. Poverty, the rapacity of absentee landlords, and the scarcity of water were more pressing concerns, as Moscow was told by its own agents and military on the ground. Iranian rulers, including the former Shah, had periodically tried to ban the Turkic language, which was deeply resented. But the laws were invariably disobeyed. Over the centuries the various ethnic groups in Iran had gotten along together reasonably well with no serious bloodshed. The Russians, though, were feared by all the region's ethnic groups, not only the Azeris. True, the rulers in Tehran were distant and cared little for Azeri feelings, but at least they were fellow Muslims. Apart from a small number of communists and ultra-nationalists in Tabriz, few people felt kinship with the Azeris across the border in the USSR, who had to endure life under the godless and sinful Soviets.

Biriya, in particular, knew he and the Soviets faced an uphill struggle to win over hearts and minds for the ADP. Soon after the coup he resorted to traditional methods of persuasion. Tribal leaders and prominent figures brave enough to voice opposition were jailed and a few were murdered. Dissent was quickly silenced.

One of the few Western observers who had seen the takeover coming was John Wall, the British Consul in Tabriz. Wall had been monitoring troop movements and café talk in the bazaar and wrote a series of warning telegrams to London, to which he seldom received a response – until the coup. Now he was pessimistic for the future. He saw how his Soviet equivalent behaved more like a commissar in one of the Baltic states than a diplomat in a foreign country. 'The Russians are more determined than ever to maintain their hold on the province,' he reported in mid-December. 'There is no railway to Tehran, but there is to Baku and that is where "autonomous" Azerbaijan is heading . . . [it] feels more like a part of Russia than of Iran.'[5]

*

Stalin did not care in the slightest about the national aspirations of the Azeris. He loathed what he regarded as petty chauvinism. In the Soviet republics, when he thought any of his own subjects wanted autonomy, his first instinct was to react with brutal repression. Typically, his way of dealing with the 'national question' was to uproot entire ethnic groups and transport them thousands of miles from their homeland to unfamiliar territory as a way of teaching them a lesson about nationhood. This is what he did to the Kazakhs, Kalmyks, Chechens, Tatars and many others, murdering millions along the way. But he was willing to use nationalism and to play ethnic politics when it suited him.

Stalin's objective in Iran was never to annex a new territory and impose a Soviet system there, as he was to do in Eastern

Europe. His principal aim in the region was simpler and more modest: he wanted an oil concession in southern Azerbaijan. His allies, Britain and the US, would end the Second World War possessing drilling rights in what was by far the world's biggest oil-producing nation, and he saw that unless he staked a claim now, the Soviet Union would not. So he was willing to bully the Iranians, and risk the wrath of the Western powers, in a bid to get them. It was the world's first oil crisis.

For much of the Second World War, Iran had been occupied by the Soviets and the British. All the Allies considered Iran vital to their effort against Nazi Germany. After the Germans invaded the Soviet Union in June 1941 and the Big Three alliance was formed against Hitler, most of the supplies the Soviets needed were shipped by the United States to the Persian Gulf. It was the obvious supply route, and the lifeline without which the USSR might not have survived, as even Stalin grudgingly admitted. It started with a trickle, but when America entered the war after Pearl Harbor, weapons, ammunition, machine tools, war materiel on a vast scale, as well as food, were sent to southern Iran. From there it went by road to the Soviet Union, which shares a 1,700 km border with Iran.

An initial problem for the Allies was that Iran had been neutral in the conflict with Germany. Its ruler, Shah Reza Pahlavi, and most of the clique of soldiers and aristocrats around him had strong pro-Nazi sympathies. During the 1930s Iran had developed close trading ties with Germany and there were hundreds of German businessmen, political advisors and spies in Tehran. In August 1941 Britain and Russia jointly exerted pressure on the Shah to expel the Germans, knowing he would be reluctant to comply. As the British Foreign Secretary, Anthony Eden, was told by officials from the India Office, 'The greatest benefit would be drawn from the elimination of the Shah.'[6]

Russian troops entered Iran from the north and a British force invaded from the south. The Iranian army put up token resistance. On 16 September the Shah abdicated in favour of his inexperienced twenty-one-year-old son, Mohammed Reza, who until then had been excluded by his father from politics or any kind of public life. One of the new Shah's first acts was to expel all Germans. The Iranians may not have been unhappy to see the back of their corrupt, despotic and dissolute ruler, who himself had seized power seventeen years earlier in a military coup, and whose opponents often tended to 'disappear'. But the manner of his going was widely seen in Iran as insulting and the foreign interference was deeply resented, especially by the urban middle class.*

Within weeks seventy thousand Soviet troops occupied northern and western Iran, guarding the supply routes and using Tabriz as their base. About fifty thousand British soldiers controlled the south of the country, the crucial Gulf ports and the area around Tehran. The Tripartite Agreement signed by the Shah gave the occupying armies sweeping powers over Iran's security, defence and internal politics, but only for the duration of the conflict. The agreement stated that the Occupation forces would withdraw within six months of the end of the war. After VE Day, the Iranians took back political authority of the country and wanted to see the swift departure of foreign troops.

The British began winding down their garrison soon after the defeat of Japan three months later, but the Russians remained in force. On the whole, during the war the Occupation forces had got on well. Despatches from the British Ambassador in Tehran, Sir Reader Bullard, for example, praised the efforts of the Soviets to help feed the population in their zone when there was a local food shortage. But after the war distrust quickly surfaced. It seemed as though the nineteenth-century Great Game was being

---

* Reza Pahlavi was taken prisoner by British troops and kept under house arrest, initially in Mauritius and then in Johannesburg. He died in July 1944 in South Africa from a heart attack, aged sixty-six. His son remained on the throne until he was overthrown in the Islamic Revolution of 1979 led by the Ayatollah Khomeini. He died in 1980.

replayed, with Britain and Russia again vying for influence in Central Asia. However, one important new factor altered this Kiplingesque picture: for the first time the United States became a significant presence in Iran, and elsewhere in the Middle East.

Before the war America had virtually no trading ties with Iran, and only low-level diplomatic relations. Even those were placed in jeopardy in 1936 when the Iranians withdrew their ambassador for nearly a year during a dispute following the appearance of an article in the *New York Daily Herald* that called Reza Shah ill-mannered and likened him to 'a stable boy'. Otherwise, Iran was barely noticed by analysts in the State Department. Yet by 1943 President Franklin Roosevelt had declared that Iran's security and prosperity were vital to the future strategic needs of the US. At the end of 1944 there were more than five thousand Americans in Iran – technicians, engineers, economists, political officers, and spies. Some were managing the Lend Lease programme of aid to the USSR; others were effectively in charge of the Iranian finance department and public health service. As Wallace Murray, head of the State Department's Near East division boasted, the US 'would soon be in a position of actually running Iran, through an impressive body of American advisors.'[7]

US influence in Iran depressed British officials of the old school, who rightly saw it as a sign of waning British prestige. Bullard sent a series of splenetic telegrams complaining about the vulgarity and 'showiness' of the pushy Americans who did not know how to behave 'in front of Persian grandees'. But it deeply disturbed the Soviets, and Stalin in particular, who now recognised the Americans as a powerful new rival in areas where Russia had historically claimed an interest.

Stalin could see that when the war came to an end the Soviets would have occupied parts of Iran for several years but, as he complained to other magnates in the Kremlin, they might have to withdraw without getting anything out of the country. That, he declared, was unacceptable. Iran produced more oil than the rest of the Middle East put together. For thirty years the British had possessed sole drilling rights through the Anglo-Iranian Oil company, which operated the biggest refinery in the world at Abadan. Soviet intelligence knew that in September 1943 two US companies, Standard Oil of New Jersey and Sinclair Oil, began secret negotiations with the Iranian Government for an American oil concession in southern Iran.

More worryingly, according to Beria's spies, the other Allies were trying to block the Soviets from acquiring drilling rights in the north. 'The British, and possibly the Americans, secretly work against a transfer to us of oil fields,' he reported to the Soviet Politburo in the summer of 1944.[8]

In September Stalin despatched one of his favourites, a deputy Foreign Minister named Sergei Kavtaradze, to Tehran to negotiate for oil. The talks did not go well. According to a Russian transcript of his interview with the Shah, the Soviet official began by complaining that 'we are not satisfied with the present state of relations between our two countries'. Then he demanded 'as our right' a licence, with immediate effect, permitting the USSR to explore for oil in Iranian Azerbaijan for five years. He was turned down and told that no decisions would be made about oil concessions until after the war was over. Kavtaradze was indignant and accused Iran of 'pursuing a one-sided policy that discriminated against the Soviet Union.' Later, he told the Iranian Prime Minister that the decision would have 'unhappy consequences . . . you are disloyal and unfriendly to the Soviet Union.' It is unlikely, however, that if he had behaved with more finesse Kavtaradze would have fared any better. The Iranians were determined to refuse the Soviets a permanent toehold in their country.[9]

Stalin was unsurprised that his emissary returned home empty handed. But he did nothing hasty to pursue his goal of an oilfield on the USSR's southern frontier, which he thought would also give him a secondary prize of acting as a buffer zone to secure that border. At this stage, winning the war and keeping on good terms with the Western Allies were far higher priorities. But within weeks of the German surrender the Soviets renewed their efforts. Kavtaradze was sent to negotiate in Tehran once more and was again turned down. Now the Iranian government said that the Majlis would decide, after new elections and when foreign troops had left Iranian soil. It was this that prompted the Soviets to use the threat of a separatist revolt in Azerbaijan to exert more pressure on Iran, with the hapless Ja'far Pishevari as their tool.

The Soviet leadership in Moscow decided on the timing of the coup in Tabriz. It went ahead when Stalin thought the Iranians had played for time long enough. He calculated that now the war was over he had little to lose, though he turned out to be badly mistaken. The Western Allies became convinced that Russia's interference in Iran was the prelude to a full-scale invasion of the Middle East and Turkey, though there was little solid evidence.

The day after Pishevari made his 'autonomy' declaration, Iran appealed to Britain and the US for help. A local dispute principally about oil was thus turned into a potentially dangerous international incident, setting a pattern of cold war crises for years to come. The world would grow familiar with the mistrust and misunderstandings of the 'superpowers' (though that term had not yet been coined), the poor intelligence sources on both sides, the highly inflated rhetoric, the fear of showing weakness. The Americans demanded that the Soviets cease backing the rebellious breakaway movement and allow the Iranian government to reassert its authority in Tabriz. The Soviets said their actions were necessary to restore order and to protect the Red Army garrison there.

The wrangle over Iran nearly torpedoed the Moscow Foreign Ministers' Conference, which began the week before Christmas 1945. The meeting was supposed to settle outstanding issues like the peace treaties in Korea and Italy, the composition of new governments in Hungary, Romania and Bulgaria and the establishment of a peace commission for China. But Iran overshadowed proceedings, especially when Stalin announced that Russia no longer intended to honour an agreement made at the Potsdam Conference of the Big Three in July to withdraw its troops from Iran by 2 March the following year. He said he feared 'subversion and sabotage in Baku', though that was deception. All sides agreed to meet again in the New Year to discuss the Iran question, but instead they had reached a stand-off.[10]

One man made no attempt to hide his anger and frustration. President Harry Truman had spent the eight months since he moved into the White House trying to work out how to deal with the Soviets. As he acknowledged, he had been inconsistent, even contradictory, which had got him to the point, as he told one of his chief aides soon after Christmas, 'when we might any day be at war with Russia over Iran'. Now he made up his mind to follow a clear policy. At the beginning of January 1946 he wrote to his Secretary of State, James Byrnes:

> The Russians have been a headache ever since Potsdam. The presence now of Russian troops in Iran and the fact that Russia stirs up rebellion there . . . is an outrage if ever I saw one. There isn't a doubt . . . that Russia intends an invasion of Turkey and the seizure of the Black Sea straits to the Mediterranean . . . Unless Russia is faced with an iron fist and strong language, another war is in the making. The only language they understand is 'how many divisions do you have?' I do not think we should play compromise any longer . . . I am tired of babying the Soviets.

It had taken less than six months for wartime partners in the most destructive conflict in history to become enemies – as they were to remain for the next four decades.[11]

# 2

## The American Century

'War is hell ... but America had a hell of a War,' the astute columnist Walter Lippmann said soon after VJ Day. The US experience of World War Two was entirely different from that of every other combatant nation. There was much hardship, to be sure, and loss of lives. But America was the only country to emerge from the conflict better off than when it entered it in 1941. No attempt had been made to invade and occupy the country; no cities were destroyed by bombs. There were no refugees roaming the American countryside, desperately searching for food and shelter as in much of Europe and Asia. There were no direct war casualties from military action in mainland America. Around 420,000 Americans from the services died in combat or went missing in action, which, given the scale of the fighting on three continents, is a modest number. British losses, at around 330,000 service personnel, were lower, but from a population about a quarter of America's size. And combined American and British losses were fewer than Russian deaths in the Siege of Leningrad alone.[1]

America's economy boomed as never before. Its annual GNP doubled between 1940 and 1945 from $102 billion to $214 billion. Unemployment fell from 14.6 per cent to a historic low of 1.2 per cent. The war dragged the US out of the Depression. There had been rationing on a range of products such as milk, sugar, gasoline, rubber for tyres, some meats and vegetable oils, and even typewriter ribbon. But for most people, living standards improved dramatically as incomes rose by more than 50 per cent. The war was a leveller economically, unusually so in American history. The share of income of the top 5 per cent of the population fell by almost a fifth and remained that way until the gap began widening again in the 1970s.

America was the granary of the world, and its industrial workshop. At the beginning of 1946 more goods were manufactured in the US than in the rest of the world put together. During the war, America had created a new financial system that ensured the US dollar would become the world's chief trading currency, which it continued to be well into the twenty-first century. Most Americans believed not only that US soldiers had done most of the fighting to win the war but, justifiably, that American money had bankrolled the Allies to help with the rest.

Immediately post-war, Americans wanted a brief period to celebrate victory. After that, the demands were equally uncomplicated. Dean Acheson, an advisor to the President who would become US Secretary of State three years later, put it in straightforward fashion. 'I can state in three sentences what the popular foreign policies are among the people of the United States. 1. Bring the boys home. 2. No playing Santa Claus. 3. Don't be pushed around.' They also wanted the security that wealth could provide.

Before the war the only substantial US military base outside homeland America was in the Philippines. But Pearl Harbor marked the beginning of America's development as a military superpower. In 1946/47 the defence budget was $13 billion, 36 per cent of national spending and thirteen times more than it had been for each of the nine pre-war years. It was to remain at similar levels for the next three decades. By the end of the war, new naval and air bases had been leased in the Americas, in Iceland, Greece and Turkey, in Korea and the Middle East. More than half a million US troops were stationed in Europe. As it turned out, many thousands would remain for the next forty years – and America would be the strongest military power in Europe. But however counter-intuitive it might seem in retrospect, at the time it was assumed on both sides of the Atlantic that the GIs would soon return home. When the final details of D-Day were being planned in spring 1944, the US military's top brass asked President Roosevelt how long he expected occupation troops to stay in Germany and elsewhere after the war was won. The Commander-in-Chief was explicit: 'At least a year, maybe two,' he replied. But not more.[2] That was still America's clear intention throughout 1946. It changed only when the Big Three alliance began falling apart and perceptions in Washington hardened about the USSR's objectives in Europe. Meanwhile, America's allies – including the Soviets – believed the same. Winston Churchill wrote a note to the British cabinet before VE Day emphasising the point: 'We must not expect that the United States will keep large armies in Europe for long after the war,' he said. 'I doubt there will be any American troops in Europe four years after the cease-firing.'

There was to be no return to isolationism. US soldiers, engineers and an army of idealistic bureaucrats would remake Japan as a modern democracy in the American image, but disarmed so it could never again pose a threat to its neighbours or to the United States. And though the plan was to bring the troops home, it was never the intention to withdraw from European peace-making and diplomacy. An American president had been the driving force behind the Treaty of Versailles after the First World War. Woodrow Wilson's idealistic 'Fourteen Points' gave self-determination and independence to groups of newly free nations in the defeated Habsburg and Ottoman empires. But Wilson couldn't carry the American public with him in his visionary idea of collective security 'that will make the world safe for democracy'. The US Congress rejected membership of the League of Nations, one of the several reasons it was doomed to fail. In the 1920s American banks, encouraged by successive US governments, tried to bail out certain European countries bankrupted by the war. American loans funded Germany's war reparations to the French and the British. After the Wall Street

Crash America withdrew into itself in an attempt to deal with the Great Depression; the New Deal put America first and there were no foreign loans while Europe spiralled into catastrophe.

But after World War Two, American policy-makers insisted it would be entirely different. The US would stay the course, remain involved and accept global commitments. 'Europe is too important to be left to the Europeans,' said one of the most influential presidential advisors. The balance of power had shifted inexorably. A new attempt would be made to create an international body to keep the peace: the United Nations, with America taking a lead role as one of the world's four 'policemen'.

The main difference, however, became clear in the first post-war year. The US had a rival that posed a challenge, not only militarily and politically but ideologically, in a way that fascism never had. A confident America had saved the world from Hitler and Japanese imperialism, with wartime exports of arms and food. Now it would export its ideals of democracy, free trade, open markets and liberty in order to ensure the peace. It was put eloquently – and directly – to the leaders of the Soviet Union a few weeks after the end of the war by Harry Hopkins, one of Franklin Roosevelt's closest confidants and well known as a strong supporter of America's alliance with Russia:

> I have often been asked what interests we have in Poland, Greece, Iran, Korea. Well, I think we have the most important business in the world – and indeed the only business worthy of our traditions. It is this: to do everything within our diplomatic power to foster and encourage democratic governments throughout the world. We should not be timid about blazoning to the world our desire for the right of all peoples to have genuine civil liberty. We believe our dynamic democracy is the best in the world.

The tone of ideological conflict was set.[3]

*

Throughout 1946, Harry S. Truman was one of the most unpopular presidents in American history. Widely respected later as the leader who turned his country into the global colossus America has been since World War Two, he was dismissed as a lightweight for much of his first term in the White House. He was lampooned in the press as a political pygmy compared to his predecessor. Cartoons had portrayed Roosevelt as a boxer in a ring out-punching his opponents or, more often, as a nimble acrobat balancing on a high wire – misleadingly, as Washington insiders and everyone in the media knew he was wheelchair-bound and couldn't walk unaided. Truman was invariably depicted as a passive weakling. Bumper stickers on cars read 'To err is Truman'. A recording was made using a play on the lyrics of a popular song: 'I'm just mild [wild] about Harry.' In a Gallup poll at the start of 1946 only 9 per cent of the public thought a Democrat could win the Presidential election in two years' time.

To succeed America's longest-serving president, an immense figure on the world stage, would have been a hard act for anybody to follow. But an impression soon took hold that Truman just wasn't up to the job. The conventional view from the 1960s onwards has been that Truman was a 'nearly great' president, that he called the big things right. Biographers hailed him as 'a backwoods politician who became a world statesman'. Some depicted his story, the man from Independence, Missouri, as an epitome of the American Dream: an ordinary man whose extraordinary strength of character led him to triumph over adversity. But in his first couple of years in office it seemed that the bespectacled, plain-looking, simple-sounding Midwesterner who spoke so prosaically was unfit to take the place of the suave, sophisticated political genius whose uplifting rhetoric had inspired the nation in peace and war for a dozen years. The late President had certainly shared this view. Roosevelt was a great leader, but he had one glaring fault: he did nothing to prepare his successor for office. Though, in his first Inaugural Address in 1933, he had declared that 'no one man is indispensable', he didn't seem to believe it. Even one of his close aides, a loyal admirer, admitted that 'Franklin Roosevelt's idea of the Presidency was himself in the Oval Office.'[4]

Roosevelt was warned in 1944 that, with his severe heart problems and weak lungs, he would be very lucky to survive a fourth term. But he ignored medical advice and ran for election anyway, believing that his famous luck would hold. He had barely known the running mate his aides had selected for simple political reasons: in order to win a convincing victory in 1944 the Democrats needed to shore up votes in the Midwest and parts of the south. Truman had not sought nomination – a factor in his favour in Roosevelt's eyes – and he needed a lot of persuasion to be on the ticket. The two met just twice in the eighty-two days between the inauguration and the President's death, and in the last of those meetings – on the eve of his departure for the Yalta Conference – Roosevelt with his usual insouciance told his deputy 'not to bother me unless it is extremely urgent.' Many on the President's staff mocked the new Vice-President, whom they labelled 'The Second Missouri Compromise'.*

Truman had never even set foot inside the 'map room' in the White House – the equivalent of today's 'situation room' – where the President, the Joint Chiefs of Staff and their intelligence advisors met each afternoon to review the progress of the war. He had not been told about the development of the atomic bomb, nor any significant military secrets. He was given no inside information about the personal dealings between the 'Big Three' leaders and never shown their correspondence. He saw no files about the USSR, nor had any ideas about the President's post-war plans that he could not have read in the *New York Times.* Roosevelt never thought he would die and be replaced by Harry Truman. When he

---

* The first was in 1820, when Kansas was granted statehood, in an attempt to balance the number of 'slave states' with 'abolitionist' ones. It was not altogether a success and failed to prevent the American Civil War some four decades later.

suffered a fatal stroke in Warm Springs, Georgia, on 12 April 1945, his successor had almost no experience in foreign affairs – at a grave point in America's most critical conflict. He had left America only once, as an artillery officer during the First World War, commanding a gun battery in France. His superiors reported that he showed a flair for leadership and was remarkably cool under fire.

Truman had seen for himself how ill Roosevelt was. A few days before the election he told a friend that the President 'is in such a feeble condition . . . pouring cream into his tea he got more in the saucer than the cup. There doesn't appear to be any mental lapse, but physically he is going to pieces. I am very worried about him.' Yet he was genuinely surprised when Roosevelt died and, just three weeks short of his sixty-first birthday, he was thrust into a position he was ambivalent about accepting.[5]

Truman carefully crafted a modest, no-nonsense demeanour and favoured homespun platitudes – 'the buck stops here', for example – which he would pronounce with a noticeable Missouri twang. Most of this was real, but much was 'spin', similar to the way in which he would exaggerate later, adding 'colour' and, on occasion, telling downright lies about himself and others in his memoirs. Harry Truman was far more complex than the image he cultivated. Privately, like so many presidents, he was foul-mouthed, though unlike a large number of them, he was entirely devoted to his wife. His sins were late-night bourbon and poker sessions with highly dubious cronies, mostly fellow Freemasons. Detractors who knew Roosevelt's smart set were unimpressed by the visitors attracted to Truman's White House which, according to one, 'evoked the lounge of the Lion's Club of Independence, Missouri, where the odour of the ten-cent cigar competed with the easy laughter of the risqué story.'

He was modest but could be petulant; in reality he had a high opinion of himself. He admired Roosevelt enormously but could see his faults and he never fawned. He confided privately a day after Roosevelt's death that 'I don't believe the US wants any more fakers as presidents – Teddy [Roosevelt] and Franklin were enough'.

A snappy dresser, Truman invariably wore a double-breasted, light-coloured suit. He sometimes changed shirts two or three times a day. He had a congenital eye disease – which he lied about in order to get into the army reserve – and was the only American president of the twentieth century to wear spectacles at all times, even in the White House swimming pool. 'Without them I'm as blind as a mole,' he admitted. Even with strong prescription glasses he had distorted vision.* He had little of the false bonhomie adopted by many politicians. Charles 'Chip' Bohlen, one of his principal foreign service aides and later US Ambassador to the Soviet Union, described him as 'the coldest man I ever met. He didn't give a damn for me or for anyone else in the world as far as I could see.' Yet Bohlen grew to admire him enormously as 'the President who brought this country into the twentieth century.'[6]

Truman came from humble stock. He spent a decade in his youth as a dirt-poor farmer on family land that was later repossessed by the bank. After World War One, he opened a haberdashery store in Independence that famously went broke. Strictly in character, he never filed for bankruptcy; as a senator a

---

* Truman's excellent biographer David McCullough says that as a small child the future president was diagnosed with extreme long-sightedness because he had 'flat eyeballs'. My friend the ophthalmologist Wendy Franks offers an interesting observation on his poor eyesight. She explains: all infants with normal eyes are born longsighted. As they grow, their eyeballs grow too and the refractive error corrects itself by school age. Myopia, short-sightedness, at birth is rare and often caused by serious eye disease. But acquired myopia is common in literate societies. It seems that the eyeball can grow bigger, resulting in short-sightedness, due to prolonged reading. The magnified view of the eyes produced by corrective convex spectacle lenses gives a goggle-eyed appearance very different from the concave lenses of the short-sighted boffin. Truman's eyes were very unusual because his long-sightedness was caused by an unusually flat curvature of the cornea. Now we know why the President could barely see a thing.

decade later he was still paying off his creditors. In money matters he was personally incorruptible and honest, one of the few presidents to have left the White House significantly poorer than when he entered it. Yet he owed his entire political career to a notorious racketeer.

For two decades between the wars, 'Boss' Tom Pendergast controlled Kansas City business and the State of Missouri's elected offices. The Pendergast 'machine' was sophisticated. It went beyond stuffing ballot boxes and other vote-rigging tactics. It turned politics, prohibition, prostitution and gambling into thriving enterprises, the profits of which could be invested into more legitimate areas. Truman never took cash for favours, thus squaring his conscience, but he depended on the Pendergast machine to deliver, by hook or by crook, large lopsided majorities for 'his' candidates. Typically, Truman stayed loyal to Pendergast well after it was politically expedient to do so, and even after Pendergast was convicted of tax evasion and sent to Leavenworth jail, Truman defended him. 'He has been a friend to me when I needed it,' he said. 'I am not one to desert a ship when it is about to go down.' Besides, Truman admired Pendergast, '. . . even if he did own a bawdy house, a saloon and a gambling establishment, because he was a man of his word.' He was not 'a hypocrite like the snivelling church members who played with whores, drank and sold out to the Big Boss on weekdays but then repented on Sunday.'[*][7]

In office, President Truman grew into a generous, near visionary internationalist on the world stage, but in many ways he was

---

* Pendergast resorted to ordering contract murder at least once. One of his lieutenants was a fixer called Johnny Lazia, who 'controlled' the Kansas City Police Department, known to be one of the most corrupt in the US. In 1933 he helped a well-known gangster, Charles 'Pretty Boy' Floyd, flee after he gunned down four police officers. Floyd got away with the murders, but Federal officers went after him for tax fraud. He was freed on bail. But the 'machine' feared Floyd might reveal damaging information and took no chances. He was shot before the trial hearings by an unknown assailant, but the orders clearly came from Pendergast.

a man of his place and time. His diaries and private letters are littered with the casual racism of his era; he invariably called Mexico 'Greaserdom' and used terms like 'nigger', 'coon', 'dago' and 'Jew clerk'. When he referred to New York City at all, he usually called it 'kike town'. In a letter to his wife he wrote: 'I think one man is as good as another so long as he is honest and decent and is not a nigger or a Chinaman ... It is race prejudice, I guess, but I am strongly of the opinion that negroes ought to be in Africa, Asians in Asia and white men in Europe and America.' Yet one of his closest friends, his partner in the failed haberdashery business, was a practising Jew, Eddie Jacobson, whom he had met in the army. He was aware of his racism and said he tried to fight it. As President, he spoke out more forcefully for civil rights for African Americans than any of his predecessors since Abraham Lincoln, including the 'New Deal' President, FDR.[8]

Truman felt no inferiority complex when he entered the White House, though he disliked the 'snobbery' of the smooth Ivy League officials who prospered in the Roosevelt administration, particularly those from the foreign service – 'the men in striped pants', he called them. He sensed he had to exert his authority early on and needed to look decisive. His chief fault at the beginning of his presidency, as his admirers admitted, was that he sometimes made up his mind too quickly. 'He gave the impression that he would decide first and then think things through later,' said Henry Wallace, his predecessor as Vice-President, and Commerce Secretary until Truman fired him – decisively – later in 1946. He knew his own weaknesses and strengths. A year into his presidency he told one of his poker-playing chums, with false modesty, 'I may not have much in the way of brains but I have enough ... to get hold of able people and give them a chance.'[9]

Truman liked to see things in black and white. He urged his aides to bring him straightforward solutions to problems which could be presented to him on a single sheet of paper, or as Charles Bohlen once said, 'two at the most'. But the biggest problem the

US faced, or Truman believed that the US faced, was how to deal with the Soviet Union and its dictator – and there was no simple answer. He was receiving conflicting advice. 'Stop babying the Soviets' was an instinct, not a policy. Throughout much of 1946 he was searching for ways to turn his instinct into firm and practical action.

# 3

## The Russians: 'A Tsarist People'

At around nine p.m. on 25 January 1946 a nervous-looking man with a long but neatly brushed goatee beard was ushered into Stalin's office in the Kremlin. He was Igor Kurchatov, forty-three, one of the most talented Russian scientists of his, or any other, generation. With Stalin were two other much-feared Soviet potentates, Vyacheslav Molotov, the Foreign Minister, and Lavrenti Beria, the notorious head of the NKVD, or secret police. The meeting lasted just over an hour. It set the course for the nuclear arms race during the Cold War – and for the atomic age.

Stalin wanted to know what progress had been made in creating a Russian atom bomb. Kurchatov was straightforward. Progress had been slow because of lack of resources, he answered. Stalin was clearly uninterested in the science, but was keen to hear what the weapon could do for the security and prestige of the USSR. He told Kurchatov that possessing the Bomb was now the nation's top priority – 'it is our Task Number One' – and the scientists would be given everything they needed to achieve it. 'It is not worth doing on a small scale,' Stalin said. 'It is necessary for the work to be done broadly, on a Russian scale . . . It is not necessary to seek cheaper paths.' He promised that the scientists and engineers on the project would be treated well, given honours and prizes, cars, dachas, and extra food privileges, luxuries few Soviet citizens ever saw. 'Surely it's possible to ensure that several thousand people can live very well . . . and better than well. If a child doesn't cry, the mother does not know what she needs. Ask for whatever you like. You won't be refused.'[1]

Beria was relieved of the day-to-day cares of running the NKVD, but made a deputy premier with general responsibility for State security. The sacrifice was immense for a nation devastated by war and it distorted the Soviet economy for decades to come. But Stalin, convinced that the USSR needed the bomb to survive, did not count the cost.

The Soviets had been relatively unconcerned about atomic weapons until the bombing of Hiroshima and Nagasaki. Stalin knew about the possibilities of nuclear fission, and had been aware for three years that the Americans and British were building a 'new, experimental super-bomb'; his spies had told him. But he had also picked up on a telling point made by one of his scientists. Until early 1942 the scientific journals in the US and Britain had been full of theoretical papers about fission and particle physics. Then, abruptly, they stopped and nothing appeared about the latest work. 'This silence is not the result of an absence of research,' the distinguished physicist Georgi Flerov wrote to Stalin. 'A seal of silence has been imposed and this is the best proof of the vigorous work now going on abroad.'[2]

Stalin took note. He had seen intelligence reports from John Cairncross in Britain, the well-placed Fifth Man in the Cambridge spy ring, who was Private Secretary to Lord Hankey, a member of the War Cabinet. These reports referred to a project that British scientists estimated would take two to five years to complete in a joint effort with the US. At this point, though, Stalin was more concerned about weeks and months – the Soviet Union's position, with much of the country occupied by the Germans, was critical. Even if a bomb was feasible, it couldn't be built in time to make a difference to the war in the USSR, and he knew from other reliable intelligence sources that the German scientists were no more advanced than the Soviets in developing a weapon. In the autumn of 1942, more preoccupied by the battle in Stalingrad than theoretical physics, he authorised a modest nuclear project led by Kurchatov, reporting to Molotov, and ordered increased spying efforts in the US on what became the Manhattan Project.

When Stalin went to the Potsdam Conference in July 1945, he knew that the Americans were ready to test the bomb. So when Truman approached him casually after the third day of conference sessions and told him 'we have just tested a bomb of unusually destructive force' (though, carefully, he did not use the words 'nuclear' or 'atomic)', the Vozhd (Leader), barely reacted. He calmly replied, 'I am glad to hear it. I hope you will make good use of it against the Japanese.' When he returned to his villa soon afterwards he told Molotov what had happened. The commander of Soviet land forces in Europe, Marshal Georgi Zhukov, the mastermind of the Battle for Berlin, was also there, as was one of Molotov's young deputies, Andrei Gromyko, who reported the conversation in his diary: 'They are trying to raise their price,' the Foreign Minister, a man almost as ruthless as his master, said. 'Let them,' Stalin replied. 'We can talk to Kurchatov and get him to speed things up.'[3]

It was only after the destruction of Hiroshima that Stalin seemed to realise that the bomb had changed the military balance, and '. . . that cannot be allowed', he told Beria and a group of scientists on the day the second bomb was dropped, on Nagasaki. Dropping the bombs, he said, was an 'act of super-barbarity . . . there was no need to use it. Japan was already doomed.' He repeated what he had told Molotov at Potsdam, that the Americans and British 'are hoping that we won't be able to develop the bomb ourselves for some time . . . They want to force us to accept their plans for Europe and elsewhere in the world. Well, that's not going to happen.'

There is no record of any discussion about whether it was worth devoting vast resources to building a bomb. It was simply a given that the Soviets would try to match the United States.

Stalin did not doubt for a moment that it was essential and urgent. Western diplomats, too, realised it was inevitable. 'Victory over Germany . . . made the Soviet leaders confident that national security [was] at last within their reach,' wrote the British Ambassador to Moscow, Sir Archibald Clark Kerr, at the end of December 1945. 'Then plumb came the atomic bomb . . . at one blow the balance which had seemed set and steady was rudely shaken. Russia was balked . . . when everything seemed to be within their grasp. The 300 divisions were shorn of much of their value.'[4]

How to deal with the new reality? Until his scientists could arm him with a weapon, Stalin would simply carry on as though the bomb wasn't there and refuse to be intimidated, while the Americans worked out how to react. He knew from his spies that the US did not have many atom bombs ready for use – three or four at the end of 1945, nine by the middle of 1946 – not enough to deliver a knockout blow against the USSR and its armies. He hoped he could get a Soviet weapon by the time America's nuclear forces were large enough to pose an overwhelming threat.

Lavrenti Beria was the obvious choice to take charge of Task Number One. He was a monster, a mass murderer and a sexual predator on an epic scale, but he was also an exceptionally able organiser. Every task Stalin assigned him, from running purges, torture chambers and foreign espionage rings to handling huge construction projects with the use of forced labour, Beria had delivered with a chilling, ruthless efficiency. This would be no different. Though he was highly intelligent, unlike many of the other Soviet potentates, Beria never comprehended the science behind the project, not that it was an essential qualification for the job. Neither Roosevelt nor Churchill had ever understood the intricacies of the Manhattan Project, only the military power it would give them.

Until Hiroshima, Beria had been deeply sceptical that the bomb would work. All the intelligence reports from the atomic spies passed across his desk and as one of his aides at the NKVD,

Anatoly Yatskov, said, 'Beria suspected disinformation from these reports, thinking [the Americans and British] were trying to draw us into huge expenditure of resources and effort on work which had no future. Beria remained suspicious about the intelligence even when work on the atomic bomb was in full swing in the Soviet Union. Once when an agent was reporting . . . [on new] information, Beria said to him "If this is misinformation I'll put you all in the cellar." '[5]

Even the mention of Beria's name struck fear in most people – one of his Politburo colleagues, Anastas Mikoyan, said, 'Just one remark like "Beria wants this done" worked absolutely without fail.' But for the bomb project the executioner realised he had to use more subtle methods. He won the scientists' loyalty by protecting them from others in the gargantuan Soviet bureaucracy and understanding that, for effective and creative scientific work, they needed the kind of intellectual freedom all but unknown in the USSR. He let them be. On occasions he would try to be pleasant, in an ingratiating, unctuous manner. Beria was introduced to the brilliant young research physicist Andrei Sakharov, who would later become 'father' of the Soviet Union's much more powerful H-bomb. Sakharov recalled that Beria's 'plump, moist and deathly cold handshake' reminded him of death itself.[6]

The Soviets were fortunate in finding Kurchatov. He was a brooding Russian intellectual of the old school, most of whom had been wiped out in the purges of the 1930s. Kurchatov had kept his head down during the terror. A man of broad literary and artistic tastes, as well as a supremely gifted scientist, he inspired affection – 'a great soul, like a teddy bear, no one could ever be cross with him.' But he was also fiercely patriotic and as practical and ruthless as he was imaginative. 'He was complex, multi-layered, ideally suited for secret work,' one colleague recalled.[7]

Kurchatov was shown most of the intelligence material obtained by the Soviet spies in America during the war. By far the most valuable source was the physicist Klaus Fuchs, an émigré

German communist who went to Britain in the early 1930s and was assigned by the British as one of their representatives on the Manhattan Project. He understood the science in a way the others did not. Kurchatov said the information 'yielded huge, inestimable significance for our state of science ... It allowed us to bypass many labour-intensive phases of our working out problems and to learn about new technical ways of solving them.' Fuchs's information also gave Kurchatov the appearance of possessing the Midas touch, a colleague recalled. Given the choice of two or three different ways of approaching a technical problem, Kurchatov seemed always to know which was the right course to take. As Molotov said later, 'It was a very good intelligence operation by our Chekists [intelligence agents] ... they neatly stole what we needed.' But, ultimately, spying was not the crucial factor in the Russian bomb project. Soviet technicians and scientists were extremely able, and once they were given the political backing, huge resources and uranium they needed, they got there by themselves. It was estimated later that the stolen intelligence gave the Soviets a head start of around eighteen months to two years.[8]

Meanwhile Stalin allowed the scientists the kind of leeway given to few Soviet citizens. As long as they produced the goods. 'Leave them in peace,' he told Beria after meeting Kurchatov. 'We can always shoot them later.'[9]

*

Stalin afforded grudging respect, if not admiration, to the other leaders of the 'Big Three'. He saw Franklin Roosevelt and Winston Churchill as major players that he could do business with on a more or less equal basis. He had little but contempt for their successors, however. Harry Truman was 'a noisy shopkeeper' who displayed poor intellect. As for Clement Attlee, he regarded the new Prime Minister in London as a lightweight, 'a fool who doesn't know how to use power'. He simply couldn't understand how a figure with the stature and gifts of Churchill had lost the general election in Britain in July 1945, which was yet another reason to distrust 'bourgeois democracy'.[10]

At the beginning of 1946 Stalin was the only one of the victorious triumvirate still in place. But aged sixty-seven he was not the man he had been. The gap could hardly have been greater between the heroic figure of Soviet propaganda, the High Pontiff of the communist faith, and the rather sickly-looking man now in the Kremlin. He had been handsome in his youth, even dashing, though never physically prepossessing or impressive in large groups. He now looked shorter than his five feet four inches, and had developed a pronounced paunch that was not hidden by the baggy trousers and grey square-cut tunics that hung loosely around his body. Even on ceremonial occasions, when he often wore the trademark white uniforms he had designed himself, he looked stout. He shuffled, and his withered left arm hung stiffly at his side. The pockmarks on his skin from a childhood bout of smallpox were more pronounced. His moustache was scrawny, coarse and streaked with nicotine stains from the pipe he liked to fill with tobacco from cigarettes. His teeth were badly discoloured, and his eyes yellowish where once they had been amber – but they still lit up 'in a flash of menace and fury' when he heard something which displeased him.

The Soviet leader still had a phenomenally good mind and read voraciously, everything from Russian and European history to American poetry. If his exceptional memory was beginning to fade just a little, it nonetheless remained a powerful force. He always seemed to have an apt quotation to hand. At one of the social engagements at the Yalta Conference a few months earlier he had at length quoted Walt Whitman to the American delegation – as well as reams of statistics about US steel production. Stalin hugely impressed foreign leaders and diplomats; 'Smart as hell,' said Truman, who presumably did not know what Stalin had said about him.

Anthony Eden, who had seen Stalin in action at all the wartime conferences, said towards the end of the conflict that he would make him first choice as chief negotiator for any team going into any conference: 'He never stormed. He was seldom even irritated. By more subtle methods he got what he wanted without having seemed so obdurate.' Eden's most senior official, Sir Alexander Cadogan, agreed. He wrote to his wife from Yalta that Stalin was much the most impressive of the Big Three. 'He sat there for the first hour and a half or so without saying a word. There was no call for him to do so. The President [Roosevelt] flapped about; the PM [Churchill] boomed, but Joe just sat there, taking it all in and being rather amused. When he did chip in he never used a superfluous word and spoke very much to the point.' In an official minute around the same time, Cadogan wrote simply of Stalin, 'he *is* a great man'.[11]

Stalin had always been a patient man. While he rose gradually to absolute power over the Communist Party and the State, he was always calculating, waiting for the right time to act. But now he was often irascible, irritable and unpredictable. 'In the last years, Stalin began to weaken,' said Molotov, his obedient lackey for decades. 'Sclerosis comes to all with age in various degrees, but in him it was noticeable.' He lost his temper and became conceited, 'which was not a good feature in a statesman.' Another of his underlings, Nikita Khrushchev, agreed that after the war 'he wasn't quite right in the head ... He was very jittery. His last years were the most dangerous. He swung to extremes.' He could still charm and manipulate, but he now grew increasingly autocratic.[12]

There was no longer any pretence of anything other than one-person rule. Even during the Great Purge of the 1930s and the early years of the war, there had been a nod to a more collegiate ruling style. Now Stalin simply issued instructions. 'Sometimes he would listen to others if he liked what they were saying,' recalled Khrushchev. 'Or else he might growl at them and immediately, without consulting anyone, formulate the text of a Resolution of

. . . the Council of Ministers and after that the document would be published. It was completely arbitrary rule.'

He took immense interest in the private lives of those close to him but, over time, as he grew ever more isolated from ordinary life and the Russian people, these numbered only the other members of the ruling elite. 'He often appeared unannounced at their homes to try to establish what the hierarchy was within their families,' recalled Lavrenti Beria's son, Sergo Beria, who was often present at these visits. ' He made sure the families of his underlings did not see too much of each other – he feared friendships would lead to coalitions against him. He did not allow them to be absent for even a few hours without knowing where they were. A conversation between them of any length aroused his suspicion. He did not like them to have evening parties at their own homes. Any meeting without his supervision was suspect in his eyes.'

Stalin's social life was confined to these 'business associates'.[13] Several times a week, at his insistence, Kremlin power brokers and, occasionally, visitors from other, mostly Eastern European communist parties would dine with him, usually at Kuntsevo, his dacha about fifteen kilometres west of Moscow. Refusal to attend was unthinkable. Here, work and 'relaxation' blurred seamlessly in 'Rule by dining room', as one Stalin biographer put it. They were ghastly bacchanals at which Stalin's cronies would be ritually humiliated in order to provide entertainment for the Red Tsar. But they could be deadly serious. Once, after one of these drinking bouts, Khrushchev was on his way back to his Moscow apartment with another Party chieftain, the planning supremo Georgi Malenkov. With visible relief, he sank back into the seat and whispered, 'One never knows if one is going home or to prison.'[14]

As he got older Stalin turned more vicious to his entourage, men who – after him – were the most powerful people in the Soviet Union, and who inspired fear amongst their own underlings.

He had always demanded obedience and endless sacrificial work from his subordinates. But as time wore on, he demanded supreme sycophancy, too. After the war he took long breaks, spending three or four months of the year away from his capital, usually at a villa near Sochi in the Crimea. These absences were not necessarily a relief to his circle back in the Kremlin, as the leader was often particularly moody and difficult when away from Moscow, and he humiliated them from afar with a string of rebukes by telegram. They learned to be even more wary when the leader was out of town.

In the months following VE Day and throughout 1946 Stalin was angry with Molotov, a faithful communist from pre-revolutionary days, whom Lenin had nicknamed 'Iron Arse' because of his stiffness and formality. Leon Trotsky, an acute observer who loathed Molotov, described him as 'the personification of mediocrity'. Yet to outsiders, Molotov – the only man to have shaken hands and exchanged pleasantries with Hitler, von Ribbentrop, Churchill, Roosevelt, Truman and Mao Zedong – seemed the most likely candidate to succeed to the top position if anything happened to Stalin.

In the Western press, rumours began to appear that the Great Dictator's health was ailing. One Norwegian paper called Molotov 'the second citizen of the Soviet Union'. A small piece in the *New York Times* on 3 December 1945 claimed that 'the Soviet Politburo has sent Stalin on vacation' and a Reuters report on the same day announced, wrongly, that Molotov was responsible for a relaxation of press censorship in the USSR. This was all Stalin needed to put Molotov in his place.

At the time, four of the most senior members of the Politburo shared power, and the workload, under Stalin: Molotov, Malenkov, Beria, and the wily Armenian economics expert Mikoyan. Two days after the *New York Times* story appeared, Stalin sent them a vitriolic cable from the Crimea blaming Molotov for permitting wrongheaded articles to be published in the foreign press 'containing lampoons against the Soviet Government.' Separately he wrote to three of the group, excluding Molotov:

None of us has the right to change the course of our policies unilaterally, but Molotov has accorded himself this right. He gives foreigners an impression that he has his own policy distinct from that of the Government and of Stalin, and the impression that with Molotov the West can do business . . . Why? And on what grounds? . . . I thought we could confine ourselves to a reprimand of Molotov. But that is no longer enough. I am convinced that Molotov does not much value the interests of our state and the prestige of our Government, so long as he gains popularity among certain foreign circles. I can no longer regard this comrade as my first deputy . . . I send this only to the three of you. I have not sent it to Molotov as I do not trust the conscientiousness of some of those around him . . . I ask you to summon Molotov and read this telegram to him in full . . .

They did as they were told: 'We summoned M . . . he admitted that he had committed many serious mistakes, but he regarded the lack of trust in him as unjust and he shed some tears.' It was not enough to mollify Stalin. Molotov had to show total obeisance, and his fawning response makes for uncomfortable reading even today. He cabled Stalin on 6 December admitting that he had erred on the side of 'false liberalism and committed a gross opportunistic mistake which has brought harm to our state.' He went on: 'Your . . . message is filled with deep distrust towards me, both as a Bolshevik and a person, which I take as a most serious warning for all my future work. I shall try through deeds to regain your trust, in which every honest Bolshevik sees not personal trust but also trust of the Party, which is dearer to me than my life.'

Molotov was demoted and further humiliations followed, including the arrest and imprisonment of his beloved wife, Polina, but he remained at the highest levels of Party and State, albeit suitably chastised and terrorised.[15]

*

For Soviet citizens, Stalin *was* the state, its architect in the 1930s and its deliverer in the Great Patriotic War. For most communist believers throughout the world he was still the keeper of the flame, and after the war the personality cult built around him grew to inflated proportions. Pictures and busts of him were everywhere in the USSR. 'When he spoke in public you didn't want to be identified as the first one to stop applauding,' one old Bolshevik recalled.

Stalin said it was simply a political tool and that socialism needed heroes: 'The Russians are a Tsarist people . . . they need Tsars,' he told his clique. But he took elaborate trouble to burnish the image, attending to the smallest minutiae with his usual meticulous attention to detail. In 1946 he edited a short biography of himself that would be published on 1 January the following year. He went through the text personally with the utmost care; it was too important a job to be left to anyone else. When he wasn't satisfied he added sentences. The master of the Soviet Union and its new empire added to the manuscript in his own hand: 'Comrade Stalin's genius enabled him to divine the enemy's plans and defeat them. The battles in which Comrade Stalin directed the Soviet armies are brilliant examples of operational military skill . . . Although he performed his task as leader of the Party and the people with consummate skill and enjoyed the unreserved support of the entire Soviet people, Stalin never allowed his work to be marred by the slightest hint of vanity, conceit or self-adulation.'[16]

# 4

## Stunde Null – Zero Hour

They were still finding bodies near the coalface a month after the accident. Three days before the New Year, as the afternoon shift was coming to an end at the colliery in Peine, just east of Hanover, forty-six miners plunged to their deaths and dozens more were injured when a cage (elevator) taking them to the surface fell hundreds of feet down the pit shaft. The mine was in the German industrial heartland of the Ruhr, so vital for the economic rebirth of the country, and an area that fell under British jurisdiction. An inquiry was set up immediately. At the end of January 1946, Arthur Street, the British Occupation zone's most senior civil servant, concluded that the disaster was caused by carelessness and human factors that could have been prevented.

Safety regulations in the mine had not been enforced because of a dangerous shortage of senior engineers with mining experience, Street told the British Military Governor, Field Marshal Bernard Montgomery. A cable in the mine shaft that was supposed to have held the cage in place had snapped. The regulations stated that all transportation equipment for miners should be checked regularly – at least once a week. But the pit shaft had not been examined for many weeks as the colliery no longer had a safety manager. 'The clamp which holds the cable in place was not properly adjusted . . . the second shaft which should have been used to evacuate the injured was not in working order and the cage doors were improperly fitted,' Street's report said. More than half the managers and senior engineers in Germany's coal mines had been removed in the past few months because they had been members of the Nazi Party, Street reminded Montgomery. They had included those at Peine.[1]

A few days after concluding his report, Street was again called in to investigate, this time following an even more deadly accident. Early in the afternoon of 20 February a massive gas and coal dust explosion ripped through the Monopol-Grimberg mine at Unna, around twenty kilometres east of Dortmund. Nearly five hundred men were trapped underground. Just weeks earlier most of the mine's inspectors and managers had been fired because of their Nazi affiliations. They had been replaced, as a temporary measure, by long-retired inspectors who were no longer up to the job, or young men who had been press-ganged to work in the mines but had very little experience. The rescue crew sent to free the trapped miners had no training and was totally incompetent to handle a disaster of this scale. There was only one manager left at the Unna colliery with any expertise or knowledge of the mine. But as Street told Montgomery in his second report on a Ruhr mining disaster in weeks, this man, a chief inspector, was unfit for work.

'Towards midnight on the day of the explosion it became clear that operations were not proceeding to any set plan, although ample material and sufficient appliances had been provided,' said Street, and the inspector in charge was suffering from a serious breakdown. 'He was unable to concentrate on his work and ... [was] extremely nervous.' A week earlier he had been denounced by workers at the mine as an enthusiastic National Socialist and arrested by occupation investigators, whose job was to cleanse Germany of fascism. He was released pending further enquiries and was, for the time being, allowed to return to work. But he was a broken and terrified man – 'not suitable to be in charge of rescue work,' Street stated. In the early hours of the morning the former director of the mine – a well-known Nazi Party member from the early 1930s, much loathed in the neighbourhood – was released from jail to manage the crisis. With some quick and effective action he was able to save 57 of the trapped miners, but 417 men died. It was the worst coal-mining disaster in German history.

The two accidents might well have happened anyway. It is unlikely that the absence of senior mining officials in Germany at the time was the only, or perhaps the principal, cause of the disasters. But many Germans believed that it was and saw their occupiers' efforts to seek out and condemn 'ordinary' Nazis as unjust, futile and counterproductive. More to the point, the Allies, at least the British, Americans and French in the Western zones, soon came to see things the same way. The accidents at Unna and Peine starkly highlighted the dilemma the Allies faced – and marked the turning point of the Occupation, transforming it from an act of retribution into an experiment in paternalism; from reforming zeal into crowd control. The Germans were starving, and millions of desperate refugees were streaming into the occupied zones. The most pressing need was to revive the country's failing economy and rebuild its ruined social structure. Without the mines to fuel the engine of German industry, it couldn't be done.

And it couldn't be done without the Nazis. A month after the explosion at the Monopol-Grimberg mine, Arthur Street wrote to his superiors in London. 'We are very much alive to the dangers inherent in too drastic a policy of de-Nazification in industry. These . . . [mining] disasters may well be an indication that we have already gone dangerously fast in pressing our present policy.' In the first six months after the war 333 mining officials in the British zone had been fired, jailed, or suspended while they were investigated for Nazi Party affiliations. Within weeks of the Unna disaster 313 of them had got their jobs back.[2]

*

The Germans called it Stunde Null – Zero Hour. Of course there is no such thing, in life or history; nothing starts from nowhere. But with total defeat, unconditional surrender and occupation by foreign armies, it seemed that way to the Germans. More than five and a half million of them had died in a war that left their country all but destroyed physically and morally. Simply to survive amidst the chaos and rubble required a major effort of body and mind. And resilience. Between fourteen and fifteen million Germans were homeless, not including the eight to nine million former slave labourers the Nazis had imported from the lands they conquered, concentration camp survivors, and prisoners of war roaming the countryside or in 'displaced persons' camps. It was the biggest refugee crisis anywhere in the world, before or since.

The cities were eerie places. George Clare, a soldier who had lived in Berlin before the war, returned for the first time in early 1946 and described it in his memoir *Berlin Days*:

> The most striking impression was not visual but aural. The 1938 Berlin had assaulted one's ears with lively and strident crescendos, harsh ... high decibel; a medley of blaring car horns, squeaking brakes, clanging trams, shouting newspaper sellers. But now, like slow drumbeats ... each sound rose and remained alone, the clip-clop of often wooden-soled footsteps, the rattle of a handcart, the chugging of a wood-fuelled bus, the gear crash of an army lorry. This absence of the constant roar of city life was more unsettling than the sight of bombed and shelled buildings, of jagged outlines of broken masonry ... I'd been prepared for that, but not for a city hushed to a whisper.[3]

The devastation in other cities, too, was almost complete. More than three and a half million city apartments were destroyed by American and British bombing and many hundreds of thousands from Soviet shellfire as the Red Army headed west.

Between a third and a half of Germany's entire housing stock had been destroyed, considerably more damage than the Luftwaffe inflicted on Britain during the Blitz. Cologne was 70 per cent destroyed, Hamburg 53 per cent, Hanover 51 per cent, Dortmund 60 per cent. Munich was so devastated that, returning above ground one morning from a bomb shelter, it seemed to the brilliant diarist Victor Klemperer that it 'truly did almost make one think that the Last Judgment was imminent.' To Anne O'Hare McCormick of the *New York Times*, one of the best reporters on the aftermath of World War Two, millions of people were living 'in medieval fashion surrounded by the broken down machines of the twentieth century.'[4]

The Allies had originally intended to be harsh on Germany. The American 'mission statement' after VE Day, JC1067, declared: 'It should be brought home to the Germans that . . . their ruthless war and the fanatical Nazi resistance has destroyed the German economy and made chaos and suffering inevitable . . . Germans cannot escape responsibility for what they have brought on to themselves. Germany will not be occupied for the purposes of liberation but as a defeated enemy nation.' The top priority of post-war planners was to ensure that a Germany once again driven by militarism did not use its power to start yet another conflict in Europe. And both the Americans and the British calculated that the problem of how to deal with the Soviet Union could be resolved when the victory over Germany was won.

During the last two years of the war the US had endorsed a plan by one of Franklin Roosevelt's favourite financiers, Treasury Secretary Henry Morgenthau, who had developed many of the New Deal policies of the 1930s. Morgenthau's idea was to split up Germany into small regions, entirely divest it of industry and the ability to manufacture modern armaments and 'pastoralise' the country, turning it into an agrarian, peasant economy that would be powerless to wage war on its neighbours again. But when American soldiers and officials reached Germany, they saw how unrealistic and foolhardy the plan was. Conditions were, according to the senior War Department official John McCloy, a personal emissary sent to Europe by Truman immediately after VE Day, 'worse, far worse, than you can possibly imagine' – and things needed to improve fast.

A major rethink was soon under way in Washington, led by the highly influential and experienced Secretary of War, Henry Stimson, who had been an advisor to American presidents since before the First World War. He told Truman that 'a nation like Germany can't be reduced to a peasant level without creating the breeding ground for another war.' If prosperity in one part of the world helped to create prosperity in another, as Americans firmly believed, the same was true of poverty. 'Enforced poverty is even worse for it destroys the spirit, not only of the victims but debases the victor. It would be just such a crime as the Germans themselves ... perpetrated against their victims. It would be a crime against civilization itself ... [Morgenthau's proposals] are an open confession of the bankruptcy of hope for a reasonable economic and political settlement of war.' Truman was told something similar by one of his predecessors, former President Herbert Hoover, when they met at the White House after the war was won. 'You can have vengeance or peace, but you can't have both.'* Truman was convinced. He ditched the Morgenthau plan, and soon afterwards ditched Morgenthau too, unceremoniously firing him. Truman even went as far as describing Morgenthau as 'a blockhead and a nut, who doesn't know shit from apple butter'. This was perhaps overly harsh, since even if he didn't know much about Germany, Morgenthau, a successful banker, certainly 'knew' money.

The British had already reached the same conclusion: a punitive peace would be disastrous and would leave Europe devastated, unable to recover. A Cabinet minute to the Foreign Office in the autumn of 1945 made the argument plainly: 'Unless we do what we can to help, we may lose next winter what we won at such terrible cost last spring ... Desperate men are liable to destroy the structure of their society to find in the wreckage some substitute

---

* Another example of homespun advice to the President on how to treat the Germans came at the end of 1945 from Truman's Secretary for War, Kenneth Royall. 'You can starve 'em, shoot 'em or feed 'em.'

for hope. If we let . . . [Germany and Europe] go cold and hungry we . . . [will] lose some of the foundations of order on which the hopes for worldwide peace depend.' The Russians saw things differently. Around twenty-five million Soviet citizens had been killed in what they called the Great Patriotic War, eight million of them soldiers. The Germans had raped and pillaged their way through thousands of villages in Russia, Ukraine, Byelorussia; now a defeated Germany must pay reparations for their crimes and never again be in a position to wage war on the USSR. To the Soviets, the revival of Germany and the rest of Europe, particularly Western Europe, was of minor importance; another reason that the partnership between the wartime allies began to dissolve, ending their marriage of convenience.[5]

*

At the end of the war the Western Allies had no clear idea of what they would or could do in Germany. George Kennan, one of the State Department's most senior post-war policymakers, later recalled, 'At the moment we accepted . . . responsibility we had no programme for the rehabilitation of the economy of our zone.' But while they were making up their minds, conditions for the German people worsened. For many survivors, the months after the war were harder than anything they had experienced during it. Since the end of 1943, when many Germans had begun to realise they were losing the war, a remark had become commonplace in Germany: 'Better enjoy the war; the peace will be terrible.' A poor harvest, disrupted transport links and a bad winter had depleted already low food stocks. The division of the four Occupation zones – American, British, French and Soviet – had been decided after the Yalta Conference in February 1945. By then victory in Europe was assured, but nobody knew for certain exactly where the Allied armies would be when, eventually, the Germans surrendered.[6]

The food shortages were most acute in the British zone. The

British occupied the industrial powerhouse of Germany, but there was little agricultural land. The region was unable to feed itself and depended on food from the traditional German farming lands in the east – Thuringia, Saxony, Pomerania – now controlled by the Soviet Union. A British Foreign Office minute to Churchill shortly before he left office warned that 'German misery . . . will be on a scale unknown in Europe since the Middle Ages'. And so it proved.[7]

During the winter of 1945–46 there was mass starvation in Germany, with the British zone by far the worst affected. Montgomery had said at the end of the war that he had little sympathy if the Germans went hungry as 'they had brought it on themselves.' Months later, having seen for himself the results of malnutrition, he changed his mind. In early 1946 he wrote an urgent note to the Cabinet warning of a 'catastrophe' if no extra rations were sent. 'There would be famine conditions to an extent which no civilised people should inflict on their beaten enemies,' he said. At nearly the same time General Lucius Clay, Montgomery's American counterpart, sent a similar cable to his superiors in Washington. 'Some cold and hunger . . . [is] necessary to make the German people realise the consequences of a war which they caused,' he wrote. 'But this . . . suffering should not extend to the point where it results in starvation and sickness.' Clay also told officials in London that rations in the British zone 'can hardly maintain life.'[8]

The United Nations Relief and Rehabilitation Administration, which was feeding refugees in displaced-persons camps in Germany, but not German citizens, recommended that an adult who worked needed 2,430 calories a day 'as subsistence'. In the British zone, the average daily consumption in the autumn of 1945 was 1,500 calories; by February 1946 that had decreased to 1,100. It was enough to survive, but only just, and not for any sustained work.

Early that year, Konrad Adenauer, appointed Mayor of Cologne when the city was liberated and later a much-celebrated Chancellor of West Germany, was removed from his post by the British occupation force after complaining, amongst other things, about the food shortages. He wrote to friends and admirers in Switzerland to beg for extra food and vitamins for his son, penicillin for his wife and cheese and Nescafé for himself. He said that without help from outside, his family could not have survived the eighteen months after the war. Yet the martinet Brigadier John Barraclough, when he sacked Adenauer, told him that he was 'politically unreliable and a troublemaker.'* The historian Ernst Jünger who, as a Nazi fellow traveller and apologist for Hitler actually *was* politically unreliable, also received extra food from friends and readers, who dipped into their own rations to help feed him. But he spoke for many when he told the British Occupation authorities that the rations for most of the people he knew were half what they had been the previous autumn: 'This is a death sentence for many who up to now have only been able to keep their heads above water with the greatest effort, above all children, old people and refugees.'9 Apart from humanitarian concerns, some British Occupation officials, and planners in Britain, worried that hunger would damage German revival and lengthen the Occupation which was costing the Exchequer so dear. On these starvation rations the Germans were not strong enough to dig the coal and

---

* Adenauer would never forget the treatment he received immediately after the war and still smarted from it many years later. He was summoned to appear before Barraclough and two other British officers and told gruffly that he could not sit in their presence. The Brigadier read out a letter dismissing him and banning him from all political activity. He was ordered to leave Cologne and return to his home village, Rhöndorf. Not long afterwards the British, on advice from the Americans, realised how much they needed him as a reliable, anti-communist voice, and encouraged him to set up the Christian Democratic Union, which presided over the German 'economic miracle' of the 1950s and has been in power for most of the period since the war. Despite his treatment, Adenauer nonetheless preferred the British to the Americans, who had originally appointed him mayor before they handed over the responsibility to the UK. At first he was flattered and delighted to accept – until he was told by a US officer, with no humour intended, that it may have had something to do with his name beginning with an A.

roll the steel on their own, sufficiently to bring about recovery. An editorial in *The Times* of London made the point simply: 'The evidence of a deterioration in German physique over the last few months as a result of malnutrition is irresistible, and of all the forces inhibiting economic recovery in Germany this is the most far reaching. It reduces the efficiency of industrial workers both directly by its effect on health and indirectly by drawing them from their jobs into the search for off the ration food. The normal rate of absenteeism exceeds 20 per cent.' Britain increased food supplies to its Occupation zone and rations began to improve markedly from the late summer onwards – but at considerable cost to Britain itself. Rations at home were reduced, in order to increase supplies to Germany.

With hunger came disease. There was no influenza epidemic like the one in 1919 that wiped out millions of people throughout Europe, but other diseases were rampant. In Berlin, where the sewage system had been destroyed, rotting corpses were still polluting the water supply in the spring of 1946. The city's infant mortality rate was 66 for every thousand live births, around eight times higher than before the war. Robert Murphy, General Clay's political advisor, reported back to Washington at the beginning of 1946 that, among the homeless sheltering in the Lehrter railway station, an average of ten people a day were dying from malnutrition, exhaustion and various diseases. Half the children in Berlin suffered from rickets, and TB was at five times pre-war levels. In the British zone there were a thousand new cases of typhoid a month and two thousand of diphtheria, while pellagra, dysentery and impetigo, all diseases associated with malnutrition, were common.[10]

*

'They send us chicken food – and expect us to thank them,' the popular historian and lecturer Johannes Semler told an audience in Erlangen in July 1946. The Germans were not grateful, particularly when, as they saw it, the 'help' they received came with so many strings attached. The Western Allies might have given up on the idea of punishing the German people, but not of blaming them. The Germans resented Occupation troops on the ground and foreign officials dictating what they did. But most of all they loathed their new masters' air of moral superiority.

The Allies firmly believed in German collective guilt, that all Germans were responsible for the rise of Hitler, for starting the war, and for the atrocities committed during the conflict. Most Germans either did not understand the accusations in the first place or were too preoccupied in finding a roof over their heads and putting food in their stomachs to worry about philosophical notions of guilt. It was not until the late 1950s and 1960s that a long reflective period of introspection began. In the aftermath of the war, only a minority were able to see themselves as others saw them. Most Germans seemed to believe that as they were the ones who had lived through Nazism and had lost the war in humiliating defeat, they were the misunderstood victims.

A powerful version of this 'narrative of self-pity', as one future German politician later described it, is told in the first, semi-autobiographical, novel of the Nobel Laureate Heinrich Böll, *Kreuz ohne Liebe.** His hero, Christoph, who had been fighting in the Wehrmacht since 1939, is filled with despair and world-weariness:

> I want no more. It is horrible to have been a soldier in a war
> for six years and always to have had the wish that it would be
> lost; to see the collapse and at the same time to know that
> whatever power succeeds it and kicks the daylights out of the

---

\* One of the few books by Böll not translated into English (yet). It was written in 1946/1947, but was published only in 2002, seventeen years after his death. A literal translation of the title would be 'Cross Without Love', but that is not as poetic as the author would probably have wished. I am indebted to Giles McDonogh's wonderful book *After the Reich* for drawing my attention to the novel.

corpse of this state will quite probably be equally diabolic. The devil possesses all the power in this world and a change of power is only a change of rank among devils.

He had little love or admiration for his conquerors:

Do you believe that these people who conquer us, with their rubber soles and tins of spam, will ever understand what we have suffered. Do you believe they will understand what it feels like to be showered with their bombs and shells and at the same time to be sullied by this diabolic state; what it means to be crushed by these two millstones? They simply cannot have suffered as much as us . . . there is a hierarchy of suffering in which we will remain the victors, without the world ever learning or understanding what it was we felt.[11]

The feeling of resentment was more directly put by the anti-Nazi Tilli Wolff-Mönckeberg, in a series of unsent letters to her adult children. Then in her mid-sixties, she had been born into privilege and wealth. A diary entry from the 1890s records 'Prince Bismarck to lunch . . . Herr Johannes Brahms to dinner'. Now she wrote to her daughter:

People are bowing and scraping to the English, trying to find favour. I do understand that W [her husband] is deeply depressed and has no hope for his own particular world. Now he is disillusioned by the limitless arrogance and dishonesty with which they treat us, proclaiming to the whole world that only Germans could have sunk so low in such abysmal cruelty and bestiality . . . that they themselves are beyond reproach . . . And WHO destroyed our beautiful cities, regardless of human life, of women, children and old people? WHO poured down poisonous phosphorous during the terror rounds on unfortunate fugitives, driving them like living torches into the ruins? WHO dive-bombed homeless peasants? . . . Who was it . . . I ask you?[12]

The Americans imagined they could 'reform' the people by compelling them to watch films about the horrors of the concentration camps; adults were only given their ration cards when they entered the movie theatre. In Frankfurt, the writer Stephen Hermlin went to a screening of a film about the camps at Buchenwald and Dachau. 'In the half light of the projector, I could see that most people turned their faces away after the beginning of the film and stayed that way until it was over . . . that turned-away face is the attitude of many millions.'[13]

Church leaders and politicians spoke for the vast majority. The Catholic Archbishop of Cologne, Joseph Frings, was no Nazi and had indeed bravely opposed the Nazi regime. Now he stood up to the Allies. 'The Führer took decisions on his own and at most consulted his closest advisors,' he declared in a sermon in Cologne in what became for the next couple of decades the conventional view of most Germans to the Third Reich's crimes: 'As for the atrocities, most Germans first heard about them from the BBC afterwards . . . The German people are much more the victims than the perpetrators of these atrocities . . . The whole nation cannot be considered guilty . . . many thousands of old people, children, mothers, are wholly innocent, and it is they who now bear the brunt of the suffering in this general misery.'*

---

* Frings was lucky to be alive in 1946 and had known much personal loss. In 1942 he survived a bomb blast at his home in which his sister was killed. A few months later he was again unhurt in an air-raid shelter when two nuns died and five others were badly injured. One of his brothers was killed in an air raid in Magdeburg, another in a Russian camp. The Archbishop gave his name to a German word that is still commonly used today – 'fringsen'. It means to 'help yourself' in very particular circumstances; in other words that stealing is justified when one is in dire straits, for example when starving people resort to theft to feed their families. The idea derives from a sermon Frings gave in the freezing winter of 1946 when he appeared to condone stealing coal from Allied supplies if there was no other way of obtaining fuel. 'We live in times when we have to help ourselves to little things that are necessary to keep ourselves alive and to maintain our health, if we may not obtain them from our work or by requesting them.' In fact, in the next sentence he went on to

Kurt Schumacher, the leader of the Social Democratic Party, a courageous anti-Nazi who spent eight years in Dachau before and during the war, was personally affronted by the Allies' moral indignation. In particular he loathed the British officials who treated Germans 'as though they were the Pukkah Sahib condescending to the natives.'

Schumacher wrote in early 1946:

> You cannot imagine what a frightful effect the propaganda attempt to impose 'collective guilt' on the German people has had on the German opponents of Nazism. The men and women in our country who even before 1933 risked so much in the fight against Nazism ... who after the assumption of power, at a time when the present victorious powers were still concluding state treaties with the Hitler regime, were working underground and were being put in prison and concentration camps. *They* should recognise *their* guilt. They do this in no way and in no circumstances.[14]

Some Allied voices agreed. Hans Hebe, a German Jewish exile to America and a talented journalist, returned to Germany after the war with the American Occupation force, and was responsible for setting up new newspapers and magazines in the American zone. German writers were then rigorously censored, banned from criticising the Occupation armies, but they were free to tell Hebe that they were tired of being forced to watch films about Nazi atrocities and of being lectured to by the Allies. Hebe told his bosses that, 'The idea that the nation should look back, questioning and repenting ... [is] the concept of a conqueror ... the people only worry about how to fill their stomachs and their stoves.'[15]

But he was largely ignored. A more common view was that of

say that this behaviour 'had gone too far ... and God will not forgive you.' But people only seemed to grasp his initial point.

another Jewish exile, George Clare, who returned to Berlin with the British army's Intelligence Corps in 1946. He loathed the Germans' 'constant whingeing about the injustice of their fate and their inexhaustible self-pity in defeat which ensured that one could not forget how pitiless they were in victory. A nation with the mark of Cain pretended it was composed of Abels. They cursed Hitler . . . but not for the crimes committed in their name (or with the willing help of many). They cursed him for betraying their trust and loyalty by giving them in return . . . a truncated Germany, its soil drenched in German blood.'[16]

*

The Occupation armies had been promised swift demobilisation. But while they waited to go home, many were determined to make the best of their lot. At first, Allied generals issued strict edicts against fraternisation of any kind with Germans. Relations between victors and vanquished were to be strictly official and formal. The Supreme Allied Commander, Dwight D. Eisenhower, ordered American soldiers not to have any contact with locals. They could not visit German homes; no drinking with Germans in bars was allowed, nor shaking hands; no playing games with German children or sports with adults; no inviting them to Allied concerts, cinemas or parties. GIs faced a sixty-five-dollar fine for breaking the rules. Similar orders were issued by British commanders, mainly, as they admitted, as a sop to public opinion at home. Most crucially, there was to be no contact between soldiers and German women. It was hardly surprising that the rules proved impractical, almost impossible to enforce and so frequently disobeyed, they had to be dropped – first by Montgomery and then by the Americans.

Briefly, a new, now long-forgotten, 'F' word – to 'frat' – entered the lexicon. 'We were healthy young men away from home, the war was over . . . frankly a lot of us thought of little else but fratting,' one Guards officer recalled years later.[17] For German women, friendships – or more – with Allied soldiers – were often the difference between life and death for them and their families; the GIs and Tommies gave them food, milk, medicines, and even luxuries, such as cigarettes and stockings, that they had been without for so long. A song by the satirist and cabaret performer Gunther Neumann became highly popular:

> Johnny took me like a lady,
> And we traded, nothing shady.
> Two pounds of coffee so I'd do it,
> Fruit juice cans so I'd renew it.
> Hot we got with burning skins,
> For a couple corned beef tins.
> But for chocolate – Hershey Bar
> I went further much than far.[18]

The conquerors had other attractions, too. There was an acute shortage of men. Two German men out of three born in 1918 did not survive World War Two, and a third of all children in Germany had lost their fathers. In the Berlin suburb of Treptow in February 1946 there were just 181 men for 1,105 women aged between eighteen and twenty-one. Major Arthur Moon, a Guards officer, was struck by what he saw: 'In our thousands of miles that we travelled Germany, the most outstanding fact of all was the total absence of men aged between seventeen and forty. It was a land of women, children and old men.' The Lucky Strike cigarettes, fresh coffee, nylon stockings and chocolate bars were appealing, but for the most part the relationships were not just transactional. American and even British men seemed far more attractive than the crippled veterans, returned prisoners of war, with the weariness of defeat about them, and the old men who were left in Germany. The occupiers seemed glamorous and desirable – not least since so many foreign films, books and music had been banned in the culturally oppressive Third Reich. A waitress explained to the

German/American playwright and film maker Carl Zuckmayer, who returned to his home in Berlin with the American forces, that she was no longer remotely interested in German men. 'They are too soft. They are not men any more . . . in the past they showed off too much.'[19]

For Allied troops, as George Clare recounted with some relish, it was 'liberty hall' in Berlin, even while the 'no frat' rules had been in place. Billets and barracks throughout the city 'were full of Anglo-German relations being repaired at a grass roots level . . . one never went into any bedroom, including one's own, without knocking first.' Walter Slatoff, a GI who later became a professor at Cornell University, wrote an article aimed at parents of American troops stationed in Germany:

> Imagine your own 18–19-year-old son removed entirely from your supervision, given an almost limitless amount of money, granted a power over women equal to that of Van Johnson or Clark Gable, fed a steady diet of lies and stories calculated to inspire suspicion, hate and cynicism and placed among a people who had lost all moral standards. The women of Berlin are hungry, cold and lonesome. The GIs have cigarettes, which will buy food and coal. The GIs have food . . . taken in large quantities from the Red Cross. The GIs have warm nightclubs. And the GIs provide a kind of security and meaning in an otherwise meaningless city. The result is an aggressive and wholesale manhunt in [Berlin]. They stand in front of nightclubs, parade up and down the streets and in front of the Red Cross Clubs. 'Ich Liebe Dich' has become no more meaningful than 'How Do You Do?'[20]

Social liberals were as shocked as moralists by illegitimacy levels. Nearly a hundred thousand babies were born to unmarried women in Germany in 1946, around a third of all births and three times the 1945 rate. Officially recorded abortions were more than twice that number, but the real, hidden, figure was assumed to be many times higher, though nobody knows for certain the exact figure. The cost of an abortion in 1946, illegally and dangerously obtained in back streets, was high, around a thousand marks – or, in the currency used far more widely, two cartons of Lucky Strikes and a half pound of coffee. A perhaps happier outcome was the number of GI brides: around twenty-five thousand in 1946/1947.

Venereal disease was rife. The rate of gonorrhoea throughout Germany in the year after the war was staggering. At one point in early 1946, in one Scottish regiment alone, of 800 men, 108 were infected. Oddly, rates were higher among Americans, despite the generous distribution to US troops of condoms and potassium permanganate pills. In 1946, according to the US Defense Department, 250 out of every 1,000 American troops had gonorrhoea. 'VD follows VE' went the popular saying.

The war utterly changed the German family. No longer would women be confined, as long tradition and the Third Reich had it, to *Kinder, Küche, Kirche* (children, kitchen, church). A study by a German researcher soon after the war found that:

> six years during which wives had to shift for themselves and increasingly replaced men in almost all fields of economic activity, had gone a long way in developing their confidence and self-reliance, in violation of the Nazi-fostered traditional subordination of the German wife to the husband. The . . . defeat of the regime that had stressed 'manly virtues' . . . decreased the respect women had for men in general; and their husbands in particular. The returned soldiers were . . . dispirited and unable to adapt themselves to the chaotic post defeat conditions . . . but still expecting their wives to revert to prewar patterns [of family life]. Men having been indoctrinated to feel like 'supermen' were, in varying degrees, unable to deal in a dignified manner with the Occupation forces in the role of subordinates, often discrediting themselves in the eyes of their wives through awkward obsequiousness.[21]

The victors were seldom cruel, but often they were heedless, and laughably ill-informed about the people whose land they were occupying. The handbook given to British post-war troops stationed in Germany contained advice that does not seem entirely helpful. The 'average German . . . is primitive because of his admiration for medieval cruelties,' it stated. They had an 'inferiority complex', a 'guilt complex', a dual personality that lacked balance. Most Germans were 'highly emotional and wallow in self-pity.' It went on:

> The ordinary German, the husband and father, will derive pleasure in carrying out orders involving the infliction of torture and suffering. Yet in between he will take out the photo of his wife and children and slobber over it . . . the Germans are not divided into two classes, good or bad Germans. There are only good and bad elements in the German character, the latter of which generally predominate. But the Germans can be divided into two other classes, namely the leaders who plot and plan and the led who blindly follow, and those two are equally dangerous.[22]

Possibly the men on the ground were reading too much of this material, which could explain the common attitude described by a junior officer in a British tank regiment, Lieutenant Christopher Leefe, stationed near Hanover in 1946. He tells how a small boy was caught trying to steal food from the officers' mess. Leefe was present when the thief was questioned:

> The point is that none of us could have cared a bit for that little boy. He was probably an orphan, his father died on the Eastern Front, his mother under a pile of ruins and here he was, starving and risking his life climbing up drainpipes in the middle of a British tank regiment. So what? We didn't feel any compassion for him or any of the Germans . . . Now we commandeered their homes, commandeered their Mercedes, commandeered their women. I would say . . . 70 per cent of young Englishmen

thought that way. Most of us were having a bloody good time and believed we could get away with anything.[23]

Brutality by the Western Allied troops was rare, especially compared to the rape and pillage conducted by Soviet forces, and was nothing compared to the wartime behaviour of the German troops as they laid waste the lands of the *untermenschen* Slavs in Eastern Europe and the USSR. But there were isolated cases. Four hundred and eighty-seven American soldiers were tried for rape in the first eighteen months of the Occupation, and it is likely that considerably more cases were covered up and never made it to court. Letters home reveal stories that were censored for nearly half a century and have only recently come to light. 'I mail you and daddy a watch', one GI wrote to his parents. 'I hope you like it . . . It is one I got off a German captain. Ha Ha. He did not like it so I got mad and let him have it . . . if you get what I mean. He forced me to shoot him and for me, I loved to shoot him.' Another wrote, 'We did see many, many prisoners these last few days. Yes, a delightful sight. I always did want to boot one of these Heinies in the pants and I did to my heart's content.'[24]

Some prisoners and suspected war criminals were beaten and otherwise mistreated by American and British interrogators though, again, on a small scale compared to what was happening in the Soviet zone and in Eastern Europe. The worst case was of SS officers accused of murdering eighty-four American prisoners of war in December 1944, outside the Belgian village of Malmédy during the Battle of the Bulge. One hundred suspects were interned in Schwäbisch Hall, a gloomy castle near Stuttgart, and put through 'enhanced interrogation procedures' that would have been very familiar to the Gestapo. Confessions were extracted under torture. Prisoners were kept in solitary confinement for weeks and subjected to sleep deprivation and extremes of hot and cold – one German soldier was placed in a dark cellar up to his hips in water for five weeks. Prisoners were also subjected to mock trials, and to terrifying mock executions. One of them later recalled that his hands were tied behind his back, a hood was placed over his head, he was marched outside and the guards told him he was to be hanged. They led him to some steps, which they said led to the gallows. As a drum was beating, they lifted him off the ground and tied a rope around his neck. Then they told him the execution had been postponed. This was repeated with many other prisoners.

Of the many hundreds of prisoners who passed through Schwäbisch Hall, 139 complained about their treatment. An American commission of inquiry at the end of 1946 found that 137 of them 'had their testicles permanently and [irreparably] damaged by kicks received from the American war crimes investigation team.' Their report said that 'the screams of the prisoners at Schwäbisch Hall could be heard throughout the local town.' General Clay said he was appalled by the behaviour of the American inquisitors, yet he rejected the prisoners' appeals, saying they were not innocent men. 'Unfortunately, in the heat of the aftermath of the war, we did use measures to obtain evidence that we would not have employed later.'[25]

*

Post-war Berlin was the crime capital of the world. There were 240 reported robberies a day, an increase of 800 per cent on pre-war figures, and that was known to be a small percentage of the true number. Even the well-protected were not safe from thieves. Gangs of children jumped on to the backs of lorries to pilfer anything they could lay their hands on. There were many cases of Allied soldiers chopping at the young thieves' hands with bayonets to deter them. Doctors in Berlin's hospitals treated scores of children with severed fingers. 'All notions of ownership have been completely demolished,' wrote the author of the powerful memoir *A Woman in Berlin*. 'Everyone steals from everyone else because everyone has been stolen from.' And in her diary for 1946, Ruth

Andreas-Friedrich recorded that 'life here was a swapping game, where objects passed from one person to another with nobody knowing who the owner was.'[*26]

The Nazi currency, the Reichsmark, was now worthless and the Occupation Marks, which the Allies printed in an attempt to stabilise prices and create some form of money tender, had an inflationary by-product the Allied officials had not foreseen. It distorted prices in the (small) legal market and raised prices to high levels that most people could not afford in the (very large) black market. The real currency used every day, at a time when most people smoked, was the cigarette, invariably the American brand Lucky Strike. But there was cigarette inflation, too. At the start of 1946 one Lucky Strike bought four ounces of bread, but by the summer less than half that. 'The cigarette is the be-all and end-all,' a report sent by the British Control Commission's economic unit to the Foreign Office said. 'Together with chocolate and alcohol derived from Allied stores and canteens, the cigarette is probably one of the biggest threats to financial stability in the country.' The point was echoed by an American official. 'The trouble is that American cigarettes as a medium of exchange brings prices out of all proportion when Americans are dealing with Germans. A couple of cartons of cigarettes would buy a piano, if the buyer had a way of transporting it.'[27]

Berlin, according to one reporter, 'had the black market to end all such markets,' centred on the Tiergarten. There, 'crowds of soldiers gather for trade both legal and illegal, meeting Germans hoping for a quick sale . . . Germans who traipse hopefully to the Tiergarten with their household goods in prams and rucksacks

---

* Her memoir was originally published anonymously and her identity was kept fairly well hidden except in publishing circles. After her death in 2001, though, she was revealed as the journalist Marta Hillers. Ruth Andreas-Friedrich, a socialist and active in one of the very few resistance groups in Nazi Germany, wrote one of the most moving and engaging diaries covering the last days of Hitler and the start of the Occupation.

want food, cigarettes and foreign currency. Red Army men who lug along suitcases of bills representing their back pay for several years want cameras, clothing and, specially, watches. The Americans, British and French who drive up with pockets bulging with saleable gadgets want money.'[28]

Allied soldiers, mainly the Americans, could make vast sums on the black market in a giant scam that cheated desperate Germans and Russians – and the American taxpayer at the same time. At the US Army Post Exchange stores, the PX, a GI could buy a carton of Lucky Strikes for a dollar. A Soviet soldier would pay $100 on the black market. A Mickey Mouse watch cost a GI $3.95. A Russian would pay $500, and perhaps as much as $1,000 for a camera that cost an American soldier $14.95. Back home, a US private could buy a car from the huge profits made at the Tiergarten. The US military was shipping more watches, chocolate and cameras to Berlin than to soldiers in the rest of the world put together. It took the US Department of Defense and the State Department a while to discover what was going on. The scam relied on the printing of the new currency used by Allied troops, Occupation Marks. In the spirit of Allied cooperation, the new currency was printed on plates shared by the US and Soviet authorities. Far more was printed than could possibly be legitimately spent. American soldiers could convert the new currency into real US dollars at the rate of ten to one, but Russian soldiers were paid in Occupation Marks, which they couldn't take back to the USSR and change into roubles; they had to spend them in Germany – and did so on watches, wine and women.

The US Army was supplying the heavily subsidised goods sold to the GIs and buying back the otherwise worthless currency. Eventually an economist in Washington worked it out. The amount of Russian-printed Occupation Marks sent back to the States was enormous. 'Transmission of funds out of [Germany] by US troops exceeded the amount of pay and allowances to a ratio of six or seven to one,' an inquiry by a team of Lucius Clay's accountants reported. In the first months of the Occupation soldiers had sent home to America eleven million more dollars than they received in wages.

'Berlin is the most immoral city in the world. It corrupts everyone who sets foot in it,' Frank Howley, an economist with the American Occupation army, wrote in a report to the Defense Department in Washington at the beginning of 1946. But Berliners had to try to make ends meet and could not afford to be too prissy about how it was done. As Bernhard Botting, a Berlin doctor, recalled: 'It was considered most dishonourable to abstain from the black market as long as members of one's family were starving . . . Not to do so because of some code of honour or other was not a good thing. One has to be careful about getting moral issues mixed up.'[29]

The Occupation authorities all made half-hearted attempts to clean up the black market, but throughout 1946 they recognised that it was essential if the Germans were to be fed, clothed and housed. As Lieutenant-General Sir Frederick Morgan reported to the British Foreign Secretary, Ernest Bevin, the black market was necessary not only in Germany but elsewhere in Western Europe, too. 'It is hardly an exaggeration to say that every man woman and child . . . is engaged to a greater or lesser degree in illegal trading of one kind or another. In fact, it is hardly possible to support existence without so doing.'[30]

# 5

## Austria Forgets Its Past

In Vienna a routine from comic opera was enacted two or three times a day around the Ringstrasse, the majestic boulevard that circles the old city. Like Berlin, Vienna was occupied by the four powers, in apportioned sectors. But in the First Bezirk, or district, in the centre of town, responsibility was shared, with command revolving between them each month. The Ring and the intricate pattern of small streets leading from it were patrolled by the 'four curios' – a jeep manned by a military policeman from each of the four occupying powers, sporting easily identifiable national markings.*

Austria itself was a curio – a part of the defeated Reich, it was not treated as a conquered nation, but as 'Hitler's first victim'. For many who had fought against the German armies it was an entirely undeserved status, a stroke of good luck that had more to do with the rivalry between the great powers than with truth or justice. In 1938 most Austrians had supported the Anschluss. From a population of seven million there were more than 700,000 Nazi Party members, and more than 1.2 million Austrians served in German military units of one kind or another. Austrians were

---

* The commanders, four generals, also took lead responsibility each month and tended to heartily dislike each other. The bitterest feud was over HQ allocations. The British nabbed the Schönbrunn Palace, where the commander, Sir Richard McCreery, occupied the room that had once served as Napoleon's quarters – much to the chagrin of the French commander, General Jean de Lattre de Tassigny.

disproportionately represented in the SS – and among the guards and officials who ran the concentration camps.

All this was quickly forgotten in a collective amnesia that was encouraged by both the Eastern and Western allies, if for different reasons. They were sound reasons, but nonetheless many people were shocked. George Clare, who returned to Vienna, where he was born and raised, as a British Intelligence Corps officer, commented, 'Having mentally mislaid the Hitler years, they filled the void with Austrian nationalism, so rare in 1938 . . . Everything German was out, even the way the Viennese spoke that language.' He noticed at once how educated Austrians who habitually used a soft, Viennese-tinged High German, which he knew as the German spoken in Bavaria and Berlin, now deliberately used 'the rough dialect of the low-rent Vienna suburbs' to show how Austrian they were. Men would display their identity even with their choice of headgear. 'Austria was in fashion, as symbolised by the ubiquitous peasant hats few would have worn in Vienna before the war. They sprouted on many heads that, not long ago, had sported the brown or black caps of the SA or SS.'[1]

Austria became an important stage in the theatre of the Cold War, a centre of espionage, intrigue and mystery, the backdrop for scores of spy novels and thriller movies. Conditions there were better than in most of Germany, but rations were low and people went hungry for a long time after the conflict was over. And despite the patrols by the military police, Vienna was a dangerous place – especially at night. As the American novelist John Dos Passos, a correspondent there for various US newspapers in autumn 1945 and much of 1946 reported, 'As in medieval days . . . you went abroad at your own risk.'[2]

The West wanted the Austrians on their side, particularly the Viennese. Vienna was a predominantly Western city, surrounded by the Soviet East, and Soviet troops – it was, as the Russians continually reminded the Austrians, two degrees of latitude further east than Prague. And the Soviets wanted to keep a toehold in Western territory – indeed their troops did not leave Vienna for almost ten years. As a result, the Allies left the Austrians alone to settle their own accounts – with each other, with the past and with Hitler. People were desperate to deny any Nazi affiliations; only 23,000 Austrians – most of them Nazi Party members – were ever investigated for any crimes. Of these, 13,000 were found guilty of mostly minor charges and 30 were executed. Around 60,000 civil servants and local officials lost their jobs – more than half of whom were reinstated by the middle of 1947.

Immediately after the war Karl Renner, now seventy-five, was wheeled out of retirement by the Soviets to take over as Chancellor of a newly independent Austria, which had split from the Reich. It was hard for the Russians to find anyone who had not been compromised in the Nazi years that they could accept as reasonably friendly to the USSR. Renner was a compromise candidate the Allies could recognise as an interim leader, though it took the Americans some time because he was a socialist, albeit a mild one not far to the Left of some of the New Dealers in the US administration. Renner was a figure from another age, with his frock coat, pointed beard and elaborate manners straight out of the court of Emperor Franz Joseph. He had been the first President of the Austrian republic in 1918 after the collapse of the Habsburg Empire and now, as another new, Cold War, world was born, he found himself running a government of liberals, socialists, communists and assorted 'anti-fascists'.

Nearly a quarter of Vienna had been destroyed by Allied bombs; a quarter of a million people were homeless. But under the dust and the rubble the city still possessed a kind of charm. John Dos Passos sent a vivid dispatch of life there as Vienna was trying to rebuild: 'The city still wears the airs and graces of a metropolis . . . Vienna is an old musical comedy queen, dying in a poor house, who can still shape her cracked lips into a confident smile of a woman whom men have loved, when the doctor makes his rounds of the ward.'[3]

# 6

## The Spy Comes In from the Cold

On the evening of Sunday 3 February the American journalist Drew Pearson broke a sensational scoop on his NBC radio show. He reported that a Soviet spy had surrendered himself to the Royal Canadian Mounted Police in Ottawa and revealed 'a gigantic Russian espionage network inside the United States and Canada.' Pearson was one of the most respected and popular broadcasters in the US and his weekly show *Drew Pearson Comments* often attracted audiences of more than twenty-five million. On this evening he reported that 'the Russian told Canadian authorities about a series of agents planted inside the American and Canadian governments who were working with the Soviets.' Pearson had only part of the highly complex story – he didn't know that the defection had taken place nearly six months earlier and that the American, British and Canadian governments had been sitting on the information. Pearson did say, however, that the Canadian Prime Minister, Mackenzie King, had recently made 'a special trip to Washington' to give President Truman full details.

The broadcast marked the start of the Gouzenko affair – the first major spy scandal of the post-war years, with the kind of intricate plot and counter-plot that would spawn countless espionage novels and movies. Just as Pearson's main source hoped it would, the scandal sparked a wave of spy hysteria that profoundly changed public attitudes towards the Soviets in America, Britain and much of the West.

The Director of the FBI, J. Edgar Hoover, had given Pearson

the bones of the story. He calculated that it would help to prod the Truman administration into taking a firmer hand against 'subversion' and communism at home and abroad. It emerged years later, long after both he and Pearson were dead, that Hoover himself was the 'Deep Throat' and had partially leaked the details in a series of telephone conversations with Pearson in the weeks before the broadcast – they even spoke on the morning the show aired.[1]

*

Igor Gouzenko was an obscure cypher clerk for Soviet Military Intelligence (GRU) at the Russian Embassy in Ottawa. Aged twenty-six, married with a daughter, and another child on the way, he enjoyed life in the West. Fearing that he was about to be punished for some minor security lapses by being sent back to Moscow, on the evening of 5 September 1945 he left the Embassy carrying 109 secret documents. Always keenly interested in money, first he tried to interest the press. He went to the offices of the *Ottawa Journal*, which sent him packing and missed the best scoop it was ever likely to get. Officials at the Canadian Ministry of Justice thought he was a hoaxer and turned him away. Finally, he went to a Mounted Police station where officers took him seriously.

The documents Gouzenko stole proved that the Soviets had for years been searching for atomic and other military secrets and had planted agents – 'sleepers' – who had risen to senior positions in the American and Canadian governments. They established that the Soviets' principal espionage agency, the NKVD (later the MGB, then the KGB), was handling a separate group of spies and agents and was operating on a far bigger, more systematic scale than Western intelligence agencies had imagined.

The Canadians debriefed Gouzenko for months, before establishing a new identity for him. With great originality, they gave him the new name George Brown, and arranged to pay him a retainer of US $500 a month plus a lump sum of $100,000.* They handed most of the material to the Americans and British. It did not, as some spies, politicians and thriller writers suggested later, reveal details about the Soviets' theft of the Manhattan Project secrets. That was the work of other defectors and a separate spy ring altogether. But Gouzenko's treasure trove actually named Soviet agents of influence in North America, and provided good clues of how to find the names of others.

Remarkably, the three governments did little with the information – partly from inertia, partly as calculated counter-intelligence tradecraft to set traps to catch other spies, but mainly because they were concerned about the potential diplomatic and political fallout of a major espionage scandal. The Soviet Union was still supposedly an allied power and at this stage neither the US nor Britain could see many advantages in a clear break with the Russians.

After Pearson's revelations the Western press was full of the story, no matter how hazy the details, and the pressure grew on the Canadians to act. The following Sunday, 10 February, though most of Pearson's programme was about other subjects, he reported as an aside that 'arrests were imminent' in the Canadian spy sensation. At that point, however, they actually were not, but at dawn on 15 February, sixteen people were arrested, including a dozen Canadian civil servants, and charged with espionage offences.

---

* Though living in hiding, Gouzenko became well known on American talk shows in the 1950s – always wearing a white hood over his face and head, looking like something from the Ku Klux Klan. He was a highly intelligent man and spoke well – about espionage, and of life in the USSR. He wrote an indifferent autobiography, *The Iron Curtain*, but an excellent novel about Stalin, *The Fall of a Titan*. It is a pity he wrote no more fiction. He was extremely litigious, threatening to sue journalists regularly whenever there were unflattering references to him. His family back in the Soviet Union were badly treated by the merciless MGB. His mother spent weeks in the infamous Lubyanka prison, was almost certainly tortured, and died soon after her release. His wife Anna's parents and sister were jailed for five years, and her niece was sent to a state orphanage.

Five days later, in the UK, MI5 arrested the British physicist Alan Nunn May, a lecturer at King's College, London. He confessed that during the war, while on secondment to the National Research Council of Canada, which was building a nuclear reactor near Montreal, he had passed atomic secrets to the Soviets. He said he did not feel he had committed treason, rather he had 'acted rightly'. The only thing he regretted was that he had given a tiny amount of highly radioactive processed uranium-235 to the Russians via a courier, who had handled it without wearing protective clothing and as a result would be seriously ill for the rest of his life. In Canada nine people, including a member of parliament, were jailed in the aftermath of the spy scandal.[2]

There were no immediate arrests in America, though amidst the spy hysteria some senior government figures were investigated as suspected Soviet agents. They included the Treasury official Harry Dexter White, who had represented the US at the Bretton Woods conference in 1944 that set up the World Bank and the IMF; and the State Department's Alger Hiss, the first chief of America's office at the new UN. Both were disgraced; White died of a heart attack shortly after testifying; Hiss, who had been a Soviet agent, was jailed for three years for perjury.

The Gouzenko affair had a profound effect on the US and its President. Truman's popularity – already low – dived further; he had a disapproval rating of nearly 70 per cent, a record then, and a depth to which even Richard Nixon, at the height of the Watergate scandal, never descended. Truman admitted to confidants that the spy hysteria had put him under additional pressure and, perhaps inevitably, America over-reacted to the Red Menace. Igor Gouzenko was as responsible as anyone for the mood that followed, a mood which Joseph McCarthy, who was elected to the Senate nine months after Drew Pearson's story was broadcast, found it all too easy to hijack. Within a few months Truman issued an executive order forcing all government employees to take a 'loyalty oath' and the FBI, along with the tax authorities, found themselves investigating thousands of suspected communists or fellow travellers. Even private companies were firing staff on political grounds.[3]

In Britain the fear of communist incursions never reached American levels of frenzy and hysteria, but Attlee chaired a Cabinet Committee on Subversion, a few score civil servants were investigated by MI5, some academics lost their posts at Oxbridge colleges, and employees at the John Lewis Partnership department store had to sign an anti-communist pledge. But the British were, as usual, fairly relaxed about ideology. Most people were 'simply too preoccupied to worry,' as the novelist Pamela Hansford Johnson recalled: 'The ordinary person was too busy coping with the daily problems . . . he sees the ruins of the War all around him – along the railway lines as he goes to work, on the bus routes. He sees the place where the pub was and the children's play area on the cleared site. He's still wondering how long it will take to tidy them all up. He hasn't got round to contemplating new ruins . . . and despite a sporadic hullabaloo in the newspapers he . . . doesn't see Russia as a threat to himself.'[4]

For the Russians, though, the consequences were immediate. Donald Maclean, one of the Cambridge spies who later defected to Moscow rather than face being unmasked as a traitor, was then a senior British diplomat working in Washington. He told a Russian interviewer not long before he died in 1983 that the result of the Gouzenko affair was that most of the valuable intelligence the Soviets had obtained earlier was 'now blocked . . . [they] managed virtually overnight to freeze all active . . . intelligence in the United States.' By the end of February 1946, the Soviets' spy networks, so painstakingly established over many years, had been completely shut down.[5]

# 7

## Austerity Britain

In February 1946 the most unpopular man in Britain was a sixty-seven-year-old East Ender called Smith. Sir Ben Smith was the Labour Government's Food Minister and MP for the docklands constituency of Rotherhithe. A cockney with a sharp wit, he had been one of London's first drivers of a motorised taxi cab, a salt-of-the-earth trade unionist of the type that filled Labour's benches in the House of Commons after its landslide victory in the General Election the previous summer. For most of his political career Smith had been well liked as a plain-speaking, moderate, consensus figure, a Party loyalist. But then he was given the thankless task of running the post-war Ministry of Food and his lot rapidly changed.

As a result of critical shortages of staple foods, worse even than at the height of the German submarine campaign against British supply ships, on 5 February Smith was forced to announce further restrictions on domestic food rations, reducing them to hardship levels unknown even during the war. The next day demonstrators stood outside the Ministry's Whitehall headquarters with placards bearing the slogan 'Starve with Smith'. It did not help that the Minister was a rather heavy-set man, given to corpulence.

Food rationing had been a familiar routine during the war. If there were complaints about the strict allowances throughout most of the conflict – six to eight ounces of meat a week, four to eight ounces of bacon, six to eight ounces of cheese, four ounces of tea, between eight ounces and a pound of sugar – it was generally accepted they were adequate and fair. For a short while after VE Day there were hopes that rationing might end. 'People hoped for a release from the grinding privations of wartime life, which had done much to put the Labour government so resoundingly in power,' Susan Cooper, a wife and mother who endured the queues necessary to feed her family recalled: ' . . . release from the small, dull, makeshift meals; from darkness and drabness and making do, from the depressing, nerve-aching, never ending need to be *careful*.' But soon Britons began to realise just how bad their economic plight was, and that things were unlikely to improve quickly. Britain imported the bulk of its food, many suppliers demanded payment in US dollars and within months of its victory, Britain was plunged into the first of the balance of payments crises that would dog the country for the next twenty-five years.[1]

The Food Minister's announcement came on a miserable grey morning in London and sent the nation into deep gloom. Rations were cut by nearly half on almost everything from bacon and poultry to sweets and soap powder. The average adult allowances were down to thirteen ounces of meat a week; one and a half ounces of cheese; six ounces of butter and margarine; one ounce of cooking fat; two pints of milk, and one egg. 'It sounds depressing . . . it looked worse,' remembered Cooper. The additional detail in the announcement was grimmer still: rice, or what there was of it, would disappear from shops entirely; all of a sudden families were deprived of a food that itself had come from austerity. During the war dried egg, though hardly a delicacy, had become a staple in the British diet, most of it imported from the United States at vast cost – nearly $10 million a year. Smith now declared that such imports would have to cease. 'I simply don't know how I can lay my hands on the money,' he said.[2]

By reputation and tradition the English are obedient and patient – hence the various clichés in the language about the right way to face adversity. 'So they pull in their belts, put their shoulders to the wheel, grin and bear it, make the best of a bad job, keep chins, peckers and upper lips stiff,' remembered a housewife who lived, and queued, through that period. The famous patience all but snapped during the 'shrinking loaf' scandal that erupted a fortnight after the new rations regime was announced. Bread had not been rationed during the war, though the quality had suffered. 'People had got used to grimier bread, throwing away the dirty bits,' recalled Susan Cooper. Now the British loaf was not only grubby, it was smaller.

The Ministry had come up with a scheme which they imagined would induce people to lower their wheat consumption without them quite realising it, or doing anything about it. They reduced the size of the two-pound loaf by two ounces to twenty-eight ounces and the one-pound loaf to fourteen ounces, lopping a couple of large slices from each, while maintaining the price. They anticipated that people would continue to buy the same number of loaves, saving three hundred thousand tons of wheat a year. But this dim-witted attempt to bamboozle people instead caused deep resentment and, predictably, made almost no difference to the amount of bread actually consumed. It did, however, effectively end the hapless Smith's political career and hastened the introduction of bread rationing. It was this, more than anything else, that brought home to the public the meaning of 'austerity' and the uncertainty of Britain's place in the world.*

The bread scandal was directly linked to the food crisis in Germany, particularly in the British Occupation zone, where rations had been so severely reduced to an average of 1,100 calories a day. By comparison, even the lower rations announced by Ben

---

* Smith was fired from the Government in May 1946 and stood down from Parliament at the same time. He was appointed chairman of the newly created West Midlands Coal Board. He was replaced as Minister of Food by the Old Etonian John Strachey, who had flirted with Marxism in the 1930s, but was by now mainstream Labour. Soon the placards were reading 'Starve with Strachey', which scans somewhat better.

Smith's ministry provided for around 2,500 calories. During the winter, a campaign had been launched to change export regulations and allow people to send food parcels to Germany, which had been banned under wartime rules that still applied. The campaign was headed by Victor Gollancz, a left-wing publisher and veteran of various liberal causes, whose parents had emigrated to Britain from Germany in the late nineteenth century. He had visited Germany in the autumn after the war and published powerful articles describing the appalling conditions there. With a few well-connected friends and collaborators (or 'hand wringers' as a member of the Cabinet put it) Gollancz, whose uncle was a rabbi in London, appealed for large-scale humanitarian relief to help the German people.

In *Leaving Them to Their Fate: The Ethics of Starvation in Germany*, Gollancz wrote:

> I am a Jew. Sometimes I am asked why, as a Jew, I bother about people in whose name infamies have been committed against my race, the memory of which, I fear . . . may never die. I am sometimes asked this, I regret to say, by fellow Jews who have forgotten . . . the teachings of the Prophets. I feel called upon to help suffering Germans precisely because I am a Jew; but not at all for the reasons imagined. It is a question . . . of plain, straight common sense, undeflected by that very sentimentality that deflects the judgment . . . of so many. To me three propositions seem self-evident. The first is that nothing can save the world but a general act of repentance in place of the present self-righteous insistence on the wickedness of others; for we have all sinned, and continue to sin most horribly. The second is that good treatment and not bad treatment makes them good. And the third is – to drop into the hideous collective language which is now much the mode – that unless you treat a man well when he has treated you ill you just get nowhere; or, rather, it will give further impetus to evil and head straight for human annihilation.[3]

The campaign was surprisingly influential. But it was not as persuasive as *Germany: A Defeated People*, a documentary directed by Humphrey Jennings, which sparked strong reactions not only from the liberal intelligentsia, but from the general public, too. The film showed columns of exhausted prisoners of war, civilians living amidst rubble and bedraggled orphaned children playing in dirt. It was accompanied by a thoughtful, if harsh, script blaming the Germans for their own fate. The conclusion, though, appealed to reason rather than emotion: 'We have an interest in Germany that is purely selfish. We cannot live next to a disease-ridden neighbour.'

It was an idea echoed by Noël Coward's satirical song 'Don't Let's Be Beastly to the Germans', which had been popular during the war, and was now re-released:

> Don't let's be beastly to the Germans
> When our victory is ultimately won,
> It was just those nasty Nazis who persuaded them to fight
> And their Beethoven and Bach are really far worse than
>     their bite
> Let's be meek to them
> And turn the other cheek to them
> And try to bring out their latent sense of fun.
> . . .
> Let's be sweet to them
> And day by day repeat to them
> Sterilisation simply isn't done.
> Let's sympathise again
> And help the scum to rise again.
> But don't let's be beastly to the Hun.

Although the Chancellor of the Exchequer, Hugh Dalton, was privately set against giving extra help to Germany at a time of stringent austerity at home, arguing that at a cost of £80 million a year, 'what we are doing amounts, essentially, to us paying reparations to the Germans', the British press response was surprisingly balanced. A *Daily Mirror* editorial argued that the British had no choice but to help feed the Germans. 'In saying this we suggest no sympathy for the German people ... It is not a feeling of compassion which prompts us to emphasise the importance of dealing with the situation. It is a practical matter which makes action imperative. The longer Europe is allowed to sink into the bog, the longer it will take to raise up – the longer the occupation will have to go on.' The *Sunday Pictorial*, which had been firmly anti-German since before the First World War, opined that 'For the sake of Europe and ourselves, for the safety of our Occupation troops ... Germany must be prevented from becoming a plague spot and a danger to the world.'[4]

*

In 1946, most Britons knew that the country was broke. But few realised just how desperately. Survival, and then victory, had come at vast cost. Britain had been the world's largest creditor nation in the mid-1930s; now it was the biggest debtor. Britain had been saved from defeat by the Nazis; it had stood alone against a powerful enemy and, morally at least, could hold its head high. But economically the country was almost ruined. The war had cost more than a quarter of the nation's total wealth. The Churchill government had been forced to borrow massive sums and sell overseas assets wholesale under the Lend-Lease scheme, which had kept the country supplied with both war materiel and food. But within days of the guns falling silent in Europe, America had abruptly halted Lend-Lease. The British Government had been warned it would happen, but the suddenness of the move shocked the new administration in London, which was faced with an immediate financial crisis.

British debts at the end of the war were approximately £3,500 million ($14 billion at that time). In April 1945, Lord Keynes, then the world's most eminent economist, concerned that the UK would be unable to survive the next five years, prepared a paper for the Cabinet. He argued that British industry had been totally focused on military production and would need a lengthy period to re-equip for peacetime; it would take years for Britain to free itself from food import dependency; and the country was entirely out of foreign exchange reserves. He calculated a shortfall of $5 billion (about £1,300 million) for the next three years, assuming that the Treasury could delay repayment of the foreign debt it already owed for that period. 'Where is this money to come from?' he asked. Without help, and a lot of it, 'we have not a hope of escaping what might be considered, without exaggeration, a financial Dunkirk.'

As a result, in the autumn of 1945, during the last few months of his life, Keynes was despatched cap-in-hand to the US to beg for a loan. It was no easy matter. Keynes had believed he would be welcomed with warmth in Washington as the representative of America's staunch ally. He was to be disappointed, however. Instead of the 'gift' of £1,500 million and an interest-free loan of £3,500 million that Keynes sought, and thought he would obtain, he was offered £3,750 million at 2 per cent interest, with payments (made in dollars) spread over the next fifty years. And even that was subject to the approval of Congress. There were other shocks in the small print. Britain had to forgo the system of 'imperial preferences' that made it harder for British colonies to trade with countries outside the Commonwealth, and, more seriously, the Americans insisted that sterling must become a freely convertible currency within a year of the loan being agreed. That, as Keynes realised, would have disastrous consequences: a year on, there was a 'run on the pound' that forced a devaluation, which ate into the principal of the loan.[*5]

In 1946 the 'special relationship' was not as special as it would

---

* At the same time Canada, which had also done well economically out of the war, agreed to lend Britain a much-needed £1,500 million on more favourable terms than America had offered. The Canadian loan was also approved by Ottawa far more quickly and became available for use as a credit line earlier.

become. It seemed to many in Britain that it was a comforting and convenient myth, largely for home consumption, to cushion the shock of national decline. And many Americans were worried by how often the British used the phrase. Dean Acheson called it 'a dangerous intellectual obstacle to Britain's acceptance of a largely European role.' Britain and the US had fought side by side in two world wars, shared a language and many cultural links, but immediately after the war their interests were not always the same, and seemed for a short period actually to conflict. It is difficult to understand now but there were significant areas of tension, mostly caused by Britain's determination to cling on to the bulk of its Empire, while America was beginning to extend and exert its global influence. Somewhat ironically, it was the Cold War and the challenge of jointly confronting the Soviet Union that restored a relationship that was beginning to falter. Stalin brought Britain and the US closer once again.[6]

The loan negotiations caused rancour on both sides of the Atlantic. The British thought the Americans were ungenerous, that the tough terms begrudged aid to its ally and friend in its hour of most need. The Americans believed they were being open-handed and were irritated by apparent British ingratitude and feeling of entitlement. As Harold Wilson, later Prime Minister but then a junior member of Attlee's Cabinet, ruefully observed, 'There's nothing so irrelevant as a poor relative.'*[7]

It became a commonplace remark that 'beggars can't be choosers'; at the time Britain was a beggar nation, but one that could not admit to it. The Chancellor, Hugh Dalton, disliked the terms of the loan (nobody much liked them), but, as he said, 'What is the alternative? All these hopes of better times to follow in the wake

---

* Wilson was pro-American but not slavishly so. He was a young and highly gifted economics don at Oxford in the 1930s and one of Britain's youngest ever Cabinet Ministers. He was paraphrasing a quotation from one of *The Last Essays of Elia* by Charles Lamb: 'A poor relation is the most irrelevant thing in nature – the hail in harvest – the ounce of sour in a pound of sweet.'

of victory would be dissipated in despair and disillusion' without the money. When the loan was debated in the House of Commons just before Christmas 1945, twenty-three Labour MPs voted against, including a future Labour leader, Michael Foot, a young left-wing firebrand in those days, Barbara Castle, a leading Labour figure for the next three decades, and the moderate, usually pro-American future Prime Minister James Callaghan, who called the loan terms 'economic aggression by the United States'.

The sense of grievance in the UK swelled as opposition to the loan surfaced in the United States, where it took months of wrangling throughout the spring before Congress finally approved it. *The Economist*, staunchly Atlanticist, and at the time an authoritative conservative organ, spoke for many in its editorial column: 'We have at present no real option but to accept the American offer . . . But we are not compelled to say that we like it. And we do not. Our present needs are the direct consequence of the fact that we fought earliest, we fought longest and that we fought hardest. In moral terms we are creditors – and for that we will have to pay $140 million p[er]a[nnum] for the rest of the twentieth century. It may be unavoidable, but it is not right.' The argument scarcely differed from the point made by the socialist *New Statesman*: 'It is clear that on the matters that most affect Britain today, the United States is nearly as hostile to the aspirations of Britain as . . . [it is] to the Soviet Union.'[8]

A bitter jingle was soon frequently playing at nightclub cabarets:

> Our Uncle Which art in America,
> Sam be thy Name
> Thy Navy come, thy will be done . . .
> Give us this day our daily bread
> And Forgive us our un-American activities.*

---

* In diplomatic and political circles in London another piece of doggerel was often quoted to make a similar, if more snobbish, point. Lord Halifax was the British Ambassador to Washington until the spring of 1946:

Frosty notes went back and forth across the Atlantic. The Foreign Secretary, Ernest Bevin, one of the most anti-communist members of the Government, told his Private Secretary, Pierson Dixon, that 'Britain was faced with increasing hostility and distrust between the US and the Soviets . . . each of whom sought to strengthen its own position without regard to our point of view.' A low point was reached when the Cabinet agreed on a resolution, worded personally by Attlee, declaring that 'we should make clear to the US Government that it was impossible for us to work with them if they constantly took action . . . affecting our interests, without prior consultation with us.'[9]

In the US, opposition to the loan came from disparate groups. The Right objected to large-scale foreign lending on principle, while the Left objected to British imperialism on principle; the Irish lobby, the Jewish lobby and some business leaders believed Britain was in such a parlous position it could never repay the debt. Emmanuel Celler, an influential Democrat from New York who was a power on the House Finance Committee, explained the objections succinctly. The money would 'be used to promote too much damned socialism at home and too much damned imperialism abroad,' he said.

In February and early March it looked as though the loan would stall in Congress, but Truman canvassed hard for it personally, claiming later that 'I pulled every string I possibly could for that loan.' It passed eventually in the early summer, partly on a tide of anti-communist feeling, and partly because most American business leaders and foreign policy experts were starting to see that the rehabilitation of Europe was urgent and vital for American political and economic interests. One of the White House officials responsible for arm-twisting in Congress in favour of the loan

In Washington Lord Halifax
Once whispered to Lord Keynes
It's true they have all the money bags
But we have all the brains.

made the argument clear: 'The economic arguments in favour of the loan are on the whole much less convincing ... than the feeling that it may serve us in good stead in holding up a hand of a nation we may badly need as a friend because of impending Russian troubles.'[10]

Before the loan went through, though, money was so tight that the War Office had to cancel naval manoeuvres in the Middle East because of the cost of oil – a desperate position for the government, as Cabinet papers show. Keynes was adamant, however, that on economic grounds if no other, Britain had to divest itself of much of the Empire, which 'is not running at a profit'. It was one of the principal planks of his post-war financial plan. The country could simply not afford the upkeep of colonies that were a drain on its finances, he told the Government. Cutting back on 'imperial profligacy' was the obvious place to save money. A significant part of Britain's debt was the result of expenditure in Africa, the Middle East and India, and Keynes calculated that running and policing the empire would cost around £1,400 million a year: 'It is this expenditure which is *wholly* responsible [his italics] for our financial difficulties. Unless ... [this is brought] under drastic control at an early date, our ability to pursue an independent financial policy in the early post-war years will be fatally impaired.' His was a rare voice at that point, and the timing was not right – yet. Thus, Keynes's argument fell on deaf ears. 'It was the age of austerity, but not in the UK's view of its own prestige,' as one historian, who lived through the period, observed.[11]

The cost of maintaining Britain as a 'great power' was immense, but few doubted that it was crucial politically, and as important psychologically. The country might be bankrupt, but the British in 1946 were not ready to give up ideas of imperial glory, even if reality dictated that one or two colonies might have to be abandoned. This meant, primarily, keeping a global military presence – difficult to do cheaply, as many empires throughout history have found. Before the war, Britain's military had cost around £16 million a year to run; two years after the war it was £200 million. In 1946 Britain had a million and a quarter men (and a very few women) under arms, albeit down from around five million at the height of the war; fleets in the Atlantic, the Mediterranean, and the Indian Ocean; a China station based in Hong Kong, and other bases in a dozen countries and colonies from the West Indies to Aden and Malaya, as well as one hundred and twenty full RAF squadrons. All would be retained, despite acute financial hardship at home. The American Ambassador to Britain, John Winant, cabled back to Under-Secretary of State William Clayton, in Washington, after the loan terms were finalised: 'The British are hanging on by their fingernails . . . in the hope that somehow or other, with our help, they will be able to preserve the British empire and their leadership of it.'[12]

*

In Britain, the end of the war was not Zero Hour, but the general election of 1945 had seemed like a clear break from the past. The overwhelming scale of the Labour victory might have shocked Joseph Stalin and Winston Churchill, but few people in Britain were all that surprised. Voters had not passed judgment on the six years of war, but on the decade before that. The dole queues of the 1930s and the Jarrow Marches were more evocative than Alamein or the Dambusters. Modest, colourless Clement Attlee – 'the sheep in sheep's clothing' as Churchill once called him – was a moderate, ascetic, manifestly decent man who fitted the austere times. As one of Churchill's own Tory backbenchers, Harold Nicolson, admitted, 'Compared to Winston, he is like a village fiddler after Paganini . . .' yet 'poor Clem' had a far greater hand in shaping contemporary Britain than did his illustrious predecessor.[13]

Britain's post-war Prime Minister was often compared with Truman, for the reason that they were both unassuming figures who succeeded obviously 'great' leaders with immense personalities. Neither man ever rose to heights of inspirational eloquence; both were prosaic. In most other ways, though, they were very different, and at first disliked each other intensely – another cause of Anglo-American friction immediately after the war. They grew to respect each other, but their early correspondence is filled with curt notes and occasionally ill-tempered complaints.

Attlee's success in rising to the top of politics – in keeping the Labour Party's ever-warring factions together for nearly two decades as leader, in winning an incontestable mandate for change, and as Prime Minister of a government that made an enduring difference to modern Britain – should puzzle nobody. If Churchill's geopolitical vision was of a grand sweep, Attlee understood the times and the country in a way that his predecessor did not. He was a subtle, sometimes surprisingly imaginative, organiser of people. He had a thin, reedy voice compared to Churchill's rich cadences, but he possessed singular self-confidence – a quality noted by his close colleagues, though seldom by his opponents, who invariably underestimated him. He was nowhere near as humble as he looked or sounded, but was content to seem overshadowed by more charismatic Labour figures such as Ernest Bevin and the totemic leader of the Left, Aneurin Bevan. In one of the cricketing metaphors he loved to use, Attlee used to say he was team captain, if not the star player, happy to bat anywhere in the order that he was needed.

As Churchill's Deputy Prime Minister in the wartime coalition, Attlee had been totally loyal. 'Churchill won the war; Attlee's eye was on winning the peace,' one of his aides said. Quietly, with no fanfare, he took control of the deputy's office to coordinate domestic policy, touring devastated cities around the country, talking about the New Britain that would emerge after the war. He did not speak about socialism, which he did not believe in anyway. He agreed with Keynes that the post-war period would 'produce a craving for social and personal *security*'. It is a word Attlee used repeatedly. 'The problems and pressures of the post-war world . . . threaten our security and progress as surely as – though less dramatically than – the Germans threatened them in 1940. We need the spirit of Dunkirk and of the Blitz sustained over a period of years . . . Labour's programme is a practical expression of that spirit applied to the tasks of peace . . . It calls for hard work and energy and sound sense.' He talked of 'safety nets' to shield families against the effects of unemployment, and 'social provision against rainy days.'[14]

The creation of basic welfare provisions, the renewal of Britain's cities, an urgent housing programme and the establishment of the National Health Service were presented by Labour as an extension of the wartime spirit of togetherness. If the British could pull together to defeat Hitler, they could find a way to provide homes and jobs for the people. It captured the mood of the times, not only in Britain but throughout most of Western Europe, and in other countries with an entirely different political culture, like Japan. Post-war, it was not only those on the Left who argued that the *laissez-faire* free market had failed lamentably. The inability of the ruling elites to do anything about the Depression, mass unemployment, the trade slump and extreme nationalism had led to chaos, fascism, war – the virtual collapse of European civilisation in many pessimists' eyes. There had to be an alternative way, a method of planning a better society to avoid a repetition of the disastrous twenties and thirties. Only a benign State, or so it seemed to a majority, could solve the large-scale problems and had the ability to organise people and resources for collectively useful ends – as it had mobilised the population in time of war.

The details varied, but across Europe governments established free education, medical care, and social insurance of one kind or another; built homes, and encouraged full employment. They were policies that became the consensus, generally accepted even by the Conservatives in Britain. In some countries, like France and later West Germany, welfare and education provision were enthusiastically embraced by the Right. The cost was not prohibitive at the start. In Britain, over the first five years of the Attlee Government, the new social provisions cost less than 9 per cent of GNP, though proportionately that was nearly three times more than had been spent before the war. Provision, at first, was designed to cover basic needs, Attlee's idea of *security*. People were willing to pay at a time when there were genuine shortages, 'precisely *because* times were difficult . . . it seemed like a guarantee of minimum standards of fairness,' as one writer who lived through the period recalled.

Some future historians – and politicians – later identified this period as the start of the 'welfare problem' of bloated benefits systems, a 'culture of dependency' and economically illiterate ideas of building a New Jerusalem from above. Many have asked whether the Attlee government was too 'socialist' – were all its reforms needed? Was it good or bad for Britain? The argument seems sterile and the questions naïve. It is obvious in hindsight where things subsequently went wrong, and where future generations made mistakes by spending too much, but was this the fault of Attlee's government? From the perspective of the time, it is hard to see how democratic politicians could have acted any differently and been elected. They were responding to national moods. The intellectual case, at that time, for a return to pre-war policies was thin. The elites, new and old, now saw the alternative challenge as communism. Leading Tories on the opposition benches admitted that if they had won the election in 1945 they would have done more or less the same as Labour in the immediate post-war years, except perhaps for nationalising the coal mines. Moderate welfare reforms, a state-subsidised health-care system of one sort or another, the 'social market' as it became known, ideas of redistributing wealth, seemed a reasonable balance of economic 'freedoms', and, more importantly, a political imperative.

Attlee was hardly a revolutionary. He argued that his practical, moderate, decent Fabianism was designed to *prevent* revolution. His policies at home, he said, were of a piece with Labour's foreign policy, which challenged Soviet-style communism throughout the world. Poverty, want and insecurity would always be breeding grounds for Marxism, he argued.

*

Despite its reforms, the Attlee government was in many ways deeply conservative. According to Anthony Howard, one of the most acute observers of those times, 'Far from introducing a "social revolution" ', the overwhelming Labour victory brought about the 'greatest restoration of "traditional" social values since 1660. The war had buried the dinner jacket; it had reduced famous public schools to pale, evacuated shadows; it had abolished the caste system in the civil service; it had eroded most of the social barriers in Britain. The Labour Government tried to take over the citadels of economic power – while the Conservatives, with a better understanding of reality, went quietly and without fuss to restore and recreate the environment in which they could begin to flourish again.'*[15]

---

* As was noted by some. Not everything had changed, despite the Blitz, a Labour Government and rationing. Life remained merry for a few. Early in 1946 Henry 'Chips' Channon, the socialite Tory MP, described in his sparkling political/social diary attending 'the fashionable, carefree Carcano-Ednam wedding reception'. He reported: 'I remarked to Emerald [Cunard] how quickly London had recovered from the war and how quickly normal life had been resumed. After all, I said, pointing to the crowded room, "this is what we have been fighting for".'

# 8

## A Performance at the Bolshoi

Six days after Drew Pearson broke the Gouzenko story, Stalin made a rare public appearance. Even more unusually, he made a speech. The leader was seldom seen in public after the war, apart from the major high days and holidays of Soviet communism such as May Day and the anniversary of the Revolution on 7 November. He made very few set-piece speeches, sometimes fewer than one a year. He was no great orator, but on 9 February he gave a thirty-five-minute address at a rally in Moscow's Bolshoi Theatre for the next day's 'elections' for the USSR's highest legislative body, the Supreme Soviet. In Russia's one-party state, it was a rubber-stamp body, but politicians from Stalin downwards, State officials, and the people dutifully went through the motions.

Stalin reached no heights of rhetoric, though he was clearly understood by his live audience of a thousand or so Party apparatchiks and the millions who heard him on radio. He wrote the speech himself – even taking the trouble personally to insert instructions at key points about what the audience reaction should be. The final draft of the speech before it was delivered includes the words 'warm applause', 'laughter', 'cries of approval' and 'furious applause' at the end of some paragraphs – culminating in 'furious applause and standing ovation'.

Amidst his unwieldy Marxist–Leninist gobbledegook, it became clear that Stalin had dispensed with the spirit of the Big Three alliance, as well as the letter. There was not a single friendly word in it for the Western powers, beyond admitting that the war had 'been won in cooperation with an anti-fascist coalition of the United States and Britain'. Now, he said, the USSR must redouble its efforts to turn the country into a superpower to rival the West in one decade – 'to surpass in the near future the achievements of science beyond the borders of one country', which was a clear hint at the nuclear weapons race soon to come. He demanded renewed efforts 'to increase the level of our industry . . . threefold in comparison with the pre-war level'. That, he said, was the only way to ensure Soviet security 'against any eventuality'. By the time Stalin sat down, Soviets had realised that their leader wanted them to work even harder to rebuild their war-shattered nation; they must abandon any hopes of greater freedoms or any relaxation of the dead weight of State oppression which might have accompanied victory. Instead, he had called for renewed ideological purity and Bolshevik rectitude.[1]

In Stalin's eyes, Russia had grown lax during the war, principally to please the West. All that would now change. Russia, in the words of Stalin's daughter, Svetlana, would again become 'half prison, half barracks' as it had been before the war.[2]

Soviet troops, in particular, had cherished high hopes of peace, quiet and some longed-for prosperity when they returned from the Front. Aleksandr Yakovlev, who later became the father of *glasnost* and *perestroika* as one of the chief reformist advisors to the last Soviet leader, Mikhail Gorbachev, was twice seriously wounded; once so badly that he carried a limp for the rest of his life. He was awarded the Red Army's highest honours, but when he returned home, despite the propaganda surrounding Russia's victory in the Great Patriotic War, he could see the harsh conditions that actually prevailed: trainloads of prisoners of war being sent to Siberia, malnourished children, and the return of lengthy jail sentences for minor offences. 'It became obvious that everyone lied,' he said of the Party ideologists.[3]

Stalin saw threats everywhere, even from those who were starving. The war left famine in its wake, the worst in the Soviet Union since the 1920s and early 1930s. The 1945 harvest was poor, followed by terrible weather in Ukraine, drought in Moldova and unseasonable rain which destroyed crops in Siberia. The following year's harvest was one of the worst on record. The grain crop was a third of its 1940 level, the potato yield less than half. Between one and a half and two million people died from starvation. And the famine was exacerbated by ideology: the Soviets were sending large quantities of food to East Germany and other parts of its new empire in an attempt to prop up the popularity of local communist parties. They were also stockpiling food in case growing international tensions led to war.

The Kremlin used the same methods that had been adopted in the 1930s – grain was requisitioned from the collective farms and the peasants were accused of hoarding. Stalin sent his henchmen to demand delivery of the quotas of grain each region had been ordered to hand over to the State. Unsurprisingly, the results were the same; the famine worsened.

Typically, Stalin had little sympathy with the victims and blamed them for their own plight. Khrushchev was sent to Ukraine, as he had been in the 1930s when he was Party Secretary there. He was hardened to suffering in the Soviet countryside and had caused a good deal of it himself, sending thousands of people to their deaths in the camps. Now he reported that famine in Ukraine was 'dire' and that people were resorting to cannibalism. Stalin reproved him: 'This is spinelessness. They're trying to play tricks on you. They are telling you this on purpose, trying to get you to pity them and get you to use up your grain reserves.'[4]

The State raised prices and halted bread rationing among workers in rural areas, but not the peasants on farms, meaning they had virtually no bread though they were producing the grain to make it. The same day, the little economic freedom that they possessed was taken away. Farmers on collectives were banned from growing produce for themselves on the tiny plots of land they had been allowed before.

Thousands of people who complained about the famine publicly were sent to the Gulag. Predictably, theft of food increased. In the summer and early autumn of 1946, 53,369 people were charged with stealing bread; three-quarters of them were sent to jail. New laws were introduced to raise sentences from three months to three years; at the stroke of a pen Stalin personally increased the sentence to five years – and more for repeat offenders. Starving people were sent to labour camps for years for stealing potatoes lying in a field.

In Ukraine, some people fought back. Partisans from the Ukrainian Insurgent Army, the UPA (Ukrayins'ka Povstans'ka Armiya), fought a low-level guerrilla campaign against Soviet forces, predominantly in western Ukraine and the eastern part of Poland in the Carpathian mountains, where at one point it numbered more than 30,000 soldiers. The UPA's dream was an independent Ukraine of ethnic Ukrainians and for much of the war they had been fighting Poles as hard as they had fought Soviets. The sporadic fighting was little more than a minor irritant to the Kremlin, though Stalin took no chances. He sent more than 100,000 troops of his own, and pressed the Polish army to join the Russians in combating them. He used tried and tested methods – between 1945 and the end of 1947 more than 182,000 Ukrainians, mostly peasants or civilians who had nothing to do with the UPA, were despatched to the Gulag. The UPA fought on until the end of 1949, when they were finally crushed by the Soviets, though at the cost of over 1,200 Red Army casualties.

*

In his Bolshoi speech, Stalin had not listed his grievances against the West, but his catalogue of them was growing: the Western Allies were interfering where they had no business in Eastern Europe, showing no understanding of Russia's legitimate security concerns; they were trying to stop him gaining an oilfield in Iran; the US was building military bases from Iceland to Panama, from Japan to the Mediterranean, in many places where it had shown no interest before; it was objecting to the USSR securing reasonable reparations from Germany for the destruction it had wreaked.

But chief among Stalin's resentments was that the US had refused to grant the Soviets a loan. As with Britain, the Americans withdrew Lend-Lease immediately after VE Day; Congress had approved the aid only up to the end of the war. But it was halted so abruptly that ships bound for the Soviet Union with much-needed supplies were ordered to turn around mid-voyage and head back to the US. Stalin was indignant and told Truman, via an emissary from Washington, that it had been 'unnecessary ... brutal even' and would not be forgotten. Truman realised later that he had made a mistake, but the damage was done.[5]

The Soviets had first requested a loan a year earlier. Molotov had tried to negotiate $6 billion at an interest rate of 2.25 per cent, saying that the money would be used for heavy industrial and transport equipment to help rebuild the Soviet economy. He was told that the US would think about it. Months passed with no answer. In November 1945 Truman despatched an inquiry team led by the Mississippi Senator William Colmer, a fervent segregationist and long-time anti-communist, to Moscow. The Colmer Commission advised against giving any money unless the Soviets provided verifiable statistics on industrial and military production, withdrew their troops from Eastern Europe and subscribed to US principles of free trade. The Soviets would not accept these terms, as the Americans well knew. 'It was a total insult,' one of Molotov's aides said – an insult made worse when accompanied by the lame excuse that the official paperwork for the loan application had somehow 'been mislaid during the transfer of records from the Foreign Economic Administration to the State Department.'

By the time Stalin rose to speak at the Bolshoi Theatre he knew the loan would not go through. He was not surprised, but it was a big factor in a speech that many people in the West saw as a cold ideological justification for Cold War or, as the Supreme Court Justice William O. Douglas called it, 'the declaration of World War III.'[6]

# 9

# The Declaration of Cold War

In his diary, President Truman described 1946 as 'The year of decisions'; he now began to take some in an attempt to solve his dilemma of how to 'stop babying the Soviets'. The Gouzenko affair, the continuing row over Iran and, as he saw it, Russian pressure on Turkey to acquire a military base on the Bosphorus Straits, the takeovers in Romania and Bulgaria, and now the Bolshoi speech, all signalled to Washington that the Soviets were becoming increasingly 'aggressive'. Having entered office knowing so little about foreign policy, Truman now began listening to advisors who would stiffen his resolve.

It has often been said that Roosevelt had been too 'weak' to stand up to the Russians, too ill, too 'naïve'. But he knew a confrontation with the Soviets would almost certainly come at some point. His priority, though, was to win the war against Germany and Japan, and *then* deal with Stalin. Before his death he was beginning to take a much harder line.

On 1 April 1945, less than a fortnight before he died, in one of his last cables to Stalin, Roosevelt wrote:

I cannot conceal from you the concern with which I view developments of events of mutual interest since our fruitful meeting at Yalta ... The decisions we reached there were good ones and have for the most part been welcomed with enthusiasm by the peoples of the world, who saw in our ability to find a common basis of understanding the best pledge for a secure and peaceful world after the war. Precisely because of the hopes and expectations that those decisions raised, their fulfilment is being followed with the closest attention. We have no right to let them be disappointed. So far there has been a discouraging lack of progress made in the carrying out . . . of the political decisions which we reached at the conference . . . I am frankly puzzled as to why this should be . . . and I must tell you that I do not fully understand in many respects the apparent indifferent attitude of your government.

He went on to say that the USSR's wish to dominate Eastern Europe, particularly Poland, 'would be unacceptable and would cause the people of the United States to regard the Yalta agreements as having failed . . . and the difficulties and dangers to Allied unity which we had so much in mind, will face us in an even more acute form.' Roosevelt was more explicit in his last note to Winston Churchill, sent two days before his death. 'We will need to consider most carefully the implications of Stalin's attitude and what is to be our next step.' On the day he left Washington for Warm Springs, Georgia, where he died, he told a journalist he trusted, Anne O'Hare McCormick, of the *New York Times*, 'Stalin is not a man of his word . . . either that or he is not in control of the Soviet government.'[1]

A short while earlier, on 24 March, Roosevelt lunched with an old friend, Anna Rosenberg Hoffman, at Hyde Park, his home in upstate New York. She recalled that, 'He held a telegram and got quite angry. He banged his fists on the arm of his wheelchair and said "Averell [Harriman] is right. We can't do business with Stalin. He has broken every one of the promises he made at Yalta."' And it was to Averell Harriman, polo-playing multi-millionaire businessman, old friend of the late President, and former Ambassador to Moscow, that Truman now turned. Harriman was a sombre-looking man who thrived on being a behind-the-scenes power broker and international fixer. He inherited a fortune from his father, the railroad tycoon E. H. Harriman, and he made another one personally in shipping, banking and oil. He had been sympathetic to the USSR – until he got there, saw life in the Soviet Union for himself, and began to deal with Soviet officials. 'Any negotiation . . . always seemed like you had to buy the same horse twice.'*²

In the last months of the war, Harriman's suspicions about Russia's future ambitions grew. He flew back to Washington from Moscow on his own aeroplane – Harriman was one of the first private citizens in America to own one – to tell Truman personally to stop being emollient and to start challenging the Soviets:

> These men are bloated with power. They expect they can enforce acceptance of their decisions without question upon us and all countries. Unless we take issue with present [Soviet] policy there is every indication the Soviet Union will become a world bully wherever their interests get involved. We can divert this trend, but only if we materially change our policy towards the Soviet Government . . . [not] any dramatic action but a firm . . . quid pro quo. Russian plans for establishing satellite states are a threat to the world and us. Unless the USSR changes, there's the prospect of a barbarian invasion of Europe.³

Harriman's political advice was underpinned by a strong ideological basis. Two weeks after Stalin's Bolshoi speech, the State Department in Washington received what would become one of the central documents of the Cold War, the so called Long

---

* Many Russians were mystified by Harriman's hangdog look. The USSR's former Foreign Minister and wartime Ambassador to Washington, the highly sophisticated Maxim Litvinov, came to know Harriman well. He often used to quip, 'How can a man with so many tens of millions look so miserable all the time?' It was Litvinov who early in 1946 called the Cold War right, telling Harriman's successor that the best either side could expect was 'an armed truce'.

Telegram. At the height of the Gouzenko spy scandal and debate in the White House about how to deal with the Soviet Union, the chargé d'affaires at the Embassy in Moscow, George Kennan, was asked to assess what the USSR's next step would be. Kennan had studied Russia and its history for many years, had worked there off and on since 1934, and was without doubt the State Department's foremost Russia expert. He sent back a 5,500-word cable (not the 8,000 words of many accounts, but nonetheless long for a telegram) of considered analysis and cogent historical background.

Kennan was probably the most influential American diplomat of the second half of the twentieth century, 'the court intellectual of the cold warriors', as he was later described by the historian/diplomat Arthur Schlesinger Jr., who on the whole admired him. A haughty, patrician figure, quick to take offence, Kennan had an abiding contempt for politicians: 'Our national leaders in Washington had no idea at all, and would probably have been incapable of imagining, what a Soviet occupation, supported by the Russian secret police of Beria's time, meant for the people subjected to it,' he wrote in his memoirs.[4]

But he knew what politicians wanted to hear and the Long Telegram provided it. 'At bottom of the Kremlin's neurotic view of world affairs is a traditional and instinctive Russian sense of insecurity,' he wrote. Russian rulers from Ivan the Terrible to Stalin preferred 'to keep their people in darkness rather than risk illumination by contact with foreign ideas.' Even 'Westernisers' like Peter the Great sought to 'limit contacts with the rest of Europe; they were fascinated by Western technology, rather than political ideas.'

Marxism was 'the figleaf' that gave the Soviet leaders intellectual respectability – they were not merely paying lip service. 'No one should underestimate the importance of dogma in Soviet affairs . . . the basic Soviet instinct . . . [is] that there can be no compromises with rival power and the constructive work can start

only when communist power is dominant. We have here a . . .
force committed fanatically to the belief that with the US there can
be no permanent *modus vivendi*. For them it is desirable and necessary that the internal harmony of our [country] be disrupted,
our traditional way of life destroyed, and that the international
authority of our state be broken, if Soviet power is to be secure.
Impervious to logic or reason . . . [the USSR] is highly sensitive to
the logic of force. For this reason it can easily withdraw – and
usually does – when strong resistance is encountered at any point
. . . [The West]) should be drawn into a tight bloc around the US
to contain any Soviet expansion.'

Central and Eastern Europe had proved indigestible to the
Russian nationalism of the Tsars 'and would do the same to communism', he said. There was little difference between the
'heavy-handed generals and commissars who now command the
capitals of Europe and the Tsarist satraps of old'. Revolts over time
would 'shake the structure of Soviet power.' The economic system
had taken root in the USSR, where expectations were low, but
elsewhere people were 'unlikely to accept a standard of living as
low as that of the Soviet people.'

Kennan was farsighted. The Soviet Union, he said, grew the
seeds of its own destruction. Imperial overstretch would mean
'that Russia would probably not be able to maintain its hold successfully for any length of time over the territory it has today
staked its claim if the West stood firm against Soviet bullying and
if the Soviets were [kept] within the areas it had conquered in the
War.'*

---

* Brilliant and highly influential though Kennan undoubtedly was, a visionary in
many ways, he had some strangely outdated ideas. He was not enthusiastic about
women's suffrage. His letters and diaries are full of observations such as 'women tend
to be more high-strung, unsatisfied, flat chested and flat voiced in the US than in
other countries and would lead more meaningful lives if they returned to family
picnics, children's parties and the church social.' He was an unashamed elitist and
thought democracy was over-rated. 'We ought to create a panel . . . of outstanding

It was the birth of the idea of 'containment' of Soviet expansion, a principle that Truman would adopt with enthusiasm and which the United States would adhere to for the next forty years until the Soviet Union and its empire collapsed – as Kennan foretold that it would.[5]

\*

Just as the Soviets had carefully built up spy networks in the United States and Europe, so too had the Americans in Germany and Eastern Europe. There were hundreds of them watching the new enemy, as the Soviets were fast becoming. The CIA was not created until the spring of 1947, but the US had a large number of separate espionage agencies under Hoyt Vandenberg, the Director of Central Intelligence. Vandenberg told Truman in early March 1946 that there was no sign of 'unusual Soviet troop movements or military activity of any kind' anywhere in Europe or the Middle East.[6] The Russians declared that they were demobilising fast, and the available intelligence established that this was true. By the end of 1946, from 11.5 million Red Army soldiers at the height of the war, numbers had decreased to only 2.8 million – similar to the combined number of American and British troops in Europe (2.45 million).

The Soviets had torn up a set of tracks on the main railway lines heading West from Berlin and their Occupation zone, and took them to the Soviet Union as war reparation, which 'did not suggest they were planning an invasion of Western Europe'. The

people that would comprise perhaps 500–1,000 souls' appointed by some 'detached authority such as the Supreme Court. From this group the nation's leaders should be chosen.' He was a diplomat in Germany for the years before the US joined the war and had some odd notions about the Nazis. 'It cannot be said that German policy is motivated by any sadistic desire to see other nations suffer under German rule. On the contrary, Germans are most anxious that their new subjects should be happy in their care . . . they are willing to make what seems to them important compromises to achieve their results and they are unable to understand why these measures should not be successful.'

Military Intelligence Division of the War Department reported to Truman that 'Soviet strength for total war is not sufficiently great to make a military attack against the United States . . . (or its Allies) anything more than a hazardous gamble.'[7]

Numerous reports all said the same thing. General Eisenhower, just returned from command of Allied forces in Germany, told Truman that 'the Reds do not want war . . . They have gained just about all they can assimilate.' General Marshall, Admiral Forrest Sherman, Deputy Chief of Naval Operations, and the other Joint Chiefs of Staff said: 'The offensive capabilities of the US are manifestly superior to those of the Soviet Union. Any war between the US and the USSR would be far more costly to them than to us.' They had no atomic weapons, were unable to launch a surprise attack and, according to the best intelligence and logistics experts in the War Department, they didn't *feel* strong, despite their assets. It would take them at the least fifteen years to overcome the losses in manpower and equipment sustained during the war; a decade to replace the loss of technicians and engineers, fifteen years to build a strategic air force, and fifteen to twenty years to build a navy.[8]

It was not military attack the West feared, but mass starvation and the breakdown of order among America's Allies. 'The pall of fear hanging over Europe . . . [is] preparing the continent to fall into Stalin's hands like ripe fruit,' said the Under-Secretary of State, Dean Acheson. The Director of Central Intelligence told Truman directly: 'The greatest danger to security of the United States is the possibility of economic collapse in Western Europe.'[9]

# 10

## The Abdication Crisis

Prince Naruhiko Higashikuni was the first member of the Japanese imperial family to break ranks and say it publicly. On 27 February 1946 he told a journalist from the *New York Times* that Emperor Hirohito should abdicate in favour of his son and a regent be nominated until Crown Prince Akihito, then aged twelve, came of age. Higashikuni, the Emperor's uncle by marriage, was one of the few members of Japan's ruling circle in the 1930s to have opposed war in Asia and to have warned against embarking on a route bound to result in conflict with the United States. After Pearl Harbor he had continually sought ways to bring about peace. Following Japan's surrender in August 1945, he became Prime Minister, charged with overseeing the cessation of hostilities and reassuring the people that the Japanese empire was secure, despite the defeat. After two months he retired voluntarily, but he remained one of the most influential members of the government. Now he admitted that in Tokyo court circles the idea of abdication had been discussed for months; just a few days earlier he had told the Emperor in a private audience that he should stand down. He had said the same thing at a Cabinet meeting. Hirohito, he declared, bore 'moral responsibility' for the nation's defeat, 'to the dead and to his bereaved subjects'.

These unprecedented comments caused a sensation. Japan was a strictly hierarchical society. The imperial family and leading aristocrats seldom spoke out of turn or manifested any sign of disloyalty. A few days later the Emperor's youngest brother,

Prince Misaka, declared that Hirohito should accept responsibility for defeat and graciously volunteered himself as the regent. Another brother, Takametsu, was also suggested. Despite hunger and extreme hardship being uppermost in most Japanese minds, much of the country was talking about the possible abdication. The censored press, however, barely mentioned the issue, although there was a huge stir when one of Japan's foremost poets, Miyoshi Tatsuji, published an essay urging the Emperor to step down as he had been 'extremely negligent in the performance of his duties . . . [and] was responsible for betraying the loyal soldiers who had laid down their lives for him in battle.'[1]

But the most powerful man in the country had decided against abdication. General Douglas MacArthur, the proconsul in charge of America's occupation of Japan, was insistent on Hirohito staying on the throne – and whatever MacArthur wanted in post-war Japan he got. America would remake Japan from the top down and turn it from semi-feudal despotism into a model twentieth-century democracy rooted in Western precepts of freedom. The Americans would impose democracy by fiat on Japan, whether the Japanese wanted and liked it or not, but they would do so using imperial institutions, including the existing civil service. They adopted as their principal ally and functionary in the task an Emperor who just weeks earlier had been regarded by his people, and by himself, as a descendant of the gods. Despite such obvious ironies, the creation of the new Japan was a remarkable achievement – practical, efficient, bloodless – and of lasting importance in re-ordering not just Japan but, by example, much of the Asian continent.

At the beginning of 1946 neither princes nor poets would have dared to question Emperor Hirohito's right to rule, despite the humiliation of total defeat. But early in the New Year, the Emperor issued a statement proclaiming himself human. It was the first stage of a process that turned Hirohito from an absolute ruler, literally worshipped by his people, into a constitutional monarch.

The statement, or 'Declaration of Humanity', was not written by the Emperor, or indeed anyone at Hirohito's court. It was drafted by a mid-level officer of the American Occupation authority. MacArthur – referred to by everyone in Japan, including himself, as SCAP (Supreme Commander for the Allied Powers) – wanted the Emperor to make a public relations gesture that would both help to keep him on the throne and avoid a war crimes trial. The statement was designed to be heard in Washington DC and London as loudly as it was in Kyoto and Okinawa. Its author, Lieutenant-Colonel Harold Henderson, an advisor to SCAP's Education Department, had been wrestling with the wording for some days.

By his own account, Henderson finished the draft in his lunch hour, lying on a bed at the Daichi Hotel in central Tokyo, where many of the senior American occupation soldiers were billeted, 'imagining what it would be like to be the Emperor of Japan.' He came up with a simple two-paragraph statement which had profound implications. The Emperor said he 'looked forward to a new world with new ideals, with humanity above nationalism as the great God. The ties between us and the nation do not depend only on myths and legends . . . and do not depend at all upon the mistaken idea that the Japanese are of divine descent, superior to other peoples and destined to rule them. They are the bond of trust, of affection, forged by centuries of devotion and love.' The statement refrained from saying in plain language that Hirohito was a man – by 'a subtle use of esoteric language' the Emperor had only to descend 'part way from heaven', as the highly conservative constitutional expert Joji Matsumoto claimed. But it identified the Emperor with less archaic notions of sovereignty, which were new to Japan – and to Hirohito. Until the unconditional surrender, days after the bombs fell on Hiroshima and Nagasaki, he had shown little interest in democracy or in the people's will. But his advisors and SCAP warned him that he needed to burnish his image as a peace-loving, European-style figurehead who had been betrayed by the ruthless military men around him if he wanted to preserve the monarchy, to remain on the throne – and to stay alive.[2]

Many influential figures in Washington, including most of the senior military brass, wanted the Emperor deposed, tried as a war criminal and executed. The British, Russians, Australians, Koreans and Chinese all pressed President Truman to start proceedings against him. Neither Attlee nor Stalin could understand what the Americans were waiting for. A Senate resolution and the Joint Chiefs of Staff instructed MacArthur to 'proceed immediately to assemble all available evidence of Hirohito's participation in and responsibility for Japanese violations of international law.' But MacArthur hesitated. He was convinced that the monarchy, with Hirohito continuing as Emperor, was vital for the stability of Japan and to bringing about the revolutionary changes to the country he was planning. Hindsight suggests he was probably right.[3]

MacArthur knew very little about Japanese history or culture, but a close advisor on his staff, and a personal friend, Brigadier-General Bonner Fellers, knew a great deal. Fellers had studied Japanese and visited Japan often between the early 1920s and the late 1930s. His cousin Gwen, to whom he was very close, was married to the Japanese diplomat Terasaki Hidenari, who had been posted to Washington for many years. Fellers wrote a series of intelligently argued briefing papers which seemed to MacArthur much more informative than the superficial material he was receiving from home.

A few months before the end of the Pacific war, Fellers had advised MacArthur:

An absolute and unconditional defeat of Japan is the essential ingredient for a lasting peace in the Orient. Only through complete military disaster and the resulting chaos can the Japanese people be disillusioned from their fanatical indoctrination that they are the superior people, destined to be overlords in Asia. Only stinging defeat and colossal losses will prove to the people that the military machine is not invincible and that their fanatical leadership has taken them the way to disaster ... There must be no weakness in the peace terms. However, to dethrone or hang the Emperor would cause tremendous and violent reaction from all Japanese ... Hanging the Emperor would be comparable to the crucifixion of Christ to us. All would fight and die like ants. The position of the militarists would be strengthened immeasurably. An independent Japanese army responsible only to the Emperor is a permanent menace to peace. But the mystic hold the Emperor has on the people ... properly directed need not be dangerous. The Emperor can be made a force for good and peace provided the military clique [around him] ... is destroyed.

After the war Fellers said that it had been the Emperor's decision to surrender and that he had personally ordered his seven million soldiers to lay down their arms. 'Through his acts, hundreds of thousands of American casualties were avoided ... therefore, having made good use of the Emperor, to try him for war crimes would, to the Japanese, amount to a breach of faith. We would have alienated the Japanese.'[4]

MacArthur was convinced, and set about persuading Washington to support the monarchy in general and Hirohito in particular. At the end of February 1946 he cabled Eisenhower, saying that he had investigated the Emperor's role over the past decade and that no evidence had come to light linking him to war crimes – a disingenuous claim as nobody had looked very hard. Indeed, they had quite deliberately not tried to find documentary proof or a paper trail of any kind.

MacArthur also reminded Eisenhower that the Emperor was 'a symbol which united the Japanese.' If he were indicted:

Japan would experience a tremendous convulsion ... it would initiate a vendetta for revenge ... whose cycle may not be complete for centuries . . . Destroy him and the nation will disintegrate. Civilised practices will largely cease and a condition of underground chaos and disorder amounting to guerrilla war . . . will result. All hope of introducing modern democratic methods would disappear and when military control finally ceased, some form of intense regimentation, probably along communistic lines, would arise. A minimum of a million troops would be required, which would have to be maintained for an indefinite number of years. A complete civil service might have to be recruited, running into several hundred thousand.[5]

At the beginning of March, George Atcheson, the State Department's man on the spot, reported to Truman in favour of Hirohito, less colourfully and effusively but with essentially similar advice. 'The Emperor is a war criminal . . . and the emperor system must disappear if Japan is ever to be really democratic. Nevertheless, in the present circumstances chaos would be best avoided and democracy served if Hirohito stayed as emperor and war crimes charges dropped.' Abdication was 'a potentially attractive future course but best postponed.'[6]

Truman reluctantly agreed that keeping Hirohito and the monarchy was the lesser of two evils. This was when the essential myth of modern Japan – nurtured over many years to come – was born. Hirohito had to be presented as a man of peace, hoodwinked by others – a ceremonial figure who had no choice but to go along with everything the soldiers around him wanted, from the invasion of China and the ambitious plans to conquer a vast Asian empire, to war with America and the British. There is, however, a mass of evidence that categorically proves the opposite: that he knew of and approved the war aims, including the timing of the Pearl Harbor attack; that he was a more than willing participant, and that he did little to halt the atrocities committed by his troops.

Hirohito, then in his forties, was an intelligent, extremely well-educated man, but he was also inflexible and unimaginative. He was not usually reflective nor, as those who knew him admitted, a deep thinker. He had considered abdication in order to devote his time to the real passion of his life, marine biology. But on the advice of his Cabinet he rejected the idea on the grounds that it would 'encourage republicanism.' He also realised that if he were no longer Emperor and thus useful to the Americans, it would be much easier for them to charge him with war crimes.

The ultimate pragmatist, Hirohito never acknowledged that his actions had been in any way criminal, nor that the war and its conduct had been morally wrong, only that they had been a mistake. In a private letter to his son, the Crown Prince – sent a few months after the war, when the future Emperor Akihito was twelve, but which did not surface until the 1980s – Hirohito showed little insight, let alone remorse. He blamed the incompetence of his generals and made no mention of democracy or the pursuit of peace. Instead, he told his son, 'our people lost the war because they took the US and Britain too lightly.' The military had failed to grasp the big picture. 'They knew how to advance but not how to retreat . . . had the war continued [we] could not have protected the three holy regalia* and the people would have to have been killed.' It was a chilling admission from a once godlike ruler who was now revealed as all too human.[7]

*

The Emperor's Holy War had cost the lives of at least 2.7 million of his subjects. In a decade and a half of conflict – Japan had first invaded China in 1931, annexing part of Manchuria, and then again six years later – 1.74 million soldiers were killed in battlefields stretching from the Great Wall of China to the northern tip of Australia. In the two and a half years after the war reached the

---

* The imperial mirror, sword and jewel. Since the seventh century, emperors had promised to protect the regalia, as a central part of the enthronement ceremony.

home islands almost a million people died in the carpet-bombing of Japanese cities and prime agricultural areas. The country was devastated – 'cowed and trembling before . . . [a] terrible retribution' thundered MacArthur, who liked grandiloquent phrases. The destruction of Japan was significantly greater than the Allies had inflicted on Germany, even before taking account of the effects of radiation from the two atomic bombs that ended the war. Around two-thirds of all homes in Tokyo were destroyed, 57 per cent of homes in Osaka and 89 per cent in Nagoya. As people fled to the countryside, many cities became ghost towns.

The Japanese military had deliberately underestimated the damage in case it encouraged defeatism. But at the end of January 1946 a US Strategic Bombing Survey conducted for SCAP showed that, at the time of Japan's surrender, its capacity for continuing the war had been exaggerated. Harry Truman's personal envoy, Edwin Locke Jr., came to the same conclusion a few months after VJ Day. 'The American officers now in Tokyo are amazed that . . . the resistance continued for as long as it did,' he reported to the President. 'The entire economic structure of Japan's greatest cities has been wrecked . . . Five million of Tokyo's seven million population . . . left the city.' Around the same time, a team of American economists calculated that Japan had lost more than a third of its total wealth and around half its potential income, not including the assets from its hugely profitable Asian empire. Japan was dependent on shipping but had lost more than 80 per cent of its entire merchant fleet from Allied attacks in the Pacific and the home islands.[8]

Amidst the rubble of the cities, one of the saddest sights was that of orphaned children with white boxes hanging around their necks. The boxes contained the ashes of their relatives. In some cities, more than a quarter of the population was homeless – with a mass influx returning home from the front. More than five million Japanese were repatriated in the eighteen months after the war. Around 80 per cent were soldiers and the rest were colonists and their families from the empire Japan had conquered but had now lost. They were seldom welcomed back with open arms. Soldiers, in particular, were widely despised – and this in a country where propaganda, and long tradition, had conditioned its people to hold officers and men from the Imperial Army as the fount of all honour. 'We were not invincible, as we had been told by our superiors,' one officer recalled wearily, many years later. 'The big shock was coming home and being shunned. People did not look us in the face.' Army and people together were not 'a hundred million hearts beating as one', as the military mantra went. The people now regarded soldiers not as returning heroes but as discredited failures, and treated them as pariahs. But it was not only that the military had failed lamentably in its mission and left the country starving and ruined: since the defeat, the public had also been inundated with information about the atrocities Japanese soldiers had committed in China, the Philippines, Korea, Indonesia, and South-East Asia. Japan had been dishonoured in the eyes of its own people, for which the Japanese blamed their own soldiers.

But in the immediate aftermath of defeat questions of honour took second place. For at least the next two years food remained the biggest issue for most Japanese. Much of Japan had gone hungry long before the surrender. Shortages had been acute since the fortunes of war had turned in favour of the Western Allies and by the end of 1944 the majority of Japanese were malnourished. South Korea and Formosa (Taiwan) had been colonies since before the First World War and had produced large amounts of food for the home market.* But the sinking of Japanese ships in the Pacific meant that these supplies were not getting through. American bombing of the cities had also disrupted food distribution, and

---

* Japan annexed Formosa from the Chinese in 1895. After war with the Russians in 1905, and a long-drawn-out diplomatic wrangle, Japan acquired the Korean Peninsula in 1910.

1945 saw the worst harvest since 1910. At the end of autumn 1945 the country was almost entirely out of rice. Thousands had starved to death and officials warned that ten million people now faced imminent starvation. They were exaggerating, but their panic prompted swift action from the occupying army.

MacArthur's first, decent, instinct was to alleviate hunger and avoid famine. He cut through red tape, ordered the seizure of 3.5 million tons of food that the US Army had stockpiled for emergencies and had it shipped to Japan. The Joint Chiefs of Staff and the House Appropriations Committee were indignant and demanded an explanation, but he responded with customary arrogance:

> Under the responsibility of victory the Japanese are now our prisoners, no less than did the starving men of Bataan become their prisoners when the peninsula fell.* As a consequence of the ill treatment, including the starvation of Allied prisoners in Japanese hands, we have tried . . . Japanese officers upon proof of responsibility. Can we justify such punitive action if we ourselves in reversed circumstances, but with hostilities at an end, fail to provide the food for sustaining life among the Japanese people over whom we stand guard?[9]

This impressed the Japanese immensely and 'kindled a light of hope in hearts that despaired', according to the otherwise anti-American historian Yamahoka Akira.[10]

The food imports did more than anything else to make the Japanese accept defeat and occupation. The supplies were basic Western foodstuffs: wheat, corn, flour, sugar, dried milk and tinned corned beef. They were not part of the traditional Japanese diet, but kept people alive, even if 'hunger was a constant companion'. Instead of rice, the new staples were a thin, watery gruel and

---

* The Bataan Peninsula was MacArthur's former HQ in the Philippines, from which he was forced to retreat in the spring of 1942.

a form of steamed stale bread usually fed to cattle. Necessity forced people to experiment. By the middle of 1946 newspaper advice columns were headlined 'Let's Catch Grasshoppers', and 'How to Eat Acorns'. But occasionally letters were published from middle class ladies, who complained that American beans caused embarrassing levels of flatulence – 'the new rations makes one so ill mannered', said one.[11]

As in Europe, health officials recommended that subsistence for working people should be 2,200 calories a day. But throughout 1946 and well into the following year, most Japanese survived on barely half that. And, as in Europe, the black market was a huge problem. Sufficient food was supposed to have been distributed through official 'compulsory deliveries'. But vast amounts were siphoned off by established criminals, and new gangs, many of which were composed of demobbed soldiers. The price of illicit goods rose inexorably – by the end of 1946 the cost of black-market rice was thirty times higher than the legal market price. Even two years later the price was seven to ten times greater. Everyone who could afford to, and many who could not, resorted to the black market as the only way of properly feeding their families. Of course, this meant that the very poor, the sick and the elderly suffered even more acutely. Nearly a million and a quarter Japanese were arrested for black-market activities in 1946, but far more were never caught. As an editorial in a popular newspaper said, 'In today's Japan the only people who are not living illegally are those in jail.'[12]

*

There was a joke popular in post-war Japan about General MacArthur. Invariably, it went, he confused the title Supreme Commander with Supreme Being. His egotism, self-regard and vanity were legendary. So were his energy, brainpower, determination and air of total calm. He was an authentic war hero at a time when they were badly needed. Nobody ever doubted his personal physical courage. It had been shown dramatically when, at the end of August 1945, he landed at Atsugii air base as a conqueror, ready to accept the surrender of the Japanese Imperial Army. He, and a small entourage of unarmed officers, escorted by a tiny force, were surrounded by 300,000 Japanese troops still armed to the teeth. Just one lone gunman could have killed him and his aides. MacArthur, still handsome and fit at the age of sixty-five, looked on totally unperturbed as his men began to disarm the Japanese, who stood by astonished. Churchill said later that 'of all the amazing deeds of bravery in the war, MacArthur's personal landing . . . was the greatest of the lot.' It was a masterstroke of public relations, and no general understood the importance of appearances as instinctively as did Douglas MacArthur. Atsugii was a potent symbol that the Americans had come in the spirit of conciliation, not vengeance. A Japanese observer at the time, the historian Kazuo Kawai, described it as 'an exhibition of cool personal courage . . . [but] it was even more a gesture of trust in the good faith of the Japanese. It was a masterpiece of psychology, which completely disarmed the Japanese apprehension. From that moment, whatever danger there might have been of a fanatic attack on the Americans vanished in a wave of Japanese admiration and gratitude.'[13]

MacArthur's men loved him, but throughout his career he was almost universally hated by officers of similar rank and above, who observed his vaunting ambition at first hand. Considering how many powerful enemies he made in the army and politics, it is amazing that MacArthur rose to the heights he did. He had been decorated many times for acts of conspicuous bravery on the battlefields of France during the First World War. But while his commanding officer, the venerable General John Pershing, pinned the medals on him, he was also writing home that he loathed MacArthur, whom he said was no better than 'above average' in military efficiency and ranked him thirty-eighth out of forty-five in talent among US brigadier generals. 'He has an exalted opinion of himself,' wrote Pershing, a feeling shared by scores of Mac-Arthur's officers. The public adored a hero, though, and when he married the fabulously rich, if flighty, J. P. Morgan banking heiress Louise Cromwell Brooks in the 1920s, one newspaper headlined the match 'Mars Marries Millions'. His stock rose even higher among the people, if not among his fellow officers, when a comment the bride made to her brother – 'He may be a general in the army, but he's a buck private in the boudoir' – found its way into the gossip columns.[14]

Roosevelt, too, had always disliked MacArthur personally, but he admired him as a leader of men and realised his importance as a war hero. There had always been mutual distrust – MacArthur made no attempt to hide his right-wing Republican views – but it flared into the open in 1933. It was at the lowest point in the Depression and Roosevelt, who had been President for just a few months, wanted to cut the army budget and redirect federal spending towards domestic New Deal programmes. At a meeting of the Joint Chiefs of Staff, MacArthur stormed into a rage as the other starred generals looked on. 'When we lose the next war and an American boy, lying in the mud with a bayonet through his belly and an enemy foot on his dying throat, spits out his final curse, I want the name not to be MacArthur, but Roosevelt.' Roosevelt was indignant. 'You must not talk like that to the President,' he snapped back.[15]

Truman despised him, but could find no plausible reason to refuse his appointment to Japan as SCAP, recommended by the Joint Chiefs at least partly because they didn't want him in Europe, or specifically, in Washington. Truman, as his aides recalled, sometimes looked tense and irritable merely at the mention of MacArthur's name. 'Mr Prima Donna, Brass Hat, Five Star MacArthur,' the President complained in his diary. 'He's worse than the Cabots and Lodges . . . They at least talked to one another before talking to God. Mac tells God right off. It is a pity we have such stuffed shirts in high positions. Mac's a play actor and bronco man.'*[16]

Yet Truman gave him enormous power, and virtual independence in wielding it. His standing orders stated: 'You will exercise our authority as you deem proper to carry out your mission. Our relations with Japan do not rest on a contractual basis, but on unconditional surrender. Your authority is supreme.' For six years MacArthur had more power over 70 million Japanese than Truman possessed in the United States over 200 million Americans. Ambassador William Sebald might have been the State Department's man on the spot in Tokyo, but he had to ask MacArthur's permission before seeking an audience with the Emperor or any senior Japanese government officials. 'Never before in the history of the US had such enormous and absolute power been placed in the hands of a single individual,' Sebald said after his tour of duty in Tokyo was over.[17]

America's task was immensely ambitious and it needed a man of MacArthur's dash, bravado and self-confidence to carry it off. Just before embarking on his journey to Japan, as an aide-memoire to the orders he was given days earlier by Washington, he wrote a list outlining his Initial Post Surrender Priority for Japan. From a later American standpoint, during much of the Cold War for example, it would seem a liberal manifesto, coloured by the New Deal, and rather different in emphasis from the aims of future US governments. MacArthur wrote: 'First . . . destroy military power. Then, build structures of representative government. Enfranchise the women. Free political prisoners. Liberate farmers. Establish a

---

* Truman loathed the 'Boston Brahmins' and was heard more than once to quote the jingle about New England snobbery, attributed most commonly to John Collins Bossidy at a Holy Cross Alumni dinner in 1910:

> Here's to dear old Boston
> Home of the bean and the cod.
> Where Cabots talk only to Lodges
> And Lodges talk only to God.

free labor movement. Encourage a free economy. Abolish police oppression. Develop a free and responsible press. Decentralise political power . . .'[18]

The Supreme Commander possessed the messianic zeal for the challenge and believed instinctively, as did European imperialists of old, in the superiority of the white man and in the purity of his civilising mission. The Occupation, which lasted six years and eight months – twice as long as the war between the US and Japan – was entirely American-run. Nobody else was allowed any say – and certainly not the Koreans, the Chinese, the Vietnamese, or the Filipinos, the conquered peoples who had recently suffered far more at the hands of the Japanese than had America. Other Asian countries' opinions were never sought. The Americans seldom liked to hear it, but race played a profoundly important role in the Occupation.

MacArthur himself barely saw any of the Japanese over whom he ruled. He never socialised with them – off-duty his relaxation time consisted chiefly of watching cowboy movies with his cronies and his second wife, Jean, a loyal, rather matronly figure, with whom he lived happily until he died. According to his private secretary, Faubion Bowers, 'only sixteen Japanese ever spoke to him more than twice and none of those were under the rank, say, of Premier, Chief Justice or President of the largest university.'[19] Yet he grew immensely popular. MacArthur's own simple reasoning was that 'the oriental mind adulates a winner'. An equally straightforward explanation is that the Japanese were familiar with authoritarian rulers who regarded themselves as godlike. Nearly half a million people wrote to him and he kept thousands of their letters meticulously filed. Most were filled with cringe-making gush. He was often called 'Japan's living saviour'. One correspondent said, 'When I think of the generous measures your Excellency has taken instead of exacting vengeance I am struck with reverent awe as if I was in the presence of a God.' And an elderly man told MacArthur that each morning he worshipped the

SCAP's picture as he used to do with the Emperor's. He was sent huge numbers of gifts – from silk kimonos to ceremonial tea pots to confectionery.[20]

One of MacArthur's big weaknesses was that he surrounded himself with yes-men, cronies who never challenged his assumptions. 'His egotism demanded obedience not only to his orders but to his ideas and person as well,' said the playwright, journalist and Ambassador to Italy Clare Boothe Luce, who had known him well for decades and, in many ways, admired him greatly. 'He . . . relished idolatry and surrounded himself with sycophants.' There were around one and a half thousand SCAP officials under him in mid-1946, a figure which doubled the following year. Many were idealistic and full of reforming zeal. They believed that they were building a new society in Japan, a society that would bring peace and stability. But many others were too busy having a good time.[21]

In Japan, as in Germany, Washington at first decreed that there should be no fraternisation between Occupation forces and the Japanese. But there were nearly half a million American troops in Japan throughout most of 1946 and the regulations were flouted so often they became pointless and unenforceable. MacArthur reversed the orders. 'They keep trying to get me to stop all this Madam Butterflying around,' he told one of his aides. 'I won't do it. I wouldn't issue a non-fraternization order for all the tea in China.' Historically, the home islands had been so cut off that the GIs were the first foreigners most Japanese encountered. And the Americans knew next to nothing about the Japanese. It was an entirely unequal relationship, victor and vanquished, powerful and powerless.[22]

To the young American men of the Occupation army the Japanese seemed exotic, particularly the women. The GIs were fed enormous amounts of absurd propaganda. 'The flat-chested, button-nosed, splay-footed average Japanese woman is about as attractive to most Americans as a thousand-year-old stone wall. In fact, less so,' claimed a widely read article in the *Saturday Evening*

*Post* headlined 'The G.I. is Civilizing the Jap'. But American troops seemed more than willing to ignore the blemishes. Many of the senior officers in the army and SCAP's civilian officials kept Japanese mistresses. More than ninety thousand illegitimate babies were born to Japanese women in the first three years of the Occupation. Propaganda the other way labelled American men as frightening and abusive, with no manners. Many Japanese were surprised to find that the truth was rather different. The women's magazines were full of letters such as this, written by a thoroughly respectable young woman from the south of the country. 'I find them [American soldiers] . . . courteous, friendly and perfectly at ease. What a sharp and painful contrast to the haughty, mean and discourteous Japanese soldiers who used to live in the barracks near my home.'[23]

Most rank-and-file GIs had little or no contact with the Japanese people. The only women they met were prostitutes. Prostitution, especially the idea of American soldiers 'defiling' Japanese womanhood, presented a problem to the Japanese authorities, who had their own ideas about the 'needs' of the American military. They assumed the US troops would behave as their own soldiers had done, taking 'comfort women' as trophies of war from the territories they had colonised. As a result, they employed 'comfort women' for the GIs, advertising in the press for volunteers. Hundreds of brothels were established to service the troops, segregated by rank and, of course, by race, with entirely separate facilities for black GIs. Naturally, most of the women who volunteered did so out of desperate financial necessity, but some turned out to be from reasonably comfortable middle-class families and were acting out of a patriotic desire, as the Government put it, 'to perform the great task of defending Japanese women'.

The GI geishas were required to take an oath of awesome pomposity:

> Although our family has endured for three thousand years, unchanging as the mountains and valleys and the rivers and

grasses, since the great rending of August 1945, which marked the end of an era, we have been wracked with infinite, piercing grief and endless sorrow and we are about to sink to the bottom of parlous, boundless desperation ... The time has come, an order has been given, and by virtue of our realm of business we have been assigned the difficult task of comforting the Occupation army as party of the urgent national facility of post-war management. This order is heavy and immense, and success will be very difficult. We absolutely are not flattering the Occupation force. We are not compromising our integrity, or selling our soul. We are paying an inescapable courtesy and serving to fulfil one part of our obligations and to contribute to the security of our society. We dare say it loudly: we are but offering ourselves for the defence of the national polity.

In other words, everyone had to make sacrifices. Despite the fine words about patriotism, crime syndicates quickly took control of most of the 'official' brothels and the women working in them were effectively bought and sold. In the spring of 1946, by which point it was estimated that a quarter of the GIs who used them were infected with venereal disease, MacArthur closed the brothels down.[24]

\*

SCAP officials, higher up the social ranking, lived extremely well – far better than they could have done in suburban America. Their houses had been requisitioned from Japan's upper classes and they were looked after by large retinues of servants, paid for, to the resentment of hungry Japanese, by their government. Bowers even had two cooks, one for Western food and one for Japanese. He later acknowledged that 'I and nearly all the Occupation people I knew were extremely conceited and extremely arrogant and used our power every inch of the way.' George Kennan, as a senior State

Department official, was despatched to visit and report on SCAP. He was appalled by what he saw. MacArthur's entourage competed bitterly for the boss's attention and the atmosphere of intrigue was 'reminiscent of the latter days of the court of the Empress Catherine, or of the Kremlin under Stalin,' he cabled to Washington. He felt contempt for the noisy 'colonial types' enjoying their supremacy over another race and said of the Americans in Tokyo that they were 'startlingly Philistine . . . indulging in luxury and exhibiting idleness and boredom.' The wives of the officials 'behaved as though the purpose of the war had been so that they might have six Japanese butlers with the divisional insignia on their jackets.'[25]

The scope and ambition of the American project in Japan were astonishing. As one historian put it, America 'set about doing what no other Occupation force had done before: remaking the political, social, cultural and economic fabric of a defeated nation and in the process changing the very way of thinking of its people.'[26] On the whole the Japanese would accept the Occupation, and willingly import the ideals of democracy and the free market. But there would be plenty of resentment at their liberators' arrogance and institutionalised racism. The paradox was that for the six years of Occupation it would be the anti-imperialist US that took up the 'white man's burden'.

# 11

## Rape and Pillage

While the Americans transformed Japan, Stalin set about creating an empire in Europe. He saw no difference between his actions and those of the United States in the Far East. Towards the end of the war he had told Milovan Djilas, a Yugoslav communist visiting Moscow, 'Whoever occupies a territory also imposes on it his social system. Everyone imposes his system as far as his army can reach. It cannot be otherwise.'*[1]

Germany and its capital were the Soviet Union's new prize possessions. The symbolic importance of the Red Army having conquered Berlin, discovering Hitler's remains outside his bunker and flying the hammer and sickle flag on the ruins of the Brandenburg Gate were of inestimable value to Stalin as a declaration of who had won the war and who would now make the peace. Germany's wealth was a prize too, and the Soviets now ruthlessly raided the country for booty, both official and unofficial. The untold riches, by Russian standards, of what the Russian troops found as they fought their way west shocked and appalled them. They would exact revenge for the thirty thousand towns and villages the Germans had devastated following their invasion in 1941 – and for the estimated seventeen million dead Soviet citizens.

---

* Typically, Stalin found a historical reference to back up his point: *cuius regio, eius religio.* It translates as 'Whose realm, his religion' and was the basis for the Peace of Augsburg in 1555, which allowed each German prince in the Reformation to decide which religion his people would follow. The principle was codified in the Treaty of Westphalia in 1648 that ended the bloody, religious/ideological Thirty Years War.

Despite the destruction from the war, Germany was still far better off than the USSR, where most of the Red Army soldiers and their families lived in great poverty and squalor. 'How well these parasites lived,' Lieutenant Boris Itenberg wrote to his wife from somewhere in East Prussia. 'I saw ruined houses, abandoned furniture, dozens of other signs of an incredibly good life . . . you would be amazed at what you see. Chairs, sofas, wardrobes. They lived so well. Why did they need more? They wanted a war – and they got one.' Dimitry Shchegolev, an infantry officer, was billeted outside Berlin 'in a small block of flats previously occupied by railway clerks. Each flat is comfortably furnished. I saw in the larder even as the battle was raging . . . home-cured meat, preserved fruit, strawberry jam. The more we penetrate into Germany, the more we are disgusted by the plenty we find everywhere . . . I'd just love to smash my fist into all those neat rows of tins and bottles.'[2]

Resentment was further stoked by propagandists like Ilya Ehrenberg, who was widely read by the Soviet troops he accompanied as a reporter on the Front: 'Don't count the days . . . count the number of Germans you killed today.' Germans, he declared, 'deserved no mercy of any kind.' In addition, Red Army officers told their men that there was no need to justify cruelty to the enemy. 'This is not the time to speak of Law and Truth. The Germans were the first to take the road beyond good and evil. Let them be paid in kind a hundred fold.' The troops did what they could to obey. 'The disaster that befell this area with the entry of Soviet forces has no parallel in modern European history . . . The Russians swept the native population clear in a manner . . . [unknown] since the days of the Asiatic hordes,' George Kennan reported to the US State Department in the spring of 1945. This was an exaggeration, especially given the behaviour of German forces in Poland and the USSR, but it is true that the Soviets were not seen as liberators – not in Germany, nor, for the most part, elsewhere in Central Europe. The atrocities they committed would be remembered with bitterness for the next four decades of Occupation.[3]

However, in one important way, conditions were better for Germans under the Soviet Occupation than in the American and, certainly, the British zones. There was more to eat. Most of the prime agricultural land that had traditionally fed the country was in Eastern Germany – Saxony, the Prussian lands, Thuringia, Pomerania. Despite the post-war chaos in the transport and distribution networks, the Russians were surprisingly efficient in getting food supplies to the cities. Yet more surprisingly, when food stocks were low, the Soviets sent extra supplies to Germany, even during the winter of 1945–46, when famine ravaged much of the USSR and more than a million and a half Soviet citizens starved to death. In the Soviet-controlled sector of Germany, though there was not enough food, there was almost no starvation – a point which Russian officials made sure to highlight to Germans living under American and British Occupation.

But there was a heavy price to pay for this largesse. Nobody knows for certain how many German women were raped by Soviet troops in the immediate euphoria of victory. It was seldom mentioned in Germany until decades afterwards; certainly not in Eastern Germany, where the subject was completely taboo until the fall of the Berlin Wall in 1989. In the spring of 1946 between 150,000 and 200,000 'Russian babies' were born in the Soviet zone, the vast majority of whom were brought up as orphans. Of all children born in Berlin between January and April, it is estimated that one in six were fathered by Russians. The number aborted was far higher – according to some medical opinion, between five and eight times higher. Besides the ordeal of rape itself, 'venereal disease as a result of rape by a Russian was part of a woman's lot in that period. Syphilis and gonorrhoea were rife,' as one woman who had been repeatedly assaulted recalled. Around 10 per cent of rape victims were infected, tens of thousands of women. Getting hold of antibiotics, which offered a good chance of a cure, was a difficult and expensive business in the Soviet zone. In the barter system operating in Berlin, a supply of the necessary drugs would cost a hefty half kilo of coffee, or maybe five cartons of Lucky Strikes.

The continued rapes undermined any hopes the Soviets might have had of converting Germany to communism. Senior Red Army officers and their political advisors knew how much they were hated and feared. As Andrey Smirnov, a high-ranking Soviet official at the time, admitted to a British diplomat, 'There are more Communists in the Western part of the country, which has not been in touch with the Red Army, than there are in Berlin.'[4]

As a result, the Russians began to impose stiff punishments on undisciplined offenders and by the late summer of 1946, rapes by Soviet soldiers were rare. But there were still random outbreaks of violence against women, as many victims remembered. 'These days have become dangerous to many,' Ruth Andreas-Friedrich wrote in her diary:

We visit Hannelore Thiele . . . She sits huddled on her couch. "One ought to kill oneself," she moans. "This is no way to live." She covers her face in her hands and starts to cry. It is terrible to see her swollen eyes, terrible to look at her disfigured features. "Was it really that bad?" I ask. She looks at me pitifully. "Seven," she says. "Seven in a row. Like animals." Inge Zaun lives in Klein-Machnow. She is 18 years old and didn't know anything about love. Now she knows everything. Over and over again, 60 times. "How can you defend yourself?" she says impassively, almost indifferently. "When they pound at the door and fire their guns senselessly. Each night a new one, each night others. The first time when they took me and forced my father to watch, I thought I would die." . . . "They rape our daughters, they rape our wives," the men lament. "Not just once but six times, ten times, twenty times." . . . Suicide is in the air. "Honour lost, all lost," a bewildered father says, and hands a rope to his daughter, who has been raped twelve times. Obediently, she goes and hangs herself from the nearest window frame.[5]

*

Immediately behind the frontline troops, the Soviets despatched small 'initiative groups' of communist émigrés who had left Germany around the time the Nazis came to power. Their task was to covertly prepare the ground for communist control of the Soviet zone. At this stage, it was vital that they do nothing to antagonise the Western Allies. Three teams of a dozen apparatchiks were sent. The most important was the group that arrived in Berlin two days before Germany's final surrender, while hand-to-hand fighting continued amidst the rubble of the city. It was led by the dour, fifty-one-year-old Walter Ulbricht, handpicked by Stalin to be proconsul of Russia's new German domains, which he would remain until his death a quarter of a century later.

Born in Leipzig, Ulbricht was active in the German trade union movement after the First World War, and was elected to the Reichstag as a communist in 1928. He fled the Nazis in 1933, first to France, then to Spain as a Comintern agent in the Civil War. His specialty was organising purges of Republicans who were not seen as sufficiently loyal to the USSR and to Stalin and he is said to have ordered scores of them. In 1940 he found his way to Moscow. Colourless and humourless, Ulbricht had not been one of the best-known communists in the pre-Hitler days, only second-, perhaps even third-rate, compared to some of the sophisticated, intelligent and cultured Party leaders who did not survive the Nazi purges. In fact, the death of potential rivals was the best way for him to rise so high, and he was chosen for his willingness to follow orders and his supine loyalty to the Kremlin.

Gustav Regler, a Comrade who knew him in Spain, and in exile in Moscow during the war, described him as entirely 'innocent of theoretical ideas or personal feelings'. He had 'a face stiff with malice that was conscious of its own ugliness. He sought to relieve it with a symbolical Lenin beard around the plump chin, a hairy appendage that did not, however, rid his fawn-like mouth of any of its petit bourgeois arrogance. His eyes, the right sharply observant and the left half-closed, were hidden behind a schoolmaster's glasses. He had the look of a lapsed priest who visits shady houses.' Another long-time communist, a young woman who knew him before he left Germany, recalled, 'You really got cold just looking at him.' And an aide who worked for him closely remembered his 'vicious temper'.[6]

At first the KPD (German Communist Party) activists behaved impeccably and could claim some real achievements, such as getting the water supply system and electricity working and the metro running. They encouraged a lively press and re-established the old political parties, including their far more popular rivals on the Left, the Social Democrats, which was more than the Western Allies did. In the American and British zones censorship was heavy and it was nearly a year before the parties were allowed to operate freely.

In the Communist Party's early post-war propaganda there was no mention whatever of socialism or Marx. In fact, it was stated unequivocally that 'instituting the Soviet system in Germany would be wrong.' But this was a lie since the Party was taking control by stealth. Wolfgang Leonhard, one of Ulbricht's lieutenants who came with him from Moscow, was given direct instructions on how to proceed. Local mayors could be 'bourgeois' or Social Democrats, but deputies should be 'loyal' and report to the Communist Party. 'We must have completely reliable comrades whom we shall need to build up the police. It's quite clear. It's got to look democratic, but we must have everything in our control.'[7]

The leading Nazis were arrested, as they were in all the liberated countries in the West. Most were sent to the infamous Sachsenhausen and Buchenwald concentration camps, where many communists had been imprisoned by Hitler. Hundreds were later executed, following cursory trials before 'People's Courts' run by loyal Communist Party members. Over time, more than 520,000 'fascists' were arrested in the eastern part of Germany, many of them sent to the Soviet Union into the great maw of the Gulag, or to labour camps above the Arctic circle. In Eastern Germany the process was not simply about 'de-Nazifying', as it was, with varying degrees of success, in the Western zones of Germany. It merged with the Soviets' principal goal of getting rid of anyone who might in future potentially stand in the way of a communist takeover. As early as February 1945 Beria wrote to NKVD officers at the front in East Prussia with a list of those who must be arrested. It contained obvious targets – members of the SS, senior army officers, government officials, concentration camp guards, the big landowners. But more ominously the order included 'newspaper editors, authors of anti-Soviet literature and other enemy elements.'[8]

One of the Party's first acts was to set up its 'sword and shield', a secret police force which, when the East German state was established later, became the Stasi (Ministerium für Staatssicherheit, or Ministry for State Security). From the first, the force was modelled almost exactly on Soviet lines and operated with the help of NKVD advisors. It used the same codes and methods of code breaking. At first it even adopted the same method of sewing the pages of files together with a thread through the top left hand corner of a page; officers called each other Chekists, as they continued to do in the USSR. An internal document from its earliest days, prepared for Ulbricht, showed where the organisation's loyalty and heart lay: 'The Soviet Chekists under the leadership of Lenin and the Soviet Communist Party created the basic model of socialist state security organs . . . to learn from the Soviet Union means to learn to win . . . to learn to disarm even the most sophisticated enemy.'[9]

Ulbricht looked with suspicion on the German people, whom he could never forgive for having allowed Hitler to seize power. He thought his compatriots were deeply unreliable and that the

German working class was, in the classic communist analysis, subject to 'false consciousness'. More simply put, they didn't know what was good for them – so the communists would tell them. While German politicians and church leaders in the Western zones were denying the idea of German 'collective guilt', Ulbricht accepted it – albeit with a self-serving Marxist twist: 'All the more is it necessary that in every German individual the consciousness and the shame burns, that the German people bear to a significant extent guilt and responsibility for the war and its consequences,' he said:

> Not only Hitler bears guilt for the crimes that were committed against humanity. Also bearing their portion of guilt are the ten million Germans who in 1932 cast their votes for Hitler in free elections, although we Communists warned that "He who votes for Hitler votes for war." Bearing their portion of guilt are all those Germans who spinelessly and meekly looked on as Hitler gathered power in his hands, as he smashed all democratic organisations . . . and let all the best Germans be locked up, tortured and decapitated . . . The tragedy of the German people consists of the fact that they obeyed a band of gangsters. The German working class and the productive part of the population failed before history.[10]

Nevertheless, for a brief period, the obedient Ulbricht followed the edict of his master in Moscow and tried to 'look democratic'. The KPD were relatively well organised in getting basic services running: Berlin's transport system, devastated by US bombing raids and the Soviets' final assault on the city, was operating efficiently by the autumn. The slogan 'Junkers' Land in Peasant Hands' was initially popular among tenant farmers, and a raft of new Red Army officers were despatched to replace the loathed 'conquerors' of Berlin. East Germany's new Commander-in-Chief, Marshal Vasily Sokolovsky, was an unexpected choice, not least because he was a cultured, unassuming man without the swagger and ruthlessness of so many top Soviet generals. His chief political commissar, Vladimir Semenov, was equally unusual. Then only thirty-five, Semenov was a bright, highly educated philosophy scholar. The first thing he did after he was appointed was to read all the archival documents he could find in Berlin on the history of Napoleon's occupation of the German states. (There is little evidence, however, that they were much use to him as a guide to post-Second World War conditions.)

For a while Berlin enjoyed a lively arts scene, with freedoms unknown since the days of the Weimar Republic. The theatres reopened, staging all kinds of 'bourgeois' plays, and a few socialist ones the Nazis had branded 'decadent'. The first performance for fifteen years of Bertolt Brecht's *The Threepenny Opera* was at the Hebbel Theatre, one of the playhouses left intact after the bombing of Berlin. On the opening night, a storm of applause from the full house greeted Brecht's famous line: '*Erst kommt das Fressen; Dann kommt die Moral*' – 'First comes grub; then comes morality'.

The concert halls were full. Newspapers were launched that contained some decent writing and offered liberal opinions – even the Red Army newspaper, *Tägliche Rundschau*, was permitted liberties that its counterpart in Moscow could never have got away with; a lively satirical magazine, *Ulenspiegel*, was full of wit, and clever cartoons mocking both the Soviets and the Americans. The first complaints that it was allowed too much freedom came not from the Soviets, but from the US Army authorities. 'We bubbled with activity and believed the golden age had begun,' recalled the founding editor, Buchenwald survivor Herbert Sandberg.*

But it could not last since Stalinists did not know how to live

---

* Later, the Americans did much to encourage a lively, free press and the revival of culture of all kinds. But at the start of the Occupation they were much more careful, hilariously so at times. There was strict censorship of newspapers, books, plays and films in the Western zones. The Americans banned thirty-four films sent to Germany to promote the American Way of Life. Huge successes in the US like *Gone with the Wind* (1939) and *The Grapes of Wrath* (1940) were considered too negative. Some

with criticism. By the spring of 1946 a resolution from the Party leadership determined that it was now time 'to launch the struggle against reactionary influences and tendencies'. Editors were leaned on and papers became noticeably more boring, more shallow, and more pro-Soviet. With over a quarter of a million Russian troops still on German soil, people knew that saying what they really felt about the USSR could be a risky business.[11]

Some verse that appeared first in *Ulenspiegel* may not have been great poetry, but it struck a chord among Berliners:

> Welcome Liberators!
> You took from us eggs
> Meat and butter, cattle and feed.
> And also watches, rings and other things.
> You liberate us from everything, from cars and machines.
> You take along with you tram cars and rail installations.
> From all of this rubbish, you liberate us.
> We cry from Joy.[12]

Apart from the violent attacks on German women, the greatest cause of resentment under Soviet Occupation was the huge amount of war reparations the USSR demanded – and the brutal way in which they were exacted. One of Russia's main post-war aims had been to get what it saw as just recompense for the devastation the Germans had wreaked in their short-lived Occupation. Most of the fighting and dying in the European war had taken place on the Eastern Front and civilians had suffered the most. In Byelorussia, in less than three years of warfare, nearly 20 per cent of the population had been killed, with some towns changing hands three or four times. In parts of Ukraine and the Caucasus one in six had died. The Germans had scorched the earth as they

---

books were banned, including Spengler's philosophical work *The Decline of the West*.

retreated. Stalin had continually told the Western Allies that he would be expecting reasonable reparations.

Neither Churchill nor Roosevelt liked the idea, but at the Yalta Conference they had accepted it. The Soviets came up with a figure for the cost of the destruction caused by the Nazis: $128 billion, although they never attempted to explain how they arrived at the calculation nor was it based on evidence of any kind. The Americans, and more reluctantly the British, agreed on $10 billion as a 'basis for negotiation'. At Potsdam Truman tried to talk Stalin out of claiming so much from Germany. He said he felt no outrage at their thirst for revenge: 'The Soviets had been thoroughly looted by the Germans over and over again, and you can hardly blame them for their attitude.' But he argued on practical grounds that it might be better if the German economy was revived. 'If you want milk you have to feed the cow,' he said in typically homespun fashion. Stalin was doubtful. He did not see 'why Wall Street bankers should be paid first' and remained adamant about reparations.[13]

From the moment of victory the Russians sent 'reparations teams' to rip the heart out of Eastern Germany's infrastructure and industry and transport it back to the USSR. 'Take everything,' Vladimir Yurasov, the officer in charge of one of the teams, told his men. 'Take all of it. What you can't take, destroy. Leave nothing for the others, not a single bed, not even a chamber pot.'[14]

Factories were carefully disassembled, along with every bolt and nail, and sent to the Soviet Union where they were just as carefully put back together again. According to German historians, between a third and a quarter of all East Germany's industrial capacity was taken by the Soviets. The Americans estimated that the Russians took 80 per cent of machinery in their sector within the first fifteen months of the Occupation.

'They ... dismantled the refrigeration plant at the abattoir, tore stoves and pipes out of restaurant kitchens, stripped machinery from mills and were completing the theft of the American

Singer sewing machine company when we arrived,' an American Occupation official reported. 'They had disassembled much of the S-Bahn overground metro, one line of the Berlin to Potsdam railway track and much of the central telephone exchange.' They took the animal feed from the Leipzig zoo, and a few months later, in the autumn of 1946, they took most of the animals too. Often Russian soldiers forced German workers to dismantle their own factories and put the machinery on trains bound east. Once, near Leipzig, the NKVD surrounded a football stadium, stopped the game mid-match and took the men in the crowd away to disassemble a factory.[15]

Edwin Pauley, the American Reparations Commissioner, saw the scope of the Soviet pillage with his own eyes. Pauley, a multi-millionaire oilman and a hard-headed realist, was outraged. On one tour of Berlin he nearly caused a dispute between the Occupation powers. With his own camera he took a photograph of freight cars loaded down with industrial plant and machinery from a factory. A Russian guard spotted him, threatened him with a rifle, jabbed him with his bayonet and arrested him. Pauley's escort, an American colonel, found him, showed the Russian soldier his 'four powers' pass and his .45 pistol. The Soviet sergeant realised he was outranked and let the Commissioner go, but it was nearly a tricky diplomatic incident. Soon afterwards Pauley wrote angrily to the State Department, deeply disturbed that Russians were clearly uninterested in restoring Germany's economic potential.[16]

Under the Potsdam agreements the Soviets were entitled to take some reparations from Western zones of Germany and the British and American sectors of Berlin. But Pauley thought they had already taken more than their ration. 'The effect of these removals will be ... [the] complete destruction of employment opportunities in the area. What we saw amounts to organised vandalism, not only against Germany but against the US forces of occupation.' His aides had a list of twenty American companies that had been nationalised by the Nazis, but might have been expected to return to their pre-war owners. The Soviets had taken equipment from an IT&T plant 'down to even small tools', and machines from IBM, Gillette, Ford Motors, Woolworth and Paramount Pictures. 'Russia is a vacuum into which all moveable goods . . . would be sucked,' he told the President. 'There's nothing we can do to stop them taking whatever they want from their zone but we ought to give them nothing from the western zones.'[17]

Pauley's Soviet counterpart on the Reparations Commission, Ivan Maisky, who had been Ambassador to London during the war, was one of the best-liked Russian officials among Western diplomats. Charming, an intellectual, he was the opposite of a typical grey Soviet bureaucrat, and would patiently explain that Russia had been so devastated in the war that reparations were necessary if the USSR were ever to catch up with the West. He pointed out that the Americans were taking vast amounts in reparations too, which was true but in a less clear-cut, physical way. The US had spirited away many scientists, technicians and engineers, as well as technical data and information of great commercial value – substantial 'intellectual reparations' – worth, he argued, a similar amount to the plant and machinery the Soviets claimed. Pauley agreed that all these had been taken, but argued that they were 'recent German technical advances for immediate uses in war' and were therefore 'clearly reasonable war booty.' It was a moot point.

The German communists knew the damage this was doing to their cause. Leonhard recalled a conversation with a fellow Party official one evening as they watched a Red Army truck filled with seized goods leaving barracks. 'That's the enemy, over there,' his comrade said. 'What, the Germans?' said a surprised Leonhard. 'Oh no, our reparations teams.'*[18]

---

* Even Molotov admitted later that the Soviets made serious mistakes on German reparations. 'The situation should have been handled very carefully, but was not . . . we should have considered what the people in Eastern Germany would think of us if we took everything from them . . . it undermined the new Germany we were

*

Apart from the 'official reparations', Russian soldiers were still looting informally on a vast scale well into the spring of 1946. 'The Soviets acted like Conquistadores accumulating booty, not ascetic Bolsheviks,' a Russian historian said. The senior commanders, like Marshal Zhukov, set a bad example for their men, turning his homes into museums. According to a later NKVD report, his dacha near Moscow contained 'dozens of boxes of silverware and crystal, along with 44 rugs, 55 valuable classical paintings, 323 furs, 400 metres of velvet and silk . . . the entire house was furnished with every kind of foreign luxury . . . a huge canvas depicting two naked women' hung over the Marshal's bed. Apart from the doormat 'there was not a single item manufactured in the Soviet Union'.[19]

Stalin was aware of what they were doing and gave his approval when he issued an order permitting officers to send back to the USSR goods weighing up to five kilos, with no questions asked about what was being despatched. But the most senior officers took far more than that. His own chief bodyguard, General Nikolai Vlasik, used his time at the Potsdam Conference to extract some 'war reparations' of his own. He returned to Moscow with a hundred-piece porcelain dinner service and dozens of crystal vases and wine goblets. He later said that all senior Soviet security officers had received similar china, but he did have a hard time explaining how a horse, a bull and two cows had ended up in his ancestral home in Byelorussia.

Air Marshal Aleksandr Golovanov dismantled Goebbels's country villa piece by piece and had it flown back to Russia. The NKVD's top man in Germany, Ivan Serov, plundered a treasure trove that allegedly included the Belgian crown jewels. In the first year of the Soviet Occupation an inventory of the 'trophy bri-

---

building.' On the other hand, he said, taking German industrial plant and booty helped the economy of the USSR so, in his terms, not all bad.

gades' states that officials and army officers sent back to the USSR 100,000 railcars full of various 'construction materials' and 'household goods' from Eastern Germany, 6,000 pianos, 495,000 radios, 188,000 carpets, around a million 'pieces of furniture', 264,000 wall clocks, 6,000 railcars with wallpaper and 588 with china and other tableware, 3.3 million pairs of shoes, 1.2 million coats, 1 million hats and 7.1 million 'dresses, shirts and items of lingerie.' For the Soviets, according to one German official, 'Germany was a giant shopping mall where they did not pay for anything.'[20]

On a more modest scale Western soldiers looted too. An American officer, Lieutenant Joe Reader, managed to spirit away the priceless medieval Quedlinburg Bibles from Thuringia, and other US officers stole masterpieces from Frankfurt's Städel Gallery. Many years later the gallery got them back. Two officers from the American Women's Army Corps stole $1.5 million-worth of jewellery from Princess Mary of Hesse. The Krupp family mansion in Essen was requisitioned by British officers. Nothing of any value remained in it by the time the soldiers left. The novelist Colin MacInnes was a soldier with the British Occupation forces throughout 1946. 'The things stolen varies with each man's nature,' he recalled. 'Looting is irresistible to anyone who had not a real indifference to possessions or a rare sense of duty. The opportunities are enormous. Even for those who are not thieves by nature, the attraction of what seems at first a delightful game is overwhelming.'[21]

# 12

## 'Woe, Woe to the Germans'

Edvard Beneš was President of Czechoslovakia for the second time. After Hitler's invasion in 1938, he had spent seven years in exile, but returned to Prague in triumph after Germany's defeat. As head of the Czech Government-in-exile based in London, he had been popular with his British hosts and at sixty-one was a quintessential Central European intellectual with the manner of a dignified schoolmaster. If he felt any resentment at the Munich Agreement between Britain and Nazi Germany, which had effectively handed Czechoslovakia to Hitler, he never showed it. Unlike, say, Charles de Gaulle, the prickly head of the Free French, he was always diplomatic, acknowledged the hospitality he received and caused few political ructions with the Allies. Beneš had the reputation of being a liberal man of sound judgement, wisdom and impeccable democratic credentials. He was also one of the most enthusiastic and ruthless practitioners of ethnic cleansing in European history.

In the two years after the war Beneš expelled more than two and a half million Germans from Czechoslovakia, often with no notice of any kind. Nor did he seem to care how many died in the process. He expropriated the property of the ethnic 'Sudeten' Germans, the majority of whom were from families who had lived in Czechoslovakia for generations. It was payback – not only for the barbaric Nazi years, but also because they had been of the ruling caste before independence in 1918. In 1943, while still in exile, Beneš had issued a chilling decree: 'We have decided to eliminate the German problem in our republic once and for all. The entire German nation deserves the limitless contempt of all mankind. Woe, woe, thrice woe to the Germans. We will liquidate you.'[1]

Later, back home in Prague, he called not only for a 'definitive clearance of the Germans from our country, but also a clearance of German influence'. At no point did the Allied powers express any disapproval. Churchill's Cabinet accepted the expulsions as 'inevitable . . . even desirable', and in December 1944 the Prime Minister told the House of Commons, 'Expulsion is the method which as far as we have been able to see will be the most satisfactory and lasting. A clean sweep will be made. I am not alarmed at the prospect of the disentanglement of the people, nor am I alarmed by these large transfers.' Stalin encouraged Beneš, telling him, 'This time the Germans will be destroyed so that they can never again attack Slavs.'[2]

Beneš was popular at home, principally for his anti-German policies, as were the other leaders around him in a post-war coalition government that included the liberals of his own party, communists and conservatives. The Justice Minister, Prokop Drtina, was cheered when he said, 'There are no good Germans, only bad and even worse ones. They are a foreign ulcer in our body . . . the whole German nation must bear the punishment for their crimes.' The Defence Minister, Ludvík Svoboda, declared, 'It is necessary that we deal with this Fifth Column once and for all.'[*] All the main churches approved of the expulsions, apparently turning Christian teaching on its head. The Catholic Canon of Vyšehrad, Monsignor Bohumil Stašek, preached in a sermon that 'Once in a thousand years the time has come to settle accounts with the Germans, who are evil and to whom the commandment "love thy neighbour" does not apply.'[3]

Moreover, the Czechs, as they often pointed out, had international approval for expelling the Germans. In Article XII of the

---

[*] Svoboda is one of the most common of Czech surnames, meaning 'freedom'.

Potsdam Agreement the three victorious Allied governments recognised 'that the transfer to Germany of German populations, or elements thereof, remaining in Poland, Czechoslovakia and Hungary, will have to be undertaken.' Article XIII also justified why this needed to be done quickly. It was almost as an afterthought that the agreement concluded: 'Any transfers that take place should be effected in an orderly and humane manner.' It was silent on the means of willing this to be, amidst the chaos of postwar Europe.

Early in 1946 Prague Radio declared that the Potsdam Agreement on population transfers had been 'the greatest diplomatic and political victory ever achieved by our nation in its long historical fight for existence against the Germans'. Few people at the time seemed much concerned with the plight of the German exiles. There were vast numbers of other refugees in Europe, and the details of the scale of Hitler's 'final solution' were emerging. But the journalist Anne O'Hare McCormick – an almost lone voice – described the forced expulsions as 'one of the most inhumane decisions ever made by governments . . . [supposedly] dedicated to the defence of human rights.'[4]

From the moment of liberation, the Czechs took the Nazis' anti-Jewish legislation and applied it to the Germans. All ethnic Germans had to wear a large letter N (for *Nemec*, or German) sewn on their clothes, as Jews in the Nazi years had had to display the Star of David. Germans were not allowed to enter public parks. They were permitted in shops only after Czech and Slovak customers had finished, which often meant that there was nothing left for them to buy. They were banned from purchasing certain goods, particularly foods like milk, cheese or meat. They were branded enemies of the state, meaning that their property could be confiscated at any time. Dozens of 'German' villages were burned to the ground, and many of their inhabitants left hanging from trees.

In Prague, forty-two thousand Germans, most of them born in the city and whose forebears had lived in the Czech lands for centuries, were interned. Some of the most prominent were murdered. One of the best known, Professor Albrecht Kurt, an eminent psychologist and the last rector of the German university was arrested at the Institute for Neurology and Psychiatry, then beaten and lynched by a mob outside the hospital.

Assorted buildings were taken over as makeshift prisons – baroque palaces, the riding school modelled on the famous Spanish institution in Vienna, the Education Ministry and the city's main labour exchange among them. The Scharnhorst school was the most notorious. An elite college, it had been open to all until the Nazi invasion, but since 1938 had been exclusively for Germans. After liberation, over a period of many months, well into the summer of 1946, thousands of Germans were jailed there, and scores were murdered. Groups of ten prisoners at a time, including women, children and old men, were led down a corridor to the courtyard and shot. Others were then forced to strip the corpses and bury them. Students were pulled through the streets to Wenceslas Square, where gasoline was poured over them and they were set alight.

Thousands of Germans were marched to the former concentration camp at Terezin, better known as Theresienstadt, the so-called 'model ghetto' to which the Nazis had invited groups of foreign dignitaries in a crude attempt to show how enlightened their policies were on the Jewish question. Between 10 and 15 per cent died in the hundred or so kilometres en route to the camp. The Russian occupiers watched and did nothing. American troops were also nearby and saw what was happening but they, too, made no attempt to interfere.

Behind the facade at Theresienstadt conditions were ghastly, almost as bad as they had been under the Nazis. Years later a survivor recalled the appalling scenes there. Groups of five to six hundred Germans would arrive at a time. They were separated into groups of men, women and children, led through a tunnel into a muddy courtyard, being beaten along the way by Czech guards. Those who were too old or ill were killed on the spot.

Once in the courtyard the prisoners were again made to run a gauntlet of beatings. Many of those who fell were personally killed by the camp commandant, Alois Pruša, who had himself been interned there by the Nazis. His daughter Sonja, in her twenties, once boasted that she had killed eighteen Germans and was proud of her achievement.

The entire German population of Brno, the third largest city in Czechoslovakia, was ordered to leave with almost no notice and trek more than sixty kilometres to the German border. As they left, they were pelted with stones, pieces of wood, rotten food – anything that came to hand – by Czechs who had known them all their lives. They were given no food or water. Those who staggered along the way were beaten with rifle butts, including old people and pregnant women. Those who couldn't get up were shot. A sympathetic Czech soldier, Joszef Kratochvil, recalled later that he saw the route 'lined with dead people, old men and women . . . children, and women who had been raped . . . [lay] collapsed in ditches.' Of the twenty-three thousand people who left the city it is estimated that six thousand died.[5]

Civil engineer Kurt Schmidt survived the Brno death march, but instead of reaching Germany he was interned in a camp set up for Germans near Strahov, close to Prague. His incarceration was harrowing:

We were forcibly reminded of death by the executions which took place in full view inside the camp. One day six youths were beaten until they lay motionless. Water was poured over them (which the German women had to fetch and carry) and then the beating continued until there was no sign of life left. The terribly mutilated bodies were deliberately exhibited for days next to the latrines. A 14-year-old boy was shot, together with his parents, because it was alleged he had tried to stab a guard with a pair of scissors . . . the women were routinely attacked and abused by guards and the men were powerless to protect them. If any man had tried to protect his wife he would have risked being killed . . . [The guards] often did not even trouble to take the women away – amongst the children and in full view of all the inmates of the camp they behaved like animals. During the nights one could hear the moaning and the whimpering of these poor women . . . Day and night there was no peace . . . it was as if one had entered hell.[6]

Although by and large Soviet observers ignored what was happening, some were shocked by the brutality of what they witnessed. Even a man as tough and violent as Ivan Serov, the Soviets' most senior secret policeman in Central Europe, and later head of the KGB, professed disapproval. From the Soviet zone in Germany, he reported to his boss, Beria: 'Every day around 5,000 Germans arrive from Czechoslovakia, most of them women, old people and children. Without any future, or the hope of anything better, many end their lives by suicide, cutting open their veins.' Marshal Zhukov, commander of Soviet forces in Europe, told Stalin personally that far too many people were being expelled – albeit for practical reasons. The eastern part of Germany was struggling to cope with the influx. But Zhukov was ignored.[7]

Altogether, between June 1945 and June 1947 around 1.4 million ethnic Germans arrived in the American and British zones of occupied Germany and 786,000 in the Soviet zone. Nobody has counted exactly how many died. The numbers are notoriously difficult to verify. The Germans in the aftermath of war claimed that 280,000 died, but that was an overstatement. The Czechs put the figure at less than 25,000, which is equally wrong. The best estimate is likely to be around 210,000, a number arrived at many years later from Soviet sources made available after the collapse of communism.

Throughout the communist years the Czechs barely acknowledged what had happened to their German population. Even after the Velvet Revolution of 1989, it was infrequently mentioned.

Instead Czechs refer to *odsun* – a strange euphemism literally translated as 'spiriting away', which hardly describes what actually happened. More than half a century later the expulsions were defended by older Czechs who had lived through them. Like so many Czechs of all classes at the time, one woman in her early eighties remained unrepentant. 'We hated them. People who had survived the concentration camps were returning and they described what had happened to them there. The fact is that people hated the Germans, genuinely hated them, so much that there was a spontaneous reaction and the feeling was that if they liked the Third Reich so much, they could go there.'[8]

*

The redoubtable Marion, Countess von Dönhoff made a dramatic escape from her East Prussian *schloss*. The thirty-five-year-old aristocrat and journalist, who had evaded death after taking part in the failed von Stauffenberg plot to assassinate Hitler in 1944, rode to safety in Germany's western zone on her favourite mount, Alaric. It was a journey of eleven hundred kilometres and took ten days. The resilient countess – who later became publisher of the newspaper *Die Zeit* – turned a painful ordeal into a remarkable adventure. Most of her fellow ethnic Germans expelled from Poland after the war were less fortunate. They faced brutality and humiliation.

With the collapse of the Habsburg and Ottoman empires after the First World War, new countries had been created. Many borders were adjusted, but people generally stayed where they were. After the Second World War the opposite happened. With the exception of Poland, no European borders changed. By agreement reached between the Allies during the war, eastern Poland was absorbed into the Soviet Union and the Poles were compensated with Pomerania, Silesia and East Prussia – western regions which had been part of Germany. As a result there were major population movements of Ukrainians and Poles in the east, which

reopened bitter, bloody conflicts going back centuries, culminating in 1995/1997 in vicious warfare. The border change left almost
seven million Germans in what was now Poland – and the Poles
wanted them out. The Western Allies had no more sympathy for
their plight than they had shown to the Sudeten Germans.
Churchill again commented favourably, saying that the transfers
were 'reasonable' and once, at a dinner with aides during the Yalta
Conference, used matchsticks to illustrate how people would be
moved across frontiers. And Stalin told Władysław Gomułka, the
post-war communist leader of Poland, 'You should create such
conditions . . . that they want to leave themselves' – a suggestion
echoed by the Catholic Bishop of Katowice in Silesia: 'The sooner
they leave of their own accord the better.'[9]

As in Czechoslovakia, the expulsions were extremely popular.
They had been a war aim of the exiled Polish leaders and were
endorsed by the new post-war government which was composed
principally of Soviet-imposed communists. Before he died in a
plane crash in 1943, Władysław Sikorski, head of the Government-
in-exile in London, was beginning to move towards accepting new
post-war borders for Poland, though with reluctance, which
would almost certainly mean that the Germans should 'be forced
to draw back . . . [to the West].'[10]

Sikorski's successors in exile went further. They were not only
intent on reducing the size of German territory in Pomerania and
Silesia, but were also aiming for a much harder and more compli-
cated target: the removal of age-old traces of Germanisation in
these lands. 'It is more than just the removal of German signs or
memorials, it is purging the sap of Germanization from every part
of life, the removal of Germanization from the people's psyche.'[11]

The government's main instrument would be the Polish forces.
In a letter to his troops in the spring of 1945, General Karol
Świerczewski, Commander of the Polish Second Army, explained
exactly what they were doing:

An unlikely communist dictator: Ja'far Pishevari, leader of the rebel People's Government of Azerbaijan, whose Soviet-sponsored coup in the north of Iran was the first Cold War crisis between East and West.

РЕАЛЬНОСТЬ НАШЕЙ ПРОГРАММЫ
—ЭТО ЖИВЫЕ ЛЮДИ, ЭТО МЫ С ВАМИ,
НАША ВОЛЯ К ТРУДУ, НАША ГОТОВНОСТЬ
РАБОТАТЬ ПО-НОВОМУ,
НАША РЕШИМОСТЬ ВЫПОЛНИТЬ ПЛАН.
И. Сталин

After the war, Stalin was suffering from various ailments, and even his clique of Kremlin magnates knew he was failing mentally, but his carefully burnished personality cult portrayed him as a man of strength and vigour.

Winston Churchill, on 3 March 1946, making his 'Iron Curtain' speech: a phrase that defined an era.

A food queue in the ruins of Hamburg. A defeated people eked out an existence, but hunger and disease were rampant.

The Germans called it Stunde Null – Zero Hour. The ruins of Berlin where nearly two-thirds of the city's homes had been destroyed by bombing between December 1941 and May 1945.

The Red Army on the march. Of all the combatant nations, the Soviets had suffered the most during the Second World War.

The May Day parade in Belgrade. The people celebrated peace, but their leaders were determined to seize the power in Eastern Europe that military victory had given them.

Prime Minister Clement Attlee (*above right*) and Foreign Secretary Ernest Bevin: the two main pillars of Britain's post-war Labour Government, which tried to transform the country while confronting national bankruptcy.

Though during the war bread had never been rationed in the UK, in Austerity Britain bread rationing began in the summer of 1946. Rationing of other foods continued, for some things like meat, until six years after the war.

After the Second World War, Europe confronted its biggest ever refugee crisis. More than eleven million people went through the displaced-persons camps established by the United Nations Relief and Rehabilitation Administration. For much of 1946, UNRRA was run by the colourful and fiery former Mayor of New York, Fiorello LaGuardia (*centre*).

UNRRA helped prisoners of war, orphans, former slave labourers of the Germans and millions of people whose homes had been destroyed. Some of the camps, like the one below in Bavaria, were for Jewish survivors of the Holocaust.

America came out of the war as the world's mightiest military power. As the saying went: 'War is hell, but America had a hell of a war.'

The Supreme Commander of the Allied Powers, General Douglas MacArthur, with Hirohito, the Emperor of Japan.

In Japan everything was in short supply after the war. Here, in Tokyo, a queue forms for people to collect their cigarette ration.

MacArthur was widely respected in Japan, although the American occupation was not always popular. But in the Philippines he was revered. When he returned to Manila, which he liberated from the Japanese during the war, he was mobbed by adoring crowds, with people clambering on roofs to get a view of him.

We are transferring the Germans out of Polish territory . . . in accordance with directives of . . . [the Allies]. We are behaving with the Germans as they behaved with us. Many have already forgotten how they treated our children, women and old people . . . One must perform one's task in such a harsh and decisive manner that the Germanic vermin do not hide in their houses but rather will flee from us of their own volition . . . and will thank God that they were lucky enough to save their heads. We do not forget that Germans will always be Germans.[12]

The Russians encouraged the expulsions, even though some Red Army officers and Soviet diplomats affected shock and outrage. With no forces on the ground, the Western Allies were powerless to ensure that the 'population transfers' were orderly and humane – but there is little evidence that they even tried.

Thousands of people at a time were rounded up and given no more than an hour or two to bundle up a few possessions before they were told to leave for 'somewhere' across the new border, in Germany. They were mostly women, children and old men. Young men had been carted off to war and were either dead, or displaced and had not found their way 'home'. Early in 1946 Anna Keintopf, a farmer's wife from the village of Machswender in Pomerania, set off with her three small children, along a road thousands of others had already taken. The border was sixty kilometres away, through a landscape blasted by war. They came across their first dead body within five kilometres – a woman whose corpse was swollen with decay. From there on, bodies were common at the sides of the road – bodies of women, of children, of animals. Sick people lined the road, unable to move. Many were ill from drinking contaminated water, including her daughter.

'Sometimes we did nine kilometres a day, sometimes a little bit more. I often saw people along the road blue in the face and struggling for breath, and others who had collapsed from fatigue and never got to their feet again,' she said later. They slept on the road or, if they were lucky, found a barn or farm outhouse. There were continual raids by Polish bandits, which the guards did nothing to halt. The nights were terrifying. Shots rang out repeatedly, fired at people trying to protect either their property, or women and girls from rape. At one point, Keintopf reported:

> A terrible scene was enacted before our eyes. Four Polish soldiers tried to separate a young German girl from her parents whom they struck with rifle butts, particularly the father. He staggered and they pushed him . . . down the embankment. He fell down and one of the Poles took his pistol and fired a series of shots. For a moment there was silence and then the screams of the two women . . . mother and daughter pierced the air. They rushed to the dying man . . . The young girl was taken away – either to be raped or used as slave labour.

Just before they reached the border the column was halted, and they were made to pass through a line of Polish soldiers:

> Some people were taken out of the column and forced to . . . go onto carts with all they had with them. No one knew what this meant, but everyone expected something bad. Some people refused to obey. Often it was single individuals, particularly young girls, who were kept back. Mothers clung to the girls and wept. Then the soldiers tried to drag them away by force and if they did not succeed they began to strike the people with rifle butts and riding whips. One could hear the screams of those who were whipped. I shall never forget.

Anna and her children did, however, make it across the border and ended up in Western Germany.[13]

Thousands were taken by rail – on transports not unlike those used just months earlier to take Jews to their deaths. One survivor recalled that it took weeks to progress a few score kilometres. The trains moved achingly slowly and often they were deliberately kept in sidings for days. 'Men, women and children were all mixed together, tightly packed in the railway cars which were locked from the outside. When the wagons were opened for the first time I saw from one of them ten corpses were taken and then thrown into coffins . . . I noticed that several people had become deranged. The people were covered in excrement.'[14]

Many of the Germans were interned in concentration camps before being expelled. The most notorious was the Zgoda camp at Świętochłowice, in Silesia, where in sub-human conditions of hunger and starvation more than two thousand of the five thousand inmates died within a few weeks. Zgoda had been one of the small satellite camps of Auschwitz; now Jewish inmates had been replaced by Germans. Its young commandant, only in his twenties, was a Polish Secret Police officer, Aleksy Krut. He commanded a group of guards all aged between seventeen and twenty-three. The mistreatment of prisoners was systematic from May 1945. Krut said that he could do to the Germans in five months what it had taken the Nazis five years to do to the Jews – and he was barely exaggerating. Inmates were tortured by guards, then by *kapos* – German prisoners recruited for the task with the threat of immediate death if they refused – and finally by prisoners forced by camp staff to beat one another. Zgoda was closed at the end of November 1945, but other camps remained open throughout 1946.

Nearby, at Gliwice, was a camp where, according to prisoners who survived, inmates 'had their eyes beaten out with rubber cudgels . . . work parties [who] were buried alive in liquid manure,' and one man 'had a toad forced down his throat until he choked to death' while guards looked on laughing.[15]

At Lambinowice camp in south-west Poland around 6,500 prisoners were said to have died within a few months. The camp was run by another young man in his twenties, Czeslaw Geborski, 'a depraved . . . [man] who only made himself understood with kicks.' One of his most notorious guards, Johan Fuhrman, is alleged to have 'struck a baby dead whose mother had pleaded with him for some soup for her child.' According to one well-documented story, a group of German women and young girls was sent from the camp to exhume a nearby mass grave of hundreds of Russian prisoners of war killed by the retreating German army. When the grave was opened up there was an appalling stench. 'As the corpses lay out in the open the women and girls were forced to lie face-down on top of these slimy and disgusting corpses. With their rifle butts the Polish militiamen shoved the faces of their victims deep into the . . . decay. In this way human remains were squashed into their mouths and noses. Sixty-four women and girls died.' Between 40,000 and 60,000 Germans died in the camps, and more than 100,000 died on the roads and railways towards Germany.[16]

Between 1945 and 1947, around 630,000 Germans were thrown out of Hungary and 700,000 from Romania, where they had lived for centuries. More than 60,000 Hungarians were expelled from Slovakia and 100,000 from Yugoslavia. Ukrainians were thrown out of Poland and Poles from Ukraine in an ethnic war that had begun in 1943 and ran parallel to the conflict against the Nazis, but continued, with brutality, afterwards. Despite Germany's millions of war dead, its population was much bigger afterwards, inside its new borders – from around 60 million in 1939 to 66 million at the end of 1946. The result was that, after the Second World War, Europe was more ethnically homogeneous than it had been for many centuries, and would remain so until immigrants from outside the continent began to arrive in large numbers from the 1960s onwards. The Jews had all but disappeared, and the Germans were not wanted anywhere outside Germany. Vast populations had been forced to uproot in the biggest refugee crisis the world had ever seen. Hitler had dreamed of an ethnically pure Europe. Paradoxically, Germany's defeat ensured that by the end of 1946 his dream was, to a great extent, a reality.

# 13

## 'Anywhere but Home'

At the end of February, Marshal Zhukov was summoned back to Moscow from his headquarters in Berlin. The recall had nothing to do with the purloining of war booty. Zhukov had been the saviour of Moscow, the mastermind of the decisive battles at Kursk and Stalingrad, and the conqueror of Berlin. He was widely admired at home, and by commanders of the Western Allies, especially General Eisenhower, and it was this that brought about his downfall. Such a popular war hero was a potential threat and Stalin was determined to put the Marshal in his place.

The Marshal's phones and homes were bugged as Stalin sought evidence that could be used against him. The NKVD reported that at a party held at Zhukov's dacha in the autumn of 1945 those present had hailed the Marshal as the Great Commander of his generation, 'the victor over Germany.' Next came testimony from the so-called Aviators' Case, a separate but simultaneous investigation into Air Marshal Aleksandr Novikov.

Under torture, the celebrated Novikov, known as 'the father of the Soviet Air Force', claimed that Zhukov 'tries to belittle the leading role of the Supreme Commander-in-Chief in the War.' That post, of course, was Stalin's. 'Zhukov is not embarrassed to over-emphasise his own role as an army leader . . . and he even declares that all the main plans for military operations were worked out by him.' Novikov also alleged that Zhukov had established a clique of soldiers around him, loyal to him alone, and that he had even awarded a medal – undeservedly – to the popular singer Lydia Ruslanova, with whom Novikov claimed Zhukov was having an affair.*[1]

Zhukov was ordered to appear before the Supreme Military Council, where he was ritually humiliated. Stalin told him his conduct was 'intolerable'; Beria and Molotov accused him of 'Bonapartism' – in the Marxist canon the worst charge that could be made against a soldier. They wanted him purged, sent to the Gulag and, although they did not say so outright, shot. But Stalin hesitated. Zhukov was too popular and, to an extent, protected. He was removed from his post, however, given a lowly job as military commander of the Odessa region, and publicly vilified. Much of the vast haul of loot he had shipped back from Germany was confiscated, as was the early draft of his memoirs, which was shown to Stalin, who told the Marshal to 'leave history writing to historians.' The official Soviet news agency denounced him as 'an exceptionally power-loving and self-obsessed person who loves glory, demands respect, expects submissiveness and cannot bear dissent'. The Ministry of the Armed Forces issued a statement that declared: 'Having lost all sense of humility, and carried away by personal ambitions, Marshal Zhukov, believing that his achievements had been undervalued, ascribed to himself in conversations with subordinates the preponderant role in the conduct of all the major operations in the Great Patriotic War, including those operations in which he was not at all involved.'[2]

Some of Zhukov's friends and supporters in the army were less fortunate. The phone calls of other senior officers were routinely

---

* Ruslanova was among Russia's biggest singing stars in the 1930s and by Soviet standards a vastly wealthy woman. She was married to one of Zhukov's favourite officers, Lieutenant-General Vladimir Kryukov, and it seems she did have an on-off-on-again love affair with the Marshal. She was a huge hit singing patriotic songs at concerts for Soviet troops during the war – a Russian equivalent of the British singer Vera Lynn, though with a racier private life. At Zhukov's request, just days after Berlin fell, she sang to troops in front of a still smouldering Reichstag. She suffered for her association with Zhukov, as did her husband. He was jailed for treason for ten years following Zhukov's demotion and she spent five years in the Gulag.

monitored. The record of one conversation between General Vasily Gordov, a confidant of Zhukov and a commander both at Stalingrad and the Battle for Berlin, and his chief of staff, General Fedor Rybalchenko, was shown to Stalin. During the call both men remarked that life in the West was far better than in the Russian countryside where millions of people went hungry, with Rybalchenko commenting, 'the newspapers just lie. Only the government officials live well, while people are starving'; and Gordov wondered, wistfully, if it might be possible to go live in the West. Both were against Stalin's by then fairly obvious policy of confrontation with America, which they worried would end in war. 'Before ten years have gone, they will whip our ass,' said Rybalchenko. 'Our prestige has been declining. Nobody will support the USSR.' Later Gordov, talking to his wife too close to an NKVD microphone, said that there would probably be 'everything in abundance' if collective farms were abandoned. 'People have a right to better lives . . . They won the rights of battle. Stalin has ruined Russia.' Soon afterwards Gordov, his wife and Rybalchenko were arrested, and rotted for years in the Gulag.[3]

Despite Stalin's distrust of his military commanders, he did not institute a wholesale purge of the officer class as he had done in the 1930s. Instead he turned on another large section of the Red Army – the Soviet prisoners of war captured by the Germans or their allies. He held them in utter contempt, believing them to be cowards or traitors for disobeying orders not to surrender, or – even worse – dangerous, because they had spent time in the West and might have been infected by foreign influences, habits and ways of thought. He believed that any soldiers who had seen what life was like in the West needed to be watched carefully. More than a million Soviet POWs had died in the first year of the war – three times more than the total number of Britons killed in six years of war. But there were more than two million still alive, some in camps, many of whom had been used as slave labour by the Nazis.

The prisoners of war did not expect a heroes' welcome, but

they might at least have had their suffering under the Germans acknowledged and been made to feel wanted in the USSR. Instead, fewer than one in six returned to their homes and families or to their pre-war civilian lives. Most were sent to 'filtration' camps, where they were interrogated by the secret police about their activities outside the USSR. Many thousands were shot out of hand if they had cooperated with the German army, even if it had been as forced labour. More than 900,000 men and some women, returned to face repression of one kind or another, either in the camps amid the Arctic wastes or in compulsory 'work battalions' for several years. Around 10 per cent were forced to re-enlist in the army for a decade. In early 1946 an American diplomat said that the Embassy knew 'of only one single instance in which a repatriated prisoner has returned to his home and family in Moscow . . . Repatriates are met at points of entry by police guard and marched off. Trainloads are passing through Moscow and continuing East. Then passengers are being held incommunicado.'[4]

Typically, Stalin came up with a historical reference to justify his deep suspicion of his own troops. He referred often to the soldiers who had returned from the Napoleonic wars resentful, disappointed and angry. In December 1825, many Russian officers had rebelled against Tsar Nicholas I. The Decembrist uprising was suppressed, five of its leaders hanged and several hundred of their supporters exiled to Siberia. Stalin might just as easily have considered 1917 and events in which he personally took a part. The February Revolution that year had begun with mutinies among soldiers both at the Eastern Front and in barracks in Russia. A comment that was first attributed to Yakovlev was frequently quoted after the dictator's death: 'Stalin made two mistakes. He showed the Russians to Europe – and Europe to the Russians.'

*

Millions of other Soviet citizens were also terrified of returning to the USSR: Ukrainians who wanted independence from the Soviet

Union; 'White' Russian anti-communists who had fought with the Germans in rebel groups, such as the former Red Army General Andrey Vlasov's Russian Liberation Army; Cossacks from the Kuban and other areas of the steppes, who longed for ancient freedoms to roam; Poles who found themselves on the wrong side of a border change; workers who had been taken as slave labourers by the Germans; assorted groups of Jews, Caucasians and others who, amidst the chaos of war, had somehow managed to find their way west. There were around two million people 'who were willing to go anywhere on earth except home,' as the Paris correspondent for *The New Yorker* since the 1920s, Janet Flanner, wrote. Accurate figures are hard to come by, but the best estimate is that more than half were immediately killed or sent to prison camps and around a third faced other forms of repression. They had, however, no choice but to return.

The Western Allies had made a deal with the Russians in 1944 that all Soviet citizens would be repatriated after the war. Later, the politicians involved in the negotiations claimed that they had no idea what would happen. This is disingenuous at best, a lie at worst. The British Foreign Secretary, later Prime Minister, Anthony Eden, justified the agreements on grounds of *realpolitik*. 'We cannot afford to be sentimental about this,' he told Churchill, who did not like the deal but knew he had little choice but to go along with it. 'After all, most of them had been captured while serving in German military formations, the behaviour of which . . . has often been revolting. We surely do not want to be saddled with a number of these men.' The most senior Foreign Office lawyer, Patrick Dean, was under no illusions either, 'In due course, all those with whom the Soviet authorities desire to deal must be handed over to them, and we are not concerned with the fact that they may be shot or more harshly dealt with than they might be under English law,' he told ministers. Only one member of the War Cabinet, the Minister for Economic Warfare, Lord Selborne, is on record as opposing forced repatriation. He wrote to the

Prime Minister that 'sending these people back to Russia will mean certain death for them'.[5]

Eden, though, had made a verbal agreement with Molotov, which he said was binding, that the Soviet citizens would be sent back 'whether they were willing to return or not.' Molotov was insistent on the wording and was clear about the implications. He was as cynical as his boss, Stalin, with whom, one afternoon during the purges in 1938, he had co-signed an order to execute 'saboteurs and Trotskyists' – 'all 3,167 to be shot' the document stated – and then left his office to go to the Kremlin cinema to relax with other Soviet magnates by watching a Western. Later he could admit that many of the purge victims were probably innocent, but was still convinced that 'they could not be trusted'.[6]

Despite the repatriation agreement, Churchill thought highly of Molotov:

A man of outstanding ability and cold-blooded ruthlessness ... his slab face, his verbal adroitness and impenetrable manner were appropriate manifestations of his qualities and skill. I have never known a human being who more perfectly represented the modern conception of a robot. And yet, with all of this, there was an apparently personable and keenly polished diplomatist ... in the conduct of foreign affairs. Sully, Talleyrand, Metternich would welcome [him] to their company, if there is another world to which Bolsheviks allow themselves to go.

Significantly, more people tended to agree with Alexandra Kollontai, the most glamorous of Bolshevik revolutionaries, who described Molotov as 'the incarnation of greyness, dullness and servility.'*[7]

---

* Molotov could occasionally surprise, though. He wrote the most passionate love letters to his wife, Polina Zhemchuzhina, a leading communist in her own right, who in 1948 was arrested on the orders of Stalin. Molotov may have been a model Kremlin lickspittle but he summoned up the courage to abstain on a vote in the

The Americans were more mealy-mouthed about sending people 'home'. Officially, Washington maintained the line that their fate could not be foreseen. Averell Harriman, hardly a naïve man, a confidant of presidents, and an ambassador to Moscow who had spent more time with Stalin than any other Westerner, a man who understood the nature of power, continued to claim that it was:

> . . . inconceivable to . . . [us] at the time that any appreciable number of the liberated Russians would refuse to return home . . . [we] had no reason to suppose the Soviet state would treat them as deserters or dangerous. We were thinking of the welfare of our own prisoners, some 75,000 men who, without exception, could not get home quickly enough. We had not thought hundreds of thousands of them would refuse because they had reason to suspect they would be sent to their deaths or to Beria's prison camps. That knowledge came later . . . Eisenhower and his staff were fearful that, if they did not send them back, the Russians would seize on one pretext or another to hold up the return of American prisoners from Eastern Europe.[8]

American troops, aware of what was going on, did the dirty work their political masters ordered them to perform. The forced repatriations continued throughout 1946 and well into 1947. At the end of January in Kempten, Bavaria, US troops were ordered to remove several hundred Ukrainians who had sought refuge in a church. 'Soldiers entered . . . and began to drag people out

---

Politburo on whether to send her to the Gulag – before eventually toeing the line and approving it. He wrote rather moving letters, if not literary masterpieces, often calling her 'my pleasure honey'. Typical examples: 'Polinka, darling, my love. I'm overcome by impatience and desire for your closeness and caress.' And, 'I want to kiss you impatiently, and kiss you everywhere, my adored sweetie.' He also had a dry sense of humour. Once he overheard people referring to him by his nickname, Stone Arse, attributed to Lenin. He interjected: 'Strictly speaking, what Lenin called me was Iron Arse.'

forcibly . . . They dragged women by the hair . . . and beat the men with rifle butts. One soldier took the cross from the priest and hit him with his rifle . . . Pandemonium broke loose. The people, in a panic, threw themselves from the second floor of the church and they fell to their death or were crippled. In the church there were suicide attempts.' An American diplomat told his superiors at the State Department, 'Our troops find it not only shocking but incomprehensible when Soviet refugees targeted for extradition bite each other's jugular veins rather than submit to repatriation.'[9]

In one incident at Dachau, when American soldiers tried to move 300 Ukrainians onto a train, eleven committed suicide in front of them. Just before dawn on 24 February, sixteen hundred troops, with tanks, surrounded the Plattling camp in Bavaria. According to the commanding officer's report, 'Truck headlights and camp searchlights shone on GIs as they loaded . . . [the Russians] onto waiting lorries. Again the barricades went up . . . again men hanged themselves and were cut down; again heads smashed windows and necks met glass fragments in the frames; again . . . wrists bled from razor blades and home-made knives. It was a wonder only five died.'[10]

British troops, too, repatriated thousands of Russians to the USSR from their Occupation zone in Germany. They had to perform a similar task in Austria when they returned many thousands of Yugoslavs to the tender mercies of Marshal Josef Broz Tito, the communist dictator who had taken over in Yugoslavia. Tito was as brutal as his one-time mentor Stalin, with whom he was later to fall out but with whom he shared a taste for bloody revenge against enemies, real or imagined. Churchill called Tito 'the great Balkan tentacle' but that did not prevent him making a similar deal to the one he had made with the Soviets. With British help, Tito's partisans had liberated Yugoslavia from the Germans – and won a bitter civil war against anti-communist forces. Around thirty thousand soldiers of the Slovenian Home Guard, a collaborationist army which had fought with the Germans against Tito's

Partisans, and of the Ustashe, the Nazi puppet regime in Croatia, were being held as prisoners of war by the British in Austria. Tito demanded their return so he could mete out justice – and show his people who was the new boss in Yugoslavia. The British Government handed them over.

The commander of Allied forces in Italy and Austria, Field Marshal Harold Alexander, later Lord Alexander of Tunis, one of Churchill's favourite generals, ensured that the job, unpleasant though it might be, would be done with supreme efficiency. From camps in Carinthia, 27,000 men were sent across the border to Yugoslavia. They were given no warning and told their destination would be Italy. Most did not know until the last moment that they were being deceived. The officer in charge of repatriating one group of Slovenes reported later: 'The platoon were only able to continue this harrowing task by constantly reminding themselves that former events had clearly proved that had the boot been on the other foot the kicks would have been no less savage.' Another officer, who complained that the whole business 'is most unsavoury and British troops have the utmost distaste for carrying out the orders', was summoned to HQ and admonished by his superiors. Anthony Crosland, later a Labour Foreign Secretary, described the events in Carinthia that winter 'as the most nauseating and cold-blooded act of war I have ever taken part in'.[11]

When they crossed the border, between ten thousand and twelve thousand Slovenes were immediately force-marched along the Drava river to Maribor, a small town where the Partisans had set up a concentration camp. There they were joined by other prisoners from Croatia, whom Tito claimed were soldiers or officials of the Ustashe. Most were killed during late 1945 and the first half of 1946 in the forests of Kocevje. The usual method was for the Partisans to take groups of two hundred or so, march them to the edge of deep ravines by an escarpment known as the Kocevski Rog and there either shoot the prisoners or throw them over the edge alive. The walls of the ravines were then blown up, ensuring

between officers and men. 'There was no sele
them,' an eyewitness said. 'Everyone brough
doomed to die.'[12]

Between fifty and fifty-five thousand men
were killed either in the forest or at the camp
conditions were appalling. There, the Croats w
the worst treatment – two hundred members of
movement, boys and girls aged between fourtee
thrown into the ravine and buried alive. Many
few miles from Maribor town, where deep tren
to bury them. They were lined up on the side
shot.

One miraculous survivor described the sce
the Partisans undressed us, tied our hands beh
wire and then tied us together two by two. 'f
trucks to the east of Maribor. I managed to unt
my hands, but I was still tied to the other office
to huge ditches, where . . . [below us] there
bodies piled up. The Partisans started shooting
was only slightly injured when he was throw
bodies, and then more were piled on, hiding hi
tisans were through shooting our group they
bury us because there was room for more . .
more victims. I managed to untie myself from
and crawled out of the mass grave.' He esca
burial teams that arrived later to 'tidy up' and
oners were dead.[13]

The Civil War in Yugoslavia was no blood
flicts in the 1940s – and less vicious than s
themselves had murdered vast numbers. At the

Sebe_9781101910283_1p_all_r3.indd   150

Croatia, four hundred thousand Jews, more than a hundred thousand Serbs, and many thousands of Tito's Partisans had been killed. The executions were later justified by the Yugoslav communists in a straightforward, if chilling manner. Milovan Djilas, who was a high-ranking Yugoslav communist for more than a quarter of a century before himself falling foul of Tito, said many years later: 'Yugoslavia was in a state of chaos and destruction. There was hardly any civil administration. There were no properly constituted courts. There was no way in which the cases of twenty or thirty thousand people would have been reliably investigated. So the easy way out was to have them all shot and have done with the problem.' Tito himself was equally matter of fact, explaining in the 1950s that elsewhere in Europe, for example in France and Italy, many people guilty of war crimes had gone free because the process of de-Nazification had been conducted in the courts. Tito had dispensed with the legal system entirely. 'We put an end to it once and for all,' he said.[14]

# 14

## 'This Chinese Cesspit'

In the spring of 1946 America's chief emissary to China was in buoyant spirits. General George Marshall was the master planner behind America's victories in Europe and the Pacific, a supremely gifted organiser revered by both Roosevelt and his successor, President Truman, who called him 'the greatest military man that America has ever produced – or anywhere else for that matter.' Marshall believed he had achieved a diplomatic breakthrough that had eluded peacemakers before him: brokering a historic deal to end the Civil War in China that had continued, off and on, for nearly twenty years between the recognised government, the Nationalist Kuomintang (KMT), headed by Chiang Kai-shek, and communist insurgents led by Mao Zedong.

On 4 and 5 March, Marshall had held talks with Mao and his advisors at the communist leader's fortress headquarters in Yen'an, north-east China. Marshall, though a strong anti-communist, was impressed by 'Chairman' Mao personally and by the discipline of Mao's troops and close political aides. Ever the realist, in the few months he had been in China, he was convinced that sooner or later – preferably from the US point of view, later – it was inevitable that the communists would take power there.

Marshall reported to Washington immediately after he left Yen'an that a settlement of the Civil War, or at least an enduring ceasefire, was within reach. 'I had a long talk with Mao Zedong and I was frank to an extreme,' he told President Truman. 'He showed no resentment and gave me every assurance of co-operation.'[1]

Marshall was much less enthusiastic about Mao's rival, Chiang, a man of deft political skills, who liked to be called the Generalissimo. Chiang had done much to modernise China and had a reputation as a successful military leader, following a series of campaigns against powerful warlords who had split the country apart after the Empire collapsed in the 1900s. He had united much of China under the KMT. Though the US supported Chiang with arms and money, it did so with ever-decreasing enthusiasm as the Nationalists lost popularity, sank further into a mire of corruption and failed to deal with China's woeful economic condition. Nevertheless Chiang, a man of ascetic tastes but great vanity, told Marshall that, in principle, he too would accept a ceasefire.

Of the sixty million or so dead in the Second World War nearly a quarter were Chinese. It is a grim statistic rarely mentioned in Western accounts. After the Soviet Union, China suffered the greatest war casualties. Around fifteen million were killed – twice as many as German, British, French and American deaths put together – in a conflict that lasted nearly three years longer than the war in Europe. In 1937 the Japanese had invaded for a second time, having annexed Manchuria in 1931. Japan's Occupation was brutal. Prisoners were rarely taken. As an act of wanton destruction it is hard to match the cruelty of the Japanese blowing up the dykes on the Yellow River. A million and a half hectares of China's prime agricultural land was immediately flooded, causing acute famine for millions. It took decades for the dykes to be repaired and rebuilt.

When the war with Japan was over, the killing and the dying went on for the Chinese. The KMT had tried since 1927 to crush an armed revolt by the communists. Chiang came close to doing so in the early 1930s but never managed it. The Nationalists held the majority of the country and were in control of a population of around 430 million, including the most fertile farmland and most of the big cities, but the communists controlled much of the north and east – territory that included more than 150 million people;

the Nationalists tried to remove them to no avail. There was a stalemate. Life for most Chinese was poverty-stricken and violently repressive, no matter which of the rival rulers they lived under. Mao was already experimenting with the totalitarian methods of permanent purge for which he later became notorious when he seized power in a united China. The KMT started out as a mildly socialist force that emerged following the ouster of the last of the imperial dynasties, the Qing. After Chiang Kai-shek became its head in the early 1920s, it turned into a military dictatorship – known for its seediness, graft and incompetence.

China was one of the poorest nations in the world and getting poorer. It was ravaged by inflation. In 1946 the government deficit was four times that of the previous year, and would rise six-fold by the start of 1947. The cost of living in Shanghai was 900 times the pre-war level. According to one economist, 'In 1940, 100 Yuan bought a pig; in 1943 a chicken; in 1945 a fish; in 1946 an egg and in 1947 one third of a box of matches.'[2]

During World War II, China became vitally important to the Americans. Japan had occupied most of eastern China and Manchuria, but not all of the country. The US needed the Chinese to continue the fight against Japan, ensuring that as many Japanese soldiers as possible remained in China, away from the American troops in the Pacific islands. During the Occupation the KMT and the communists maintained an uneasy alliance, though there were occasional skirmishes and plenty of mutual bitterness. Both sides were waiting for the Japanese to leave China before resuming the Civil War. Roosevelt did not despatch troops in any significant numbers to help the Chinese war effort, but he sent Chiang a group of high-level military advisors, a war-chest of weapons that included heavy guns and fighter planes, and large sums of money.

The American mission ran into immediate problems. Heading it was General 'Vinegar' Joe Stilwell, a tough, abrasive, straight-talker with a fine military record but few diplomatic graces. He was just the wrong personality to deal with the smooth, tricky and subtle Chiang Kai-shek, and they hated each other on sight. Stilwell told the journalist Theodore White from *Time* magazine, 'The trouble in China is simple. We are allied to an ignorant, illiterate, superstitious peasant son of a bitch.' In his diary he was even more splenetic, referring to Chiang, for reasons unexplained, as 'The Peanut' or, more easily understood, 'The Rattlesnake'.[3]

Not long after he arrived in China, Stilwell told the War Department, 'Anything that is done in China will be done in spite of not because of . . . [Chiang] and his military clique . . . The army is generally in a desperate condition, underfed, unpaid, untrained, neglected and rotten with corruption. We can pull them out of this cesspool but continued concessions have made the Generalissimo believe he has only to insist and we will yield.' Later, he told Washington, 'The Chinese Government is a structure based on fear and favour, in the hands of an ignorant, arbitrary and stubborn man.' Chiang, who may have been arbitrary and stubborn, but was certainly not ignorant, fed poison about Stilwell to influential friends in the US, such as the publisher of *Time*, Henry Luce, and several senior Republicans in Congress. To one, he complained that Stilwell was 'a man who does not place much value on organization, concrete planning and overall implementation.'[4]

Stilwell now discovered what had happened to $500 million in gifts and loans that America had granted to China the year after the US entered the war. Much of it had disappeared into the bank accounts of Chiang's cronies, mostly to his wife Mei-ling's brother, the Foreign Minister T. V. Soong. Soong had negotiated the loans and based the terms on unrealistic exchange rates, which made himself and his family a fortune but which worked against the State. A significant amount of the government deficit was a direct result. The endemic corruption of the Nationalist Government was among its main failures, alienating the rulers from the middle-class urban dwellers who should have been its natural supporters against the communists. The flow of stories in the Western press about graft and corruption in China continued to anger large sections of opinion in America, without whose backing the KMT would have been hard-pressed to survive. Chiang knew his clique were on the take. He wrote in his diary that even his close aides were 'indulging in extreme extravagance, whoring wildly and gambling with no restraint . . . they brag, swagger, extort and stop at nothing.' But he did nothing to restrain them.[5]

Chiang also knew that the Soong family had raided the country's gold reserves, but the Generalissimo indulged his wife. They had an unconventional marriage, certainly by the standards of most Chinese people in those days. Mei-ling had been educated at an Ivy League college in the US, and was an attractive and seductive woman well known for using her feminine charms. Stilwell called her 'Madame Empress' and was not alone in finding her grand airs galling. Roosevelt had loathed her ever since she had embarrassed him at a White House reception by calling for more American aid and money for the KMT. He said he didn't want her sitting anywhere near him again, or in his line of sight, as 'she would try to vamp' him. He told his wife, Eleanor, that 'despite impressions of her as a delicate, sophisticated lady who wore elegant silk dresses with slits down the sides, she's as hard as steel.' Truman said he 'didn't want her anywhere near Washington.' Both presidents had probably heard about Madame Chiang's affair with Wendell Willkie, who had been Roosevelt's Republican challenger in the 1940 election.*[6]

---

* Their affair apparently began when Willkie, married to a librarian, Edith, was sent on a bipartisan tour to China by Roosevelt in early 1943 and, according to Stilwell, the Republican politician, then aged fifty-one, was 'immersed in soft soap and adulation' by Madame Empress. A detailed account of the relationship came from a more reliable source than Vinegar Joe. The American publisher Gardner Cowles, not a man who exaggerated or made up stories, accompanied Willkie on the trip. One evening in Chiang's wartime capital, Chonqing, Willkie left a formal reception early. So did Mei-ling. Cowles had a room adjoining Willkie's and 'at around 4 a.m. a very buoyant Willkie appeared, cocky as a young college student after a successful night with a girl. After giving a play by play account of what happened between him and Madame Chiang, he concluded that he had invited her . . . to return to Washington

At least Chiang had tried to fight the Japanese invaders, though with only moderate success. Mao had made virtually no attempt at all, but after the communists took power they worked hard to create the myth that it was they who had led the main armed resistance to Japan. It helped to give them legitimacy, but the claim was based on a lie: in fact, as the Red Army commander Lin Biao admitted privately, after a few early defeats against far better equipped and trained Japanese troops, 'we kept our powder dry.' The communists wanted to keep their army in the north intact, ready for use later against what Mao saw as the principal enemy: the KMT. It was a policy that the Soviet Union's envoy to China, Petr Vladimirov, understood but could not endorse, telling Molotov that the Chinese communists 'have long been abstaining from both active and passive action against the aggressors.' Towards the end of the war he cabled Moscow to explain that Mao's armies 'were strictly ordered not to undertake any vigorous operations or actions against the Japanese, down to retreating under an attack and seeking a truce.'[7]

Mao spent most of the war in his hilltop hideaway in Yen'an, building up his own power, refining his personality cult, and trying out different forms of administration in the regions he controlled. It was then that Mao initiated the Chinese versions of collectivised farming that would continue well into the late 1980s and the 'rectification campaigns' supposedly based on 'honest self-

---

with us.' Cowles pointed out that perhaps it wouldn't help his chances of election in 1944 (he hoped to run again) if he stepped off the plane with the Chinese leader's wife. Cowles went on: 'She was one of the most beautiful and sexy women either of us had met but journalists were already gossiping about how the two were flirting in public.' Cowles was sent to withdraw the invitation to Madame Chiang. When he told her, according to Cowles, she scratched her fingernails down the sides of his cheeks, leaving marks that remained for more than a week. Mei-ling told Cowles, and others, that on their wedding night Chiang had said to her that he believed in sexual intercourse only for the purpose of procreation, and as he already had children from a previous marriage they would not make love 'in the normal way' – as she delicately put it.

criticism', but which, as one Chinese historian put it, resulted in 'thousands of people being rectified to death.' The Americans sent a team to Yen'an – the 'Dixie Mission', as it was called in America because it was entering 'rebel' territory. Chiang allowed eight American soldiers and officials unlimited access to Mao, who completely charmed them. They reported to Washington that Mao was essentially a democrat, a mild agrarian socialist in a country of impoverished peasants, a great admirer of the American Revolution and of the US, who wanted nothing more than to cooperate with the KMT to modernise and reform China. The two journalists who accompanied the mission, Theodore White and Annalee Jacoby of *Time* magazine, noticed that Mao seemed to enjoy an unhealthy degree of pleasure in being the object 'of panegyrics of . . . almost nauseating slavish eloquence.'[8]

But all the Americans missed the big story – easily done, given Mao's stringent efforts to hush it up. The communists were critically low on funds. They relied on a traditional Chinese crop to arm their troops, feed the people, as collective farming was already failing, and support the lavish lifestyles of Mao and his chief apparatchiks: opium. Chinese records show both the extent of the operation and the care the communists took to cover their tracks. The opium was handled by what the communists called the 'Local Product Company'. Sales were recorded as foreign trade in 'special product', and sometimes 'soap'. Mao banned opium use in areas he controlled but it was nonetheless produced in great quantities in Yen'an, transported in strict secrecy and security under armed guard outside the province and sold by trusted merchants throughout the rest of China and abroad.

The Russians knew of this illicit business venture, and on occasion would point out to Mao that drug dealing was not a worthy trade. Vladimirov reported to Moscow that the Chinese 'recognised it was regrettable', but Mao and his circle 'decided to give opium a vanguard role' because it brought in so much money. A million boxes weighing half a kilo each a year were sold to middlemen – and then on to dealers throughout Asia – amounting to 40 per cent of the communists' entire income.[9]

Mao and Stalin had an uneasy relationship from the start. Mao understood that he needed Russian support and that he could not win the Civil War without it. But being a supplicant to Moscow piqued his enormous vanity. Stalin might have been the leader of the communist movement throughout the world, but Mao had ideas of his own which, given the chance, he would implement as an alternative to the Soviet model. On the whole, he kept his mouth shut and appeared to be a dutiful follower, but he loathed being number two to anyone. Mao wrote to Moscow, begging to visit Stalin so they could 'discuss revolutionary tactics'. Twice in 1946 dates were fixed, but on both occasions Stalin cancelled at the last minute. Later, after he had seized power in China, the Chairman wrote: 'He wanted to prevent us from making a Revolution, saying we should not have a Civil War and should co-operate with Chiang Kai-shek, otherwise the Chinese nation would perish. But we did not do what he said.'[10]

Stalin feared that Mao could become his rival as the fount of all socialist wisdom. But he was ideologue enough to realise that it would be a great victory for socialism if the most populous nation in the world joined the communist camp. It would affirm that history was on the side of Marxism. On the other hand, if six hundred million Chinese were led by a young upstart (Mao was fifteen years Stalin's junior) following an independent line, the victory would leave a bitter taste. Warily, Stalin helped the Chinese communists with supplies and money, but never as much as Mao wanted. However, he also recognised Chiang as the legitimate President of China, telling the Chinese Foreign Minister, who visited Moscow in 1945, that he was prepared to do a deal with the Nationalists for territorial concessions in northern China in exchange for a 'guarantee of Chinese integrity' – in other words to try to halt Mao's insurrection. He also told Soong, 'As to communists in China, we do not support and do not intend to support them. We want to deal honestly with China and the Allied nations.' But as he frequently did, Stalin was attempting to deceive both sides.*[11]

*

In the last few months of the war, Vinegar Joe Stilwell was fired. The Americans felt that his feuding with Chiang was damaging the campaign against Japan. America's principal representative in China soon became Patrick Hurley, a millionaire Oklahoman oilman, a conservative Republican who had been Herbert Hoover's Secretary for War, but knew nothing about China or Chinese customs. He addressed the Chiangs as Mr and Mrs Shek, and when he visited Yen'an he surprised his hosts at a dinner by imitating Native American war cries. With deliberate rudeness, he called Mao and the highly sophisticated, erudite communist Zhou Enlai, 'Moose Dung' and 'Joe N. Lie'.

Hurley's orders were to seek a compromise between the communists and the KMT and to push for a coalition government after the war. Once he got the hang of his name, Hurley was impressed by Chiang, who convinced him that a deal was both undesirable and impossible. 'The communists are worse than beasts,' Chiang told him, and Hurley tended to agree. Nevertheless, he managed to broker direct talks between Chiang and Mao. Neither wanted to meet face to face, but Chiang wanted to please the Americans, and Stalin wrote to Mao three times begging, cajoling and finally almost ordering him to go.

They met in Chiang's capital, Chonqing. Mao insisted on travelling there on the same plane as Hurley. He felt it was the only way to guarantee that he wouldn't be killed on the journey and,

---

* Mao Zedong resented the pressure he was put under by Stalin for the rest of his life. He brought it up time and again until his dying day as one of the main reasons to distrust the Soviets. It was a cause of the Sino-Soviet split later, every bit as much as were any ideological or geopolitical reasons.

once there, he made sure two tasters sampled his food before he would touch it. A vague agreement was reached, but everyone was aware that it was window dressing. Within weeks, the Japanese had surrendered, Soviet forces had occupied a part of Manchuria, as agreed between the Allies, and Mao's troops attacked the KMT forces in the rest of the province.

Hurley thought the US administration was not doing enough to support Chiang. In December, without telling Truman first, he resigned in a blaze of publicity. As a precursor of the hysterical McCarthyite attacks that would soon grip the US, he blamed communists and fellow travellers in the State Department for 'betraying' America. He claimed, in his resignation statement, that 'A considerable section of the State Department is endeavouring to support communism generally, as well as specifically in China.' He presented no evidence, but that did not prevent an avalanche of attacks in the press and from Congress claiming that Truman was soft on communism. The President began the first Cabinet meeting after Hurley's resignation with the words, 'See what that sonofabitch [Hurley] did to me.'[12]

Truman needed someone to sort out his administration's China crisis and picked the most widely respected man in America for the job. George Marshall was the iconic military figure in the US – more admired even than Generals Eisenhower or MacArthur. He was exactly what the gentleman soldier should be: humane, wise, generous, an apolitical figure almost above criticism – at the time at least – even by the conservatives in Congress. 'The more I see him and speak to him the more I am convinced he's the great man of the age,' Truman said of him. His only personal weaknesses seemed to be an over-fondness for maple candy and pulp fiction. He had no wish to go to China and was not convinced he could do the job Truman wanted of him. For the first time in more than forty years in the services, he was no longer on the active duty list. He was sixty-five and looking forward to retirement, as was his wife Katherine, but, as he told his close aides and friends, he couldn't find a way of saying no to the President.[13]

Marshall went to China in the new year with a massive sweetener. He promised the KMT and the communists $500 million between them to help modernise China and rebuild its shattered economy if they could find a way to work together. Within the first few weeks, he negotiated a deal that both sides accepted in principle, and he was optimistic that they could make it work in practice. He stayed in China nearly the entire year, trying to see his mission through. But this was a Marshall plan that was destined to fail.

# 15

## Iron Curtain

The most potent image of the Cold War was of the 'Iron Curtain' that separated East and West by ideas as well as by armies. It is a phrase long assumed to be Winston Churchill's, from one of his most famous and influential speeches, at Fulton, Missouri, on 5 March 1946. In fact it was first popularised, in the context of the USSR and Eastern Europe, by Hitler's propaganda chief, Joseph Goebbels. It appeared in a German newspaper more than a year earlier, on 25 February 1945, just after the Yalta Conference. It is unlikely that Churchill read the article in *Das Reich*, though its main point was not entirely dissimilar to his own. 'Should the German people lay down their arms according to Yalta, the Soviets would occupy the whole of Eastern and South Eastern Europe,' Goebbels had written. 'If one includes the Soviet Union, one gigantic iron curtain would come down at once behind which the mass slaughter of the people would take place.'*

---

* The phrase derives from the safety curtain in theatres, invented in the late nineteenth century by the architect Edwin O. Sachs. As a reference to post-revolutionary Russia it appeared in 1918 in an obscure book by Vasily Rozanov, an anti-socialist tract called *The Apocalypse of Our Times*. 'With clanging, creaking and squeaking, an iron curtain is lowering over Russian history,' he wrote. Sebastian Hafner used the idea in his book *Germany: Jekyll and Hyde*, about the rise of Hitler, saying, 'In March 1933 . . . an iron curtain was rung down on Germany.' Churchill first used the term in a telegram to Harry Truman on 12 May 1945: 'An Iron curtain is drawn down upon their [the Soviets'] front. We do not know what is going on behind it,' he wrote. He repeated it in the same context a month later in a further cable to the President. At the Potsdam Conference, he used a phrase very like it directly to Stalin

The Soviets had no master plan to build an empire in Eastern Europe, as many Cold Warriors would later suggest. It had not been a war aim, nor the intention of the magnates in the Kremlin; it was just an opportunity that arose. The extent of Russia's new domains depended on how far the Red Army had gotten on the day Germany surrendered; there was no other logic to it. It was Hitler who did more than anyone else to create what became known as the 'Soviet bloc'. If the Germans had not invaded the USSR in 1941, there would have been no Soviet empire in Europe. And if the Western allies had launched D-Day earlier, the Russian conquests would probably have been smaller. Lavrenti Beria made a shrewd observation after the war when he was asked by his son Sergo if there was a way the West could have avoided the colonisation of Eastern Europe by the Soviet Union. 'One way. They should have invaded Normandy much earlier, though it would have cost the lives of more of their soldiers. If the Westerners had landed . . . months earlier, they could have got to Poland while we were still far to the East. Though they realised what mistakes they were making, they shrank from making the sacrifices . . . they are [now] paying dear for it.'[1]

Throughout much of the war Stalin had pressed the British and Americans to open a 'second front' in Western Europe to relieve losses in the USSR. Their refusal was one of the principal disagreements between the Allies during the conflict. Roosevelt might have been persuaded, and came near to agreeing on an invasion of Nazi-occupied France in 1943. But Churchill was adamantly against. He thought it was too risky and British casualties would be far too high. Both President and Prime Minister calculated that it would be better to keep the Soviets fighting the Germans in the east while the Western Allies prepared for an invasion in France

---

when he told the Soviet leader that an 'iron screen' had come down behind the Balkans. Stalin stared at him for a few moments and gruffly replied, 'That's nonsense.'

on a vast scale that would deliver the crushing blow. The strategy was put in clear terms by Sir William Strang, a senior diplomat and later the Permanent Secretary at the Foreign Office, in a memo to the British War Cabinet: 'Better that Russia occupies Eastern Europe, than Germany controls the . . . West.' If Stalin's allies had taken his advice during the conflict, there might have been no Soviet empire to speak of, or at least not one which, in Churchill's phrase at Fulton, left the Russians able to impose an Iron Curtain 'from Stettin in the Baltic to Trieste in the Adriatic.'[2]

Stalin had no clear idea of what to do with his new conquests. They did not form a cohesive whole, but were a discrete collection of nations with diverse cultures and histories, often deeply antagonistic to each other. Their main connection was that they had been overrun by the Red Army in 1944–45. Later, the Soviets would treat the entire region as one vast dominion and impose communist regimes on the Russian model throughout. But Stalin did this neither all at once nor at the same speed in every country. He thought first in terms of the USSR's security. He was not convinced that all these countries needed a Soviet-style one-party state immediately, believing that in some places the communists could co-exist with left-leaning parties in 'people's fronts' for years – even decades – laying the groundwork for a communist regime at a later date. He told Tito in the middle of 1945, 'Today, Socialism is possible even under the English monarchy. Revolution is no longer necessary everywhere.'[3]

He was in control of lands that historically hated Russia and which, between the wars, had been deeply hostile to the Soviet regime. Apart from Czechoslovakia, none had been democracies in the 1920s and 1930s. Most of them – Hungary, Romania, Poland – had been ruled by authoritarian regimes of the Right. For Stalin, the only acceptable outcome of the war was the establishment of regimes that could be relied on never to pose a threat to Russia. That did not necessarily mean they had to be Sovietised – 'being somehow neutered might do', as one observer at the time remarked. The Soviets wanted an Eastern European buffer zone of 'friendly states' to replace the interwar *cordon sanitaire*, which they believed had been designed to isolate the USSR. Soon afterwards, as relations with the US and Britain worsened, and the Cold War began, Stalin decided that the best guarantee of this was to impose communist regimes totally dependent on the USSR and obedient to the Kremlin, essentially to maintain a belt of colonies along its western borders.

Some Central European countries had been enemies during the war – Hungary, for example, enthusiastically joined Hitler in the invasion of the Soviet Union, as did Romania. Others, like Czechoslovakia and Poland, were nominally allies. All had suffered to different degrees under the Nazi Occupation, and would suffer again, if differently, under the Soviet 'liberation'. In Hungary, as in Germany, the Red Army used rape as a weapon of war: the Swiss Red Cross in the spring of 1946 calculated that, from a total female population of four and a half million, around 200,000 Hungarian women and girls were raped by Soviet soldiers during the winter of 1944–45 when Russian forces drove out the Germans. In Romania, Poland and Czechoslovakia there were few instances of rape. Hungary was forced to pay huge war reparations similar to those demanded of Germany. Around a third of Hungary's national income was simply taken by the Russians for the first few years after the war, including some of the country's gold reserves, and whole factories were transported to the USSR. That was one of the principal reasons for the unenviable record achieved by Hungary in the eighteen months after the war when hyper-inflation reached 14 quadrillion per cent (i.e. 15 noughts, or 158,000 per cent a day). In Bulgaria, the Soviets behaved with fiscal propriety and decency when they 'liberated' the country at the end of 1944.*

---

* Most Hungarians refused to be paid in money throughout 1946 after the currency collapsed. The wallpaper in many Budapest homes was decorated with large banknotes in fantastical denominations. In his marvellous book *My Happy Days in Hell*, the poet, memoirist and wit György Faludy explained the effect this had on daily life. In the summer his publisher brought out a new edition of one of his works.

In Romania, where they forced the monarch, King Michael, to abdicate more or less at gunpoint, and in Bulgaria, the Soviets installed communist regimes immediately. In the latter, where Russians had close cultural ties with the Bulgarians, they were at first welcomed. The propaganda emphasised, with a measure of plausibility, that it had been the Russians who had 'liberated' Bulgarians from the Ottomans in the 1870s and now, again, the Russians had liberated them from tyranny. Many Bulgarians accepted the official view. In some other countries the Soviets were more inclined to be patient. As in the eastern sector of Germany, they would make their administration 'look democratic', while ensuring that important functions like the secret police and state security were under their control. In all the coalitions, the communists made sure that they took control of the Interior Ministry. It was the most powerful force in people's day-to-day lives. Apart from running the police force, the Ministry appointed judges, issued identity papers, passports and exit visas, and granted licences to print newspapers and run radio stations.

Stalin told local communist officials in his new domains to tread carefully and to be content with 'an opportunistic policy'. He gave detailed instructions to local communist parties in Eastern Europe. To Gomułka in Poland he wrote: 'You must move towards Socialism not directly but in zigzags and in roundabout ways . . . avoid the temptation to adopt a premature path towards a people's democracy.' He gave similar instructions to Mátyás Rákosi, the leader of Hungary's communists, telling him to move

---

He was paid 300 billion Pengö, which before the war would have been worth around US $60 billion. When he collected his money, knowing it would have devalued by the time he'd walked through Budapest, Faludy ran to the central market a few blocks away. He spent the entire amount, he said, 'on one chicken, a litre of olive oil and a handful of vegetables.' On 5 July 1946, a one hundred quintillion Pengö note (20 noughts) was issued; when one elderly gentleman received one as wages he used it as part of the lining of his hat. The currency was stabilised the following year only with the help of the Americans, who returned to the Hungarian National Bank US $40 million worth of gold bullion they had managed to rescue from the Russians.

step by step: 'Don't be grudging with words, don't scare anyone. But once you gain ground then move ahead. You must utilise as many people as possible who may be of use to us.' It is from Stalin that Rákosi took his famous line that the communists used 'salami tactics, we took what we wanted slice by slice.' Later Rákosi was brutally frank, or rather, boastful, about how the communists took over in a slow-motion putsch. Speaking to Communist Party workers he explained: 'Our demands were always modest at first – and were then increased. For instance, first we demanded only "government control" of the banks; only later did we call for out-right nationalisation of the largest three banks. It was precision methods . . . that enabled us to defeat the reactionaries.'[4]

Ultimately, though, it was the presence of Soviet troops on the ground which ensured that the communists would get what they wanted. One of Rákosi's chief lieutenants, József Révai, Hungary's formidably intelligent future culture tsar, put it in simple terms: 'We were in a minority in Parliament and in the Government but at the same time we represented the leading force. We had decisive control of the police . . . our force was multiplied by the fact that the . . . Soviet army was always there to support us with their assistance.'[5]

\*

Stalin was willing to permit genuinely free elections in some of his new domains, at least until the communists started losing them. He wanted to avoid conflict with his Western allies. Immediately after the war he had believed that communists, supported by their liberators from fascism, would do well under 'bourgeois democ-racy'. But he underestimated how loathed the Soviets were and how little support the communists really had. Local officials knew, but could find no way of telling their Soviet masters the truth. Rákosi calculated that there were fewer than four thousand com-munists in Hungary in 1945; Anna Pauker said there were fewer than a thousand reliable Party members and fellow travellers in

Romania. In every country where elections were permitted the communists did badly, except in Czechoslovakia. Before the first free Hungarian elections in November 1945, Rákosi told Stalin that the communists could, with the socialists, win between 60 and 70 per cent of the vote and form a 'popular front' government. But they each won around 17 per cent, while the centre-right Smallholders Party won a plurality. The Soviets did not wish to risk further such humiliations so they resorted to more tried and tested methods to get their way: bribery, intimidation, threats and, eventually, violence.

Stalin was deeply suspicious of local communists who had remained underground in their own countries during the German Occupation: they might have been enemy agents or they might have independent ideas of their own. He relied on so-called 'Muscovites', whom he despatched to run the local communist parties – and, eventually, administrations – throughout Eastern Europe. Most had spent long years in Russian exile preparing for the day they would return in triumph. Many had become Soviet citizens. Handpicked by Stalin, they were sent as proconsuls of provinces in the Red Tsar's new imperium. They were chosen for their unwavering loyalty to the USSR and to Stalin personally. They had lost real contact with the land of their birth. Their children had been educated in the Soviet Union. The USSR had given them shelter, a cause to believe in and a job. Most were professional Bolshevik agitators, who had long since ceased any other work, if they had ever tried any.

Many of them had also spent time in jail for their communist beliefs. When they returned to their native lands after the war, they were not returning 'home'. They were representatives of a foreign power, furthering the interests of the USSR. They could have been despatched anywhere and served their overlords in Moscow with equal fervour and slavish obedience. Life as an émigré in the Soviet Union had been dangerous. It had been hard enough for a Russian communist to survive the purges of the

1930s: a foreigner who might be working as a Comintern agent, in regular touch with other potentially dubious strangers, was invariably mistrusted. Many had lived in Moscow's seedy Hotel Lux, surrounded by other émigrés, constantly watchful of each other – and of their own backs. Hundreds perished by the assassin's bullet, including figures hailed as heroes in the Bolshevik pantheon, like Béla Kun, head of the short-lived communist government of 1919 in Hungary. Even his status as a minor celebrity could not save him from being liquidated as a 'Trotskyite agent'.

The Muscovite lived a life of slogans, and when the slogans changed – as they repeatedly did at Stalin's whim – a life of grave danger. As one of them described it:

> The Muscovite's life was by no means enviable. Its *leitmotif* was fear. A Muscovite . . . was never safe wherever he went, least of all [in] the Soviet Union. Neither his loyalty nor long Party membership would protect him. He knew that he did not even have to commit a mistake in order to be relieved of his job, or to be arrested and tried. Muscovites knew that no such thing as permanent truth existed – because no such thing ever existed in the Soviet Union . . . [A Muscovite] knew the truth has many faces, and the only thing that concerned him was which face was on top just then. He was fully aware that at all times truth was what the Secretary General or the Supreme Body of the Party held to be truth, and therefore it did not particularly bother him that yesterday's truth had changed, by today, into a lie.[6]

Czechoslovakia was the only Central European country where the communists had large support. An industrialised nation, it was significantly better off than neighbouring Austria, and between the wars had been wealthier than either Belgium or Holland. In some elections in the 1920s and 1930s, the communists had gained a third of the vote. In the first post-war elections in May

1946, judged free and fair by both sides, they were the single biggest party with nearly 40 per cent of the vote, and formed a coalition with the liberals and socialists. While the good showing *was* pro-Soviet, it also came from an anti-German tide. It was the Russians, after all, who were helping Czechs throw the Germans out.

More important for Stalin, when Edvard Beneš was still in exile in Britain he had signed a Treaty of Friendship with the USSR which broadly gave the Russians the major say in post-war Czech foreign policy. Beneš had written to Molotov towards the end of the war with a pledge that, 'In regard to issues of major importance, we would . . . always speak and act in a fashion agreeable to representatives of the Soviet Government. In foreign affairs, the policies of the two nations should be co-ordinated from this time onwards.' Beneš was neither a fool nor a coward and he lived under no illusions: the Soviets had the power and he wanted close ties with them for practical reasons. Equally, he had no illusions that the West would protect his people from foreign domination. It was 'the West', Britain and France, who, despite their rousing rhetoric about freedom, had betrayed the Czechs at the infamous Munich Conference in 1938. Beneš's was the only Government-in-exile in Central Europe to return to power after the war. He spoke repeatedly of a 'third way' between East and West, at the same time as the divisions between them were widening. For a short while at least, Stalin left the Czechs alone and gave them the kind of leeway he did not allow elsewhere. He even held the Czechs up 'as the example of good friends and neighbours'.[7]

Another neighbour was far less willing to kow-tow to, or even to compromise with, the Soviets. Poland would become the acid test of just how much independence the Soviet Union would permit in its newly conquered territories.

*

In 1815, after the Battle of Waterloo, Tsar Alexander I was asked by the British Government what would happen to Poland following the defeat of Napoleon. The Emperor told the Duke of Wellington, the British Crown's Plenipotentiary to the Congress of Vienna, that the future could 'end in only one way for Poland – as I am in possession'. A hundred and thirty years later, the Red Tsar, Stalin, thought the same. Many Poles, including their leaders, were of the belief that the Western allies could somehow guarantee that they would regain independence after the horrors they had endured over the previous six years; years during which almost one in six Poles – five million people, three million of them Jews – had been slaughtered. But it was never going to happen.

Poland was key to the Soviets' idea of a buffer zone. It shared a longer common border with the USSR than any other European country – and its people had the bitterest hatred for the Russians. Poland stood along the main route which European invaders had historically used to march on Russia, and Stalin was determined to close down this potential enemy corridor once and for all. Throughout the latter stages of the war, and immediately afterwards, the Soviets had time and again made clear their minimum terms: Poland would be in the Russian 'sphere of influence', with a government subservient to Moscow, and there had to be a border change that would subsume the eastern part of the country into the Soviet Union. The new frontier had been part of the 1939 Hitler–Stalin Pact. The Americans and, more forcefully, the British, had tried to make Stalin moderate his demands, but he maintained categorically that they were not up for negotiation.

At the Yalta Conference, Churchill argued that independence and self-determination for Poland were a 'matter of honour' for him and for Britain 'because we drew the sword for Poland against Hitler's attack . . . Britain went to war so that Poland should be free and sovereign.' Stalin's response was stark: 'For us Poland is not just a matter of honour. It is a matter of security. A matter of life and death.' He then got up from his seat, walked around the conference room and delivered a lecture on how the armies of both Napoleon and Hitler had marched across the Polish plain en route to an invasion of Russia. 'Poland has always been a corridor for attack on Russia. Twice in the last thirty years our German enemy has poured through this corridor.' As Molotov insisted many times, Poland was a 'line in the sand. Poland was always in a difficult situation. We felt we cannot lose Poland. If this line is crossed, they will grab us too.'[8]

Like the Czech government led by Beneš, the Polish Government-in-exile during the war had been based in London. Unlike the Czechs, however, none of Poland's officials had been freely elected by the Polish people, and they were entirely unwilling to make any deals with the Russians. The loathing had deep roots, but there were more recent grounds for resentment. Poland had been carved in two by the Hitler–Stalin non-aggression pact and tens of thousands of Poles had been sent to Soviet prison camps or murdered by the Russians – including the notorious massacre of much of the Polish army's officer corps in the forest of Katyn in 1940. When, four years later, the exiled government called for a rising against the Germans in Warsaw, the Soviets did nothing to help, though their troops were not far from the city. Much to the fury of the British and Americans, the Soviets would not even allow the RAF or USAAF to fly over their supply lines to drop weapons and ammunition to the doomed Poles, whose Home Army was crushed while Warsaw was almost destroyed.

The Soviets had advised against the rising several times. Molotov warned the Poles that the USSR 'would disassociate itself from this purely adventurous affair in Warsaw' and Stalin said the rising was led by 'a handful of power-seeking criminals.' But he was being cynical. The Polish fighters were as anti-communist as they were anti-German and, if they had succeeded, they would eventually have tried to fight off the Soviets and forestall any Russian control over the country. By wiping out the Home Army – fifteen thousand soldiers were killed and around the same number of civilians – the Germans were simply doing Stalin's dirty work for him.*

The Polish exiles showed cynicism too. Soon after Germany attacked Russia, the head of the Polish Government-in-exile, Stanisław Mikołajczyk, said to an aide, 'The only thing that will settle Polish relations with the Soviet Union will be a war between the USSR and the US and Great Britain, with the latter countries on Poland's side.'[9]

Roosevelt supported Polish independence, but was exasperated by the Polish Government-in-exile. After it refused to accept the boundary changes the Soviets sought, he told Averell Harriman, the American Ambassador to Moscow:

> I don't know what the Poles in Poland think. We know very well what the Polish government in London thinks. It is predominantly a group of aristocrats looking to the Americans and the British to restore their position, landed properties and feudalistic system of the period before and after the last war. They have a basic suspicion of the Soviets and don't like Communism, which latter opinion I share with them. They think the future of Poland lies in Great Britain and the United States fighting Russia to protect Poland. I don't see that we have any interest in that kind of thing.

He thought they were being entirely unrealistic by refusing to

---

* The ill-fated Warsaw Rising has a crucial place in the narrative of Poland betrayed, by both East and West. Many military experts said afterwards that in fact the Soviets could have done little to help the Poles even had they wanted to. The Commander of the Home Army, General Władysław Anders, opposed it, later calling it 'the biggest and most reckless catastrophe of Poland.' It was mounted principally for political rather than military reasons, Anders thought. The Soviets had stopped their advance into Poland at the banks of the Vistula for a good reason: they were low on supplies and the German defence of Warsaw was resolute. The Soviets made one attempt to cross the river to send Polish units from the Red Army into the city. It was a disaster. The Red Army did not take Warsaw for another three months. Nevertheless, the suppression of the rising was a great convenience for Stalin.

compromise. When Mikołajczyk visited Washington in the autumn of 1944, Roosevelt told him in simple terms: 'There are five times more Russians than Poles. The British and the Americans have no intention of fighting Russia.'[10]

Churchill always stood up for the exiled government in public, but privately he said more than once, 'I'm sick of the bloody Poles.' When he met Mikołajczyk on 13 October 1944, after the failure of the Warsaw rising, he told him the Poles would have to accept the border changes which awarded the USSR some of eastern Poland, the so-called Curzon Line. He said the Allies had wrung from Stalin a concession that as a compensation the Poles would be awarded formerly German lands in the West.[*][11]

It was not a bad deal, Churchill argued. The Poles had to come to some reasonable terms with the Soviets and accept geographical and military realities: 'There is no choice.' Mikołajczyk refused. Churchill had been calm, but at this he started to lose his temper. 'Our relations with Russia are much better than they have ever been and I intend to keep them that way . . . Unless you accept the frontier, you're going out of business forever. The Russians will sweep through your country and your people will be liquidated. You're on the verge of annihilation.'[12]

The Soviets' policy was simply to ignore the exiled government. Molotov was unambiguous. 'We see no reason why Poland should be liberated through the efforts of the Red Army so that there may be placed in power a group which has shown a basically antagonistic attitude towards the Soviet Union,' he said. Instead of

---

\* The Curzon Line was the demarcation of the Polish–Russian border at the end of the First World War. Entire books, and long ones, have been written about whether it was fair or harsh on Poland. It was suggested at the Versailles Peace Conference in 1919 by Lord Curzon, the British Foreign Secretary, who tried to give newly independent Poland most of the areas where Polish majorities lived. The Poles did not accept it, mainly because it left out areas that had been part of the historic Polish kingdom until the eighteenth century. After World War I, when the Soviets invaded Poland but were repelled, the Poles pushed the border about 100 kilometres east of the Curzon Line. The Yalta agreement gave that territory back to the USSR.

dealing with the London government, Stalin established a rival team in the 'liberated' city of Lublin in eastern Poland, comprising mostly 'Muscovites', Polish communists who had lived in exile in Moscow, and a few communists who had survived underground during the German Occupation, then recognised the Lublin Committee as Poland's legitimate government.

At the Yalta Conference and afterwards, there were long arguments between the Allies about Poland. The British and the Americans extracted a pledge from the Soviets that there would be free elections and independence for all countries in Europe – East and West – specifically Poland. Stalin agreed to sign this Declaration on Liberated Europe, with its 'guarantees' about democracy. Molotov was surprised and asked Stalin if he was sure the Soviets should agree – 'This could have serious consequences for us.' Stalin's answer was typical. 'Go ahead and sign it,' he said, 'don't worry. We can implement it in our own way later. What matters is the correlation of forces.'[13] Long negotiations followed about the composition of a new coalition that would unite the rival Poles. Presidents and prime ministers became bogged down in details about how many ministers from each of the two groups there would be – absurdly in the view of Stalin, who said, with some justice, that the Americans were interested in Poland because of the number of US voters with Polish origins. Eventually the Western Allies agreed to recognise a new government made up of a coalition between the 'Lublin' and the 'London' Poles.

Stalin, as a gesture to mollify his allies, had assured Mikołajczyk when he visited Moscow at the end of 1944 that 'there is no need to fear. We know that Communism does not fit the Poles. They are too individualistic, too nationalistic. Poland's future economy should be based on private enterprise. Poland will be a capitalist state.' Mikołajczyk did not believe him for an instant, not least because, later in the meeting, when they discussed elections for Poland, Stalin said, 'Of course, there are some people – of the Left and Right – that we cannot allow in politics after the war.' According to the Polish leader, he pointed out that in democracy it was not always possible to dictate who could be in politics and who could not. 'Stalin looked at me as if I was an idiot and ended the conversation.'[14]

The Soviet dictator was frequently impatient about the 'hypocrisy' of the Western leaders, who so often lectured the Soviets with fine rhetoric about self-determination for smaller, weaker countries, and about democracy. He would point out that when the US and the UK had signed the Atlantic Charter, earlier in the war, which contained a sweeping statement about the freedom of people to choose the form of government they wished, Churchill had insisted on an assurance that the Charter would not apply to any of the colonies in the British Empire, including India, where a popular independence movement had long been campaigning for freedom. The Monroe Doctrine gave the US a self-appointed right to stop others interfering anywhere in the Americas – and the Americans permitted nobody else any say in the future of Japan. From Stalin's point of view the other Allies had limited rights to interfere in Poland, a country so clearly important to the USSR.

Averell Harriman, who had met Stalin many times when he was US Ambassador to Moscow, was right when he told Truman that the Soviet leader could not grasp that others believed firmly in their own ideology too. 'Stalin does not and never will fully understand our interest in a free Poland as a matter of principle. He is a realist in his actions and it is hard for him to understand our faith in abstract principles.' In a later cable he reflected that, 'Words have a different connotation to the Soviets than they do to us. When they speak of insisting on "friendly governments" in their neighbouring countries, they have in mind something different from what we would mean.'*[15]

---

* Harriman was the American who met Stalin the most often and for the longest time. They frequently spent hours in conversation. He was fascinated by him as everyone else was. After he returned to Washington from his time in Moscow, he said: 'It is hard for me to reconcile the courtesy he always showed for me personally

The realist in the Kremlin wrote to the American President, with a copy to the British government:

> You evidently do not agree that the Soviet Union is entitled to seek in Poland a Government that would be friendly to it, that the Soviet Government cannot agree to the existence in Poland of a government hostile to it. This is rendered imperative, among other things, by the Soviet people's blood freely shed on the fields of Poland for the liberation of that country. I do not know whether a genuinely representative government has been established in Greece, or whether the Belgian Government is a genuinely democratic one. The Soviet Union was not consulted when these governments were being formed, nor did it claim the right to interfere on those matters because it realises how important Belgium and Greece are to the security of Great Britain. I cannot understand why in discussing Poland no attempt is made to consider the interests of the Soviet Union in terms of security as well. One cannot but recognise as unusual a situation [in] which two governments – those of the United States and Great Britain – reach agreement beforehand on Poland, a country in which the USSR is interested first of all and most of all and, placing its representatives in an intolerable position, try to dictate to it.[16]

The British and Americans gave up on Poland, knowing they could extract no more concessions from the Soviet Union. 'The limits of our capacity to act have been reached,' admitted Churchill. They were unwilling to break up the Alliance for obvious and sensible reasons. At Yalta, and for months afterwards, they needed the Russians to carry on fighting the Germans. Berlin had still not

with the ghastly . . . [truth] of his wholesale liquidations. Others, who did not know him personally, saw only the tyrant in Stalin. I saw the other side as well – his high intelligence, that fantastic grasp of detail, his shrewdness and [the] surprising sensitivity towards people that he was capable of showing . . . I found him better informed than Roosevelt, more realistic than Churchill . . . he was the most inscrutable and contradictory character I have ever known.'

fallen, and for the US the top priority was to get a commitment from the Russians to join the war against Japan when the conflict in Europe was over. At the time of Yalta there was no certainty that the atomic bomb would work and no way of knowing how destructive it might be. The bomb would not even be tested for a further five months. The Americans believed that winning the war would require a costly and bloody invasion of Japan and they wanted the war-hardened Russians on their side.

The American military planners had been the most determined to get a deal with Stalin to bring the Russians into the war against Japan. The Joint Chiefs of Staff had sent an urgent memo to Roosevelt not long before the Yalta Conference: 'With Russia an ally in the War against Japan, the War can be terminated in less time and at less expense in life and resources . . . Should the War in the Pacific have to be carried on with an unfriendly or negative attitude on the part of Russia, the difficulties would be immeasurably increased.' The calculation for the Americans and British was simple, as it had been about delaying D-Day: more dead Russians meant fewer dead Americans and British. Stalin agreed to declare war on Japan within three months of the end of the war in Europe, a major commitment as it meant moving many divisions from Europe to East Asia.[17]

The Poles felt betrayed. Mikołajczyk protested that he was 'exhausted, bewildered and, most of all, abandoned' after dealing with Churchill, Roosevelt and Truman. General Władysław Anders, the head of the Polish Home Army and a brave and popular leader, told Churchill he had 'sleepless nights' about the way the Western Allies had 'sold Poland to the Soviets . . . you have signed . . . [our] death warrant.' As the Cold War developed, the view gained strength among 'revisionist' historians and many Western politicians that the East Europeans were 'sold out' by the Allied leaders who had won the war against Germany. From the 1970s onwards, until well after the Soviet Union fell, that became the authorised view; the word 'Yalta' turned into a synonym for betrayal and the appeasement of communism. But it is as hard from a distance to see a feasible alternative as it was to the main players at the time, who were not naïve and ineffectual figures, and who for the last few years had been broadly right on the major issues. What else could have been done? Neither the Poles nor others since have come up with a plausible or practical answer.[18]

A few days before he died, Roosevelt was told by America's first post-war Ambassador to Poland, Arthur Bliss Lane, that the US was 'betraying' the Poles. Roosevelt replied impatiently, 'What do you want? Do you want a war with Russia over Poland?' And when Truman, in the summer of 1946, was accused of not listening to the Poles, he pointed out that perhaps their expectations were somewhat high. 'I guess . . . [they] thought we should have a war to keep Poland free,' he said. 'Geography betrayed the Poles; not the Allies', as Acheson put it simply on many occasions.[19]

What, realistically, were the choices facing the Western Allies? Sir Frank Roberts, a member of the British delegation at Yalta and later a Cold War-era Ambassador to the Soviet Union, remained convinced the deal was as good as the West could get:

> We could have said 'no, we will have nothing to do with it.' In which case the Russians would have gone ahead [anyway] . . . There wouldn't even have been this, perhaps you would say, hypocritical possibility, of getting some Poles back into Poland by having elections . . . That was the alternative. We could have continued to recognise the Polish government-in-exile and said everything was wrong. But I don't see that this would have been a better position. It would have, if you like, enabled us all to feel much nicer if we hadn't given way to this terrible Stalin. But in practice I don't see how it would have helped anybody very much.[20]

Stalin thought of Poland as the Tsars had – they were always plotting something against the honest upstanding and straight-talking Russians. Invariably in novels, poems and plays, even music – the opera *Boris Godunov* is a good example – Polish kings are traditionally surrounded by sinister, corrupt and scheming Catholic priests who want to destroy the Orthodox faith, and effete Polish aristocrats whose aim is to extend their landholdings and serf-ownership.

Traditionally, in Russian eyes, the Poles were an endless cause of trouble. As Molotov said, 'The Poles never calm down and they are never at peace. They are irrational. They are always at one's neck.'[21]

One of Stalin's favourite operas was Glinka's *Ivan Suzanin* (titled, before the Revolution, *A Life for the Tsar*). It is set in 1613 during a Polish invasion of Russia. Suzanin is a Russian noble who offers to guide the foreign army towards a safe and unknown route into Russia. He leads them to a forest from which there is no escape and they are slaughtered, almost to a man. When the Poles realise they have been hoodwinked they kill the Russian 'hero' Suzanin, but their invasion has been foiled. Stalin saw the opera many times from his box at the Bolshoi – and seemed particularly to enjoy the scene in which the Poles are massacred in the forest.[22]

Some Poles fought against the Soviets and paid a heavy price. While talks about a settlement for Poland were continuing, the Russians showed the world who held the real power in the country. Sixteen Home Army officers were seized by Soviet troops in Warsaw and put on trial in Moscow. The chief defendant was General Anders's second-in-command, General Leopold Okulicki, one of the leaders of the 1944 Warsaw Rising. The sixteen were charged with organising resistance to the Soviet army, which they had in fact been planning to do, but had not yet embarked on. Okulicki was jailed for ten years, twelve others from five to eight years and three were acquitted – fairly mild treatment in those days by the standards of the USSR.

The Home Army was disbanded at the end of the war. Most Poles recognised the folly of continuing to fight against the Soviets, but armed resistance continued for a while, carried out by small guerrilla groups which the Russians took seriously, as they did all opposition. The biggest irritant, though, was WiN, Wolnoscść i Niepodległość, Freedom and Independence, led by a former Home Army officer, Jan Rzepecki. WiN was a peaceful organisation, though it existed in the murky underground. It called for protests to support democracy and, for a short while, published a newspaper, *Polska Niezawista* (Independent Poland), until Rzepecki was arrested in autumn 1946. Under torture he gave away the names of supporters and activists and WiN had to go even deeper underground.*[23]

The Poles were warned what would be in store. In an unguarded moment the Communist Party General Secretary, Władysław Gomułka, who in the early post-war period was a member of the power-sharing coalition, and who had been ordered by Stalin to tread warily, was overheard talking to an opposition leader: 'You can shout all you want that the blood of the Polish nation is being spilled, that the NKVD rules Poland,' he said. 'But this will not turn us back from our path . . . Once we have taken power, we will never give it up.'[24]

*

Churchill was buoyed by the reception he received after his Fulton speech on March 5. It caused the sensation that he had hoped for, and he was once again the centre of attention. He had been deeply depressed after losing the 1945 election and, at seventy-one, he feared his long political career might be over. He made the best of it, telling friends like Lord Alexander, the commander of British forces in Italy, that he would spend the rest of his days painting. 'I am damned glad now to be out of it . . . the newspapers bore me. I just glance at them,' he said. There were mutterings in the Tory

---

* WiN re-formed itself and continued for a further five years or so, though under constant surveillance and State harassment. Over the years it had around 10,000 members, though it was often penetrated by the secret police and its leaders were invariably arrested, tortured and jailed. Other resistance continued until the early 1950s in tiny groups, occasionally performing acts of small-scale violence.

Party that perhaps it was time to remove him as leader, though there were no real efforts to push him. But just before Christmas 1945, he did seriously consider resigning. He wrote to the Duke of Windsor, the former King Edward VIII, with whom he had remained on good terms since the Abdication: 'The difficulties of leading the Opposition are very great and increasingly I wonder whether the game is worth the candle.' His doctor, Lord Moran, was worried about his state of 'delayed shock' and exhaustion and recommended a break away from Britain.[25]

Churchill spent the first three months of 1946 in the United States, much of it painting in the sun in Florida at the holiday home of Frank Clarke, a wealthy Canadian admirer. Shortly before he left for the US, Churchill received an invitation from a Dr Frank D. McIver, President of Westminster College in Fulton, Missouri, to give a lecture 'on the world situation'. Normally such an offer, especially one from an obscure academic institution in the middle of nowhere, would have received a polite refusal. But it came with an interesting postscript at the bottom of the page. 'This is a wonderful school in my home State. Hope you can do it. I'll introduce you. Best Regards. Harry S Truman.'[26]

Churchill saw on opportunity to step back on the world stage, and to issue a warning against appeasing the USSR, as he had done about Nazi Germany in the 1930s. He told Truman that he was planning a winter visit to Florida 'for rest and recuperation' and was not planning to give any lectures. 'But if . . . as you suggest you would like me to visit your home State and would introduce me I would feel it my duty – and it would give me great pleasure – to deliver an address . . . under your aegis.' He said it was the only speaking engagement he had in mind 'and the explanation for it would be my respect for you and your wishes'.*[27]

---

* This was not strictly true. He made other speeches on the trip, which was not all a holiday as he implied, but he did not share the billing with the American President at any of the others.

Later, Truman tried to say that he had known little in advance about the content of the speech, but his claim was disingenuous. At a dinner in Washington on 11 February 1946 the two men discussed it at length. They travelled together by train from DC to Fulton, an overnight journey, and the President carefully read a draft of the speech. According to Churchill, Truman told him that 'he thought it was admirable and would do nothing but good, though it would cause quite a stir. He seemed very pleased.' On the train they also played poker, a game the former Prime Minister did not enjoy, with some of the President's Missouri cronies. Churchill lost seventy-five dollars. Later, he told the British Ambassador to Washington, Lord Halifax, that 'it had been well worth it.'[28]

Churchill went to Fulton to make headlines and he did. His live audience was 350 Westminster College students, but the world's press and newsreel cameras descended on the small town and his words were broadcast across America. When he'd finished speaking he told McIver that he hoped he had 'started some thinking that would make history', and on the journey back to Washington he described it to aides as 'the most important speech' of his career. That may have been an exaggeration, but it had profound resonance for the following four decades.

Everybody knows it as the 'Iron Curtain Speech' but Churchill had titled it 'The Sinews of Peace'. Of course he knew which soundbite would receive the most attention, but only a small part of the speech referred directly to the Soviet Union and Eastern Europe. Most of it was about the 'fraternal association' between the English-speaking peoples, the 'special relationship' he mentioned several times in the text, and the need for 'the British Empire' and the US to unite more closely to create a lasting peace. He did not specifically mention the American loan to Britain, which was then being debated in Congress, though it was clearly a factor in what he was saying. He spoke about sharing military bases, manufacturing interchangeable weapons, building institutions together – eventually sharing a common citizenship. He was the first major statesman in the world to speak openly in strong terms about the breakdown of the Big Three's wartime alliance, and that hit the front pages.

The reaction was speedy. The Soviet newspaper *Pravda* carried an editorial across three columns of its front page, blasting Churchill as a 'warmonger'. A few days later, Stalin responded personally in a rare 'interview' in the same paper, saying that the Fulton speech was a 'call to war with the Soviet Union'. Churchill, he said, clearly believed that 'The English-speaking peoples, being the only valuable nations, should rule over the other remaining countries in the world. This is a racial theory based on language . . . One is reminded of Hitler and his friends.'[29]

Truman did not endorse the speech publicly for several weeks. He waited to see the reaction at home first. He also ordered Dean Acheson, the Under-Secretary of State, not to attend a reception for Churchill the week after Fulton in case it gave the impression that the Administration approved of the former PM's views. Privately, he wrote to Stalin, in his own hand, suggesting he visit the US to make a similar speech, which he would introduce personally, as he had done with Churchill. This was never a likely event. On the whole, though, the speech was widely praised by both the Left and the Right in the US, where opinion was hardening against the Soviet Union. The press no longer portrayed Stalin as benign Uncle Joe, as they had done so often during the war. It was only in April, after most of the American papers came out in favour of Churchill, that the President dared to publicly associate himself with the speech.

There were critics but mostly the usual suspects. The former Vice-President and now Commerce Secretary, Henry Wallace, said it was an 'attack on a former ally from . . . [someone] who could not free himself from the roll of the drums and the flutter of the flags of empire.' The Nobel Prize-winning author Pearl S. Buck, on the evening after the speech, said it was a 'catastrophe, turning our destiny a dangerous way . . . we are nearer war tonight than we were last night.' Eleanor Roosevelt, widow of the former President, said it was a direct attack on the fledgling United Nations Organization and her late husband's vision of the post-war world.*[30]

At home in Britain the speech was well received and put Churchill back at the centre of the political debate. The Labour Prime Minister, Clement Attlee, had been given the gist in advance and told Churchill privately, 'I am sure it will do good.' In public, however, Attlee was more circumspect and refused to comment, saying only that Churchill had 'spoken in an individual capacity in a foreign country'. Ernest Bevin, the Foreign Secretary, told Westminster journalists – off the record – that he thought it was 'a brilliant speech'.

Some of Churchill's loudest critics came from his own party. The Shadow Foreign Secretary, Anthony Eden, hoped Churchill was not planning to 'pursue an anti-Russian crusade independent from the US', and the Tory grandee Lord Salisbury said Churchill was in danger of wrecking the bipartisan policy of firmness against the USSR by alienating the Left. He said the speech strengthened the case for Churchill to retire from leadership so he 'could say what he liked without associating the . . . [Conservative] Party with it.' But there was no move within Tory ranks to remove him as leader. Rather, his stock rose.[31]

Fulton was seen later as one of the first salvos in the Cold War, and Churchill continued to present himself as a visionary who was always right about Stalin as he had been about Hitler in the

---

* Churchill and Eleanor Roosevelt hated each other. She was far more left-wing than her husband, and a long-time critic of British imperialism. She was one of America's first delegates to the UN. Just before he left for his American trip, according to the 7 January 1946 diary entry of the wartime Admiral George (now Viscount) Cunningham, they were at a lunch together in London: 'Winston and Mrs R got into an argument about the causes of the war, which she said were economic. He denied this and said they were mostly to do with personalities with a thirst for power.' The argument descended into a slanging match, and the substance of the disagreement was never settled.

Thirties. But there is a dilemma in looking for a consistent line from Churchill on the Soviet Union. He contradicted himself many times – and often seemed to act as inconsistently as he spoke. Any politician who has been in public life for more than fifty years will inevitably leave behind hostages to fortune. One usually can find a Churchill quote – and an eloquent one – to prove or disprove almost anything about his thoughts, and he could believe in diametrically opposed ideas at the same time.

During the Battle for Stalingrad, Churchill had told Eden that the Soviets could not be allowed to control the Baltic states and eastern Poland after the war. The Russians had 'occupied by acts of aggression in shameful collusion with Hitler. The transfer of the peoples of the Baltic states to Soviet Russia against their will would be contrary to all the principles for which we are fighting this war and would dishonour our cause.' In May 1944 he told his Foreign Secretary, 'I fear that great evil may come upon the world . . . The Russians are drunk with victory and there are no lengths they may not go to.'[32]

Yet just five months later, in the so-called 'percentages deal', Churchill agreed to carve up Europe after the war, secretly sealing the fate of half a dozen countries. He described the scene dramatically. The two leaders met in Stalin's apartment in the Kremlin on the night of 9 October 1944:

> The moment was apt for business so I said 'Let us settle our affairs in the Balkans. Your armies are in Romania and Bulgaria. We have interests, missions, agents there. Don't let us get at cross purposes in small ways. So far as Britain and Russia are concerned, how would it do for you to have 90 per cent predominance in Romania, for us to have 90 per cent of the say in Greece and go 50/50 about Yugoslavia?' [Churchill picked up some paper and wrote down the deal he proposed]. Hungary was another country to be split 50/50. Casting an eye over the paper Stalin took his blue pencil and made a large

tick upon it, and passed it back . . . It was all settled in no more than it takes to set down. After this there was a long silence. The pencilled paper lay in the centre of the table. At length, I said, 'Might it not be thought rather cynical if it seemed we had disposed of these issues, so fateful to millions of people, in such an offhand manner? Let us burn the paper.' 'No, you keep it,' said Stalin.

Churchill called it the 'naughty document', and when he told Roosevelt what had been agreed, the President accepted it as a realistic arrangement. Churchill believed it was a good deal because Greece would remain in the West's 'sphere of influence'.[33]

After that meeting he wrote to his wife, Clemmie, 'I have had very nice talks with the old Bear . . . I like him the more I see him. Now they respect us and I am sure they wish to work with us. To dine with Stalin once a week . . . would be no trouble at all. We get on like a house on fire.' He told his Cabinet after the Yalta agreements, 'Poor Neville Chamberlain believed he could trust Hitler. He was wrong. But I don't believe I am wrong about Stalin,' and he once told an aide enthusiastically, 'With Stalin one could always talk as one human being to another.' There was not a hint of his famous irony when he told the House of Commons on 7 November 1945: 'How glad we all are to know that . . . Stalin is still strongly holding the helm . . . I cannot feel anything other than . . . admiration for this great man, the father of his country, the ruler of its destinies.'[34]

The percentages deal, like the Yalta agreement four months later, simply recognised the post-war facts of life. The division of Europe would have happened anyway; Soviet troops were 'in possession'. But Churchill was not entirely an innocent bystander, or even only a bit-part player. He helped to build the Iron Curtain from Stettin to Trieste.

When he returned to Britain after the Fulton speech, Churchill's appetite for politics was revived. He looked younger and was full of energy. He dealt firmly with any lingering speculation about his future. 'I have no intention whatsoever of ceasing to lead the Conservative Party until I am satisfied that they can see their way clear ahead and can make better arrangements.' His long-time crony Brendan Bracken would tell fellow Tory MPs whenever they asked, 'Winston . . . is determined to continue to lead the Party until he becomes Prime Minister on earth – or Minister of Defence in heaven.'[35]

Churchill was back on form. He told his doctor, Lord Moran: 'A short time ago I was ready to retire . . . and die gracefully. Now I'm going to stay and have them out. I'll tear their bleeding entrails out of them.' He was referring not to the Soviet Politburo, but to his parliamentary colleagues.[36]

# 16

## The Fog of War

On Monday 4 March, the day Churchill and Truman left Washington for Fulton, an urgent top-secret cable arrived in the US State Department from Robert Rossow, the American Consul in Tabriz, northern Iran. The rebel regime set up by the Soviets the previous December, with Ja'far Pishevari as leader, was firmly in control of the province. Tabriz, he said, looked like the capital of a satellite state. Now, Rossow claimed to have spotted 'exceptionally heavy troop movements' near the city. The Russians were supposed to have withdrawn their forces from Iran by 2 March – as the British had done from the south of the country, in accordance with the 1941 treaty between the Allies and Iran. But around 30,000 Soviet troops had stayed, while Stalin continued to press for the oil-drilling rights he had been seeking for many months.

Rossow was unaware of the negotiations going on between the Soviets and the Iranians over oil. He was convinced that the Russians had a more ambitious aim: the invasion of Iran followed by an attack on Turkey. He reported that during the previous night 150 truckloads of new Russian troops had crossed the border with the Soviet Republic of Azerbaijan and arrived in Tabriz, and a mechanised division, including sixteen Sherman tanks, was moving south towards Tehran. Rossow was an experienced and reliable official, trusted by his superiors.[1] The next day he sent another detailed cable: a further 100 trucks laden with supplies and twenty-two more tanks, this time Soviet-made T-34s, were heading in the same direction, and two regiments of infantry were moving towards

Iranian Kurdistan. 'Soviet reinforcements ... arriving in Tabriz night and day,' he said. 'All observations and reports indicate inescapably that ... Soviets are preparing for major military operations.' His reports were based on local information from Iranian sources, which turned out to be either mistaken or highly exaggerated – most of the troops were in fact heading away from Tehran and back towards the USSR. But they were never checked or verified, thus prompting a major military alert by the US and a renewed diplomatic crisis of the kind that would become familiar during the Cold War.[2]

Consul Rossow's next dispatch contained information which alarmed Washington, though it, too, was wrong. He reported that General (later Marshal) Ivan Bagramyan, 'a soldier with a spectacular combat record, is said to have reached Tabriz' to take over command of Soviet forces in the area, replacing a lower-ranking officer with almost no war experience. Bagramyan was a specialist in tank warfare, a hero of the Battle of Kursk and a commander in the final advance of the Red Army into Germany. In fact, Bagramyan was nowhere near Azerbaijan – he was commanding Soviet detachments in the Baltic republics – but a momentum towards conflict was building rapidly.[3]

When Truman returned to Washington from Fulton he was shown Rossow's telegrams. The last, dated Wednesday, 6 March, described Tabriz colourfully as reminiscent of 'an armed camp'. The streets were clogged with military equipment, he said. The President summoned Averell Harriman, both an expert on Russia and known to be a hawk regarding the Soviet Union: Harriman's advice was invariably to stand up to the leaders in the Kremlin. The President told him to prepare to leave for London as Ambassador to Britain. Harriman was half-reluctant, but Truman said he needed a trusted figure there. 'It is important. We may soon be at war with the Soviet Union over Iran.'[4]

The Americans had no significant forces in the Middle East, as the President well knew. At that time Britain was the principal

Western power to have major interests there. But he was determined that the US had to show strength of purpose. If the Soviets were 'bluffing' in Iran he would call that bluff. If they weren't, as he said, 'It is better to know now . . . what their intentions are.' He despatched America's most modern and best-equipped battleship, the USS *Missouri*, to the eastern Mediterranean. Its mission was to carry home to Istanbul the body of the late Turkish Ambassador to the US, Mehmet Münir Ertegün, who had died a few weeks earlier in Washington. Any vessel would have sufficed for such a routine diplomatic task, but the President chose to send the American flagship as a signal to Moscow. The navy had proposed despatching the Eighth Fleet, including an aircraft carrier, to Turkey, but Truman decided to wait and see.

At six that evening the Secretary of State, the pugnacious Southerner James Byrnes, was shown a large map of Azerbaijan and Iran, with arrows indicating where Soviet troops were thought to be and where they were said to be heading. Byrnes had been a close confidant of Roosevelt, who used to call him 'my assistant president'. He had been half-promised the Vice-Presidential nomination for the 1944 election and was deeply resentful when Roosevelt changed his mind and chose Truman instead. But he was loyal to the new President, who appointed him Secretary of State immediately after he entered the White House. Under the US Constitution, as there was then no Vice-President, Byrnes would succeed to the presidency if Truman died.

Byrnes, aged sixty-six, a consummate Washington insider and Democrat deal-maker, had tried to make the alliance with the Soviets work after the war. But he had been criticised in the press and in Congress, where anti-communism was growing into a fervent cause, for being too cosy towards the Russians. Since Truman's 'stop babying the Soviets' letter, he had turned into a hawk. That evening, he said, he had seen firm evidence that the Russians were adding 'military aggression to political subversion'. It was time to stand up to the Russians. 'Now we will give it to them with both barrels,' he declared.*5

In London, the Foreign Secretary, Ernest Bevin, according to a fellow British Cabinet minister, 'was in a great state, saying the Russians were advancing on Tehran, that this meant war, and that the US was going to send a battle fleet to the Mediterranean'. Hassan Alia, the Iranian Ambassador to Washington and a close friend of the Shah, sent a cable to Tehran warning that it looked as though 'the first shots of World War Three will be fired in Iran.'6

Officials in Moscow were perplexed by the air of crisis in Washington and London. Two weeks earlier, at a meeting of the Big Three Foreign Ministers in Paris, Byrnes dined at the Hotel Meurice with Molotov, his deputy Andrey Vyshinsky, and the French Foreign Minister Georges Bidault. Molotov had nonchalantly told Byrnes that missing the deadline for Soviet troop withdrawals 'is far too trivial a matter to disturb relations between the US and the USSR.' Byrnes seemed doubtful, and mentioned that both countries had signed the UN charter guaranteeing rights for small nations against more powerful ones, and they should both adhere to it. But he let the matter drop.

The Soviets had no intention of going to war over Iran and their support for Pishevari and the Azeri separatists was lukewarm, a tactic designed to secure an oilfield as well as greater influence in Iran. But they did not intend to show weakness. 'When dealing with the likes of these Westerners, we must never

---

* In January 1946 *Fortune* magazine carried a long, unflattering portrait of Byrnes, who was brought up in poverty by a single mother in South Carolina and made a huge success as a lawyer. 'Some of his close friends call him a fixer, a compromiser, an appeaser and worry that such a man should be the custodian of American foreign policy,' the piece ran. 'He is said to lay out three hats in the morning, so he can compromise on the one in the middle.' Byrnes remained bitter to his dying day that Roosevelt let him down over the Vice-Presidency. He believed it was because he was a Catholic. At first he was contemptuous of Truman, and sometimes showed it, though he grew to admire him. Truman said he knew that 'Jimmy always believed he should rightfully be in this job and not me.'

display lack of resolve or absence of backbone,' Stalin lectured Molotov, who took the lesson well. They continued to bluff.[7]

While Truman was bracing himself and his country for conflict, Stalin had just completed extended talks with Ahmad Qavam, the Iranian Prime Minister. Qavam, an aristocrat from one of Iran's oldest families, had been in office since the middle of January. He had spent two weeks in Moscow trying to reach a deal that would remove Soviet troops from Iranian Azerbaijan and put an end to Pishevari's rebellious autonomous republic. He returned to Tehran on Monday 4 March empty-handed, but without giving in either to Stalin's threats or his blandishments. An elegant, sophisticated sixty-nine-year-old, vastly experienced in Iranian politics (his father had been Prime Minister half a century earlier and he had sat in several of the former Shah's governments in the thirties). Qavam tried his best to steer an independent path for Iran between the rival bigger powers. He hated the idea of British and American domination over his country almost as much as that of Soviet interference. But if the choice had to be made – and it looked like it did – he would reluctantly go with the Americans. The Shah agreed with him.[*][8]

Qavam was convinced the Soviets were not planning a full-scale invasion of either Iran or Turkey. He told the American Ambassador, Wallace Murray, so in plain terms. 'Their main interest is the oil,' he said. But that did not seem to have registered in Washington. In no contemporary reports from Tehran about Soviet actions is the Russian request for an oil concession mentioned. The State Department was nearly as reticent. Briefing

---

* The Shah's sister, Princess Ashraf, accompanied Qavam on the mission and sat in on one of the discussions in the Kremlin. She described meeting the Soviet dictator: 'After a long wait, in a sinister room, suddenly the door opened and I caught sight of a man with a moustache. It was Stalin . . . what a relief. Stalin was soft and fat, and above all he was small.' The Princess made a rather better impression on Stalin, who admired her pluck. 'Just look at that tiny woman,' he told one of his cronies. 'She's a real patriot.'

papers about Iran make few references either to the Soviet negotiations for oil exploration rights in the north, or to the American
discussions for a similar concession in the south, though future oil
supplies for the West were often discussed by Churchill and
Roosevelt, and, later, by Attlee and Truman; all of them agreed
that the Soviets should not be allowed access to any oil from the
Persian Gulf. Late on 6 March, Byrnes sent a formal diplomatic
note to the Soviet Foreign Ministry demanding an explanation of
why Russian troops were overstaying their welcome by remaining
in Iran contrary to Treaty obligations. He did not receive a reply.[9]

\*

Newspapers in the West were full of the crisis in Iran. A week
earlier, a war between the allies who had defeated the Nazis had
seemed unthinkable. For much of the Second World War the press
in the US and Britain had carried large amounts of pro-Russian
propaganda. Now the same papers suggested that conflict with the
Soviets was inevitable if they did not cease their aggression. The
right-wing news magazine *Time* had regularly claimed that communism was 'skin deep' in the USSR, praising Stalin as a benign
figure who saved his nation from Hitler. Now smiling Uncle Joe
had morphed into a snarling tyrant who murdered his opponents,
had erected an Iron Curtain in Europe as Churchill had described,
and was threatening to take over the Middle East. The august *New
York Times* confidently reported that 'Soviet troops were within
25 miles of Tehran' – completely untrue, and taken from unreliable
Iranian sources; no *Times* reporter was anywhere near the area. A
few Russian tanks and troops were patrolling the roads into Azerbaijan and Iran's Kurdish region, but most of the Soviet soldiers
were still near Tabriz. The reports caused panic in Tehran. 'Hundreds of better-off residents piled their belongings on any vehicles
at hand and fled, clogging the roads to the south,' reported Murray
to Washington.[10]

The Soviets insisted that there were no forces heading towards the Iranian capital, though they pointedly refused to say when their troops would leave Azerbaijan and Tabriz. As tension mounted, American soldiers and diplomats were providing more reliable information. General Norman Schwarzkopf Sr., commander of a small force in Tehran protecting the civil advisors still in Iran, reported to Washington that there 'were no signs of any intended invasion.'* Eisenhower, chairman of the Joint Chiefs, told Truman that he was sure the Soviets were 'in no position to attack' and he was confident they had no intention of doing so. George Kennan, acting US Ambassador in Moscow, also assured Truman that no attack was imminent, cabling to the State Department, '[Stalin] has not prepared the Russian people for any such undertaking. The Russians would not blunder into a situation whose implications they had not thought through.' He said the Russians might 'probe and use intimidation ... but would [remain] this side of the line' to avoid a break with the Western Allies. Lord Halifax also advised restraint. 'Interference in Persian affairs did not necessarily amount to major Russian military operations,' he told the Foreign Secretary, Ernest Bevin.[11]

The Iranians wanted Soviet troops out of their country, and had no wish to hand the Russians an oilfield. Knowing that the US could not quickly send troops, and that the British wouldn't, Qavam asked the American Ambassador what the US was prepared to do to help Iran. Ambassador Murray said the US might not be in a position to help militarily but would be tough diplomatically; he advised Iran to put the issue before the UN Security Council. The US, Britain and other Western allies would support the Iranians. From the distance of several decades, this does not seem much, but at the time it was significant. This would be the first test for the UN as the world's new peacekeeper.

Franklin Roosevelt did not live to see its birth, but he was the

---

* His son Norman Jr. was the general who commanded American forces in the first Gulf War against Iraq in 1991.

father of the United Nations. It was his vision that created it, he had fought hard against the sceptics to launch it, and had made deals with America's rivals, notably Stalin's Russia, to ensure that it came into being. Roosevelt argued that the UN was not based on idealistic beliefs – 'globaloney' as some of his critics called it – but on a practical idea. Empires and power blocs had been unable to keep the peace; their rivalries always ended in war. 'Spheres of influence' and calculations about the balance of power were 'old world' ideas that had resulted in the catastrophes of 1914 and 1939. Roosevelt believed that the major powers could settle disputes collectively and – with the US, USSR, Britain and China acting as the world's 'policemen' – maintain peace. Stalin had backed the idea, if not entirely with enthusiasm. Truman calculated that the Soviets wouldn't wreck the UN just as it had come into being unless they genuinely wanted another war. And if they did, 'we might as well know now,' as an aide to the President said.

On 8 March Byrnes sent another formal note to the Soviets. Much sterner in tone, it was by diplomatic standards terse; the most unfriendly official communication between the two governments since the end of the war. It was scribbled down hastily by one of Byrnes's brightest assistants, Alger Hiss. 'The US cannot remain indifferent to the tensions in Iran,' it said. 'The US expresses the earnest hope that the Soviet Union will do its part in guaranteeing peace by withdrawing immediately all Soviet forces from the territory of Iran, to promote international confidence necessary for peaceful progress.' It made no threats and, as suggested by Dean Acheson, Byrnes's deputy, it left 'a graceful way out' for the Soviets if they wanted to avoid a showdown.[12]

The Iranians put the Soviet troop withdrawals on the agenda of the next UN Security Council meeting. The Russians immediately dubbed this an 'unfriendly and hostile act that could have unfortunate results', to which Qavam replied that the continued presence of Russian troops past the 2 March deadline was 'illegal'. But the Soviets were preparing their exit. They were being called bullies even by friendly governments and they wanted a settlement. 'We probed on Iran, no more, but we got no support,' Molotov said later.[13]

The Security Council meeting was scheduled for 26 March. Two days earlier, the Soviet newspaper *Izvestia* reported that the Soviet withdrawal 'begun on 2 March' would continue for the next few weeks. Stalin gave a rare interview to a Western journalist, Eddie Gilmore of the United Press, on the same day. He was conciliatory Uncle Joe again, saying that there was 'really no danger of war' and that the tension over Iran was caused 'by certain political groups who were busy with propaganda.'

Stalin hoped that the Security Council meeting in New York would be postponed, but it went ahead as planned at the UN's temporary headquarters at Hunter College in the Bronx. There were newsreel cameras present and it was broadcast live on radio. The Russian representative, Andrei Gromyko, said that as Soviet troops would be out of Iran within 'five or six weeks unless unforeseen circumstances occurred', he expected the item to be dropped. But Byrnes demanded that it should remain on the agenda 'until the last Russian soldier leaves Iran' and continued with a barnstorming speech. 'There are forty nations not represented here. They look to us to give each of them . . . [assurances] that the doors of the Security Council are open for them to present a grievance when they see a grievance affecting their national security . . . Unless the UN . . . [takes] a tough line now it will die in its infancy of inefficiency and ineffectiveness.'[14]

Gromyko, in a fury of indignation, picked up his papers, cursed in ripe Russian and stormed out of the hall – the first of many such exits over the following three and a half decades made by the future 'Mr Nyet' of Soviet foreign policy. There was no war, but the Iran crisis had profound consequences. Robert Rossow, who played as important a part in it as anyone else, later commented: 'Though not a shot was fired, the Battle of Azerbaijan was as significant in its outcome as Bunker Hill, Bull Run, or the

First Battle of the Marne.' A British diplomat in Tehran at the time put its significance in a different way: 'Above all, it was the efforts of Standard Oil . . . and Shell to secure oil prospecting rights that changed the Russians in Persia from hot war allies to Cold War rivals.' Stalin, much to his irritation, never got his oilfield. But the US did. Within a few months of the Russian withdrawal, a deal was signed giving the Americans their first oil concessions in Iran.[15]

After the Soviet troops, advisors and spies left Tabriz, the 'autonomous' government fell apart. Pishevari received a letter from Stalin that reeked of hypocrisy. Instead of receiving support, or even sympathy, the loyal Comrade was given a lecture in real-politik. Stalin had encouraged the separatist insurrection. Now he told Pishevari that there was no 'revolutionary situation in your country . . . if our forces had stayed there it would have undercut the basis of our liberationist policies in Europe and Asia . . . Western countries would hold on to where they wanted throughout the world. So we decided to pull our troops out of Iran . . . in order to grab this weapon out of the hands of the British and the Americans and unleash a movement of liberation in colonies that would render our policy of liberation more justified and effective.' He told Pishevari and his PDA to 'moderate your position' and to support the Tehran government.[16]

When the last Soviet soldier had crossed the border back to the USSR, the Iranian army brutally suppressed the revolt. Scores of PDA officials and supporters were arrested, tortured and killed. Stalin told them to cease their resistance and to retreat. A few managed to escape the Shah's bloody vengeance, Pishevari among them. He fled to Baku, in the Soviet republic of Azerbaijan, a defeated man. He died in February 1947 in a mysterious car crash. No firm evidence was ever found, but it is more than likely that the 'accident' was the work of the MGB.

# 17

## Sunset on the Raj

On 23 March three senior British Government ministers left London, bound for Delhi. Their mission was a curious one. For nearly two centuries India had been 'the jewel in the crown' of British imperialism. Now a trio of Labour parliamentarians 'tried to give away an empire but found their every suggestion for doing it frustrated by the intended recipients,' as the chief assistant of one of them, the young Labour MP Woodrow Wyatt, put it.[1]

By the time the Cabinet Mission – or, as Indians called them, the three Magi – arrived in Delhi, it was obvious that British rule would soon be over. Britain wanted to withdraw from India as soon as possible, not through altruism or careful planning, as the Government tried to pretend, but from exhaustion and weakness: 'though ultimate responsibility still rests with [your government], it no longer has the power to take effective action ... we are in fact conducting a retreat and in very difficult circumstances,' the Viceroy, Lord Wavell, reported to the King.[2]

After the war, the real issue in India was not whether the British would leave, but how they could do so without appearing to lose face. The increasingly bitter dispute was about the kind of India the British would leave behind. Could an independent India remain one state, as it had been – albeit on occasion uneasily – under the British Raj? Or were the differences between the majority Hindus and the Muslims irreconcilable; would they have to be kept apart?

The ministers would remain in India for three months, trying

– and failing – to persuade the various Indian nationalist leaders to agree on a plan for their country's future. 'Freddie' Pethick-Lawrence, head of the delegation and Secretary of State for India, declared halfway through the mission that it was 'the last chance' for a settlement that would keep India united. He was right, though the failure was hardly Pethick-Lawrence's fault. A solution to the dilemma had eluded far wiser men than him and his two colleagues, Sir Stafford Cripps, President of the Board of Trade and a future Chancellor of the Exchequer, and Albert Alexander, First Lord of the Admiralty.

To many Indian observers, there was something fitting about the principal envoy the British had despatched to negotiate away India. The colonial masters had habitually sent vigorous, decisive men, confident in their Civilising Mission, to run the Indian empire. Pethick-Lawrence, aged seventy-four, an old-Etonian Labour politician, was a 'charming old gentleman, kindly', if a 'bit of a dodderer.' Even his friends, of which, being a decent man, he had many, tended to call him 'Pathetic-Lawrence'. He was best known for having been a passionate believer in women's suffrage; he had once been arrested at a demonstration along with Emmeline Pankhurst, whom he had joined on hunger strike, and had himself been force-fed. He was well intentioned, but not the most clear-sighted thinker. As the Viceroy said, 'Lord Pethick-Lawrence had little idea why he was in New Delhi, beyond a vague desire to transfer power and give India her freedom. The question of who was to be the recipient of the power was one he had never seriously addressed.'[3]

The Cabinet Mission arrived in India soon after a series of elections, which had been staggered over the preceding three months because of the logistical problem of organising the count simultaneously in such a vast country. More than forty million people voted, around 10 per cent of the population – the biggest election ever held in India until then. It was flawed, based on outdated voter lists and on a limited franchise, and there was clearly ballot-rigging in some areas: 'hardly an election in the normally understood meaning of the term,' said A. K. Azad, who had been a leading player in Indian politics for a generation. Nevertheless, imperfect though the poll may have been, nobody doubted that the results clearly reflected the people's mood. The purpose was supposed to have been to choose provincial governments throughout the country, completely made up of Indians for the first time. But as campaigning went on, it became a plebiscite on one issue: whether Muslims should be granted a separate state, Pakistan – 'land of the pure'. Overwhelmingly, the Muslims voted in favour.[4]

The fight for freedom from the British had been led by India's biggest political party, the Indian National Congress. The party had been formed in 1885 by elitist, pro-Western lawyers and business people as a polite pressure group to campaign for more rights for Indians under the Raj. But since the 1920s, Mohandas Gandhi had transformed the Congress into a mass nationalist party of four million members, and many more sympathisers, demanding *swaraj* (freedom), and using the revolutionary tactic of non-violent civil disobedience, *satyagraha*, which the British found hard to counteract. Gandhi became, in the words of one Congress activist, not only the most famous Indian, but also the best-loved since the Buddha, and was universally called Mahatma – Great Soul.

Gandhi's mixture of spiritualism and hard-nosed deal-making had infuriated the administrators of the Raj. 'He may be a saint; he may be a holy man . . . but of this I am certain; he is one of the most astute, politically motivated and bargaining little gentlemen I have ever come across,' one India Secretary said during the Thirties. Stalin would simply have ordered his NKVD to shoot Gandhi and the other Congress leaders in the back of the neck. The British kept jailing him, thereby increasing his popularity.

By 1946 Congress's main opposition was no longer the British, but the Muslim League. That, too, had begun life as a cosy club of upper-class Indians, seeking a limited range of extra privileges for

Indian Muslims. However, under the leadership of Mohammed Ali Jinnah, the League grew rapidly to a membership of more than two million and its message became increasingly religious and separatist in tone. The Congress had initially attracted many prominent Muslim members – including Jinnah – and while the British were the common enemy, the two communities worked together for one objective: to end the British Raj. But Congress, under Gandhi's religious inspiration, had become more overtly Hindu as it grew into a mass movement. Muslims, just over a fifth of India's population of around four hundred million, were concerned for their future in a country called Hindustan. Congress claimed to speak for all Indians and still called for a united, plural country, but by 1940 the Muslim League was demanding a separate Islamic homeland. To complicate matters yet more, in the north and west of India there were millions of Sikhs, a smaller minority, trapped between the two larger communities as they grew further apart.

In the elections Congress had won nearly 90 per cent of the seats nationally, and held power in all except one of the provincial governments, but the League won overwhelmingly in areas where Muslims formed a majority of the population. As Jinnah had told his followers, every vote cast for the League was a vote for Pakistan, every vote against was for a Hindu Raj. 'That is the only choice and the only issue before you,' he had said repeatedly during the campaign, throughout which the rhetoric had grown harsher, more divisive and more fundamentalist from both sides. Congress campaigned at religious festivals, used Hindu icons in campaign leaflets, encouraged saffron-clad holy men to support the Party and linked abhorrent religious practices such as the slaughter of holy cows with anti-League, anti-Muslim tirades. The League, for its part, used Islamic precepts to the same end. At polling booths, Party activists would hold the Koran in one hand and a Hindu text or the image of one of the Hindu gods in the other, and ask voters which they would choose before hustling them to cast their ballot.

Moderate religious leaders, like the highly respected scholar Maulana Shabbir Ahmad Usmani, urged their followers to support the League: 'Any man who gives his vote to the opponents of the League must think of the ultimate consequences of his action in terms of the interests of his nation and the answers that he will be called upon to produce on the Day of Judgment.' Those (now few) Muslims who supported the Congress were said to be 'Muslims in name but Hindus in action – half fish, half fowl'. A leading Congressman, Vallabhbhai Patel, had said on the hustings, 'Pakistan is not in the hands of the British government. If Pakistan is to be achieved the Hindus and Muslims will have to fight. There will be a civil war.' A prominent member of the League, Liaquat Ali Khan, replied simply, 'The Muslims are not afraid of civil war.'[5]

The British had wanted to maintain a united India and beat a dignified retreat to the sound of trumpets, boasting that their stewardship of India for two centuries had been glorious. As the High Victorian imperialist Macaulay had said in the 1850s, when Indians had been educated 'into a capacity for better government . . . it will be the proudest day in English history.'[6]

Two weeks after the Cabinet mission arrived, on 11 April, the Prime Minister authorised the Partition of India as a last resort, though the decision was to be kept highly secret. Pethick-Lawrence and his two colleagues were to stay throughout Northern India's hottest season and attempt to reach a deal that would preserve unity, but could – if they 'were satisfied that there was no other basis on which an agreed settlement could be reached' – accede to a separate Muslim homeland. The most senior official in the Indian Civil Service, Sir Penderel Moon, had told Attlee at the start of the year: 'It is now abundantly clear that the Pakistan issue has to be faced fairly and squarely. There is no longer the slightest chance of dodging it.'[7]

Violence between Muslims and Hindus spread across India. It began with isolated cases but riots and organised gang murders grew in intensity – in Bombay (now Mumbai), in the United

Provinces, in Bengal. Gandhi's policy of non-violence was the chief tactic that had helped to weary the near-bankrupt British into submission. It was of little use now.

There was a depressing sign of what was to come in Ahmedabad when, soon after the elections, the Mahatma sent a group of workers to calm growing inter-communal tensions in the city. Two of them were killed when they tried to intervene to halt a riot. Despairingly, their co-workers wrote to Gandhi for help. 'Our Congress workers, Shri Vasant Rao and Shri Raja Bali, went out on . . . [their] quest and fell a prey to the *goondas*' [gang members'] knife. They laid down their lives in the pursuit of an ideal and they deserve all praise. Yet no one else had the courage to follow in their footsteps. They have not the same self-confidence. If they had it, there would be no riots, and even if riots broke out, they would never assume the proportions or the form the present riots do.'[8]

The safest people in India were the British. Amidst the violence, nobody harmed colonial oppressors, who could move freely around the cities and towns. One British newspaper editor, Desmond Young, was bemused one afternoon when 'the start of a street fight was delayed to allow my wife to cross the road.'[9]

*

In the autumn of 1938, India's most influential political and cultural magazine, *Modern Times*, had published a bitter attack on one of the most admired Nationalist leaders, the Congress President, Jawaharlal Nehru. Headlined 'No Caesars', it hit hard against the President's arrogance and the way he presented himself as 'a god-like' figure:

What lies beneath that mask? What desires . . . what will to power, what insatiate longings? Men like Jawaharlal, with all their capacity for great and good work, are unsafe in democracy. He calls himself a democrat and a socialist, and no doubt he does so in all earnestness, but every psychologist knows how the mind is ultimately a slave to the heart and logic can always be made to fit in with the desires and irrepressible urges of a person. A little trust and Jawahar might turn a dictator, sweeping aside the paraphernalia of a slow-moving democracy. His conceit is already formidable. It must be challenged. We want no Caesars.

The piece was signed with the pen name Chanakya, an ancient Indian political philosopher, and caused an outcry amongst Nehru loyalists. But the real author was later revealed: Nehru himself. It was a typical example of his love of mischief, his sense of humour, his enjoyment of the ridiculous – and his political acumen. Though plainly an elaborate joke – the magazine was published by one of Nehru's best friends, 'Bibi' Nandu – it was obvious that the story would come out at some point and would reflect well on him.[10]

Nehru was the undisputed leader of the practical wing of Congress, if not its spiritual conscience. At fifty-six he was still handsome – one of the few politicians to have toiletries named after him, like 'Nehru Brilliantine' and 'Nehru Hair Tonic'. Almost everyone who knew him was charmed by his smile and sense of fun, though occasionally his patrician manner could irritate. Descended from the highest caste of Kashmiri aristocracy, the Kashmiri Hindus, often called Pandits, he was educated at Harrow and Trinity College, Cambridge, and his upbringing mattered to him; even towards the end of his life he could be heard occasionally to sing the Harrow fag song, 'Jerry, you duffer and dunce'.

He had known nothing about the way ordinary Indians lived until he returned to India from London in 1912 after he was called to the Bar. He saw the poverty and squalor as if for the first time, and blamed the British for keeping his countrymen 'backward'. He fell under the spell of a non-ideological socialism – and of Gandhi, who recognised his talent and handpicked him as leadership material for the Congress. In return, Nehru called Gandhi his 'adopted father'. He had physical courage, too. In the *swaraj* campaigns in the twenties and thirties, the British beat him up many times – he saw his mother viciously hit about the body with sticks by police until she bled. He was jailed for nearly ten years in total, including almost two years during the war. But nonetheless the British respected him. According to the novelist Nyantara Sahgal, 'What is so comforting is that the man at the helm of affairs is so much like an English gentleman.'

Although politically shrewd, and a clever tactician, Nehru often acted emotionally, even passionately. He was immensely attractive to women. He had an arranged marriage when he was twenty-six to Kamala, the teenage daughter of a friend of his father, but they spent long periods apart and she died of TB in Switzerland in 1936. 'I overlooked her,' he admitted. He had many lovers, of whom the best-known – and most-gossiped about – was Edwina Mountbatten. But his affair with the social activist Mridula Sarabhai lasted many years, as did a relationship with the highly popular actress Devika Rani. He was linked for some time with Padmaja Naidu, the daughter of the leading Congress supporter and generous Party donor, Sarojini Naidu. Pamela Hicks, Lady Mountbatten's daughter, later said of Nehru, 'It was impossible to be a woman and not be attracted to Pandit-ji.'[11]

The public was seduced, too. Nehru was a powerful orator and his popularity increased as independence came near. He was all but unchallenged as the obvious leader of a free India. But despite his charm and humour he could be aloof. As the writer Nirad Chaudhuri, who knew Nehru well, said: 'He disliked anyone fawning on him, as well as the usual Hindu reverent manner . . . [his] English gentleman's manner was adopted only when one spoke to him in an English which approached his in accent. To anyone who had a Hindi or Bengali accent he would almost behave like an Englishman to a "native" . . . I wondered how he endured the English of a normal Congressman.'[12]

By 1946 Nehru was becoming frustrated by Gandhi, who

increasingly spoke only about mysticism, vegetarianism and the importance of sexual abstinence – not issues Nehru saw as essential for the future of an independent India, an India he knew he would lead. He did not say, as some Congress officials now openly did, that Gandhi was perhaps becoming a little senile, but he wrote that *Bapu* (father, the name he invariably called Gandhi) was 'going around with ointment trying to heal one sore spot after another on the body of India, instead of diagnosing the cause of this eruption of sores, and participating in the treatment of the body as a whole.' Nehru's biggest problem, however, was not Gandhi, whose powers and influence were on the wane. He now faced what was to be the most crucial battle in his rivalry with Mohammed Ali Jinnah and Muslim nationalism.[13]

\*

Jinnah lacked Nehru's charm and easy manner. He was quick to take offence and slow to forgive a slight. But he was every bit as clever, shrewd and sophisticated – and even more of a snob. In 1946 Jinnah was sixty-nine, a tall but stooping figure, painfully thin and, although he didn't know it, already suffering from the lung cancer that would kill him within three years. Few men can claim to have founded a country; when Pakistan came into being, largely thanks to him, it was the fifth most populous nation in the world.

Born in Karachi to privilege and wealth – if not quite in the same league as the aristocratic Nehrus – Jinnah was sent to London to train for the Bar at Lincoln's Inn. When he returned to India he built a hugely successful practice, specialising in commercial law. He was soon the highest paid barrister in the country, earning a reported £25,000 a year, a fortune at the time. One of his peers at the bar admired his prodigious abilities: 'Jinnah was a poor lawyer, but a superb advocate. He had a very striking personality and the presentation of a case as he handled it was a piece of art.'[14]

He was said to be 'cold and unemotional', interested only in the law and politics, but in his early thirties he fell in love with Ruttenbai 'Ruttie' Petit, often described as 'the most beautiful girl' in Bombay. Ruttie's father, Sir Dinshaw Manockjee Petit, was one of the richest Parsee merchants in the city. His daughter was only sixteen when she met Jinnah and Sir Dinshaw took out a restraining order against him to stop them from meeting. But the couple waited until Ruttie was of age and then married, although Sir Dinshaw never approved.

The marriage shocked the Parsee and the Muslim communities. By this stage Jinnah was an up-and-coming Congress and Muslim League politician, but a firm believer in Muslim–Hindu unity to force the British out of India. He was not known to be deeply religious or observant of Islamic customs. He always wore Western clothes, owned more than two hundred suits, favoured spats and was said never to have worn the same silk tie twice. He occasionally drank beer and whisky. Ruttie was glamorously turned out in the most up-to-date outfits from Paris or London. She had 'advanced' views about women's rights, and ran a fashionable salon in the Jinnahs' grand villa in the Malabar Hills. Although she converted to Islam, it was purely for the sake of form. Once, when Jinnah was out campaigning, Ruttie arrived, emerging from a Rolls Royce flamboyantly dressed and bearing a tiffin basket. At the top of her voice she said, 'Look, J, I have brought something delicious for lunch – ham sandwiches.'

But in the late twenties, the couple grew estranged. Ruttie moved into a suite at the Taj Hotel in Bombay and later went to Paris. Still only in her twenties but increasingly unwell, she died in 1929. Jinnah, a highly controlled man who seldom showed his feelings, broke down in tears at her funeral. He became disillusioned with life, with India and with Indian politics. He had only contempt for Gandhi's *satyagraha* campaigns and the Mahatma's Hindu spiritualism, which he said was alienating Muslim opinion of all kinds.

Jinnah moved to London and made a fortune at the English

bar. Briefly he toyed with standing for Parliament as a Labour member, but nothing came of it. One staunch Labour Member of Parliament remarked that he was not surprised the idea was dropped. In Britain, he said, 'Few people would want to be represented by a toff like that.'[15]

When he returned to India in the late 1930s, Jinnah set up home in his Bombay villa with his sister, Fatima, and his teenage daughter, Dina, and began campaigning for Muslim nationhood. History repeated itself; Dina fell in love with Neville Wadia, a man twenty years older than her and a Parsee, as Ruttie had been. Jinnah was furious. He tried to stop the marriage, and after Dina defied him and married Wadia, they barely saw one another.

In 1933 when Choudry Rehmat Ali, the former tutor to the Nawab of Bahavalpur and later a Cambridge academic, first proposed the name Pakistan in an obscure pamphlet (a near acronym from the letters of Punjab, Afghanistan, Kashmir, Sind and Baluchistan) Jinnah agreed with a parliamentary committee that it was 'a students' scheme, chimerical and impracticable', but he came to change his mind and would devote the rest of his life to it.* From 1940, when the Muslim League passed the Lahore Declaration demanding a separate state, Jinnah never compromised on that demand, although for a long period he did not specify where exactly Pakistan would be, nor how its borders could be defined.

Jinnah's opponents often said that it was his petulance which made negotiations between the two sides impossible. A different man might have been more flexible. Kanji Dwarkadas, an old friend of Jinnah's late wife, said that he felt Jinnah had been treated badly by the Congress leaders. 'His self-esteem, his pride and his

---

\* The first person to propose, in print, the idea of separating India into two nations seems to have been the philosopher and great educator Sir Sayed Ahmed Khan, whose grandfather had served in the Mughal Court. A civil servant who founded numerous schools and colleges for Hindus, Muslims and Sikhs, he wrote in 1878: 'Hindus and Muslims are two nations, even though they have drunk from the same well and breathed the air from the same city.'

feeling of being personally hurt had embittered him and he had created ghosts of suspicion and distrust all around him.' The unswerving demand for Pakistan, according to Dwarkadas, was a negotiating position; Jinnah was like a barrister arguing a brief. 'Right until 1946 he was prepared to work for a united India. All the time he was talking in terms of Pakistan this was a . . . bargaining point.' He accepted statehood and partition because 'he had rightly come to the conclusion that the Congress leaders did not want a settlement with him.'[16]

It was around this time that Jinnah made an unusual comment for a man who so ruthlessly used religion for political ends. It probably reflected his inner views. 'You may belong to any religion or any caste or creed – that has nothing to do with the business of the state . . . in the course of time all these angularities about the majority and the minority countries . . . will vanish. Indeed, if you ask me, this has been the biggest hindrance in the way of India to attain freedom and independence and but for this we would have been free peoples long, long ago.'[17]

For weeks Pethick-Lawrence tried to talk the two sides into reaching an agreement, but as the Viceroy, Wavell, reflected in his diary, 'he is no man to negotiate with the tough Hindu politicians . . . he is no poker player.' Against Jinnah he fared even worse. The leader of the Muslim League had no interest in woolly idealism and Pethick-Lawrence was a man who thought in terms of little else. 'Jinnah endured ten minutes of rambling platitudes about the welfare of the world, without showing the slightest sign of interest . . . we made no progress whatsoever.' On occasions outside the conference room when Jinnah and Nehru met, they were never seen to exchange a word. The British delegation flew back to London on 29 June empty-handed and deeply disappointed. When they departed, Wavell wrote to the Cabinet: 'The country is ripe for serious trouble.'[18]

*

For Wavell, a respected general with a reflective mind – his collection *Other Men's Flowers* is one of the most entertaining of all English verse anthologies – Britain 'made an entirely wrong turn in India twenty-five years ago .' He thought that if the Indians had been seriously offered the kind of Dominion status within the Commonwealth that 'white' territories such as Australia, Canada, New Zealand and South Africa had obtained around the time of the First World War, there would have been a good chance of keeping India united. In the early 1930s Gandhi and other Congress leaders went to London for talks and were assured that soon India would gain a kind of self-government – but not yet. No date was given, and all goodwill with the nationalists was lost when in 1939 Wavell's predecessor, Lord Linlithgow, declared war on Germany 'on behalf of India' without consulting any Indians at all. The Australian and Canadian governments, for example, were asked beforehand and made the decision for themselves. The British expected a million Indians to fight against the Germans.

Nehru, who loathed fascism and the Nazis rather more than some of Britain's ruling elite did, said that it was hard for the people of India to fight for the freedom of Poland when they themselves were under foreign occupation. 'If Britain fought for democracy she should . . . end imperialism in her own possessions and establish full democracy in India. A free and independent India would gladly co-operate . . . with other free nations for mutual defence against aggression.'[19]

The British establishment tended to believe the dictum of the most magnificent of all the imperial grandees sent to oversee the smooth running of the empire: Lord Curzon. As Viceroy at the turn of the century, Curzon had declared, 'As long as we rule in India we are the greatest power in the world. If we lose it we shall drop straightaway to a third rate power . . . The rest is redundant.' Few believed this as instinctively as did Winston Churchill, the most romantic of imperialists, who had battled all his political life to maintain British rule in India. Yet Churchill probably did as much as anyone to hasten its end.

When he was Prime Minister he had no intention of ever giving up the Jewel in the Crown. He told the War Cabinet that even if he was forced by the Indian nationalists into making some concessions, 'I would feel under no obligation to honour promises made at a time of difficulty.'[20]

Churchill regarded any notion of Britain leaving India, or even India being granted Dominion status, as 'criminally mischievous'. He retained the sentimental attachment to the idea of the Raj that he had held as a junior cavalry officer on the North-West frontier in the 1890s. Leo Amery, Secretary of State for India during the war, said, 'Winston knew as much about India as George III did of the American colonies . . . He reacts instinctively and passionately against any government for India other than the one he knew forty years ago.'[21]

When in 1942 Congress mounted its Quit India campaign of civil disobedience, Churchill regarded the Indian leaders as traitors at a time of war. He ordered the biggest crackdown against the independence movement since the reprisals following the Indian Mutiny of 1857. More than 60,000 people were arrested, including Gandhi and Nehru, and 350 were killed. Jinnah did not support the strikes and boycotts of the Quit India campaign, calculating, sagely, that if Britain won the war, it would be so exhausted and poor that it would in any case be forced to leave India of its own accord.

Churchill, famously, detested Gandhi – 'the seditious Middle Temple lawyer now posing as a fakir'. He could be surprisingly vicious. When Gandhi was under permanent house arrest – albeit at one of the Aga Khan's palatial residences, but still effectively a jail – he went on a hunger strike. As his health began to fail, Churchill suggested that he had had glucose added to his water. And even when told that the Mahatma's life genuinely was in danger (he was drifting into long periods of unconsciousness), the

Prime Minister called Gandhi 'an old humbug' and a 'rascal' and still refused to release him. He wrote to his friend the South African Prime Minister Jan Smuts: 'I do not think Gandhi has the slightest intention of dying and imagine he has been eating better meals than I have for the last week. What fools we should have been to flinch before all this bluff and sob stuff.' A good joke, perhaps, considering Churchill's girth compared to the Mahatma's, but it is hard to see how Churchill could really have thought he was furthering the cause of the British in India.[22]

In Cabinet, Churchill would explode with rage when India was discussed. Once, to the consternation of most of his ministers, he thundered: 'I hate Indians. They are beastly people with a beastly religion.' Amery's once close relationship with him was irreparably damaged because of the Prime Minister's attitude to India. 'Churchill . . . is not quite normal on the subject of India . . . he seems incapable of taking in even the simplest point but goes off at a tangent and then rambles on . . . an outsider knowing nothing of his reputation would have thought him a rather amusing but quite gaga old gentleman who could not understand what people were talking about . . . one wonders whether on the subject of India he is really quite sane – there is no relation between his manner, physical and intellectual, on this theme, and the equability and dominant good sense he displays on issues directly to do with the conduct of the War.'[23]

Amery was not alone. Lord Cadogan, the Permanent Secretary at the Foreign Office, described Churchill 'as simply drivelling' on the subject of India. And at the height of the Bengal famine in 1943–44, when between one and a half and two million Indians starved to death, one of Churchill's favourite generals, Sir Alan Brooke, was appalled that 'the Prime Minister seemed content to let India starve, while still wanting to use it as a base for military operations'.[24]

At the end of the war the only way the British could have maintained rule in India was through massive and continuing repression. With just sixty thousand troops stationed there, it was not an option. The new Labour Government committed Britain to leaving India – and meant it. But leaving quickly and honourably posed a great dilemma. Despite the romance of the Raj and the rhetoric of Empire, the British were too exhausted to hear the sound of trumpets. As the Labour Chancellor of the Exchequer, Hugh Dalton, said towards the end of 1946: 'I don't believe that one person in a hundred thousand in this country cares tuppence about India so long as British people are not being mauled about there ... To those at home there were other concerns, like the price of food.'[25]

# 18

## Refugees

He had been Mayor of New York for three terms and, before that, a Congressman for a decade; his was one of the most recognised faces in America. But, out of office for three months and away from the limelight, Fiorello LaGuardia was not a contented man. At sixty-three, still full of energy, he was impatient for something significant to do. On 31 March President Truman named him director of the United Nations Relief and Rehabilitation Administration (UNRRA). Though he was hoping for something perhaps more known and with a bigger profile at home, he grabbed the opportunity, telling his supporters that it was one of the most important jobs there could be. And so it was. The world had never seen a bigger refugee crisis, and LaGuardia was the man appointed to deal with it. Soon after accepting the post, ebullient as always, he explained to reporters who were wondering why he had taken the job: 'Go to the library and ask for a book called the Bible, New Testament, and that will tell you what UNRRA is about.'[1]

UNRRA had been established well before the end of the war. Its aid workers set up camps and hospitals close behind the Allied lines where, as they tried to feed a desperate mass of people, they saw clearly the unprecedented scale of the crisis. They worked with dedication and skill and, considering the chaos and dislocation in post-war Europe, they saved a vast number of lives. Nobody knew for sure until long after the war was over, but UNRRA officials estimated that they would have to deal with around seven million refugees. By the time the camps closed early in 1949 it was considerably more than that – around eleven and a half million. And in the spring of 1946 there were still around four million refugees, or displaced persons (DPs), in Europe, the difference being that a displaced person had a home to go to (if it could be found), whereas a refugee was actually homeless. Inevitably, perhaps, the question was one of semantics or nuance: did a survivor of Auschwitz or a slave labourer whose village had been destroyed still have a home?

The DPs included Jews who had survived the concentration camps, prisoners of war from a dozen countries, and – by far the majority throughout 1946 – slave labourers whom the Nazis had transported to Germany. By the end of 1944 Germany's entire effort, including all industrial output, was dependent on forced labour. Around 18 per cent of the workforce were, effectively, slaves. Most came from the Soviet Union (1.7 million) and Poland (700,000) and elsewhere in Eastern Europe. But at least half a million were French and many thousands were from Norway, Holland and Belgium. Technically, those from Western Europe weren't 'enforced' labourers, but more often than not they were made to sign employment papers at gunpoint. After the war, feeding them, keeping them safe and sending them home was an immense task. UNRRA was doing its best, but it was becoming bogged down; hence the need to appoint someone with the flair and drive of Fiorello LaGuardia.

LaGuardia's predecessor was Herbert Lehman, scion of the banking firm Lehman Brothers, and a great friend of Franklin Roosevelt, whom he had succeeded as Governor of New York when Roosevelt was elected President in 1932. According to one of his officials, Lehman delivered 'a mini New Deal in New York State, which combined welfare provisions generous by American standards with financial orthodoxy'. He was a major philanthropist and organiser of various Jewish charities, which is partly why Roosevelt appointed him. 'I want to see some of those goddamned fascists begging for subsistence from a Jew,' the President said, while also saying that Lehman was able, decent, and full of integrity.[2]

A friend described Lehman as a 'very nice, comfortable man, like a brown bear, swinging his little legs from the chair. Honest, brave, but slow ... somewhat lacking in charisma'. Others were less charitable. British officials concluded that he was 'ineffective', according to a report to the Foreign Secretary, Ernest Bevin, that he was 'an indifferent organiser, lacking in guts or common sense.' Dean Acheson, the Under-Secretary of State, liked Lehman personally, but would not have appointed him to a big job: 'Governor Lehman has never shown any understanding of what is required. The simplest executive task was beyond him.'[3]

The dynamic and colourful LaGuardia could not have been more different. A 'Roosevelt Republican' who supported the New Deal, he was also a legendary campaigner against Tammany Hall corruption. Only five foot two, heavily overweight and, on the face of it, unprepossessing, on the stump he was an attractive crowd-pleasing showman and, in his prime, a brilliantly effective organiser. His was a classic American Dream story. He knew a great deal about refugees from personal experience. The son of an Italian musician father and a Jewish mother, he grew up on various military bases in the American West and Midwest before returning to Europe in his early teens with his parents. His family established themselves in Trieste, then the principal port of the Austro-Hungarian Empire. LaGuardia was a gifted linguist, fluent in Italian, German, Hungarian, Serbo-Croat, Yiddish, and Romanian, as well as English.

His first job, at age seventeen, was as an interpreter in the US Consulate in Trieste. Six years later, in 1906, he returned to America to attend law school, financing himself by acting as a translator on Ellis Island. After graduation, he built up a busy law practice in a poor neighbourhood on Manhattan's Lower East Side. Relentlessly ambitious, he became a Republican politician at a time when the Democratic Party machine ran both New York

State and its greatest city amidst a stew of graft and corruption. Nonetheless, during the First World War, he rose to become New York's Attorney-General.

LaGuardia could be charming and witty, and was patently sincere about cleaning up politics in New York. From 1934 until 1945 he was one of the most effective mayors in the city's modern history, but he could also be a bully, rude and difficult to work with; even one of his great admirers, Averell Harriman, described his style as 'ranting, fist waving, screaming, and . . . irresponsible'. He was generally liked, at times loved, by the public, who recognised his guts and authenticity, but disliked by his peers. Robert Caro, an early biographer, commented: 'Men who distrusted excess distrusted him . . . he did not hesitate to play melting-pot politics, to wave the bloody flag, to appeal in one of the . . . languages in which he could harangue an audience to the insecurities, resentments and prejudices of the ethnic groups in immigrant communities . . . His naked ambition for high office, his cockiness, truculence and violent temper . . . repelled.'[4]

He spoke out loudly against fascism and communism, but was disappointed to be given only a minor role in the wartime administration, as head of civil defence. Roosevelt had supported him, despite his Republican ticket, as Mayor of New York, but did not trust him with a high-profile post of the kind he coveted. Truman, when he became President, could see LaGuardia's merits, but he wanted to back a Democrat for what looked like being a tight mayoral race in 1945. LaGuardia thought that without cross-party support he would lose, and so he retired, frustrated.

Whatever he thought about the UNRRA post when Truman offered it, once installed he put his massive energy behind the job, and above all his flair for publicity. The organisation badly needed both. He toured camps tirelessly, inspiring aid workers, as well as ensuring good photo-ops; towards the end of July 1946 he was pictured, famously, in Milan with the great conductor Toscanini. At home, he was a master of the political hard sell, understanding voters' concerns about rampant spending abroad. But when LaGuardia spoke about the responsibility of Americans to help in an unprecedented humanitarian disaster, people listened. Asked what he could do for the needy, he replied, 'Provide fast-moving ships, not slow-moving promises.'[5]

\*

Aid has always gone hand in hand with politics and so it was in 1946. The bigger and more expensive the problem, the more the politicians are involved. UNRRA had been set up by Roosevelt and Churchill at the start of 1944 with a huge budget of $10 billion. The Americans contributed three-quarters of the money, Britain and Canada the rest. The US had learned some lessons from American Relief Administration, established after the First World War, which had been deemed a failure both at home and abroad. That was partly through no fault of its own; the ARA had been overwhelmed by the problems arising from the 1919 influenza epidemic, which killed more than twelve million people in Europe alone, and rather more in Asia. But after 1918, aid had arrived too slowly – and had come with too many strings attached. The relief effort was soon bogged down in domestic politics, too. Some American states refused to give any money if it was allocated for foreign aid, and the US refused to coordinate relief efforts even with its allies. As a result America lost much of the goodwill in Europe that it had earned during the First World War.

This time it would be different. Relief was a key part of the Allies' post-war plans and America was determined to work collaboratively with other countries. Roosevelt was aware of the pitfalls, however. At the end of 1943, a report from relief experts and State Department officials had warned, 'Even if all the supplies came from the United States we ought not to play "Lady Bountiful" and expect the world to thank us for being so rich. It would make much better sense to take part in an international body which will decide where and how supplies would go.'[6]

In practice, though, it did not always work out quite like that. There was muddle and confusion as one UNRRA official, the novelist and philosopher Iris Murdoch, who had been drafted into the civil service during the war, admitted. Like so many others, she joined in a flush of idealism – in her case after her boyfriend, Frank Thompson, a young Special Operations Executive officer, was killed in the Balkans.

The London office, according to Murdoch, 'was rather too full of inept British civil servants (me for instance) uncoordinated foreigners with special ideas and an imperfect command of English . . . the result [was] pretty fair chaos . . . There were very many noble-hearted good-natured . . . people' drained by 'the general flood of mediocrity and muddle.' Murdoch also anticipated potential international tensions – UNRRA was 'not run by bowler hats from Ealing . . . who behave approximately like gentlemen but by the citizens of Milwaukee and Cincinnati and New Haven, Connecticut, let loose in their myriads to deal a death blow to tottering Europe.'[7]

More to the point, UNRRA's workload was considerably greater than expected. Originally it was supposed to send 250 teams of aid workers to help 7.7 million people, mainly in Germany. Within three months 450 teams were needed – and despatched. In some camps conditions were very poor, and continued to be so for a long time. F. S. V. Donovan, a senior official in the British military government, wrote to his superiors in Whitehall:

The actuality of conditions in the centres fell sadly short of the hopes and excitement that had filled [the DPs] when they knew the War was over and they had been liberated . . . Accommodation was often damaged and squalidly patched up with salvaged or improvised material. Water, electricity and sanitation were scarce. In the circumstances of the time such conditions were inescapable. They were better than those of many Germans, but in . . . [many] respects displaced persons were frequently worse off than they had been under the Nazis.[8]

There were severe shortages of food, too. Kathryn Hulme, director of the Bavarian DP camps in the American zone, described in a letter home to a friend the 'scramble for food' when Red Cross parcels arrived at one camp:

It is hard to believe that some shining tins of meat paste and sardines could almost start a riot . . . that bags of Lipton's tea and tins of [instant] coffee and bars of vitaminised chocolate could drive men almost insane with desire. But this is so. This is as much a part of the destruction of Europe as are the gaunt ruins of Frankfurt. Only this is the ruin of the human soul. It is a thousand times more painful to see.[9]

There was constant tension between the military and the politicians, and between the soldiers and the aid workers. At first, the task of setting up the camps and feeding the hungry was borne by British and American troops, most of whom had, only a few weeks earlier, been devoted to killing and now had to perform peacetime roles for which they were not trained. They were soon criticised for handling the task with iron discipline, as if it were a military operation.

President Truman wrote to General Eisenhower, saying he had heard the criticisms and asking if there was any truth behind the charges. He wanted a report on conditions in the camps. Eisenhower resented the attacks but replied with a temperate letter, in which he admitted that, 'In certain instances we have fallen below standards. But I should like to point out that a whole army has been faced with the intricate problem of adjusting from combat to mass repatriation . . . and then to . . . unique welfare problems.'[10]

Most of the camps were staffed by the forces until the end of 1946, when there were enough UNRRA workers in place to take over. Armies were not trained in relief work and soldiers did not always know how to deal with camp inmates. Frequently it was the officers, who were used to issuing orders, who understood the least, 'The default position was to regard it as a logistical problem rather than a humanitarian one,' an administrator at one camp concluded. Francesca Wilson, a British nurse at a camp in Bavaria, recalled losing her temper with an officer who had barked out orders to get children moved from one camp to another with no notice. She told him: 'I hate the army. Why don't you go and fight someone? Why do you meddle with civilians, with peaceable human beings? They are counters to you. You think you can move mothers and babies and sick people as you can move companies of men and batteries of guns in war. Why don't you stick with something you understand.'[11]

Another nurse was appalled by an American commanding officer of a camp who issued new hygiene rules 'by coercive and disciplinary action', with threats of sanctions if they were disobeyed. Anyone who dropped litter, or left clothing hanging on pegs, was disciplined; men who refused work were arrested, including concentration camp survivors and others who had been slave labourers for the Nazis. Women were forcibly tested for venereal disease. 'The army's talent for relief work could hardly be called top-flight,' she complained. The soldiers were often equally dismissive of the UNRRA teams, with Field Marshal Montgomery alleging that UNRRA was 'quite unable to do the job'.[12]

Many American soldiers and politicians resented paying the bulk of the cost of the camps, particularly when there were well publicised cases of gross wastefulness, farcical mismanagement or misjudgement and, occasionally, straightforward corruption. 'An international racket ... whose main purpose was the sustenance of ... political groups such as Communists', said a report commissioned by some isolationists in Congress.[13]

*

A study by British psychologists of former forced labourers from Eastern Europe in the refugee camps in the summer of 1946 found that, far from being happy to be free, large numbers, perhaps the majority, were 'bitter and touchy. The gratitude some of the UNRRA administrators and soldiers expected was not there; instead there was increased restlessness, complete apathy, loss of initiative and a great, sullen suspicion towards all authority. Many . . . [are so] cynical that nothing done even by helpful people is regarded as genuine or sincere.' This reaction seems highly predictable, but both the military and UNRRA soon gave it a name: 'Liberation Complex'.[14]

The Polish novelist Tadeusz Nowakowski spent more than a year in one of the displaced persons' camps. He said later that he would be forever grateful to the aid workers who helped to save his life and that of so many others, but he romanticises nothing in his harrowing novel *Camp of All Saints*. At a crucial moment in the narrative, his hero says, 'Suffering . . . never unites people. It only separates them; only joy can bring them together. There is no fraternity in defeat . . . the only fraternity is in victory. Nor is there such a thing as a brotherhood of arms or a common feeling based on sharing the same war experiences, the same camps and prisons. Contrary to all clichés about how suffering and injustice ennoble their victims, experiences that originate in moral defeat do not bring people together.'[15]

Post-traumatic stress syndrome was not at the time a recognised condition, but many refugees were clearly suffering from it. Marta Karman, a Polish émigré working in the British sector, discerned a pattern.

A problem a great number of the DPs had was counterbalancing the reality that was always extremely hard and often sordid and horrible for them, by calling up daydreams of their past lives until they were almost certain that, the moment they were liberated, they would find themselves in the same happy, beautiful world they knew before the war. All their past difficulties would be forgotten, freedom would take them back to a world where nothing had gone wrong . . . a paradise in which all people were good, all wives loving, all mothers-in-law charming, all husbands faithful and all homes beautiful. There was no unemployment, poverty, unhappiness. Instead of returning to paradise they found themselves in many cases in worse conditions than they were before. Long periods of inactivity gave them time to reflect . . . seeing their reality . . . and their hopes for a better life destroyed, most seek escape into drink or sex. Can anyone be surprised at the licence found in the camps.[16]

The logistical problems in the camps were exacerbated by the extraordinarily high birth rate. By the middle of 1946, 750 babies a month were born in camps in the American Occupation zone. A third of the Jewish women in the DP camps aged between eighteen and forty-five had already given birth or were pregnant. Many aid workers – often from religious organisations – expressed shock that the camps were sites of feverish sexual activity, even Bergen-Belsen, where thousands of people had suffered under the Nazis.

The diary of one well-known volunteer, Francesca Wilson, contains a few brief comments about conditions in the camps but pages about how the displaced persons, particularly the women, 'gave themselves up to debauch without restraint'. A French doctor working for UNRRA explained it partly as a result of boredom – what else was there to do in internment camps? Nevertheless, he went on to say that 'the moral standards of many of these women is very low . . . sexual irregularity has reached appalling proportions.' But even so, there were mitigating circumstances. These young women, especially survivors of concentration camps, 'had lived through hell and are now . . . [overwhelmed] by an irresistible desire for affection and forgetfulness which they seek to satisfy with every means at their disposal.'[17]

There was a more basic biological explanation, too: survival of the race. Most of the Jews in the refugee camps were not survivors of the concentration camps – there were few of those. But somehow or other, they had escaped the Nazis and they had all lost family and loved ones. They craved new ties, a new generation to live for. As one historian of UNRRA's work put it: 'Sex was not just a pleasure . . . it was an act of defiance against extinction.'[18]

# 19

## Trials and Errors

Two fine Empire buildings near the Paris Opéra housed the head-quarters of CROWCASS, the Central Registry of War Criminals and Security Suspects. The first floor of one of them, at 53 rue des Maturins, was the nerve-centre of the Western Allies' effort to cleanse Germany of Nazis. In the middle of an elegant room there stood a bulky piece of machinery, rather like a cross between a motor car engine and a printer's linotype equipment. It was a Hol-lerith IBM card index machine, the most up-to-date and sophisticated device of its kind. The FBI had one in Washington DC, as did a handful of other government departments and big corporations in America, to speed up administration and management tasks. At CROWCASS it was used to check photographs, fingerprints and personal details of suspected Nazi Party members.*

The machine was the pride and joy of American and British

---

* A full and up-to-date list of members had been rescued from destruction by a stroke of good fortune. In the last days of the war the Nazis had got rid of as many membership records and files as they could find. Party officials at various headquarters and regional offices throughout Germany did a fairly thorough job. But, through carelessness, Party chieftains had overlooked one thing: a full membership list and documentary records of every Nazi member since the Party's foundation, along with photographs, were sent to the Josef Wirth paper mill outside Munich to be pulped, but amidst the chaos of defeat nobody checked whether the thousands of bales of paper delivered had actually been destroyed. The manager of the plant, Hans Hüber, realised their importance; 'the crown jewels' for the Allies, he thought. He delayed pulping the files, and was eventually able to hand over the material to the American army.

'de-Nazifiers', who were impressed by the time it saved in the laborious task of identifying war crimes suspects from Party membership lists. But there were major drawbacks. Much of the time the machine didn't work properly, unable to run efficiently because of the unreliable electricity supply in France, where there were power cuts for much of the day.

The real problem facing the de-Nazifiers, though, was the sheer volume of the task. When the war ended in May 1945 there were eight million members of the Nazi Party, more than 10 per cent of the German population. At the start, there was plenty of zeal for punishing the serious criminals, particularly on the part of the Americans, who saw it as one of the principal purposes of the Occupation.

The initial orders given to the Supreme Headquarters Allied Expeditionary Force in Europe (SHAEF), were clear: Nazi Party members and 'supporters' should be banned from any employment other than menial labour. That included anyone 'who had profited' from the Nazis or worked for a company that gave the Party money; 'militarists' such as the Junker landowners and those who had supported the Nazis after they took power in 1933. The British were less idealistic, and less willing to spend resources on removing the Nazis. Nevertheless, they agreed that there should be retribution, followed by rehabilitation and then guidance towards creating a genuine German democracy. This was the Allies' plan when Germany surrendered.

But they quickly grasped the complexity and magnitude of the task. Mining accidents, and loss of production in other industries, would not be the only consequences if too many Nazis were removed from their positions too quickly. Nazis were needed in every area of German life. The middle classes and professionals were disproportionately represented: in Bonn 102 out of 112 doctors were members; in Cologne, a city shattered by bombing, 18 of the 21 specialists in waste management, sewerage and clean water belonged to the Party. Most secondary school teachers had

had to join almost as a condition of employment. Eighty of the 100 musicians in the Berlin Philharmonic Orchestra were members.

The problem the Allies faced was how to find people in any positions of importance who had *not* been Nazis. As Lucius Clay, who took over from Eisenhower as American military commander, said, 'Our major administrative problem was to find reasonably competent Germans who had not been affiliated or associated with the Nazi regime. All too often, it seemed that the only men with the qualifications . . . in the civil service (and elsewhere) were more than nominal participants in the activities of the Nazi Party.' Con O'Neill, one of the most senior British Foreign Office civil servants dealing with Germany, said the original harsh laws were foolish: 'As an example of systematic and meticulous imbecility, it would be hard to beat.'[1]

Lucius Clay would become one of the most important figures in Germany in the years immediately after the war. Born in Marietta, Georgia, he was tall, a swaggerer, careful about his appearance. One of his principal advisors, Robert Murphy, described him as 'a political general, who had shrewd instincts about what Washington wanted.' After West Point he spent seventeen years marking time in the Engineering Corps and saw no action during the war; an aide recalled that 'he never commanded anything with more firepower than a desk.' But Clay was a natural leader, as became clear when he joined Eisenhower's staff at SHAEF at the age of forty-nine. He said from the start that his real job was less to manage a military outfit and more to make propaganda for the West, 'to promote our ideals of democracy.' For him, food had to accompany freedom: 'There's no contest between Communism on 1,500 calories a day, and the Western way on 1,000.'[2]

One of the things he enjoyed most about the job was his office in Frankfurt-am-Main, which had been Eisenhower's. The office was in a vast monument of a building, once the headquarters of IG Farben, the manufacturer among other things of the Zyklon B used to murder Jews in the gas chambers. The building stood untouched in the middle of Frankfurt, surrounded by the rubble from American bombing raids. Eisenhower's secretary (and mistress) Kay Summersby described it: 'The building was a small city in itself. It was very elegant ... lots of marble, fountains and indoor flower gardens, great curving staircases and very luxurious offices. Several tennis courts could have fitted into Ike's office.'[3]

By contrast, the British military headquarters were in a series of unglamorous barrack buildings in Bad Oeynhausen. Montgomery was succeeded in the summer of 1946 by Air Marshal Sir Sholto Douglas, the former head of Fighter Command, whose passion was German music (he had sung in the Bach Choir before the war), and who declared at the time he took over that his mission was to 'restore normal life' to Germany as soon as possible. The civil administration, in overall charge of the Occupation and a branch of the British Government, was the Control Commission Germany – referred to invariably as Cock-Ups Guaranteed. It swelled at one point to nearly twenty-five thousand bureaucrats and was scattered throughout Germany, with branches in Hamburg, Berlin and Hanover. Its official HQ was back in London, headed up by John Hynd, Chancellor of the Duchy of Lancaster and previously a railwayman and trades union official. Inevitably, his office was nicknamed 'Hyndquarters'. Hynd said he was chosen because he had taught himself German with the help of a correspondence course, but, in fact, he had many admirers. Attlee, in his usual terse language, thought Hynd clever and able – high praise from him – and Victor Gollancz said 'there is no humaner man in British public life.'[4]

The Allies initially tried to root out the Nazis themselves. Their primary method was the *Fragebogen*, a detailed questionnaire which all adults under pensionable age in the American and British zones – around thirteen million people – were required to complete and submit to the Occupation administration. People who failed to do so could not obtain ration cards or get a job of any kind; some went to jail. At the top of the form, in bold type, was the warning: 'False information will result in prosecution by the courts of the military Government.'

The Americans made no exceptions at all, which led to some absurdities. The form had to be submitted by people who had spent years in concentration camps, or were well known to have been anti-Hitler such as Erich Kästner, author of the celebrated children's book *Emil and the Detectives*, whose work had been banned by the Nazis. It was equally pointless making Hermann Göring's wife, Emmy, complete the *Fragebogen*. She was then held in Straubing prison, while her husband was awaiting trial in Nuremberg and filled in the answers while supervised by an American prison guard:

> One of the questions was "Did you have a relative or a close friend with a high position in the Third Reich?" "Yes, my husband," I wrote. "What post did he have?" "He was not in the SS but the SA. He was a Reichsmarshal, master huntsman, Commander of the Luftwaffe . . . " I tried to remember his other titles but ended up by sighing. "Why are you sighing like that?" asked the American. "I can't remember my husband's titles anymore." "Don't worry. Just write Hermann Goering. We've got enough information on him already."[5]

The questions were designed to find out how committed to the Third Reich each and every German had been. Had they joined the Party in order to keep their jobs, were they fellow travellers who became Nazis for convenience, were they ardent enthusiasts? One of the main criteria was length of membership; anyone who had joined before 1933 was considered to be more culpable. But it was a crude device; often the answers hid as much as they revealed – and many of those responsible for the deaths of vast numbers of Jews and forced labourers were never officially Party members at all. Nevertheless, in the first nine months of the Occupation

115,000 had been detained at one point or another and 370,000 Nazis had been dismissed from their jobs.

Once completed, the questionnaires were despatched to CROWCASS in Paris and the answers were fed into the IBM index machine. On some days there were forty thousand requests for information and the system was in chaos. By March 1946 there were still seven million *Fragebogen* waiting to be processed, half of them from self-confessed Nazis. It was estimated that it would take more than two years to get through them all. The Allies simply could not cope.

On 1 April SHAEF introduced a new Law For the Liberation from National Socialism and Militarism, drafted by American lawyers: 'To secure a lasting basis for German democratic life in peace with the world, all those who have actively supported the National Socialist tyranny, or are guilty of having violated the principles of justice and humanity, or of having selfishly exploited the conditions thus created, shall be excluded from public, economic and cultural life and shall be bound to make reparation.' A new system of de-Nazification tribunal, or *Spruchkammer*, was set up under a framework designed by the Allies but run independently by German jurists and officials. John 'Jack' Rathbone, the chief legal officer in the British zone, explained the rationale: 'The Germans had created the mess. [We] thought they should clear it up. It would be jolly good for them.' The tribunals let the Allies off the hook, but as a means of meting out justice they proved farcical.[6]

*

A year after the de-Nazification process started, a joke began circulating in Germany. A man goes into a police station and gives himself up. 'I am a Nazi,' he says. The officer in charge tells him it's a bit late. 'Why didn't you come and hand yourself over to us months ago?' 'Well, months ago I wasn't a Nazi.'

The *Fragebogen* and the *Spruchkammer* tribunals were treated with almost universal derision. Prominent Germans who had been known to oppose Hitler's regime were also beginning to worry about 're-Nazification'. A Gallup poll commissioned in April by SHAEF found that 49 per cent of Germans thought that 'Nazism was a good idea badly implemented'. They blamed the Nazis – but mainly for having lost the war and leading them to disaster. More than two-thirds rejected any idea that they might be responsible for the atrocities committed in their name. Konrad Adenauer, the leading figure in the newly formed Christian Democratic Union, and one of the most respected and popular politicians in Germany, spoke out against further de-Nazification a few weeks after the tribunals were established. He said that 'the Nazi fellow travellers' should be left alone and that the de-Nazification process was taking too long. 'In the belief that many have subjectively atoned for a guilt that was not heavy ... we are determined, where it appears acceptable to do so, to put the past behind us.' Confronting Germans with Nazi crimes, forcing them to watch films of the concentration camps, educating children about the horrors that had been committed in the war were counterproductive and as likely to create a nationalist backlash as they would promote contrition, Adenauer argued.[7]

Adenauer was a politician wrestling with the practical problems of governing. But these issues also concerned some eminent philosophers. One of them, Karl Jaspers, author of seminal works on Kierkegaard and existentialism, reached similar conclusions to Adenauer. Jaspers's wife, Gertrude, was Jewish. In the Nazi period, she was forced into hiding and Jaspers had to give up his teaching post at the University of Heidelberg and was banned from publishing; if he had been less renowned he would certainly have been sent to a concentration camp.

In 1946, Jaspers published a highly influential pamphlet, *The Question of German Guilt*, which struck a powerful chord with his compatriots. Along with a series of lectures he gave when it was published, it was quoted often over the next two to three decades to justify the collective amnesia among Germans which had replaced the collective guilt that the Allies had initially hoped their vanquished foes would feel.

The Germans were not evil and should not sink into self-loathing, Jaspers wrote. 'Generalisations about the mentalities and behaviour of millions of Germans in the Nazi era are bound to be of limited application, apart, perhaps, from the generalisation that for the great main of the population, the figurative colours to look for are less likely to be stark black or white than varying shades of grey.' The Allies' Occupation was justified; 'they stop us becoming bumptious and teach us modesty,' he said. But Germans had more immediate worries:

> People don't want to hear about the guilt of the past. They don't care about the judgment of history. All they want is for the suffering to cease . . . it is the responsibility of all Germans to look clearly at the question of guilt and understand the consequences. Germany under the Nazi regime was a prison. The guilt of falling into this prison is a political guilt. Once the gates were shut, however, a prison break from within was no longer possible. Any responsibility, any guilt, attributed to the imprisoned – wherever it arose – must prompt the question whether there was anything they could do?[8]

In a lecture in Heidelberg a year after the war ended he made the point more directly:

> Thousands of Germans either sought death or were killed anyway because of their opposition to the regime. The majority of them remain anonymous. We survivors did not seek death. We did not go out on to the streets when our Jewish friends were led away, nor did we cry out until they destroyed us as well. We preferred to stay alive on the weak, if justified, grounds that our deaths would not have helped in any case. That we stayed alive is our guilt.[9]

Jaspers's most famous pupil, Hannah Arendt, made an abstract point which the German de-Nazification tribunals turned, with few philosophical niceties, into a concrete form of judicial practice. Arendt, a Jew, spent much of the 1930s and the war years in exile in the US. Author of the classic study *The Origins of Totalitarianism*, one of the first books to argue that fascism and communism were essentially two sides of the same coin, she passionately opposed the concept of collective guilt: 'Where all are guilty, nobody in the last analysis can be judged.'[10]

*

As time went on, the questionnaire became more thorough – and a lot more bureaucratic. By the start of 1946 it was twelve pages long and contained 133 questions. Some, about the state of people's health or whether Allied bombing raids had affected their sleep, had nothing to do with Party affiliations. One question in particular, which asked how Germans had voted in the election of 1932, was relevant but bitterly resented. A few were so obscure that people could not answer with any certainty, such as details of bank accounts held before the war. The *Fragebogen* sent many Germans into despair. 'Is one supposed to commit perjury because one has a bad memory?' Ruth Andreas-Friedrich lamented in her diary.

One question was regarded by many people as a trick, but the Americans were convinced it gave them an insight into German attitudes – it asked whether the respondent had ever wanted Germany to win the war. It was ridiculous, and almost impossible to answer honestly with a plain yes or no. After May 1945 it was of course unacceptable to admit to having ever hoped for a German victory. But in 1939 or 1940?*

---

* Many of the first de-Nazifiers who invented the questionnaires were exiled Jews from Germany who had gone to the US in the 1930s. They had the language skills, but were unpopular – predictably – among the Germans, but also among the senior brass in the US Army and in Congress. The best-known were leftist intellectuals, philosophers and economists from the Frankfurt School, like Franz Neumann and Herbert Marcuse – the latter became highly fashionable in California in the 1960s.

The *Spruchkammer* tribunals were mocked for a good reason. They served mainly to whitewash suspect characters who needed certificates of good character, notoriously labelled *Persilschein* – after the washing powder Persil – to show they were 'whiter than white, with all brown [Nazi] stains removed.' The initial problem was to find anyone in the legal profession who was not themselves compromised – 90 per cent of German lawyers had been Nazi Party members. In Hamburg at the end of the war, *every* judge was a member of either the Party or an affiliated organisation. It was a dilemma that would never be resolved. So Nazi judges tried cases of Nazi crimes – including those jurists who had sent people to the gallows for 'crimes' that, until Hitler came to power, had not been offences, such as sexual relations between Jews and Christians. In the American zone not a single judge was removed from the bench after the war.

The majority of the police were Nazis, too, which ought to have prevented their involvement in such cases, but did not. Kurt Schumacher, the leader of the SDP, had been assigned a five-man police guard by the British Occupation forces, who had assured him that the police force had been 'cleared of Nazis'. But on 15 May 1946 he angrily wrote to British officials to say that, after overhearing his bodyguards chatting, he found that four out of the five had been in the SS. He was also profoundly shocked to learn that the British had just appointed a notorious SS man, Lieutenant-Colonel Adolf Shult, as head of the police in the British zone. An Allied Control Commission report to the British Foreign Office explained: 'It is fairly clear that if the denazification of the police is carried to extremes there would be no police force left. With

---

Eisenhower was worried about their influence and wrote to Clay in early 1946 pointing out that some of them 'had been citizens of the US for only two to three years and are using their positions either to communise Germany or to indulge in vengeance.' He said many 'conservative people' had suggested to him in Washington that 'nobody should be allowed in a significant position in the military government of Germany who had not been an American for at least 10 years'.

conditions . . . [in Germany] as they are it would perhaps seem that the essential thing is to have a reliable police force and this cannot be achieved without some sense of security . . . The need is . . . [to] terminate the process of denazification at some stage for these reasons . . . We will surely still need the police as an instrument of military government.' In an apparently seamless transition, many senior officers kept their jobs, among them Wilhelm Hauser, Chief of Police in the Rhineland-Palatinate, who, when he was an SS officer in Byelorussia, had been responsible for countless wartime atrocities.[11]

No German institution was entirely 'cleansed'. Brown stains remained everywhere. More than three-quarters of university professors had been Party members, and even those who briefly lost their jobs were reinstated. Dr Hans Preuss, Dean of the Theology Department at one of Germany's foremost universities, Erlangen, in Nuremberg, was a fervent Nazi who, in the 1930s had organised the burning of books in the university's library written by Jews or Marxists. Preuss was sacked in the summer of 1945 but got his job back the following year. Around two-thirds of Germany's teachers had been Nazis, and at the gymnasia, the best secondary schools, the figure was higher. Thousands had been fired in the three or four months after the end of the war. In 1946, 90 per cent of them were reinstated. The British poet Stephen Spender, then a civil servant, who had been despatched early in the year to report on education in the British Occupation zone, could see why. Visiting a school in Hamburg, he asked the children what they were studying. 'Latin and biology,' they said. 'Nothing else?' I asked. 'No, sir. You see the history, geography, English and mathematics teachers have all been fired.'[12]

Many of the clergy, regardless of denomination, had also been Party members. After the sacking of numerous German civil servants, the Lutheran Bishop of Württemberg, Theophil Wurm, preached that they had suffered too much and were the victims 'of extremely skilful propaganda . . . [most] had joined the Party thinking of the public welfare. They did not identify themselves with the regime.' He was perhaps also thinking of himself. He had joined the Nazi Party in 1933, arguing that he had done so 'in good faith ... believing it could produce a religious revival,' though he later began to oppose the regime and was removed from his bishopric. The American Religious Affairs Division of the Occupation reported to Clay that it knew of 351 active clergy in the American sector. Of these, only three were defrocked. In the summer of 1946 the Catholic Archbishop of Freiburg, Conrad Gröber, nicknamed 'Brown Conrad' because of his fervent support for the Nazis, issued a pastoral letter to his flock in which he blamed the rise of Hitler on 'secularism', neatly absolving the Church and the people from responsibility for what had happened over the last dozen years.

The tribunals began by handing out light sentences, and they grew ever laxer. Only 10 per cent of cases were heard in public. In hundreds of thousands of cases, fines were issued, based on written statements, and the offenders simply 'reclassified' into a lower category. Many notorious Nazis received fines of fifty Reichsmarks. Before the war that had amounted to around three weeks' average wages. Now it was worth less than a packet of cigarettes. These ineffectual penalties brought the whole system into disrepute. Between 20 April and 20 December 1946, 41,782 cases were dealt with; of these only 116 were considered to be major, indictable offences. An American Occupation official in Heidelberg reported to General Clay that in more than 80 per cent of cases the offender would have been classified in a more serious category if the US authorities had still been in charge.[13]

Some German politicians did their best to undermine the tribunals. In Bavaria, the Chief Minister, Anton Pfeiffer, who had been a well-known anti-Nazi, believed the whole system to be 'victor's justice' and was determined to wreck it from the outset. He claimed that there were only thirty thousand Nazis in Bavaria, the birthplace of the Party, and only a handful of serious offenders,

a vast understatement. Hundreds of civil servants and other officials had been fired by the Americans in the first flush of anti-Nazi
enthusiasm. Pfeiffer reclassified 75 per cent of them, either rein-
stating them, or employing them in new posts in a different
department.

And as with everything in Germany at the time, there was a
black market in the *Persilschein* certificates. Thousands of well-
known Nazis bought letters establishing their 'innocence' from
opponents of the old regime, which were enough to get them
cleared by a *Spruchkammer*. There were even cases of Nazis
paying Jewish survivors to testify that they had hidden their
families or somehow helped Jews escape persecution. Others
simply bribed tribunal officials to clear them. According to a US
military intelligence report, this was easy enough in Bavaria:
'Nazis routinely trade endorsements of their guiltlessness and
mutually certify to their anti-Nazi attitudes and activities in the
past ... intercepted letters seem to indicate that the CSU very
commonly gives aid and comfort to former ... [Nazi] Party
members.'[14]

In many parts of the country Germans ostracised those who
worked for the tribunals or the de-Nazification programme but it
had been difficult to find qualified people prepared to do these
jobs. One American official reported from Steinach, near Nuremberg, to the effect that it had 'one of the most incompetent'
tribunals in the American Occupation zone:

The chairman's public prosecutors are ordinary farmers who
are practically illiterate. There is one young law student, who
... has carried the entire responsibility for operations. Since
neither the prosecutor nor the chairman are capable of
drawing up anything approximating adequate charges or a ...
[written] decision, this man has alternated between writing
charge sheets and ... the decisions for the chairman. Thus he
has found himself in the peculiar position of, first, drafting

charges and then drafting decisions opposing his own charges. This 'Jekyll and Hyde' situation has been a strain and . . . he is close to a nervous breakdown.[15]

*Spruchkammer* officials routinely received menacing threats. In Schwetzingen, near Heidelberg, the chairman of the tribunal was sent a letter warning him that he was committing 'a serious crime' by working for the board. 'Should an opportunity arise, you will have to bear the consequences of your actions. Think of your family.' In nearby Mauberg, the chairman resigned, saying he was 'afraid of the consequences'.

In the American and British zones, 83 per cent of civil servants originally removed by the de-Nazifiers were reinstated within three years. As the academic Noel (later Lord) Annan, then an official in the British Occupation zone, said, 'Large numbers of ardent Nazis learned that their best chance . . . was to lie low, to be employed as a clerk, and wait for the heat to die down.'[16]

*

Cordell Hull, Roosevelt's Secretary of State from 1933 to the end of 1944, had opposed the whole idea of war-crimes trials. Just before leaving office he said that, ideally, he would take 'Hitler . . . and Tojo and their arch accomplices to a drumhead court martial. And at sunrise the next morning there would occur an historic incident . . .'* Churchill was also opposed to show trials and thought the major war criminals should simply be executed without fuss. 'It would be best to line them up and shoot them,' he said, although he would change his mind in the last few months of the war. A memo from Sir Alexander Cadogan, head of the

---

* Hull was America's longest-serving Secretary of State – and is likely to remain so. He was at Foggy Bottom for nearly twelve years, throughout Roosevelt's three full terms. He won the Nobel Prize in 1945 for his work towards establishing the UN, to which he was a delegate after he resigned from the State Department on health grounds, rather than for any contribution to jurisprudence.

British Foreign Office, suggested that it would be wrong to try people like Heinrich Himmler because 'their guilt was so black that it was beyond the scope of any judicial process.' But Truman, Attlee and, crucially, Stalin wanted some form of large-scale trial to go ahead.[17]

In the eyes of most Germans, and of millions of people throughout the world who knew what was happening in the eastern half of Europe, the presence of Russian judges presiding at the war-crimes trials which began in Nuremberg in November 1945, undermined the entire process. Stalin had been determined to tell the world that the USSR could mete out judicial punishment on equal terms with the Western Allies, but the Soviet judges' participation was seen as a crude display of victor's justice. George Kennan thought that prosecuting even the top tier of surviving Nazis – the first twenty-four defendants in the main Nuremberg trial which would continue throughout most of 1946 – would be counterproductive. 'The only implication this procedure could convey was, after all, that such crimes were justifiable and forgivable when committed by one government under one set of circumstances, but unjustifiable . . . unforgivable and to be punished by death when committed by another government under another set of circumstances.'[18]

At the time there was almost no human-rights law on statute books anywhere outside the US; almost no international law of any kind nor international courts to enforce it, and only the vaguest legal concept of genocide or 'crimes against humanity'. The judges at Nuremberg had to make new laws, which would set the precedent for the system of international human-rights courts that were developed later. And those laws, drafted by American, British, Soviet and French judges, were used to hang German leaders.

Jurists throughout the world were outraged, and many argued passionately that the precedents set by the court would prove dangerous. The Chief Justice of the US, Harlan F. Stone, was appalled by what he called 'the high-grade lynching party in Nuremberg'. He said he didn't care what America's chief prosecutor, Robert Jackson, or his British counterpart, Sir Hartley Shawcross, did to the Nazis – they deserved death. But it was contemptible to pretend that this was a normal court 'conforming to standards of procedure according to common law or even to natural justice.' When he was asked to swear in the American members of the International Military Tribunal he refused, saying he 'did not wish, even in a remote way, to give my blessing or that of the . . . [US Supreme] Court on the . . . trials.'

For Allied leaders 'the trials were as much about pedagogy, teaching the Germans a lesson, as about justice or making law,' a lawyer involved with them said later. The hearings were broadcast daily on German radio, newsreels were made to show in schools and in cinemas. This did not have altogether the desired effect. A SHAEF opinion poll conducted in the first weeks of the trials showed that less than 10 per cent of Germans believed that it was unfair to bring the leading Nazis – Göring, von Ribbentrop and the clique close to Hitler – to trial. But by the summer of 1946, when the Nuremberg trials had been in session for six months, 40 per cent thought they were unfair.

Truman and Attlee shrewdly argued, however, that the process was not primarily to execute a few dozen manifest war criminals. It was important to amass evidence about atrocities – the murder of the Jews, the treatment of slave labourers, the mass rape of Slavs – and place them on record so that nobody, including the Germans, would forget what had happened.

The British felt they had botched some early cases heard in the autumn of 1945 before the Nuremberg trials began. The charges were different, not crimes against humanity but specific murders which were tricky to prove. The defence lawyers, all British, argued, successfully in many cases, that the accused had been 'obeying higher orders'. Fourteen of the thirty defendants were acquitted, five received short jail terms and eleven were hanged.

Attlee was furious and thought that the entire process had made the Allies look foolish. He told the Cabinet at the end of 1945 that there was a 'lack of drive and energy' in prosecuting cases effectively.[19]

Early in 1946, Hartley Shawcross, who also had a seat in the British Cabinet as Attorney-General, responded with a plan for 'an accelerated war crimes programme' trying fewer cases: 'There are tens of thousands of Germans responsible for millions of murders. We must set ourselves an absolute minimum of prosecuting at least 10 per cent of those criminals in the British zone. That's about 2,000 people. I am setting as an immediate minimum that we try 500 cases by 30 April 1946.' Attlee reluctantly accepted the deadline but was not wholly convinced: 'This would surely have the effect of leaving a large number of criminals unpunished and at large.' He was right. As it turned out the British reached barely two-thirds of Shawcross's revised target.[20]

It was an immense task to track down and punish all the suspects, even the 'big fish', let alone the smaller fry who slipped through the net. There were never enough qualified investigators or lawyers; the chaos in Germany and much of Europe at the time, with millions of refugees on the move or in displaced persons camps, made it harder still – though the comment from one prosecutor that 'the miracle is that we got as many as we did' seems complacent. Pursuing the Nazis was, perhaps rightly, considered less important than feeding the people and rebuilding the country. It is hardly surprising that so many criminals escaped justice. Many, however, remained at liberty not through inertia or carelessness, but as a deliberate act of policy.

Hundreds of Nazi scientists, engineers, industrialists, spies and bankers who might – and should – have gone to jail were allowed to go free because they might prove useful to the Allies. This devalued the de-Nazification process more profoundly than the lack of zeal shown by the local German tribunals. If the Allies, with their judges' courts and fine rhetoric about punishing the guilty, found pragmatic reasons to let some Nazis thrive, why should the Germans be more rigorous about prosecuting less serious malefactors? This was a question that informed Germans repeatedly asked Allied officials. They never received convincing answers.

In the US Army's highly efficient Operation Paperclip, around four hundred scientists and technicians were arrested, interrogated and, if they were of any potential use, shipped out of Germany, whatever their political beliefs or human-rights records might have been. The Third Reich's top technical brains were plundered and shared out between the US and Britain – partly as war booty, but just as important, to keep them and their work out of the hands of the Russians.

The Soviets also detained scientists and held them for years against their will in the USSR or East Germany, but they tended to get the second-raters. The cream went to the US and lived well while they designed American rockets, satellites and missiles. Some had been well-known SS members, like Wernher von Braun, General Walter Dornberger and Kurt Debus, who went on to become the first director of NASA's Kennedy Space Center in Florida.

These men were valuable commodities. 'Their future scientific importance outweighs their present war guilt,' as a report to the US State Department put it neatly, if cynically. Even lesser-known figures such as Arthur Rudolph, a devoted Nazi member since 1931, were protected. The father of America's Saturn rockets which would take astronauts to the moon, Rudolph boasted once of how he had quietly got on with his research while fifty-seven slave labourers who had been hanged were left dangling on hooks directly outside his laboratory. 'He is 100 per cent Nazi, a dangerous security threat, should be interned,' the interrogators who originally debriefed him reported.[21]

One of America's biggest successes was to land the material possessed by Professor Herbert Wagner, a scientific administrator rather than a researcher. He was located in an underground bunker in the Bavarian Alps, where he showed US specialists blueprints for sophisticated electronics, communications systems and photographic equipment which was further advanced than anything developed in the West. The technological haul taken from Germany by the US and Britain would later make considerable commercial fortunes. American economists estimated that it was just as valuable as the reparations the Russians took from the Soviet Occupation.

Most business leaders escaped any sort of punishment – even those responsible for the worst kind of atrocities. Alfred Krupp, head of the huge steel and engineering conglomerate that produced much of Germany's munitions, had employed thousands of Jews and slave labourers from concentration camps, often working them to death. He served four years in jail. George von Schnitzler, one of the bosses of IG Farben, whose company plundered Poland, manufactured the gas that murdered millions and used tens of thousands of slave labourers, was arrested on his vast estate near Frankfurt. He received the American troops who would soon take him into custody, nonchalant as ever 'wearing his trademark Scottish tweeds and English brogues, sitting with his beautiful wife, Lilly, in a room enhanced with a large Renoir over the fireplace. After offering them a brandy (which they declined) he told them "he was glad this unpleasantness is over" . . . meaning the war,' according to the report of his arrest sent to American military headquarters. At his trial, von Schnitzler admitted that IG Farben 'was largely responsible for the policies of Hitler' – an exaggeration, but he was still lucky to escape the gallows and spend a mere two years in prison before returning to a senior position in German industry.[22]

Some Nazis in the West were rehabilitated with remarkable speed, their past lives apparently forgotten. In 1946 Konrad Adenauer's private office was run by Hans Maria Globke. It was Globke who, in 1933 as a sharp young lawyer, had drafted the Nuremberg race laws, the legislative framework for the Nazis' attack on the Jews. Wilhelm Frick, Hitler's Interior Minister, praised Globke to Rudolf Hess as 'undoubtedly one of the most qualified and gifted officials in my own ministry'. Globke knew Jews were being deported east and he was aware of the plans to murder them in the death camps. He was never prosecuted, or placed in either of the most serious categories of Nazi offenders, but his role in the Nazi project was crucial. When he was Mayor of Cologne, Adenauer made him head of the appointments board for government jobs – a task he later performed in a series of CDU governments after West Germany was created, as the Chancellor's most senior domestic civil servant.

Adenauer's personal assistant was the former diplomat Herbert Blankenhorn, who had been First Secretary in the German Embassy in Washington before the US entered the war. The American Secretary of State who succeeded Cordell Hull, Edward Stettinius, wrote to Robert Murphy, the political advisor to SHAEF, with a warning: 'Racialism was one of [Blankenhorn's] favourite subjects. He was an ardent and convinced member of the Nazi Party and a member of the SS. He is not to be trusted.' When Adenauer became West German Chancellor, Blankenhorn was his chief foreign affairs advisor. One of Adenauer's financial aides, Alfred Hartman, had supervised the confiscation of Jewish property in the Ministry of the Interior, alongside Globke, in the late 1930s and during the war he had managed Germany's biggest aluminium plant, where 80 per cent of the workers were slave labourers. In 1946, the organisation that would become the German Department for Refugees was run by Rudolph Sentech. During the war Sentech had been a senior SS officer and an official in the Race and Resettlement Office, tasked with 'Aryanising' the Reich.

*

The Soviets in Eastern Germany tried, as Walter Ulbricht had put it, to 'look democratic', but old habits die hard, and they couldn't quite manage it. Predictably, when they attempted to seize power for the communists in Berlin by stealth, they were clumsy and the mask slipped.

One of Stalin's favoured 'salami tactics' to Sovietise his new empire, as the communists often described it, was to start by building 'Anti-Fascist fronts' or 'Progressive coalitions' of left-leaning parties in each country. The Soviets encouraged the socialist parties to merge with the communists, so they could, together, win free elections. The real plan, as became clear, was to position the communists so they could subvert the newly merged Party, take it over and swallow the socialists whole. It was a tactic the Soviets used throughout their new domains, reasonably successfully. And in the Russian zone of Germany it worked – up to a point. The socialists were bullied into 'uniting', but it gave the Germans yet another reason to loathe and fear the Soviets.

At first Ulbricht genuinely believed that the communists would do well in free elections and told Stalin as much. Why he thought this is a mystery. Some of his braver apparatchiks warned him that the Germans regarded them as the Russian Party and would not vote for them. A humiliating defeat would be inevitable. He took little notice. Ulbricht loathed the SDP – privately he called them 'social fascists' and said that by splitting the Left, they were responsible for the rise of Hitler. But he knew he needed them, at least for the time being. Initially he also believed the socialists would vote to merge with the communists, though he soon realised he would have a battle on his hands.

The SDP leader in the West, Kurt Schumacher, was a fervent anti-communist and his counterpart in the East, Otto Grotewohl, while further to the Left, was initially against the merger. When the creation of a new Party of Socialist Unity was suggested by Ulbricht, Grotewohl declared that the SDP, a Party with a long and proud history going back to the time of Marx, had 'a right to independence'. At the end of 1945 he made a rousing speech to the SDP faithful listing ten reasons why he disapproved of unification.

'In our membership, a deep distrust of the Communist brother party has materialised,' he said. In particular there was distrust of the communist leader. Erich Gniffke, the SDP's deputy leader, described a meeting between senior officials from the two parties early in 1946. 'Ulbricht did not look at any of us. His cold glance moved unsteadily from one to the other. When he managed to force a smile, his face was like a mask and his eyes refused to join in. We became increasingly irritated and could not hide our annoyance. In order to end the talks as soon as possible, we finally agreed to his arguments.'[23]

But Grotewohl changed his mind and, by March, he backed a merger as enthusiastically as he had opposed it a few weeks earlier. He suggested he had been bullied and was frightened for his safety. He told a British Occupation official, in confidence, that he was under great pressure and was being 'tickled by Soviet bayonets'. He said thousands of SDP members in the East had been intimidated and threatened and that Red Army officers had been told to enforce the merger 'at local level . . . the [SDP] organisation in the provinces has been completely undermined.' He said it was pointless resisting Soviet demands.[24]

The merger was approved at a dramatic conference of the two parties held in April at the Admiralspalast Theatre in central Berlin, though members did not meekly accept the inevitable. When Grotewohl rose to speak in favour of unification he was shouted down with cries of 'stooge', 'lackey' and 'we won't be raped'. Ruth Andreas-Fischer, now an SDP Berlin City Councillor, recorded the tumultuous meeting in her diary. 'The protests intensify. They turn more and more angry, more and more passionate. The speaker's . . . words drown in them, as though in a spring tide – "traitor . . . fraud . . . resign". Someone begins to sing "Onward, brothers, to light and freedom" (an old socialist rallying song) . . . His lips form the words automatically, and automatically the comrades join in. Everybody's face is glowing with pride and excitement. This time we didn't eat crow. For the first time in 13 years we have defended our freedom.' The next day the Communist Party newspaper, *Neues Deutschland*, hailed the new Socialist Unity Party, the SED (Sozialistische Einheitspartei Deutschlands). 'In this united party . . . there will be no room for any splinter groups.' Or as Andreas-Fischer put it, 'Not a one-party state, but on the other hand, no room for any other parties.'[*25]

In the Western sectors of Berlin there was a secret ballot of SDP members on the merger, but the Russians wouldn't allow the vote to go ahead in the sectors of the city they controlled. In two districts, the working-class areas of Prenzlauerberg and Friedrichshain, Party activists tried to defy the ban and opened polling stations. Soviet soldiers arrived, roughed up a few SDP supporters, closed down the voting booths and departed, taking the ballot boxes with them. Of the 32,547 registered Social Democrat voters in the Western zones, 29,610 voted against unification and only 2,937 were in favour. Yet the merger went ahead immediately. It had been the first free election since 1933. Few Germans were left with any illusions about the intentions of the Soviet Union towards their country. In the Berlin municipal elections five months later, the SDP campaigned separately from the SED. The Social Democrats obtained 43 per cent of the vote in the city and won 63 of the 130 seats. The new 'unified' Party was humiliated, winning only 19 per cent of the vote and 26 seats. It would be the last free election in Eastern Germany until after the Berlin Wall came down in 1989 and the Soviet empire collapsed.

Stalin, the supreme cynic, now had another merger in mind. This shocked even Ulbricht and other senior German communists. The Soviet leader wanted to co-opt Nazis and 'collaborators with the Hitler regime to support the communists and to operate within the same bloc as the SED'. He told Ulbricht: 'There were

---

* Ambition may have had as much to do with Grotewohl's change of heart as did fear. When the new Party was formed he got one of the top jobs. Then, when East Germany was created in 1949, he was appointed Prime Minister, the post he retained until he died in 1964.

eight million members of the Nazi Party and they all had family and friends . . . this is a very big number. For how long should we ignore their concerns?' He suggested forming a group of Nazis, welcoming them into the fold with the name National Democratic Party, and wondered if there was some former Nazi regional boss they could release from Sachsenhausen or the Soviet Gulag and place at the helm of the new organisation. 'But they have all been executed', he was told – not entirely accurately, since the German communists wanted nothing to do with the plan. Stalin simply frowned and expressed regret.[26]

# 20

## A Greek Tragedy

The future of Greece was sealed in the 'percentages deal' that had been agreed on by Churchill and Stalin in the Kremlin late one night in October 1944. According to this 'naughty document', as Churchill called it, after the war, 90 per cent of Greece would fall under Western control, essentially leaving Stalin to do what he wanted elsewhere in the Balkans, in Romania and Bulgaria. Stalin believed that major powers carving up continents was the way business should be done. Churchill, too, saw it as a perfectly acceptable arrangement, based on traditional European ideas of 'spheres of influence'.

But in March 1946, less than a year after VE Day, fighting flared up in Greece and a vicious civil war would engulf the country for the next three years. What might have remained a local battle between rival claimants to power in a relatively small country escalated into a proxy battle marking the early years of the Cold War. For the West, Greece became a crucial test case: could the spread of communism in Europe be halted?

In retrospect, it seems obvious who was going to win the Greek Civil War. The Soviets abandoned the communists and their leftist allies, leaving them to their fate and helping them only when it was too late. At first the British, and later the Americans, directed and financed a military campaign to install and support a pro-West government of centrists, liberals and Royalists who were determined to keep out the Reds.

At the time, though, defeating the communists did not look so clear-cut. When the Germans pulled out of Greece in the autumn of 1944, most of the country's mainland outside the cities was controlled by armed resistance bands who had fought the Occupation – guerrilla groups known as *andartes*. The strongest by far was the National Liberation Front (EAM) and its armed wing, ELAS, the Greek People's Liberation Army. EAM boasted 1.8 million members, out of a Greek population of 7.7 million, but it emerged later that this was a gross exaggeration of the real figure, which had never been higher than 700,000. Nominally, they presented themselves as a united resistance movement against occupation by the Axis powers, which had been as brutal as anywhere in Europe; around half a million Greeks had died either fighting or from mass starvation. Both of the leftist groups were nominally independent. In fact, they were controlled by the Greek Communist Party. The second largest Partisan group was the conservative National Republican League, EDES, which, since the German invasion of 1941, the British had supported with weapons and a small number of experienced soldiers.

The rival groups loathed one another. Greek politics had been venomous before the war, especially after the 1936 military coup led by Ioannis Metaxas, who banned all political parties, including the extremely conservative ones, but who also, with great enthusiasm, rounded up and shot thousands of leftists. During the war, the *andarte* bands in control of their own areas of Greece made an uneasy alliance against the Axis powers. They agreed to operate under the command of British generals. Although there were many skirmishes between them, they did not lead to open warfare. When large numbers of British troops arrived in Athens at the beginning of October 1944, after the Germans had retreated, the city was already in the hands of the resistance.

The Leftists were in control of the city, with more fighters on the ground and political support organized by the Greek Communist Party (the KKE). But the British brought back the government-in-exile led by the archconservative Georgios Papandreou, which had escaped to Egypt for the duration of the war, to form a 'Government of National Unity'. Churchill also made it clear that he favoured the return of the Greek monarchy.*

Predictably, the Unity Government was anything but united. The leftist members mistrusted the others, some of whom had previously close ties to the reactionary, prewar Metaxas regime. At least one government member was a well-known wartime collaborator, a general who had organised far-right anti-communist 'death squads' under the Occupation. They opposed the return of the king, George II, who had been the symbol of the pre-war dictatorship, and was still living in exile in London, at a suite in Brown's Hotel, in Mayfair, where he had spent the war. They refused to hand over their weapons to the British unless the 'royalist' forces returning from Egypt did the same, which they refused to do. The 'monarchists' made no effort to work alongside the Left, and in some parts of Greece the far-right 'security battalions' operated as death squads, rounding up opponents.

The British military had a low opinion of all the guerrilla bands, which, according to one senior officer, they saw as a 'volatile' group of amateurs who seemed to 'enjoy firing off their weapons for the sake of it.' The British expected a clash with the leftists, and Churchill instructed the commander of Allied forces in Greece, General Ronald Scobie, to prepare for a communist coup d'état at any moment. His orders were to 'use all force necessary to crush ELAS'. As the writer George Theotakas wrote in his evocative diary of the period, 'It only needs a match for Athens to catch fire like a tank of petrol'.

The leftists had not in fact been planning an insurrection, but in November 1944 changed their minds. 'We cannot follow two paths, we must make our choice,' declared the EAM general secretary,

---

* Papandreou was the founder of a political dynasty that was at the top of Greek public life for decades. His son, Andreas, and grandson, George, were prime ministers, though both of them were on the Left.

Thanasis Hadjis. They walked out of the coalition, claiming it was the puppet government of a foreign colonial power, as it had been under the Germans, and called a general strike. The spark for civil war is often said to have been the moment at which the police opened fire on a supposedly spontaneous demonstration in Syntagma Square on 4 December, killing dozens of protestors. In fact ELAS gunmen had blockaded police stations some hours earlier, as part of a coup d'état plan.[1]

The British intervened immediately to put down what Churchill called 'an armed Communist rebellion'. There were bloody battles on the streets of Athens between British troops and *andartes* from ELAS, with whom only a few weeks earlier they had fought side by side against the Nazis to liberate Greece. Churchill told General Scobie to do whatever was necessary to quell 'a local rebellion'. Heavy guns shelled ELAS-controlled areas of the city and the 'Red' suburbs. The RAF bombed 'rebel' positions that included city apartment blocks. Scores of terrified civilians, who might have hoped the war had ended with the defeat of the Germans, were killed in the crossfire.

The stage was set for bitter civil war. During the fighting, the Papandreou government, with British help, had arrested around 15,000 Left-wing suspects and deported nearly two-thirds of them to prison camps in Egypt and Palestine. The *andarte* guerrillas seized thousands of middle-class people they branded 'royalists' or 'reactionaries' and held them hostage in Athens, in their stronghold in Thessaloniki or in hideouts in the mountains. Hundreds were tortured and murdered.

Churchill faced a storm of criticism in Britain, from both left and right. The newly liberated French were appalled, and Roosevelt dissociated the American government from an 'imperialist intervention'. But there was not a word of protest from the Russians. In January 1945, officials from the Greek Communist Party went to Moscow – uninvited – to plead for help. They could not get an audience with either Stalin or Molotov. Instead, they were told by lowly officials to make a deal with the 'recognised' Greek government. At the height of the fighting, British officers asked the head of the Soviet delegation in Greece, Lieutenant Colonel Grigory Popov, what he thought of the KKE's actions. 'He shrugged his shoulders and replied that the Greek Communists had neither requested nor listened to Soviet advice.'[2]

After nearly two months of intense fighting, both sides were exhausted, and the British brokered a ceasefire in February 1945. EAM agreed to take some seats in the Papandreou Government until elections took place the following year. But they were simultaneously planning another takeover. Under the peace deal, the leftist guerrillas promised to disarm and hand over their stockpiles of weapons. They did return some, but a secret instruction to KKE Party cells ordered fighters to conceal large quantities of weapons 'for use in an hour of emergency'.[3]

By the autumn of 1945 the agreement had fallen apart. Papandreou went back on his pledge to release KKE activists and ELAS fighters from jail, saying that 'It would reinforce the communist bands with first-class graduates of the Academy of crime.' One of his chief lieutenants was even plainer: 'We are afraid that the KKE will not be sincere and will again attempt a new insurgency and a forceful seizure of power.' The 'security battalions' murdered some prominent leftists; ELAS responded by killing prominent anti-communists, especially in parts of the Peloponnese, which they controlled with an iron fist. EAM withdrew from the government.[4]

*

It was at this point that the Left made its biggest mistake, by boycotting the elections planned for the end of March 1946. The communists claimed that it would be impossible to guarantee a free vote. This might have been true, but it wasn't the point. Stalin ordered them to change their minds. He said it would be 'an ill-considered act' and 'an error' that would lead to their failure, but the KKE ignored him.[5]

By now, their leader was a dashing, charismatic figure who had spent four years in Dachau as a prisoner of the Germans, Nikos Zachariadis. He was convinced that the Left, the communists and the socialists together, could win power on their own and he was not prepared to make any compromise – not even with the Soviets. Stalin appealed to him twice to reconsider and take part in the election, but Zachariadis, who himself had ambitions to be a dictator, turned him down. He argued that the communists would be badly beaten in a corrupt poll and would look 'like losers'. Until now, Stalin had thought that the Greek Communist Party should operate like the French or Italian parties, in other words, form coalitions, lay the groundwork for 'revolution later' and 'take the path of bourgeois democracy'. Above all, he didn't want them causing him difficulties with the Western Allies.[6] He told one of his cronies: 'I advised not starting this fight in Greece. The ELAS and KKE people should not have resigned from the Papandreou Government. They have taken on more than they can handle.'[7]

The Greek communists would certainly have lost the election. But even in a rigged poll they might have made a respectable showing and gained legitimacy, as the French and Italian communists were doing. It would have been far trickier to suppress them if the communists could have shown sizeable electoral support and stuck to democratic politics. Predictably, a right-wing government won power in the election and began arresting EAM and KKE activists. 'We are not going to wait for them to make a move against us . . . we will do so first,' said an aide to the newly elected Prime Minister, Konstantinos Tsaldaris. The guerrillas returned to the hills where they had so recently fought against the Germans.[8]

Britain's postwar Labour Government continued Churchill's policy and supported the Greek Right, though it came at a price the British could ill afford. Propping up the Greek government cost more than £40 million a year, excluding the money spent on famine relief and helping Greek refugees through UNRRA. Around a quarter of a million Greeks had starved to death in the famine of 1943/44 under German Occupation. Prime Minister Attlee and his Foreign Secretary, Ernest Bevin, hoped that America would step in and contribute, which it began to do in the summer of 1946. But until then the British were on their own. Attlee was inundated with Foreign Office memos warning that, if Greece turned communist, the Russians would first move on Turkey and then on the oil supplies in the Middle East. Bevin, the most ardent anti-Soviet member of the Cabinet, warned that Britain's industrial strength would be threatened. 'Our shipping . . . a great deal of the motive power for our industry . . . the standard of life and wages of the workmen of this country are dependent on these things,' he said.[9]

*

The communists made desperate appeals to Moscow for help, sending a Party representative to Molotov to beg for aid in 'an energetic counter-attack, an armed struggle to seize authority.' Molotov turned him down flat: 'In the current situation, our Greek friends will not be able to count on active intervention from here,' he declared. He offered small amounts of money and moral support, but nothing substantial. Stalin was even more dismissive and also wanted to ensure that other Balkan states did not help the Greek communists either, which would potentially create friction with the West. He wrote to the new Bulgarian leader, Georgi Dimitrov: 'They [the Greek communists] were evidently counting on the Red Army coming down to the Aegean. We cannot do that. We cannot send our troops to Greece. The Greeks have acted foolishly.'[10]

Churchill always maintained that the Soviets kept to the 'percentages' deal: 'Stalin adhered strictly and faithfully to our agreement . . . and during all the long months of fighting the Communists in the streets of Athens not one word of reproach came from *Pravda* or *Izvestia*.' In May 1946 he told the Canadian Prime Minister, Mackenzie King, that his agreement with Stalin had allowed him to be 'busy getting peace restored in Greece. This involved the killing of large numbers of Communists in Greece. Stalin knew that. It went on for a month at least . . . He never once said a word. He held to the understanding he had given.'[11]

One country, however, did want to help the Greek communists. Yugoslavia's Marshal Tito began sending large quantities of weapons and money to the Greek Left – partly out of zeal to help comrades in need, but also to assert an independent line, what he called 'a national route to Socialism' – heresy in Stalin's eyes. Tito, who had been in Moscow exile for years in the 1930s, had in many ways modelled himself on the dictator in the Kremlin. Already he had established a terrifying secret police force, the OGPI, led by the thuggish Ante Ranković, which had murdered thousands of opponents.

Stalin distrusted the Yugoslav dictator, who he told Beria and Molotov was too 'ambitious, too ardent and full of zeal'. In Eastern Europe only Yugoslavia had liberated itself, albeit with money and weapons from the Russians and Britain – but without the need of Soviet troops. Tito resented being ordered around by Moscow, as he told his cronies in comments that he knew would get back to the Kremlin. He had ambitions to be the most powerful communist in the Balkans, which would give him a big power base. Tito resented the Soviet Union's interference in Yugoslavia's territorial demands. For months after the war the Yugoslavs had laid claim to Trieste, and thousands of partisans surrounded the city, but the British insisted that it must remain under Italian sovereignty. Tito continued to protest and threatened a full-scale invasion. Finally, the Soviets ordered him to give up his claims on Trieste and grudgingly he agreed, though he could not hide his frustration. He said he did not want to be 'small change in the politics of the Great Powers'.

Stalin now instructed the Yugoslavs to stop aiding the Greeks.

He told two senior officials from Belgrade, Milovan Djilas and Edward Kardelj, that the insurgents in Greece 'have no prospect of success whatsoever. What, do you think that Great Britain and the United States – the most powerful state in the world – will permit you to break their lines of communication in the Mediterranean? Nonsense. The uprising in Greece must stop, and as quickly as possible.'[12]

But Tito defied the Russians. He continued sending arms to the Greek communists, in increased quantities. The consequences were soon dire for hundreds of thousands of loyal communists throughout the Soviet domains. It was the first sign of the spectacular Soviet–Yugoslav split which would dominate Eastern Europe over the coming few years – and the seeds were sown for a mass Stalinist purge throughout the 'socialist camp'. Alleged Titoists would be murdered and tortured in Eastern Europe, as 'Trotskyites' had been in the Soviet Union of the 1930s. Again the Bolsheviks devoured their own children in an orgy of bloodshed. In Greece, the fighting would continue until 1949, leaving more than a hundred thousand dead, around one million homeless – and would increasingly turn into a front line in the Cold War conflict between East and West.

# 21

## *She'erit ha-pleta*: The Surviving Remnant

In his home city of Philadelphia, Earl G. Harrison had a reputation as an unemotional man, rather stolid and ponderous, fussy about detail and good order. Aged forty-six at the end of the war, a 'spare framed, square-jawed, red haired' lawyer, he had recently been appointed Dean of the Pennsylvania University Law School. He was a devout Methodist, teetotal, and a 'Roosevelt Republican' who had served in the war as Commissioner of Immigration and Naturalization. He had been an able if dull administrator, who kept a discreet, near-invisible profile. Now, in middle age, he discovered he had a flair for publicity – and for action. He was not a soldier, a thinker or a statesman. But Earl Harrison did as much as anybody to create the State of Israel.

In the 1930s he had worked tirelessly with Christian charities that raised money to help persecuted European Jews. After the war, President Truman despatched Harrison and a small team of relief administrators and medical experts to look at conditions for Jewish refugees and concentration camp survivors in Germany and Austria. The explosive reports Harrison sent back, and the subsequent inquiry commissions he chaired, shamed the US administration into supporting a Jewish State – and placed severe strains on the 'special relationship' between America and Britain. Harrison's sensational reports were one reason why the US Congress took so long to approve the vital loan negotiated with such difficulty by Lord Keynes.

'As matters now stand, we appear to be treating the Jews as the

Nazis treated them except that we do not exterminate them,' he said in early autumn 1945. He visited Belsen, which had been turned into a hospital supervised by the British Army but staffed by German doctors and nurses. By the time he got there 'the building with the fiendish gas chambers and crematoria had been destroyed.' As this remark shows, though a stickler for facts, Harrison's report was riddled with errors: there were never gas chambers at Bergen-Belsen. Thousands died there from starvation, ill treatment and disease but it was not an extermination camp. Emotional appeal trumped the detail, though. His report continued: 'Many Jewish . . . [refugees] are living under guard behind barbed wire fences in camps of several descriptions . . . including some of the most notorious . . . amidst crowded, unsanitary conditions, in complete idleness, with no opportunity, except surreptitiously to communicate with the outside world, waiting, hoping for some word of encouragement and action on their behalf.'[*][1]

Harrison argued that the United States should accept that the Jews were a nation – the first time it had been put so plainly in an official American document. 'The first . . . need of these people is a recognition of their status as Jews,' he wrote. (By contrast Britain had recognised the aspirations of the Zionists since the Balfour Declaration in 1917, which, however vaguely worded, had promised a 'national home' for the Jews.) He then made a recommendation that would pose a political problem for Truman and an insoluble dilemma for the British who, since the First World War, had run Palestine as a protectorate under a League of Nations Mandate: 'the immediate immigration of 100,000 Jews to Palestine.' He had plucked the figure out of nowhere. He had spoken

---

[*] Again, he was wrong. By this time Jews were not imprisoned. They could come and go as they pleased, certainly from Belsen, but they tended to leave only rarely. On the occasions they did, some reported being insulted, jeered, even spat at by Germans. One young Jewish man who had barely survived Belsen said that when he went outside a German complained to him that while 'we are going hungry on low rations, you are getting special meals.'

to a few Jewish leaders in the camps and to campaigners back in the US, but he never looked at whether Palestine could absorb that number 'immediately'. He spoke to no British officials, either in Germany or Palestine, let alone any Arabs, who were the majority population in Palestine by around three to one and objected strongly to new Jewish immigrants. Yet Harrison's report was quickly adopted as US policy and the 100,000 figure became the yardstick by which support for the Zionist cause was measured.[2]

Truman said that he had wept when he read Harrison's reports. But his decisions were not made on emotion. 'Palestine . . . really is the $64,000 question,' he told aides. The State Department was generally hostile to Zionism and Jewish immigration. Officials warned that if in future the US wanted to exert increased influence in the Middle East, which was a clear post-war aim, it ought to back the Arabs. There were more of them and, weak and disunited though they may have been, they were more powerful than the Jews. The American public was generally in favour of backing the Zionist cause, but nowhere near as enthusiastically as they would later become.[3]

*

Truman's diaries are full of terms like 'Jew clerk', 'smart Hebrew' and – a particular favourite of his – 'Name's Rosenberg, doesn't act like it'. Yet he had always been a moderate supporter of Jewish immigration to Palestine, if not of all the Zionist causes. As a Senator he had voted against the establishment of a Jewish state in Palestine. Now he accepted Harrison's recommendations and pledged to exert the US more energetically on behalf of the Jews, both because it was right – 'I feel obliged to assist the pitiful surviving remnant,' he told the Saudi Arabian King Ib'n Saud – and because it was politically expedient. He was frank: 'I have to answer to hundreds of thousands who are anxious for the success of Zionism,' he said. 'I do not have hundreds of thousands of Arabs as my constituents.' Mid-term elections were coming up in

November 1946 and there were key battleground states like New York and Pennsylvania – swing states in those days – where Truman said the Jewish vote would count. 'It is not just a European issue, or a Palestinian issue. It is an American issue.'[4]

The President was in tune with the public. Amidst the idealism and sincere wish to help, there was also a large amount of pragmatism in the American attitude. American Jews had not been particularly interested in Zionism until the mid-Thirties, when the Nazis came to power and there were some prominent converts to the cause. However, by 1946 America boasted the single largest Jewish community in the world. There were 4.5 million Jews in the US, mostly in the cities – 1.75 million lived in New York City alone.

The big relief charities such as the US Joint Distribution Committee, which bought land in Palestine and helped persecuted Jews to emigrate there, were mostly financed by Americans. But barely any American Jews wanted to go to Palestine and swap US citizenship for a new life in the place the Zionists wanted as the 'national home' for Jews. Between 1936 and 1946, only 494 people chose to do so – the smallest percentage of any Jewish community in the world, including the Soviet Union. American Zionism did not grow from persecution; rather the opposite. America supplied most of the finance for the Jewish national home, but not the recruits.

For many non-Jewish Americans, there was a measure of self-interest, if not hypocrisy, behind the call for large-scale immigration to Palestine. The US had done nothing to change its own stringent immigration regulations, even at a time of great urgency in Europe. There had been waves of immigration to the US during the late nineteenth century and again from 1904 to 1914. But America had closed its doors during the Depression, and even after the war the rules had not changed. That would not happen until the GIs were demobilised and had found jobs. From 1933 to 1945 there had been 365,000 immigrants allowed into America, but only 250,000 were categorised as refugees, the lowest figures for almost a century. Despite Nazi persecution there were only 160,000 Jewish immigrants in a dozen years. Even Britain, with only a fifth of America's population and often derided for its policies regarding Palestine, had given refuge to 200,000 Jews in that period.[5]

Richard Crossman, a young Oxford philosophy don turned left-wing Labour MP, was a lifelong supporter of Jewish causes, of Zionism and of the Special Relationship. He was surprised when he visited the US at the beginning of 1946:

> The average American supported immigration to Palestine because he didn't want more Jews in America. By shouting for a Jewish state, Americans satisfy many motives: they are attacking the [British] Empire and British protectionism; they are espousing a moral cause, for whose fulfilment they will take no moral responsibility, and most important of all they are diverting attention from the fact that their own immigration laws are one of the causes of the problem. I was irritated ... [in Washington] by the almost complete disregard of the Arab case. Only those very few Americans who had ... experience of the Middle East showed any understanding of the problem. The rest seemed to take it as self-evident that, once the legal title of the Jews to Palestine had been proved, there was nothing else to discuss ... they saw the Arabs as the native Indians, who were a bar to progress and 'manifest destiny' ... who would have to be pushed aside if modernity and progress were to prevail.[6]

This was also a common view among many Britons on the right. As Lord Halifax, the former Conservative Foreign Secretary and British Ambassador to the US, reported to London in January: 'The average American citizen does not want more Jews in the United States and salves his conscience by advocating their admission into Palestine.'[7]

Soon after accepting the Harrison report, Truman wrote to Attlee advising him that the British should 'immediately' allow

100,000 new Jewish immigrants into Palestine and said he would make his support for a Jewish homeland public. 'As I said to you in Potsdam, the American people, as a whole, firmly believe that immigration into Palestine should not be closed and that a reasonable number of Europe's persecuted Jews should . . . be permitted to resettle there.' What he didn't say was that the Americans themselves had allowed only 12,849 Jews into the US, under the President's Special Displaced Persons Directive.[8]

Attlee was indignant. He cabled back urgently, warning of the 'grievous harm that could be done to Anglo/US relations by putting out a figure which had been formed without consideration of the consequences for the Middle East.' He followed this with a letter in which he objected to placing Jewish refugees in a special category 'at the head of the queue', and argued that the Arabs' point of view 'as well as the Jews should be considered in regard to immigration.' Truman promptly released the correspondence to journalists at a White House press conference. Furious, Attlee fired back another angry cable.[9]

The row was patched up – temporarily. President and Prime Minister agreed to establish a joint Anglo-American Commission to look 'at the position of Jews in Europe and how it can be relieved.' The joint chairman, despite some British objections, would be Earl Harrison. For the first three months of 1946 the Commission heard evidence from hundreds of witnesses in Germany, Austria, London, Washington and Jerusalem. On 21 April 1946, in Lausanne, Harrison published his recommendations. They were essentially similar to the conclusions he had reached six months earlier – that 100,000 new immigrants should go to Palestine and that an autonomous, but not entirely independent, Jewish state should now be established. The Arabs vehemently opposed the plan from the start; the Jews broadly accepted it as a basis for negotiation. But a week later Attlee rejected the proposals out of hand, and warned that Britain would take firm action against the 'illegal' immigration routes Zionists had established to smuggle Jews from the camps in Germany to Palestine. Jewish guerrilla groups pledged to renew fighting to force the British to leave and grant them their homeland – Israel. It was this that escalated a small-scale series of skirmishes into a widespread war on terrorism – and underlined how painful Britain would find it to retreat from empire.[10]

*

The 475,000 Jews already settled in Palestine, the Yishuv, had mixed feelings about the 'surviving remnant' of European Jewry in refugee camps. In his memoir about growing up in Palestine, *A Tale of Love and Darkness*, the novelist Amos Oz, born and bred in Jerusalem, explained:

> We generally treated them with compassion and a certain revulsion. Miserable wretches; was it our fault that they chose to sit and wait for Hitler instead of coming here while there was still time? Why did they allow themselves to be led like sheep to the slaughter instead of organizing and fighting back? And if only they'd stop nattering in Yiddish and stop telling us about all the things that were done to them over there, because it doesn't reflect too well on them – or us, for that matter. Anyway, our faces here are turned towards the future, not the past.

The man who emerged after the war as the most influential Zionist leader, David Ben Gurion, agreed. For the past decade Ben Gurion had been chairman of the Jewish Agency, the organisation set up by the British officials to run Jewish services such as education. Amos Oz remembered Ben Gurion as 'a short, tubby man with a prophetic shock of silvery hair' around a bald patch, with 'thick bushy eyebrows, a wide coarse nose, the prominent, defiant jaw of an ancient mariner' and the willpower of a 'visionary peasant'. He always recoiled from the passive acceptance of fate. A combative, restless spirit, not long after the beginning of the war he had said, 'Call me an anti-Semite, but I must say this . . . we are choking with shame about what is happening in Germany, in Poland, that Jews are not fighting back. We rebel against that kind of Jewish people.' His way was 'not to plead . . . pleading is for rabbis, for women . . . Our way', he declared, was to spread the Zionist message through relentless political propaganda.[11]

Ben Gurion, born in Tsarist Poland, emigrated to Palestine, aged twenty, in 1906 when it was still part of the Ottoman Empire. A convinced socialist, like so many of the early pioneering Jews in Palestine, he had been exiled by the Turks in 1915 for 'leftist and Zionist agitation' and only allowed back when the British occupied Palestine during the First World War. He had spent forty years battling for a Jewish State and was now embarking on the most crucial phase of the struggle.

During the war Ben Gurion had feared that, by the time the Allies won, there would be no Jews left in Europe. But more had survived the Shoah (Hebrew for 'catastrophe') than he and other Jewish leaders had expected. Around 200,000 came out of the concentration camps, though 40,000 of those died within a few weeks of liberation. More than 300,000 Jews in Eastern and Central Europe had escaped the camps altogether – 80,000 Poles from a Jewish population of 3.25 million, 175,000 Hungarians and around 90,000 others. Some had lived in hiding, but most had managed to evade the Nazis and headed to the Soviet Union. After the war, the Russians encouraged them to leave the USSR. They opened their doors for Jews – but only Jews – to exit. The Poles and East Europeans were equally keen to see the Jews leave. Tens of thousands found their way to Germany and Austria, where the refugee camps were established. It struck many of these Jews on their way that of all places after the horrors of the war, it was odd that they should be so desperate to reach Germany. But it did not stop them going there; it was where they felt safest.

Ben Gurion now had another major concern. He was worried that after spending time in the refugee camps, Holocaust survivors would not settle in Palestine but elsewhere, which in practice if not theory, would weaken the Zionists' case for a Jewish State. He was furious that the American Joint Distribution Committee – invariably known as 'the Joint' – was raising money to send refugees to South America, Canada, Australia and the US. 'We should not take this matter lightly,' he told aides at the Jewish Agency. 'It is the greatest danger, not only to Zionism but to the Yishuv.'[12]

He toured the displaced-persons camps, encouraging refugees to believe that a Jewish homeland was within their grasp, that the Shoah had made it probable and it could happen soon if enough Jews agitated for it. But it was not always easy to convince them, and he confided to his diary, 'It is a long and hard road overcoming their psychology.'[13]

Ever a realist, Ben Gurion admitted that he needed to use the refugees as a weapon against the British. Many thought him cynical; his supporters thought he was practical. He had said during the war 'we want Hitler to be destroyed, but as long as he exists, we are interested in exploiting . . . [him] for the good of Palestine.' Now he made the point again. 'They . . . [the Jews in DP camps] . . . . had to operate as a political factor. In the struggle ahead we have on our side three major forces: the Yishuv and its strength, America, and the displaced persons camps in Germany. The function of Zionism is not to help the remnant survive in Europe, but rather to rescue them for the sake of the Jewish people and the Yishuv. The Jews of America and the displaced people are allotted a special place in this rescue.'[14]

He confided to an aide at the Jewish Agency: 'The disaster . . . is strength if channelled to a productive course . . . the whole trick of Zionism is that it knows how to channel our disaster, not into dependency or degradation as is the case of the diaspora, but into a source of creativity and exploitation.'[15]

Ben Gurion saw that the best way of putting pressure on the British was to encourage as many Jews from Eastern Europe as possible to go to the camps in the American Occupation zone of

Germany. When he toured the camps he made more or less the same 'stump speech' every time. 'The Americans know they will not remain in Munich forever,' he said. 'The one place . . . [you] can go is Palestine and that way . . . [you] will generate American pressure.' He told the Jews to 'bring the refugees in quickly . . . that will be the major factor for the Americans to demand their removal to Palestine. If we manage to concentrate, say, a quarter of a million Jews in the US zone it would increase the American pressure on the British, not because of the economic problem – that does not play any role with them – but because they do not see any other future for these people anywhere except Palestine.'[16]

Ben Gurion was also in the midst of another difficult battle – a power struggle within Jewry. There had always been splits and schisms within Zionism, but for decades its most eminent figure and the acknowledged leader of the movement was Chaim Weizmann. Weizmann was a political giant, vastly respected by both Jews and gentiles. His style was moderate, characterised by his often using his Establishment connections in Britain and elsewhere. He had advanced the Zionist cause further in one generation than its nineteenth-century founders could ever have imagined. His personal diplomacy, immense charm and subtle mind had done more than anything else to obtain the Balfour Declaration.

Under his guidance the number of Jews in Palestine increased nearly tenfold during the Mandate years, from a meagre handful to almost a third of the population. Jews owned nearly a sixth of the land and built a thriving city, Tel Aviv, as well as numerous villages and many more of the agricultural settlements unique to Zionism, but which appealed to idealists and socialists throughout the world – the kibbutzim.

But Weizmann was now seventy-two and his health was failing. A new generation wanted a more vibrant, active style of politics – and the ambitious David Ben Gurion put himself forward. Ben Gurion thought the Grand Old Man was too close to the British Establishment, too moderate for the times, altogether too decent, to fight the battles to come. Weizmann opposed any form of violence to force the British out of Palestine. Ben Gurion publicly agreed, but maintained links with terrorist groups and spoke of the right of Jews to protect themselves.

Weizmann made a bad political error when he appeared before the Harrison Commission and told them frankly 'that the issue was not between right and wrong but between the greater and the lesser injustice. Injustice is unavoidable and ... [you] have to decide whether it is better to be unjust to the Arabs or to the Jews.' It was the kind of scientific, detached argument that might have appealed at grand dining tables in London in the 1920s, but seemed out of touch with the more militant mood of post-war Zionism. And it alarmed Jews in the Yishuv.[17]

The feud between the two men became personal. Ben Gurion mocked Weizmann's snobbery and 'weakness', saying that Weizmann had simply outstayed his welcome on the stage. Later, in his memoirs, which ran to several hundred pages, he referred to Weizmann just twice – once solely to describe him as looking like Lenin. Weizmann, although he would later regret the comments, accused Ben Gurion of 'acting like a führer' and 'developing fascist tendencies and megalomania, coupled with political hysteria.' By the end of 1946 the abrasive Ben Gurion had ousted Weizmann from his position as head of the World Zionist Congress, the position which he had held for years. The Grand Old Man became a marginal figure, living on a past reputation.[18]

*

The Palestinian Arabs were less fortunate in their leadership. They had nobody of the stature of Weizmann to argue their case, nor somebody with the political and organisational flair of Ben Gurion to mobilise their forces. Most were pitifully poor dirt farmers. A handful of wealthy land-owning families like the al-Husseinis, Nashashibis, al-Alamis and Dajanis had possessed local power under the Ottomans, along with some Bedouin tribal elders, in a semi-feudal structure unchanged for centuries. Then the British came along – and still there was little change. The Palestinian Arabs had built few institutions while the Jews, for example, had established trades unions in the 1920s – a significant part of the Zionist project. (Ben Gurion had for many years been a union activist.) The unions bargained hard for decent wage rates for Jewish workers, with the result that even in the few places where Arabs and Jews worked together – on building projects in Tel Aviv and elsewhere – Arabs were generally paid around a third less than their Jewish workmates for the same job. This applied even when the employer was an Arab. It was a similar story with all kinds of services from education to health. The Jewish Agency was organised relatively efficiently; there was no similar body for the Arabs.

While Jewish numbers in Palestine were still insignificant the two communities rubbed along. There were occasional clashes, but on the whole they were equally poor and lived separate lives. The Turks left both sides alone as long as they kept clear of politics. There were around fifty thousand Jews in Palestine when the British took control of Jerusalem in 1917, roughly 10 per cent of the population. It was when Jewish immigration began to rise immediately after the British Mandate was established that the Arabs saw a threat and real conflict arose. Many could immediately see the consequences. As early as 1919, Ben Gurion had said, 'Everybody sees the problem between Jews and Arabs. But not everybody sees that there is no solution to it.' The diaries and letters of countless British officials and soldiers stationed in Palestine throughout the quarter of a century that the Mandate lasted said similar things. In a letter home, the future war hero, Field Marshal Bernard Montgomery, then a young general in Palestine in the late Thirties, wrote: 'The Jew murders the Arab, and the Arabs murder the Jews. This is what is going on in Palestine now. And it will go on for another 50 years in all probability.'[19]

Arab leaders always picked immigration as their principal grievance. As fascism spread, more than a quarter of a million new settlers arrived between 1929 and 1939, almost entirely from Eastern Europe. More often than not Arab tenant farmers were evicted when the land changed hands. Sporadic anti-Jewish riots became more common, but they were still rare, and were always sparked by immigration, land sales and new Jewish settlements. Yet it was the Arabs who sold land to the Jews: from 1920 onwards there was more land for sale in Palestine than the Zionist movement could afford to buy, no matter how generous the donations from America, and elsewhere in the West.

Sometimes the land was sold by Arabs who lived outside Palestine and the deals were handled by local land agents, but often it was prominent Arab leaders and spokespeople – secretly. When, during a series of violent anti-immigration riots, a Zionist organisation leaked a list of the names of Arabs who had sold land to Jews, it was headed by some of Palestine's most important dignitaries. It included Kasim al-Husseini, the former Mayor of Jerusalem and a leader of the Arab nationalist movement, and Ragheb al-Nashashibi, one of the richest and most powerful men in Jerusalem. Professed patriots in Jaffa and Gaza had sold land to Jews. Musa al-Alami, one of the most influential Arabs in Palestine, who would later represent the Arab cause at the Harrison Commission, sold the land on which the Zionists built the showpiece Tirat Zvi Kibbutz, named after an Orthodox rabbi, in the Beit She'an Valley.[20]

The Palestinians were never united, and had a divided leadership, which was taken over by the inept Haj Amin al-Husseini, the Mufti of Jerusalem. He was a disaster, taking the Palestinian cause from a failed revolt against the British in the mid-Thirties to collaboration with Hitler and, finally, to humiliating defeat in the war that followed the creation of Israel. The Palestinians could not have been in worse hands. Intelligent Palestinians argued a powerful case, but the extremists drowned them out.

Angry and frustrated, convinced that the British were against them and on the side of the Zionists, the Arabs violently rebelled in 1936. They began with attacks on Jews, but soon widened their actions to include the murder of British police and soldiers. General Montgomery suppressed the revolt easily, if brutally. Whole villages were punished in counter-terrorism operations. Around a hundred and twenty Arabs were killed in guerrilla skirmishes and nine thousand people were jailed. Many, including boys aged between seven and thirteen, were given a standard punishment of the time: the birch. More than thirty Arabs were hanged.

Yet soon, with war looming, the Palestinian Arabs secured some of what they wanted. The Neville Chamberlain Government changed course, realising that the British would need Arab support elsewhere in the Middle East in the coming conflict with Germany. At least Malcolm MacDonald, the Colonial Secretary, was honest: 'If we must offend one side, let us offend the Jews rather than the Arabs', he said. The British Government passed new laws limiting immigration to 12,500 a year and banned land sales to Jewish organisations. The Zionists were furious. Jewish terrorists launched their first campaign against the British and the Arabs – in the five months before the war they killed police officers, British soldiers and Arabs drinking in Jerusalem cafes. Around a hundred and thirty died.[21]

During the war most of the Zionists naturally backed the British – tens of thousands joined a Jewish Brigade in the British Army and the Jewish Agency's own defence force, the Haganah. But the majority of Arabs were neutral, apart from a few who joined the Mufti in Berlin and tried, unsuccessfully, to get Hitler interested in backing an invasion of Palestine.

After the Holocaust everything had changed, though the Arabs and the British both failed to see it. The British imagined they could continue as before. Remaining a Great Power meant a traditional role in the Middle East, the British Government thought – and control of Palestine was considered vital. The Arabs could not imagine that world opinion, led by the Americans but supported by the Soviets, would guarantee the establishment of a Jewish homeland.

Palestinians could powerfully argue their objections. The historian George Antonius made a passionate case before the Harrison Commission in 1946. 'We all sympathise with the Jews and are shocked at the way Christian nations persecute them. But do you expect the Muslims of Palestine to be more "Christian", more humanitarian than the followers of Christ? After what happened in Germany, Poland, Romania, etc., have we to suffer in order to make good what you committed? . . . The treatment meted out to Jews in Germany and other European countries is a disgrace to its authors and to modern civilisation. But the cure for the eviction of Jews from Germany is not to be sought in the eviction of Arabs from Palestine.'

But the rest of the world was not listening.[22]

*

The British dilemma was entirely of their own making. Britain had made similar, if not identical, pledges to two different groups of people and hoped neither would notice – or complain. It was a British official who first coined a phrase that became popular – 'Palestine: the twice-promised land'. The writer Arthur Koestler was a passionate Zionist for much of his life, but he could see the moral hazard involved: 'Here was one nation promising another nation the land of a third nation – an impossible notion.' Entire books have been written about whether Britain was deliberately duplicitous, or simply careless, by issuing the Balfour Declaration – 'His Majesty's Government view with favour the establishment in Palestine of a national home for the Jewish people' – while at the same time encouraging the Arabs to believe that they would be granted independence from the Ottomans. Either way the effect was the same. 'The British were fooling the Arabs, fooling the Jews, fooling themselves.'*[23]

---

* Robert Graves described the Balfour Declaration as a 'classic example' of a highly useful trick for writers as well as diplomats. 'A writer must formulate and observe

One of the main illusions was that Palestine was strategically important to Britain. 'Palestine is of no importance to us whatsoever,' the arch-imperialist Lord Kitchener told the Prime Minister, Lloyd George, during the First World War. In 1923 a panel of military experts, at a time when there were no thoughts in Britain of leaving India or Egypt, had concluded that there was little value in holding Palestine. A decade later, the Chief of the Imperial General Staff, Field Marshal Frederick Lambart, the Earl of Cavan, said: 'If we are to hold a garrison at increasingly broad areas of the earth's surface in order to confine foreign aerodromes at a safe distance from our own territories we shall presently . . . have to hold most of the world.' The occupation of Palestine 'had greater moral than military value', he pointed out. Power in 'the Holy Land', especially Jerusalem, was an idea, a symbol, as it has been to conquerors for three thousand years.[24]

After the war the Labour Government in Britain still had illusions of imperial grandeur. In a report to Cabinet at the beginning of 1946, Herbert Morrison, the Deputy Prime Minister, said it was vital to keep good relations with the Arab world for the sake of Empire:

> It was better to choose the possibility of localised trouble with the Jews of Palestine than the virtual certainty of widespread disturbances among the Arabs throughout the Middle East and possibly among the Muslims of India . . . The Middle East is a region of vital consequence for Britain and . . . the Empire. It forms the point in the system of communications, by land, sea and air, which links Britain with India, Australia, the Far East. It is also the Empire's main reservoir of oil. The attitude of the Arab states to any decision . . . is a matter of the first importance. Protection of our vital interests

---

certain literary principles if he wishes to be completely understood . . . Granted he may not always wish to be so understood . . . A good deal of play is made in English with deliberate looseness of phrase.'

depends, therefore, upon the collaboration we can obtain from those independent states. Unfortunately, the future of Palestine baulks large in all Arab eyes . . . To force any policy (to which they would object) and especially one that would leave us open to a charge of breach of faith, is bound seriously to undermine our position and may well lead not only to widespread disturbances . . . but to the withdrawal of co-operation on which our imperial interests depend.[25]

It is the kind of report that was already so outdated it could have been sent as a memorandum to Lord Salisbury. Yet to the Attlee Government the reasons for preventing the Jews going to Palestine seemed overwhelming.

Ben Gurion and the socialists around him felt betrayed. The British Labour Party had had a long-standing commitment to Zionism, repeatedly affirming its support for the Balfour Declaration. There had been strong links between the British Labour movement, the trades unions in Palestine and leftists throughout the world.

In 1944 the Labour conference passed a resolution: 'There is surely neither hope nor meaning in a "Jewish National Home" unless we are prepared to let Jews, if they wish, enter this tiny land in such numbers as to become a majority. There was a strong case for this before the War. There is an irresistible case now . . . after the unspeakable atrocities of the . . . Nazi plans to kill all the Jews in Europe.'

A few weeks before the 1945 election Hugh Dalton, at that time the favourite to become Foreign Secretary if Labour won, declared:

It is morally wrong and politically indefensible to impose obstacles to the entry into Palestine now of any Jews who want to go there. We consider Jewish immigration into Palestine should be permitted without the present inhibitions . . . this is not a matter for which the British alone should take responsibility . . . it is indispensable that there should be close agreement and co-operation among the British, American and Soviet governments. Steps should be taken in consultation with these two governments to see whether we cannot get that common support for a policy which will give us a happy, free and prosperous Jewish state in Palestine.

Elsewhere, Dalton made it clear to Labour colleagues that it was 'inherent in our . . . [policy] that there should henceforth be no such thing as a Jewish illegal immigrant.'[26]

But once in office the Labour leadership changed its mind. The blame for Britain's failure in Palestine has principally been laid on Ernest Bevin, the Foreign Secretary. In 1946, Bevin was sixty-five, a huge bear of a man and one of the great figures in Labour history – 'a colossus in more ways than one', Attlee called him. As the founder of the Transport and General Workers' Union, he was the most powerful trade union leader there has ever been in Britain. He was an authentic working-class hero, but never chippy – the worst insult the English middle classes can think of to describe anyone. 'He was liked as much by the London docker as by the King,' one of his most patrician civil servants, Nico Henderson, said. He ate too much, smoked too much, frequently drank too much, suffered from heart problems, kidney and liver disease and acute sinus trouble. His doctor in 1943 said 'there was not a sound organ in his body – he's a heart attack waiting to happen.'*[27]

Bevin could be short-tempered, and enjoyed nothing more than a good feud with a Labour colleague. But his reputation as a moderate, creative, responsible man of the Left is huge. As wartime Minister of Labour, Bevin was considered by Churchill to be the ablest Cabinet member in the coalition government. He is widely regarded as the most influential and successful Foreign

---

* But Bevin had a vivid sense of humour. When someone said of a rival, Herbert Morrison, 'Poor Herbert . . . he is his own worst enemy,' Bevin retorted, 'Not while I'm alive he ain't.'

Secretary since the war, right on most things – except the Middle East. Some Zionists accused him of being an anti-Semite, which is both untrue and unfair. Early in the war, Weizmann had written to friends in Palestine saying that there were 'few people in Britain who understood the Jewish Agency's problems better than him' or were 'more willing to listen to them.' It was imperial folly, not anti-Semitism, that gave him a blind spot on Palestine. But he wasn't alone. Attlee and others were equally at fault.[28]

They convinced themselves that there was a way of persuading Jews in the German camps to return to Eastern Europe. Bevin said he 'felt passionately there was no point in fighting the war . . . if the Jews cannot stay in Europe, where they have a vital role to play in the reconstruction of the continent.' His officials made the point to Weizmann, arguing that to accept the Harrison Report's view 'is to acknowledge there is no future in Europe for people of Jewish race. It is a counsel of despair that it would be quite wrong to admit at a time when conditions in Europe are still chaotic, and when the effect of the anti-Semitic policy sedulously fostered by the Nazis has not been undone. It would go far . . . to admit that there was no place for Jews in Europe . . . [our] task is surely to create conditions in which they will themselves feel it natural and right to go home rather than to admit at this stage that such conditions are impossible to create.'

How the British were in a position to create those conditions in countries like Poland, Hungary and Romania, which were occupied by the Soviets and whose people wanted the Jews to leave, was a question the officials never sought to answer.[29]

Many British diplomats outside the cloisters of King Charles Street could see how unrealistic this was. They recognised the potent appeal of Zionism to refugees and East European Jews who were heading en masse to the displaced-persons camps in Germany. The British Ambassador to Poland, Victor Cavendish-Bentinck, sent a cable that made the point forcefully, without the customary diplomatic detachment. The surviving Polish Jews, he said, 'simply do not wish to continue residence in what for them is one huge cemetery'.[30]

Most of Bevin's clashes with Zionists were over terrorism. Just before the Harrison Commission published its report, British intelligence intercepted a message from the Jewish Agency's London office and the Haganah leader, Moshe Sneh, that revealed close links between the guerrilla groups and the Agency. Bevin showed Weizmann the evidence and raged, 'Are you trying to force my hand? If you want a fight you can have it.' Weizmann never forgave him.

A few weeks later a bomb exploded at the oil refinery in Haifa. Bevin summoned Weizmann and said the incident amounted 'to a war declaration' against Britain. If they wanted a war they should be open about it and say so, then the British would give up their efforts to find a solution. 'We won't negotiate under the threat of violence. I cannot bear the English tommies killed. They are innocent.' When Weizmann referred to the millions of Jews who had been killed and who were still suffering in refugee camps, Bevin replied: 'I do not want any Jews killed either but I love the British soldiers. They belong to my class. They are working people. The problem is intolerably difficult.'[31]

*

By 1946, David Ben Gurion's principal rival was no longer Weizmann, but Menachem Begin, also a Polish Jew but a much later immigrant to Palestine. Begin was born in Brest-Litovsk in 1913, by which time Ben Gurion had already lived in Palestine for seven years and was active in nationalist politics under the Ottomans. After Poland was carved up by the Russians and Germans at the beginning of the war, Begin was arrested by Beria's NKVD as a suspected British spy and sent to the Gulag. He used to joke later, 'What became of the British agent? He soon had on his head the largest reward offered by the British police.'[32]

Begin was released in 1941 and made his way to Palestine the following year. In Poland he had been a member of the 'Revision-ist' Betar movement for Jewish Defence founded by Ze'ev Jabotinsky, but once in Palestine he became more religious and more politically extreme. A short, wiry, elegant man, he had precise movements, 'soft restless hands, thinning hair and wet lips.' With his rimless spectacles, he looked more like a bank clerk than a violent revolutionary. He believed in 'the redemption of the land' and in a 'war of liberation against those who hold the land of our fathers'.[33]

In 1944, Menachem Begin became head of Etzel, much better known as the Irgun, which had around 600 members. The Irgun began as a self-defence organisation which retaliated against attacks on Jews by Arabs. Like the Jewish Agency's militia, the 20,000 strong Haganah, and the Palmach – its special-forces unit of 1,000 highly trained men – the Irgun joined the war on the side of the British. But a small faction led by Abraham Stern split away. After Stern was killed by British police, they formed a rival, yet more extreme group, Lehi, which the British knew as the Stern Gang.

When it became clear that the Allies would win the war, Begin changed tactics. Early in 1944 the Irgun, which the British called 'the organisation', issued a 'declaration of war to the end'. The top of the declaration bore the organisation's symbol: a rifle with a map of Palestine reaching to the Iraqi border. Begin wanted to open the revolt by taking control of the Western Wall in Jerusalem – the 'wailing wall' – but the plan did not work out. Instead, the Irgun killed a British police officer as he walked through the city. Begin constantly moved around, seldom sleeping in the same place twice, and adopted a series of elaborate disguises. The price on his head was £10,000, a huge sum then.

Between them, the Irgun and Lehi made two assassination attempts on the British High Commissioner of Palestine, Harold MacMichael; attacked police stations in Jerusalem; murdered Walter Guinness, Lord Moyne, an old friend of Churchill's; and raided British ammunition dumps.

The Atomic Age. America held a monopoly on atomic bombs for only four years. Here is the twenty-three-kiloton Able being tested in July 1946 in Bikini Atoll in the South Pacific. The Soviets were working desperately to produce their own nuclear weapon, an effort Stalin called 'Task Number One'.

General George Marshall's Mission to China – an American attempt to end the civil war between the communists and Nationalists – continued throughout 1946. It ended in failure. Here, on the right, is Marshall with one of the communist leaders, Zhou Enlai, signing a short-lived ceasefire agreement.

The supreme leader of the Chinese communists, Mao Zedong, was well known for his smiles. After he won the civil war, he was responsible for the deaths of scores of millions of Chinese.

General Marshall with the President of China and the leader of the Nationalist Kuomintang, Chiang Kai-shek, and his glamorous wife, Mei-ling.

Poverty and starvation in China were rife. So was inflation. In 1946, the cost of living in parts of China was 900 times pre-war levels. An economist calculated that 'in 1940, 100 Yuan bought a pig; in 1943 a chicken; in 1945 a fish ... and in 1947 one-third of a box of matches'.

The guiding spirits of Indian independence: Jawaharlal Nehru, who became India's first Prime Minister, and Mohandas 'Mahatma' Gandhi.

The founding figure of Pakistan, Mohammed Ali Jinnah, whose determination to create a Muslim state resulted in the partition of India.

A group of communist partisans, above, are arrested in Athens. Civil war in Greece raged for more than four years and started as a local struggle between rival claimants to power in Athens. It escalated into the first of the violent proxy battles between East and West in the Cold War.

Greek communists and partisan groups: both men and women joined the resistance.

Marshal Josef Broz Tito was the only communist leader who won power without help from the Soviet Union and the Red Army. For a while he was popular in Yugoslavia, but he ran a brutal dictatorship. Stalin loathed him, and soon after the war he engineered a dramatic split with Tito, in which hundreds of thousands of people were purged and murdered in Eastern Europe.

Pro-Tito graffiti in Croatia, Yugoslavia.

The post-war Zionist leader David Ben Gurion (*above left*) used peaceful methods to pursue his cause. But he had a rival, Menachem Begin (*above right*), head of the Irgun movement, which was prepared to use violent methods to force the British to leave Palestine.

The King David Hotel in Jerusalem after it was blown up by the Irgun on 22 July. The hotel had been the HQ of the British administration in Palestine, and the bombing was the single worst atrocity in the Zionist campaign against the British Mandate; nearly two hundred people were killed.

Some rare good news in gloom-laden Britain, mid-1946.
For a while spirits were lifted – but at the end of the year, during
the worst winter the country had faced for nearly half a century,
the grim news would dominate the headlines again.

The Americans issued a postcard, below, to mark the first
anniversary of the liberation of the Dachau concentration camp.

Ben Gurion often condemned violence. When an Irgun fighter was hanged he did not mourn a martyr. 'This is not a day of mourning but of mortification,' he said. 'I am not shocked that a Jew was hanged in Palestine. I am ashamed of the deed that led to the hanging.' But he continued to keep links to the terrorist groups open and never disowned them entirely.[34]

When the war was over and the British tried to halt European immigration, Ben Gurion, Begin and the Lehi joined together in a United Resistance Command to smuggle Jews into the country. This followed an incident during which the British navy boarded a ship carrying concentration camp survivors and sent them back to Germany. Amidst the scuffle on board the vessel, three Jews were killed.

The Haganah and the Palmach confined themselves to organising the Bricha, the underground smuggling route from Germany to Palestine, but the smaller groups continued their attacks on British soldiers and police, killing dozens of them. At the beginning of June, Attlee despatched 'Monty', Field Marshal Viscount Montgomery of Alamein, as commander of British forces in Palestine. Montgomery had crushed the Arab Revolt before the war and would now do the same with the Jewish Rebellion. As Chief of the Imperial General Staff he was exasperated by Britain's position. The Government had lost control of the country, he told Attlee, 'and the winners are the Jews, who are telling the authorities "Don't dare to touch us". Things cannot go on like this'. There were 100,000 British troops 'with their hands tied . . . two a day are being killed. If we are not prepared to maintain law and order in Palestine then it would be better to get out.' Of course, the British Government wouldn't countenance that.[35]

Montgomery formed a plan that would quickly put a stop to the insurgency. On Saturday 29 June his second-in-command, General Evelyn 'Bubbles' Barker, gave the order for a full-scale attack on the Zionists. He arrested 3,000 Jews (Ben Gurion escaped as he was in Paris, and Begin, in hiding and in disguise, could not be located). Many were locked up in a fortress in Jerusalem's Russian compound that the Zionists had nicknamed Bevingrad. Barker called the attack Operation Agatha; the Zionists called it Black Sabbath.

Begin joined Lehi in planning a spectacular act of revenge. It was not long in coming, it would be bloody – and it would be a defining moment in the birth of Israel.

# 22

## 'A Jewish–Bolshevik Plot' – Blood Libels

On 1 July, an eight-year-old boy, Henryk Błaszczyk, disappeared from his home in Kielce, a large town of around 130,000 people in central Poland. Late that morning he had hitched a ride with some friends to a village twenty kilometres away where he and his family had once lived. He remembered that succulent cherries used to grow in the garden of a former neighbour, and he longed to taste them again. When he failed to return home that evening his panic-stricken parents went to the police and reported him missing. He turned up at around 7 p.m. two days later, with a full basket of fruit. Later that evening Henryk and his father, Walenty Błaszczyk, marched to the nearby police station and told the duty officers that the boy had been abducted by Jews and kept in a basement from which he had managed to escape. The father was insensibly drunk on vodka; the police did not altogether believe the boy's story and told them to come back the next morning to make a full statement.

On the way to the police station early the next day, 4 July, the boy and both his parents passed by a building at 7 Planty Street – the headquarters of Kielce's Jewish Committee. Outside the entrance Henryk pointed to a middle-aged man in a green hat, claiming that he was the one who had seized him, and that other children were being held in the building too. Minutes later police went to Planty Street and arrested Kalman Singer, the man Henryk had identified as his abductor. They beat him up before asking any questions. More police raided the building. There was no basement; they found no other children. Henryk had been fibbing because he didn't want to tell his parents where he had been for a day and a half. The boy was given a stiff telling-off by the police. Singer was released.

But it was too late. The damage had been done. The news spread throughout the town that Jews had kidnapped 'a Christian child'. A furious mob surrounded the Jewish Committee's building, ready to storm the basement and rescue the other children supposedly waiting there to be ritually sacrificed – according to the centuries-old myth that Jews used the blood of Christian children to make *matzo*, unleavened bread.* A representative from the town's Jewish community – now numbering just 380, from a pre-war population of around 20,000 – tried to quiet the crowd but failed.

Soon, hundreds of people had gathered and started throwing stones at the building. A detachment of police sent to restore order were almost overwhelmed. A company of soldiers arrived to support them and the frenzied crowd was still barely under control. Suddenly, at around 11 a.m. someone fired a shot – nobody knows exactly who. Mayhem followed. The soldiers joined the police and battered their way into the building, grabbed whoever they could find and handed them over to the lynch mob in a small square outside.

A group of fifteen or so men and women reached the third floor and barricaded themselves into a small room. One of them, a young man named Baruch Dorman, recalled what happened next:

> They started shouting at us through the door and . . . they broke in, soldiers in uniform and a few civilians. I was wounded then. They ordered us to go outside. They formed

---

* Neither Jewish nor Christian scholars are entirely sure when or where this, the original 'blood libel', surfaced, though the balance of opinion is that it first appeared in the twelfth century, passed on by Crusaders.

a double row. In the staircase there were already civilians, and also women. Soldiers hit us with rifle butts. Civilians, men and women, also beat us. I was wearing a [top] that looked like a uniform, perhaps that's why they did not hit me then. We came down to the square. Others who were brought out with me were stabbed with bayonets and shot at. We were pelted with stones. Even then nothing happened to me. I moved across the square to an exit, but I must have had such a facial expression that they recognised that I was a Jew who'd been taken out of the building, because one civilian screamed 'A Jew!' Only then did they attack me. Stones flew at me, I was hit with rifle butts. I fell and lost consciousness. Periodically I regained consciousness; then they hit me again . . . One wanted to shoot me when I was lying on the ground, but I heard somebody else say 'don't shoot, he'll croak anyway.' I fainted again. When I came to somebody was pulling me by the legs and threw me onto a truck. This was some other military, because I woke up in a hospital in Kielce.*

Later, one of the police who stayed outside in the square, Ryszard Słowaka, admitted that he and many other officers 'didn't react . . . [we] covered our eyes as people went back into the building bringing out more Jews . . . [where] people murdered them.'

Girls in their teens were thrown out of third-floor windows into the street. When the head of the Jewish Committee was spotted trying to phone for help he was shot in the back. Regina Fisz, a young mother, was forced to watch as her new-born baby was murdered – and then she, too, was killed. The massacre went on throughout the day. In the afternoon more than five hundred workers from the nearby Ludowików foundry arrived. Between fifteen and twenty Jews were beaten to death with iron bars. The

---

* Many of these accounts of the Kielce pogrom are taken from the work of the Polish historian Jan Gross, who exhaustively collated a documentary record from eyewitness evidence. His book, *Fear: Anti-Semitism in Poland after Auschwitz*, is superb – and profoundly depressing.

dead included three Jews who had won medals fighting for the Home Army – and two Christian Poles who had been mistaken for Jews. Forty-two Jews were killed in Kielce town that day and more than eighty were badly injured. Around thirty other Jews were massacred on nearby roads and local railways.[1]

*

The Kielce pogrom was the worst of the anti-Jewish massacres in the post-war years, but was by no means an isolated case. Nor were the attacks confined to Poland. In the small Hungarian town of Kunmadaras at the end of May, a mob killed three Jews and seriously injured more than fifteen others, in a similar incident sparked by the ancient blood sacrifice calumny. In Topol'čany in Slovakia, Jews had been viciously beaten up in a month-long campaign of organised anti-Semitic violence at the end of the previous year. Throughout Eastern Europe Jews were routinely threatened and scores were killed on trains. In Hungary, Poland and Slovakia, between twelve and fifteen hundred Jews were killed in the twelve months after the war ended – significantly more than in the twelve years before 1939.

It may seem inconceivable that a surge of murderous anti-Semitism could erupt so soon after the Holocaust, but it should not be perplexing. As the Polish philosopher Stanisław Ossowski wisely said a year after Kielce: 'Compassion is not the only imaginable response to a misfortune suffered by other people.' Guilt is an entirely rational reaction, especially if like many people throughout Europe, you had benefited from the murder of the Jews. 'Those whom fate has destined for annihilation easily can appear disgusting to others and be removed beyond the pale of human relations . . . If one person's disaster benefits someone else, an urge appears to persuade oneself, and others, that the disaster was morally justified.'[2]

More often than not the anti-Semitism revealed itself in a quarrel about property. When the few concentration camp survivors returned home, most found that their houses, flats or farms had been occupied by squatters who aggressively asserted their rights of possession and refused to leave. Sometimes their property was returned immediately, but it was the exception. Invariably, the authorities made it extremely difficult for the Jews to reclaim what had been theirs. This was chillingly justified by Roman Knoll, who had been head of the Polish Government-in-exile's Foreign Affairs Commission. 'Should Jews attempt to return en masse . . . [to reclaim property] people would not perceive this as a restoration but as an invasion which they would resist even by physical means.'[3]

Millions of Hungarians, Czechs, Poles and Romanians had benefited from the Holocaust, which had created an entirely new middle class in just a few years. State direction of the economy in Eastern Europe did not begin with Soviet-style post-war communism but under the authoritarian regimes in the 1930s, and was given a boost by the Nazis. The popular Polish magazine *Odrodzenie* noticed 'an entire social stratum – the new-born Polish bourgeoisie – which took the place of murdered Jews, often literally, and because it smelled blood on its hands, it hated Jews more strongly than ever.' The returning Jews were resented by the majority. People cursed their luck that of all the Jews who had 'disappeared' during the war, *their* Jews had to be the ones who came back.

Many experienced the kind of 'welcome home' of Heda Kovály, who survived Auschwitz. After the war, she returned to her former house in a village close to Prague. She recalled: 'I rang the bell and after a while a fat, unshaven man opened the door, stared at me for a moment and then yelled "so you've come back. That's all we needed." I turned round and walked into the woods. I spent the next three hours until the next train back to Prague strolling on the mossy ground under the fir trees, listening to the birds.'[4]

Typically for Eastern Europeans, especially Jews, black humour was a way of dealing with misery. A joke was often told in Budapest after the pogrom in Kunmadaras. A Hungarian Jew returns home and runs into a Christian acquaintance. 'How are things?' he is asked. 'Oh don't even ask,' the Jew replies. 'I've returned from the camp and now I have nothing except the clothes you're wearing.'

But there was nothing amusing to be found in one grisly example of how people continued to profit from the Holocaust. Well into the spring of 1946, hundreds of people were still digging up the sites of the death camps at Treblinka and Belzec, looking for gold. Rachela Auerbach was a Polish member of the Commission of Inquiry into Hitlerite Crimes. Visiting the camps, she saw a 'lunar landscape' scarred with craters and human bones scattered in all directions. 'Numerous plunderers with shovels are everywhere,' she recalled. 'They dig, they search, pulling out bones and body parts. Maybe something could still be found . . . maybe a gold tooth the Nazis had failed to find'.[5]

*

The massacre in Kielce horrified popular opinion. Anti-Semitism was 'no longer an economic issue,' the writer Wincenty Bednarczuk said in *Odrodzenie*. 'It is a moral problem, pure and simple. Today it is not a question of saving the Jews from misery and death. It is a problem of saving the Poles from moral misery and spiritual death. We imagined that the tragedy of Poland's Jews would cure the Poles of anti-Semitism. It cannot be any other way, we thought, but that the massacre of children and old people must evoke a response of compassion. The common fate suffered under the Occupation must somehow reconcile them. But we didn't know human nature. It turned out that our notions about mankind were naïve.'[6]

But many people were still trying to make capital from it. There's a Polish word, Żydokomuna, which translates literally as Judeo-communism, but which has specific connotations in Eastern Europe. It can best be defined as 'the Jewish-Bolshevik conspiracy', an idea that had powerful resonance at a time when the Soviets were beginning to impose communism at gunpoint on lands that did not want it. The theory, such as it was, posited that some leaders of the Central European communist parties were Jews, meaning that Jews generally were communists, not 'real' Poles, Hungarians or Romanians – and they wanted the Soviet Union to take over. The Catholic Church could have stepped in, but it did little to challenge the misconceptions.

After Kielce, the Church had closed ranks. The Polish Primate, Cardinal August Hlond, never made a clear, unequivocal statement condemning anti-Semitism, and he was supported in this by the vast majority of Poland's bishops. Only one condemned the pogroms in absolute terms, and he was reprimanded by his peers. The local priests did nothing to quell the tide of racial hatred that engulfed Kielce at the time. They said of the massacre of defenceless people, including women and children, that 'a misfortune took place'.

Now Cardinal Hlond suggested that Jewish communists were the cause of the troubles. 'The Catholic church opposes all murder, irrespective of where it takes place or who the perpetrators or victims are,' he said. But, he insisted:

> The miserable and deplorable events in Kielce cannot be attributed to racism . . . Numerous Jews in Poland owe their lives to Poles and Polish priests . . . and it is Jews, now occupying leading positions in state institutions, and bent on imposing a kind of regime that is rejected by the majority of the nation, who are to a large extent responsible for the deterioration of this relationship. It is a pernicious game, which produces dangerous tensions. In regrettable armed confrontations on the front of political struggles in Poland some Jews, unfortunately, perish, but the number of Poles perishing is incomparably greater.[7]

The second-ranking Polish prelate, Archbishop Sapieha in Kraków, was described even by some of his own priests and fellow bishops as 'a virulent Jew hater'. Emmanuel Mournier, an eminent French Catholic, and founder of the right centre political and cultural newspaper *L'Esprit*, met Sapieha when he visited Poland in 1946 and was baffled by 'an anti-Semitism so vivid, even amongst the high ranking Catholics . . . as if the extermination of the Jews never happened.'

The Bishop of Kielce and his priests blamed the government and the police. They claimed that most Poles had been generous to the Jews during the war, and had shown no hostility towards them during the German Occupation when they were being rounded up and killed. The trouble started afterwards, he stated:

> After the Soviet armies entered Poland and the Lublin Government extended its authority over the entire country, the situation radically changed. Enmity towards the Jews started spreading fast . . . this is a phenomenon that cannot be denied. Even Poles who belong to the ruling Party hated the Jews. The Jews are the main propagators of communism in Poland, while the Polish nation does not want communism, which is being imposed on it by force. Every Jew has a good job or unlimited opportunities and help in industry and commerce. Ministries are full of Jews . . . everywhere they occupy choice . . . positions. They are in charge of security police officers and carry out arrests. On the basis of the above reasons, one can say that Jews are responsible for the lion's share of the hatred that surrounds them. Certain communist milieus, in conjunction with the security services, which they control, induced the pogrom, which could later be trumpeted as proof that . . . fascism and anti-Semitism predominate in Polish society and as proof that the Church is reactionary.

Only the Bishop of Częstochowa, Teodor Kubina, categorically came out and said that the blood ritual claims were a myth and was shocked that so many uneducated Poles believed in it:

We declare that all statements about ritual murders are lies. Nobody from any of the Christian populations of Kielce or Częstochowa or anywhere else has ever been harmed by Jews for religious or ritual purposes. We do not know of a single case of a Christian child abducted by Jews . . . All news or stories spread on the topic are either deliberately invented by criminals or come from confused people who do not know better, and they aim to provoke a crime. They ought not to be listened to . . . We appeal to all . . . to combat with all your strength all the attempts to organise anti-Jewish excesses.

Kubina was ostracised by his colleagues. He was condemned by Cardinal Hlond and other bishops for making statements which 'are unacceptable to bishops from other dioceses on the grounds of fundamental intellectual and canonical principles of the Church.'[8]

The British Ambassador, Victor Cavendish-Bentinck, cabled London saying that he had met Hlond and asked him and the bishops to make a clear public stand against violent anti-Semitism. The Cardinal had refused. 'I was told that owing to deep anti-Semitic feelings in Poland the Bishops fear an open condemnation . . . might weaken the Church's influence. This I do not believe and I regard it as an excuse for evading condemnation of anti-Semitism in strong terms. I fear that the Polish clergy is fundamentally anti-Semitic.'[9]

The Ambassador might have added that so was the Communist Party. It understood Żydokomuna very well, and realised there was little to be gained by confronting the Kielce townsfolk. The Interior Minister, Jakob Berman, himself a Jew, was kept informed about the pogrom as it was happening but gave no orders to take firmer action to stop the rioting. More than 20,000 steel workers and miners went on strike in Łódź, not far from Kielce. At their demonstrations most of their slogans were anti-Semitic. The Party Secretary gave them a pay raise and blamed the

Jews for many of the economic ills facing the country. They were 'middle men and not productive workers', and said that the 75,000 or so Polish Jews who survived the Holocaust might be 'better off leaving the country'. Many of them did, heading to the displaced-persons camps in Germany.[10]

Later, the Government put some of the mob ringleaders on trial, though the hearings were patently unjust and the nine death sentences that were passed had clearly been decided before the trials began. None of them were police officers, soldiers or local officials, some of whom went on to be highly promoted as Communist Party officials.[11]

Communist leaders throughout Eastern Europe were sensitive to their backgrounds. In Poland, the party's General Secretary, Gomułka, whose wife, Zofia, was Jewish, continually said the communists had to appoint more non-Jewish officials. In the shorter term he suggested that some of the existing leadership change their names to hide their ethnicity. He put Zofia in charge of the vetting process.

In Hungary, several prominent Party figures were Jewish, including the leader, Mátyás Rákosi. Not to be outflanked, he grotesquely turned himself into one of the keenest anti-Semites in the country. 'You would think the Catholic Church was the largest centre of anti-State intelligence. But in reality, because Jews are everywhere, Zionism is the real centre of espionage,' he wrote to a fellow Jewish communist. A supreme cynic even by the standards of post-war Soviet hatchet-men, Rákosi was keen to recruit former fascists to the communist cause – even those whom he knew had murdered Jews under the former regime. The headquarters of the communists' feared 'sword and shield' – the secret police force, the AVO – was in the building in one of Budapest's grandest boulevards that used to house the Arrow Cross, Hungary's home-grown Nazi Party. There, in basement dungeons, the same people who once tortured Jews and communists were torturing anti-communists. Rákosi used to differentiate between the bourgeois fascists and the 'working-class fascists, the little fish', whom he welcomed into the fold. 'These little fascists aren't bad fellows really,' he told a group of Party workers. 'They were forced into fascism, see. All they have to do is pledge loyalty to us and we will happily take them in.'[12]

# 23

## The War Against Terror

Just after midday on Monday 22 July, a battered Chrysler truck with the registration number M.7022 stopped outside the side entrance of one of the best-known landmarks in Jerusalem – the King David Hotel. Nobody paid much attention when a group of youths in the flowing robes of Arab hotel workers began unloading milk churns.

The King David, opened in 1930, had rapidly become an institution. It was by far the best hotel in the city, and was invariably full to capacity. Its southern wing housed the secretariat of the British Mandate administration and the northern wing was the headquarters of the British Army in Palestine. It was teeming with British officials and soldiers and, as MI5 was based there, spies, but there was still room for some private guests. Most of them were journalists: Palestine was headline news all over the world, and the King David had the liveliest bar in Jerusalem. The basement restaurant, La Régence, decorated, oddly, in Tudor style, was the reporters' favourite place to eat.*

The Arab hotel workers carried the churns to the kitchens adjoining the restaurant, directly under the secretariat offices, but the noise disturbed a British officer, Captain Alexander Mackintosh, who went to investigate. One of the young 'Arabs' produced

---

* The King David was backed by a group of wealthy Egyptian Jews and the British financier Frank Goldsmith – father of the colourful Sir James and the grandfather of British MP Zac and the journalist and philanthropist Jemima, married for a while to the Pakistani cricketer and politician Imran Khan.

a pistol from under his robes and shot him twice in the stomach. They were taking no chances. They had been ordered not to let anybody see the churns, some of which had fuses peeping out from their lids, as they unloaded their delivery of 330 kilograms of gelignite mixed with TNT, set to detonate on a thirty-minute timer.

They made a swift getaway. As they reached the exit, a diversionary bomb exploded under a tree a hundred metres away, set off by a group of fellow Irgun fighters outside. Soldiers started firing at both groups of terrorists. Two were injured, one fatally, but they escaped in a waiting getaway taxi.

The next twenty minutes were confused, but at least three anonymous warnings were given by the Irgun. The first was to the hotel, then to the French Consulate directly opposite the hotel – 'There will be an explosion. Open your windows before the blast' – and finally to the *Palestine Post.* All were ignored. Menachem Begin was waiting nearby: 'Each minute seemed like a day. Twelve thirty-one, thirty-two. Zero hour drew near. The half hour was almost up. Twelve thirty-seven. Suddenly the whole town seemed to shudder.'

The entire southern wing of the hotel was demolished. The blast uprooted huge slabs of marble from the building's magnificent lobby and injured people in King David Street outside. One witness 'heard the thud made by a man's body as the blast flung it against the side of a YMCA recreation hall in one of the streets opposite the hotel; the body left a red patch on the white wall.' The correspondent from *The Times* of London reported that a British official in one of the offices next to the southern wing saw 'the face of a clerk next to him cut almost in two by a sheet of flying glass.' Ninety-one people died: twenty-eight Britons, seventeen Jews, forty-one Palestinian Arabs and five foreign guests. More than two hundred were injured.[1]

The attack was condemned by Ben Gurion, and this time he really meant it. 'He regarded Begin as enemy number one, more so even than the British,' an aide recalled. Begin was a danger to Zionism, and if he was allowed to run amok there could be civil war between Jews, Ben Gurion said. He even compared Begin to Hitler. 'Hitler also had boys who joined his movement and were killed to sanctify their ideal. Certain Nazis had idealistic motives, but the movement as a whole was reprehensible and destroyed the German people.' Etzel – the Irgun – was liable 'to destroy the Yishuv . . . [it is] a bubonic plague.'[2]

Ben Gurion's condemnation might have counted for more if his hands had been entirely clean. But he had a complex relationship with the hard men of violence. He was not against cooperating with them when it suited him – and then damning them when it was convenient.

The Haganah dissociated itself from the King David Hotel atrocity and claimed it had nothing to do with it. But that was not strictly true. The joint command of the United Resistance approved the attack, but after the death toll was so high the majority of moderate Zionists were outraged. The Haganah denied any responsibility and insisted it had 'no control of the details of the operation'. They were weasel words and most people knew it. The Jewish Agency quit the United Resistance Command, and from this point on contact between the moderates and extremists was more tenuous.

The extremists continued their campaign of violence. The Irgun blew up the British Embassy in Rome; they killed fourteen soldiers with a bomb at the British Officers' Club in Goldsmid House, Jerusalem, and organised a dramatic escape from Acre Prison. When one of Begin's fighters was hanged, he ordered the execution of two British soldiers for 'anti-Hebrew activities'. The dirty war went on, sapping the will of the British to stay. They turned from aggressively fighting the insurrection to defending their own men. The majority of British civilians were evacuated from Jerusalem.

Meanwhile, the Arabs looked on, most of them realising that

there would be war if the British left. Only the Arabs who lived outside Palestine, like the Mufti of Jerusalem, were confident of winning. The Jews were terrified they would be massacred.

*

In the eyes of the world, the British somehow managed to turn the King David atrocity into a public relations disaster. It was the worst single act of terrorism in nearly thirty years of the Mandate and there was a predictable outcry from the public and the press at home. In Palestine, many thought that the British Army deserved all it got and did not hesitate to say so.

At first there was sympathy for Britain in much of Europe and America, but then the reaction changed. Montgomery instructed Evelyn Barker, who had planned the arrest of three thousand Zionists – which was what prompted Irgun to plant the bomb – to emphasise to the British soldiers that they were facing 'a cruel, fanatical and cunning enemy and there was no telling who was friend or foe.' He added a warning that 'there are female terrorists too'. Any fraternisation with the locals would have to cease.*

Evelyn Barker, at fifty-two, was 'tall, thin, angular, a colonial officer of the old school, who looked like someone out of an eighteenth-century English portrait'. He had a highly distinguished military career, serving with Montgomery in Palestine in the 1930s. During the war he had won a DSO, and subsequently a Military Cross for his conduct in the battle for Le Havre. He crossed the Rhine with Montgomery into Germany and in April 1945 had liberated Bergen-Belsen. But in Palestine he was a

---

* Montgomery was notoriously anti-Semitic. Ben Gurion was told in the mid-1930s to 'watch out for Montgomery' by the British officer, Orde Wingate, who had trained the Jewish 'special night squads' immediately after the Arab Revolt. He told Ben Gurion that Monty loathed Jews 'and hated the Yishuv'. Wingate, a deeply committed Zionist, went on in the war to be a heroic commando leader in the Burma campaign. He survived numerous risky missions against the Japanese in the jungle, only to die in a plane crash in India in 1944.

disaster. He was loathed by the Arabs as a senior officer during the Arab revolt; now he would become a hate figure for the Jews as well.

Barker interpreted Montgomery's words to mean that all restaurants, bars and 'places of entertainment' would be off limits to British soldiers. Four days after the King David Hotel bomb he wrote to his officers:

> The Jewish Community in Palestine cannot be absolved from the long series of outrages. I am determined that they shall receive punishment and be made aware of the contempt and loathing with which we regard their conduct. We must not allow ourselves to be deceived by the hypocritical sympathy shown by their leaders and representative bodies, nor by the protests that they are in no way responsible for these acts . . . No British soldier is to have any intercourse with any Jew, and any intercourse in the way of duty should be as brief as possible and kept strictly to the business in hand . . . [we] will be punishing the Jews in a way the race dislikes as much as any – by striking at their pockets and showing our contempt for them.[3]

The letter was leaked, and made headlines everywhere. The line about 'striking at their pockets' shocked millions of people, especially in the United States. Instead of the earlier sympathy of a few, the balanced editorials suggesting that Britain did not have entirely easy decisions to make in Palestine, there was now scorn for the arrogance and intolerance of British colonial rule.

Attlee gave Barker a personal reprimand, and he was sent home in disgrace. But the damage to British prestige was immense and long-lasting.

The contempt for Barker would have been even greater – and the loathing the Jews had for him more profound – if people had known his private views. Barker, married and the father of a small child back in England, was having a passionate affair with one of

the most famous women in Palestine, Katy Antonius. A sophisticated Arab, widow of the historian George Antonius, she was
hostess of a fashionable salon where, as the British MP Richard
Crossman described, 'the atmosphere was terrific, with private
detectives, Zionist agents, Arab sheikhs, special correspondents all
sitting about discreetly overhearing each other.' Arab grandees,
Western diplomats and British officers dined late at Katy's villa.
But it was Evelyn Barker who would stay behind afterwards.[4]

He sent her indiscreet letters that were a queasy mixture of
schoolboy passion for her and bitter hatred for Jews. In one, he
wrote that he wept as he looked at her picture, his 'eyes going
damp with tears. I love you so much. Just think of this life and this
money being wasted for these bl***y Jews. Yes I loathe the lot.'[5]

*

Zionists in America urged Truman to exert more pressure on
Britain to accept the Harrison Commission report. Instead, the
President supported a compromise that had been negotiated by
the Deputy Prime Minister Herbert Morrison and the State
Department official Henry Grady, which would have partitioned
Palestine, given limited autonomy to both Arabs and Jews, and
permitted some new Jewish immigration, but not Harrison's
100,000. The British, the Arabs and the Zionists all rejected the
plan. Truman despaired at the Zionist response. Though now publicly a firm supporter of their cause he was exasperated, telling an
aide a few days after the King David Hotel explosion: 'I am put
out by the Jews. Jesus Christ couldn't please them when he was
here on earth, so how could anyone expect I would have any
luck?' In his diary he could still resort to crude country club anti-
Semitism. 'The Jews have no sense of proportion, nor do they have
any judgment on world affairs . . . The Jews, I find, are very, very
selfish. They care not how many Estonians, Poles, Yugoslavs or
Greeks get murdered as long as the Jews get special treatment. Yet
when they have power – physical, financial or political, neither

Hitler nor Stalin has anything on them for cruelty or mistreatment of the underdog.'[6]

Attlee called a conference in London to discuss a revised Morrison–Grady plan. It was a disaster. Ben Gurion and the Zionists refused to go. Only three Arab representatives turned up, but none from Palestine itself because the British wouldn't permit the Mufti of Jerusalem to attend – he had led the Arab Revolt in the 1930s and held private talks with Hitler.

The British were wearying of the Mandate. Ben Gurion had always thought that all they had 'needed was a push', and he was right. The King David bombing speeded Britain's retreat from Palestine. It was barely six months afterwards that the formal decision was made to pull out. Soon after the bombing, the British High Commissioner, Sir George Cunningham, had told Ben Gurion 'the people are fed up with the whole damn business.'[7]

*

After the bombing, there were disturbing anti-Semitic incidents in Britain, which shocked the Government, the Opposition and most of the public. Hundreds of people rioted in Liverpool's Myrtle Street, smashing up and looting shops owned by Jews. In Manchester there were attacks on Jews. In Bethnal Green, in east London, a Jewish Ex-Servicemen's meeting was called off, on police advice, after it was threatened by a large hostile crowd.

Churchill's was the loudest voice to call for the British to lower the curtain in Palestine. He had always supported the Balfour Declaration and Jewish causes, even though when Prime Minister he had done nothing to lift the ban on Jewish immigration, which had led to so much of the terrorism. But often he seemed to possess a very convenient memory.* Now, as the Tory

---

* Churchill was the most pro-Jewish Prime Minister there had been up till then, and probably until the late 1950s. But he was a man of his time. In his letters, and in several speeches, there are many thoughtless phrases – often linked to his visceral anti-socialism – that he might not have used if he had lived later: 'Jew commissar',

leader, he said he was appalled by 'this senseless and squalid war with the Jews in order to give Palestine to the Arabs or God knows who'. In the House of Commons he called it absurd to spend £30 million a year to keep 100,000 troops in Palestine, not just to fight a war on terror but to prevent an 'inevitable conflict between Jews and Arabs . . . To have a war with the Jews in order to give Palestine to the Arabs appears to carry incongruity of thought and policy to levels which have rarely been attained in human history.'[8]

Hugh Dalton, the Chancellor, continually tried to persuade the Cabinet to pull out of Palestine. 'The present state of affairs is not only costly to us in manpower and money but is . . . of no real value from the strategic point of view. You cannot have a secure base on a wasps' nest. It is exposing our young men for no good purpose to abominable . . . [dangers] and is breeding anti-semitism at a shocking speed.'[9]

Bevin, too, came round, and later frankly admitted the dilemma to Ben Gurion: it was about losing face. 'Palestine is not vital to England, but England does not want to admit failure,' he said. On 14 February 1947 Attlee finally agreed to end the Mandate, though he had to find as graceful a way as possible to exit. He put the entire Palestine issue in the hands of the United Nations, which created a Special Committee on Palestine to decide the future. A year later, the UN oversaw the partition of Palestine into independent Jewish and Arab states, the first countries to be created by the world's new peacekeeper. But until then the British had to police Palestine, and the killing and the dying continued.[10]

'semitic conspirators', 'cold semitic internationalists', 'subversive cosmopolitan Jewry.' Whenever he talked of Trotsky he added 'alias Bronstein'.

# 24

## 'Listen World. This Is Crossroads.'

The 166th meridian of longitude meets latitude 12 at a remote speck of land in the middle of the South Pacific: Bikini Atoll, one of the smallest in the chain of Marshall Islands. Early in the morning of 25 July 1946, on the USS *Appalachian* eight miles away, a group of American sailors, scientists and officials, and around forty international observers and reporters, were listening to the ship's loud-hailer. 'This is Crossroads. Fifteen minutes to How Hour.' The countdown continued every minute. At 8.30 a.m. – 'Five minutes to How Hour' – everyone on board was told to place a powerful pair of goggles over their eyes and to be careful when looking to starboard.

The British journalist James Cameron was among the witnesses:

> Ten seconds ... six seconds ... three seconds ... It came gently, imperceptibly to begin with; one's heightened senses seemed somehow to decelerate that first subdivided second until one saw ... the gradual maturing of an instantaneous thing. There across the field of the lens's view stretched the bowstring horizon of the Pacific. Where this ruled edge met the sky came the flash ... then, a ball, a gleaming hemisphere of purest white, a grotesque and momentary bubble, huge and growing huger, a dome rising from the sea ... now a column, a pillar of water more than half a mile across, a million tons of the Pacific Ocean leaping vertically, silently, soaring upward into the cloud base; one mile, two miles high, until it

hesitated, dropped lazily back like a mountainous snowman into the terrible cauldron of Bikini lagoon, by now a waste of murk and fog. In that initial moment ... the battleship *Arkansas* had been tossed into the air like a tiny toy, thrown vertically up and over. There was a feeling as the enormous water-dome swelled and expanded in perfect symmetry to a monstrous bulk that it would never stop developing, that it would increase indefinitely and overwhelm us, and not only us, but everybody. Then the outward movement became an upward one, where the ineffable grace of the column, the weary slowness with which it dripped its million tons back towards the lagoon.[1]

The test – codenamed Baker – was the first time an atomic bomb had exploded under water. It was detonated twenty-seven metres below the surface and established that nuclear bombs that blew up under the ocean were 'dirtier' than those that explode above ground. It was ten days before it was thought safe for scientists to get anywhere near enough to the Bikini lagoon to check radiation levels. Three and a half weeks earlier there had been another test at Bikini, of a bomb dropped by air. It had missed its intended target by a couple of hundred metres, but still destroyed some defunct German, Japanese and American ships which had been towed to the South Pacific for use as target practice.

Neither of the tests – of twenty-three-kiloton bombs, slightly more powerful than that which devastated Hiroshima, and with a minor adjustment to their detonation methods – told American scientists or the US military anything significant that they didn't already know. But they signalled to the world an end to any hopes there might have been – however slim – of a world without the atom bomb.

The Americans had a nuclear monopoly, but were unsure how to use it, or *if* to use it. Nobody in the US seriously suggested attacking the emerging new enemy, the Soviet Union, with atomic weapons – the idea that at this point there was a conspiracy of US generals and crazed physicists plotting a surprise nuclear attack on Russia is a myth. 'It might be desirable to strike the first blow,' the Pentagon's chief war planner, General George Lincoln, wrote in a memo to Truman. 'But it is not politically feasible . . . to do so or to state that we will do so.' For a start, the US did not yet have enough bombs. And what to do once they had been dropped? 'Conquering Russia is one thing,' one of the most ardent anti-Communist cold warriors in the Administration, Defense Secretary James Forrestal said, but 'figuring out what to do with them afterwards is an entirely different problem.' Eisenhower, who had initially been opposed to using the bomb against Japan, was appalled at any idea of a pre-emptive strike against the Soviets.[2]

Immediately after VJ Day some of Truman's advisors had thought they could use the leverage of the bomb; 'We have been handed a Royal Flush,' one of them said. But they didn't understand the Soviets. At a conference of Foreign Ministers in London at the end of 1945 James Byrnes tried something he imagined was humour. Were the Americans intending to use nuclear diplomacy? Molotov asked. 'Are you carrying an atom bomb?' Byrnes replied. 'If you don't stop stalling [on agreements] I'm going to pull out an atomic bomb and let you have it.' Molotov looked on unamused and said simply, 'You should be careful. The United States is not the only one making nuclear weapons.'[3]

Stalin maintained the line he had adopted from the day Hiroshima was destroyed: the Soviets must not appear to be intimidated. He told an interviewer, Alexander Werth of the British *Sunday Times*, 'Atomic bombs are supposed to frighten people with weak nerves. But they cannot decide the outcome of wars . . . [they are] insufficient for that. Of course, monopoly ownership . . . of the bomb creates a threat, but against it there exist at least two means:

a) monopoly ownership cannot last for long and b) the use of the bomb will be prohibited.'[4]

Truman found that the bomb, instead of making it easier to handle the Soviets, was making them less conciliatory. At a meeting with his friend the Budget Director, Harold Smith, Truman despaired at how stubborn the Russians were being over a range of issues. 'But Mr President, you have an atom bomb up your sleeve . . . that makes a difference.' Truman replied: 'Yes, but I'm not sure I can use it.'

*

A series of wartime agreements between Roosevelt and Churchill made it clear that they had intended to freeze the Russians out of nuclear research and keep the information to themselves. The most specific was in September 1944 when the two met at Hyde Park, Roosevelt's estate by the Hudson River in New York. An aide-memoire following the meeting said: 'The suggestion that the world should be informed regarding Tube Alloys [the code name for the nuclear project] with a view to an international agreement regarding its control and use, is not accepted. The matter should continue to be regarded as of the utmost secrecy.'[5]

The Americans now considered making an approach to the Soviets, offering to share nuclear technology. One of Truman's most trusted advisors, Dean Acheson, enthusiastically embraced the idea: 'The joint development of this discovery with the UK . . . must appear to the USSR to be unanswerable evidence of an Anglo-American combination against them.' He told the President in October 1945: 'It is impossible that a government as powerful and power conscious as the Soviet Government could fail to react vigorously to this situation.'[6]

Six months later, in the spring of 1946, Acheson was still advocating collaboration of some kind: 'The advantage of being ahead in such an [arms] race is nothing compared with not having the race.' It may be that 'long range co-operation' with the Soviets was unlikely but it would be 'impossible' if they were excluded from atomic collaboration. 'Russia will be bound to get the secret one day,' he said, suggesting that it would be best to 'approach them in a conciliatory way' now.[7]

J. Robert Oppenheimer, the 'father' of the atom bomb who had led the Manhattan Project team in Los Alamos, New Mexico, during the war, produced a powerfully argued and elegantly written report suggesting that all new nuclear research, materials and technology should be placed under an international agency, which would control the production of plutonium and thorium, the materials used to make the weapons. 'Only if the dangerous aspects of atomic energy are taken out of national hands ... is there any reasonable prospect of devising safeguards against the use of atomic energy for bombs,' he said.[8]

Many other scientists, most prominently the Nobel Prize-winning Danish physicist Niels Bohr, had long wanted to ensure that both sides had the technology to make atomic bombs.* He argued that if the weapons could be seen as a common danger they were more likely to be renounced by everyone. By the midsummer of 1946, that seemed like an idealistic pipedream.

Truman rejected the plan. And at no point did Stalin believe that the Americans or the British would share any important nuclear technology with him. If they had not done so during the war, at a time when there was close military collaboration against the Nazis, he could not imagine them doing so now. If the tables

---

* Churchill and Roosevelt were seriously concerned that Bohr would help the Russians with nuclear research. Though he did not know all the secrets of the Manhattan Project, he knew of its existence, was friendly with many of the scientists who worked on it, and as one of the greatest theoretical physicists of his age, might have been in a position to give the Soviets some crucial information. He didn't. But he had approached President and Prime Minister urging them to share research with the Soviets. A secret addendum was made to the Hyde Park agreement: 'Enquiries should be made regarding the activities of Professor Bohr and steps should be taken to ensure that he is responsible for no leakages of information, particularly to Russians.'

had been turned he certainly would not have shared any secrets with the West.

Amidst much fanfare, the United Nations Atomic Energy Commission was established to look at ways that nuclear power could be used for peaceful purposes. Throughout the spring and summer the Americans and Soviets debated a variety of ideas that would later be called 'non-proliferation' proposals, but they were window dressing. Neither side was genuinely interested in a deal. Nothing at this time would have stopped the Soviets working to build their bomb – and the Americans would not give up theirs. At the talks, the Americans came up with a proposal that the Soviets should renounce any idea of building a weapon, while the US would keep their bomb and hold it 'in trust for mankind'. This was not an attractive idea from the Soviet point of view. The Russians proposed that the US should destroy their bombs and that everyone should promise not to build the weapons in future. Predictably, the US rejected that plan.

Bikini Atoll halted the negotiations. If the Americans had any serious idea of abandoning atomic weapons, it seemed curious to many – including those who witnessed the Bikini tests – that they were building and testing bigger and better ones.

*

An equally bitter nuclear dispute now surfaced within the 'Special Relationship'. The Americans stopped sharing atomic secrets with the British. Joint work ceased immediately after the destruction of Hiroshima and Nagasaki. British scientists who had been working at the laboratories in Los Alamos and elsewhere in the US returned home soon after VJ Day. The British assumed that the cooperation would continue and research would be shared, even though most of the funding and technical resources had come from the US. To their surprise, the Americans made it clear they were rethinking the wartime agreements. The British were furious, but the Government did not want to do anything to upset the delicate negotiations over the all-important US loan so its objections were diplomatic and understated. Attlee wrote to Washington politely expressing 'disappointment' but in private, though a man barely ever known to lose his temper, he took to regularly blasting his civil servants with abuse against the Americans.[9]

Attlee thought the wartime agreements were clear. At Hyde Park, Churchill and Roosevelt had resolved that 'full collaboration between the US and the British Government in developing tube alloys for military and commercial use should continue after the defeat of Japan, unless and until terminated by joint agreement.' But the mood in the US had changed, particularly among scientists, who saw no reason why British business should profit post-war from work that American scientists had undertaken as their patriotic duty.

Professor James Conant, a former President of Harvard and the Deputy Director of the National Defense Research Committee during the war, had witnessed the first bomb test in the New Mexico desert. He claimed that the British were more interested in 'post-war industrial purposes' than military uses and was entirely against continuing the partnership. He said he was sure he spoke for the majority of scientists, engineers, and technicians who had worked on the Manhattan Project.[10]

Former Secretary of War Stimson wrote to Truman asking, 'what right do the British have to the fruits of American labor? We . . . [did] nine tenths of the work.' The President wrote to London, changing the interpretation of the wartime agreements which he said did not apply to 'commercial exchanges and industrial development . . . [only] scientific data.' A month before the Bikini tests, Congress had passed the McMahon Act; this banned nuclear exchanges with any foreign government or agency, and Truman said his hands were tied.[11]

In London, many officials and ministers were perplexed. 'We must free ourselves of financial dependence on the US as soon as possible. We shall never be able to pull our weight . . . unless we are,' Bevin told the Cabinet.[12] As a result, Britain would develop its own nuclear bomb.

It is curious how little argument there was about it at the time. Britain might have been broke, but was willing to pay the price of remaining a Great Power. The Cabinet ministers Hugh Dalton and Sir Stafford Cripps opposed the decision on financial grounds, particularly when a Cabinet Committee was told in 1946 that it would cost £30–40 million *more* than the original estimate, an overspend of 15 per cent. But they were more or less alone. The matter was kept so secret that many ministers did not even know the bomb was being planned. The go-ahead was given in January 1947 and the Cabinet Committee that recommended it said simply that 'Britain cannot afford to be left behind.' Bevin, as so often, put it more colourfully. 'We've got to have the bloody thing. And we've got to have the bloody Union Jack flying on top of it.'[13]

\*

The American engineer and inventor Vannevar Bush was one of the first men to foresee the world-wide web. He did not know how it would happen, or when, but in the early Forties he was writing about 'wholly new forms of encyclopedias' that would somehow connect together electronically and communicate with each other. He is better known, however, as the chief civilian overseer of the Manhattan Project, a deft scientific administrator who, after the war, was appointed head of the US Office of Scientific Research and Development. Bush wondered how long the Americans could keep their monopoly, and was depressed by the quality of thought among politicians and decision makers, who he considered were deluding the public. He didn't expect them to understand the science behind the bomb, but they didn't seem to grasp the politics either: 'They thought, Members of Congress . . . and the public, that there was a secret, written perhaps on a single sheet of paper, some sort of magic formula. If we guard this, we alone would have the atom bomb indefinitely.'

He knew that the Russians would construct their bomb sooner rather than later. The scientists and engineers at Los Alamos and other military laboratories thought the US 'monopoly' would last three to five years. They knew that the Russians had talented people working on their atomic projects, who had developed significant elements of the bomb independently.

Bush pointed out that the basic 'secret' of the bomb was that it was feasible and would work. 'The rest is in the details of constructing . . . [the bombs] and the manufacturing process.' He told Truman that if the Soviets put enough resources into it, which they were bound to do, 'they will do it themselves within five years.' Some of the industrialists from DuPont, Union Carbide, and Eastman, the main companies which had worked on the Manhattan Project, thought it might take the Soviet leaders even less time.[14]

But that wasn't a message the White House wanted to hear, not least since it might strengthen the position of those who wanted to share the development of the bomb with the Russians.

The military was convinced that it would take the Russians far longer – probably two decades – to develop their weapon. General Leslie Groves, widely trusted as the man who ran America's atomic project during the war, and who still managed Los Alamos, was particularly adamant. He told the President, and a Senate inquiry, that the Soviets could not get their hands on enough uranium. The US had bought the entire supply from the world's biggest producer, the Belgian Congo, and in a dramatic Commando operation, had also spirited some out of Germany at the end of the war. Groves said there was 'definitely' none in the Soviet Union or Central Europe, despite evidence from several eminent scientists, geographers and mining engineers who told the administration otherwise.

But the politicians preferred to listen to the more reassuring voices of the military planners, who had administered the manufacture of the first bomb. Groves, as one presidential advisor said, presented scientists as errant and unstable individuals who were ill equipped to determine high policy. And it was Groves who comforted Congress with his comments at a Senate Committee hearing not long before the Bikini tests. 'The atomic bomb means complete victory in our hands until another nation gets it . . . there [is] no opportunity for a nation to arm secretly.'[15]

Truman believed his military advisors, for the time being. But by the end of the year he realised America's nuclear monopoly would be fleeting. Exactly a year after Stalin had summoned Kurchatov to the Kremlin and told him to speed up work on Task Number One, on Christmas Day 1946, Soviet scientists engineered a chain reaction of fissionable material – the crucial step in building a bomb. It would be another two years before the Russians had a usable weapon, but the nuclear arms race – one of the most familiar and significant military, political and cultural features of the Cold War – would be well under way before the end of 1946.

# 25

## The Glory of France: 'Resistance in the Heart'

One summer evening, the writer Arthur Koestler hosted a small dinner for six at an Arab bistro in the St Germain *quartier* of Paris. The party consisted of some of the most famous intellectuals in Europe at the time: Koestler, with his stunningly beautiful partner and soon to be wife, Mamaine Paget, Jean-Paul Sartre and his companion, Simone de Beauvoir, and the author Albert Camus, with his wife, Francine. The evening began quietly enough; Sartre was due to give a lecture to a conference of UNESCO the next day and had planned an early night.

But after dinner the party continued on, as Paget described, 'to a little *dancing* . . . [club] with blue and pink neon lights and men with hats on dancing with girls with very short skirts.' Paget said she 'saw the engaging spectacle' of Koestler 'lugging Castor [de Beauvoir's nickname], who has I think hardly ever danced in her life, around the floor' while Sartre, equally inexperienced, 'lugged Mme Camus.'

Koestler persuaded everyone to go on to the nearby Schehé-rézade, a White Russian nightclub that had been frequented by German officers during the Occupation. The gypsy music, the vodka and champagne, and the *zakouski* canapés which were the speciality of the house took their toll. Koestler, a one-time communist who had renounced the Party and was now an ardent cold warrior, launched into a vitriolic tirade against Stalin. His masterpiece, *Darkness at Noon*, about the Soviet purges of the late 1930s, had recently been published in France and quickly sold more than

250,000 copies. Sartre and de Beauvoir were fellow travellers, if not Party members, and, as loudly, defended communism as the inevitable way of the future. Camus was somewhere in the middle.

They all got even drunker, though Camus held his liquor the best. At around 4 a.m. Koestler herded the group to a bistro in Les Halles for some fortifying *soupe à l'oignon*, white wine, more champagne, and oysters. Sartre was especially drunk. He was continually 'pouring pepper and salt into paper napkins, then folding them up small and stuffing them in his pocket.' At eight in the morning de Beauvoir and Sartre, two giants of twentieth-century philosophy, were staggering along one of the bridges across the Seine, wondering out loud whether to throw themselves in. Sartre had just two hours' sleep but managed to write and deliver his lecture later in the day – to warm applause.[1]

Despite the humiliation of defeat in the war, the German Occupation, the trauma of score-settling immediately after liberation and the continuing political and economic crises since, Paris was beginning, slowly, to recover and was . . . still Paris. For a start, if you were well-off you could get decent food and wine. There were still nightclubs with music and dancing. The salons of glamorous, fashionable women were coming back. Ideas mattered and had consequences and people argued passionately about them – so different, as George Orwell observed, from life in austerity Britain, where nobody was arguing about ideas. He wrote soon after the war: 'The English are not sufficiently interested in intellectual matters to be intolerant about them.' France had suffered less physical damage than most of mainland Europe during the war, and Paris had hardly been bombed at all, apart from a few shells from the retreating Germans after the Allied liberation. The scars were different though deep.[2]

*

The 1946 Paris Peace Conference lasted from August to October and, despite stalling from various sides, finally settled treaties between the Allies and Italy, Hungary, Romania, Bulgaria and Finland. It lacked the pomp and panoply of the Paris conference of nearly thirty years earlier after the First World War, when the formalities took place in the Hall of Mirrors at the Palace of Versailles. Then, presidents and prime ministers had stayed in Paris for many weeks, deciding the fate of empires that had endured for centuries, creating new countries at the stroke of a pen. Now, it was the foreign ministers of sixteen nations who were settling matters, and they came and went throughout the summer for a series of meetings held at the Palais du Luxembourg. Earlier, there had been a series of separate meetings involving only the Allied powers. The decisions taken on the future of the Italian colonies, on Cyrenaica and on Finnish neutrality, mattered. Far more important was the mood that was set of deepening distrust between East and West, and at times within the Western alliance.

There were frequent – and perhaps ill-advised – official lunches. At a session one afternoon Bevin noticed that the British Ambassador to France, Duff Cooper, was nodding off to sleep. 'Tell Duff I'll call him if anything happens,' he told one of his ministerial aides. Then, rather more loudly, he added, 'He's the most sensible man in the room. It's all a waste of time.'[3]

On another occasion, Bevin repeated a comment he had made previously about the Soviets. 'We'll have to accept that in some parts of Europe all that has happened is that one set of crooks has been replaced by another.'[4]

The earlier meetings exposed a simmering dispute between France and the other Western Allies. France had secured an Occupation zone in Germany, comprising most of the large coal-producing area, the Saarland. At Yalta, neither the Americans nor the Soviets had intended the French to occupy any part of Germany; both Stalin and Roosevelt wondered why a 'defeated' nation – 'a humiliated nation' said Stalin, an unimportant country thought Roosevelt – should play a role in Germany at all. Churchill argued that as a 'great European power' the French should be treated as one of 'the victorious allies'. He prevailed, but the other Allies insisted that the French zone should be carved out of the British sector. Churchill agreed, but not from a romantic notion of French glory. If, as he thought, the Americans were going to pull their troops out of Europe within the next two to three years, Britain would need to work with France as a bulwark against the Russians and he wanted, as he put it, 'to build up the French.' Churchill had also insisted the French have a seat at the top table of the UN, as one of the permanent members of the Security Council.

A French Occupation zone was vital for the French exile leader General Charles de Gaulle, who in 1944 had returned to Paris as head of the Government, an occasion marked by a huge victory parade. For him *La Gloire* was both an emotion and a practical policy. Perhaps France wasn't the great power it had been, but part of de Gaulle's extraordinary post-war bluff was simply to carry on as though it still was. He argued powerfully that French unity depended on *amour propre*.

But at the beginning of 1946 de Gaulle resigned after a series of elections had, he said, made the country ungovernable. No political party had a majority, coalitions between the communists and the Right were unstable, and no individual had the power to make decisions. De Gaulle believed he was indispensable and that the people would demand his return as the saviour of the nation, as he had been in the summer of 1944. He would wait twelve years for the call.[5]

His successors agreed with the General about the Occupation zone in Germany. The French were understandably fixated on Germany. They wanted tough reparations – as they had after the First World War – and at first proposed the complete destruction of the German economy. They tried to insist on total German disarmament and they wanted most of the industry of the Ruhr and the coal mines of the Saar handed over to France. It was a deluded plan and never likely to happen. The Americans and British wanted to rebuild Germany, and argued that French recovery needed a strong Germany. It would be pointless to impoverish Germany if France's recovery depended on German coal and steel – and German expertise.

The argument had continued since VE Day. But during the Peace Conference in the summer of 1946, the French were dismayed to learn that the Americans and British planned to merge their Occupation zones into one, which would, essentially, create a state with democratic legitimacy and economy of scale. The timing was forced by the British, who could no longer afford to feed the Germans in their own sector. Bread rationing had just been introduced at home and there were complaints about Britons going hungry so the Germans could be fed.

But the US administration had already decided that there was little point in pretending that Germany could remain one state occupied by four powers. As Kennan had predicted: 'The idea of Germany run jointly with the Russians is a chimera. We have no choice but to lead our section of Germany – the section for which we and the British have accepted responsibility – to a form of independence so prosperous, so secure, so superior, that the east cannot threaten it . . . Better a dismembered Germany in which the west, at least, can act as a buffer to the forces of totalitarianism, than a united Germany which . . . brings these forces to the North Sea.' The Americans came up with a name from comic opera – and, as the Paris Conference began, 'Bizonia' was born.[*6]

The French and their allies were not getting on. None of the Western Allies were getting on with the Soviets. The atmosphere

---

* The French finally came round to the idea of merging the zones and in 1947 brought theirs into a new state. Thankfully nobody thought to christen it Trizonia. It became West Germany two years later. Finally, they saw the logic of reviving Germany, too, and worked out a system of sharing coal and steel production. That was the first of the institutions which subsequently grew to become the European Union. Germans used to tell the difference between the Occupation zones with a joke: 'The Americans promise little but give quite a lot. The Russians promise everything but give nothing. The British promise nothing and give nothing. The French promise . . . they will always hate us.'

at the Palais du Luxembourg, newly refurbished for the talks, was growing increasingly frosty.

But some Parisians were content. The diplomats and the politicians were providing plenty of trade for the city's restaurants and nightclubs, and as the novelist Nancy Mitford, who lived in Paris for much of her life, wrote to one of her sisters: 'I'm told the *maquereaux* [pimps] stop the Peace Conference people practically as they leave the Luxembourg and offer them *l'Amour Atomique*. Aren't they heaven?'[7]

\*

Like the British, the French had to beg a loan from the US. At $2.25 billion, it was smaller than Britain's, but having to go cap in hand to *les Américains* hurt French pride. France was in disastrous economic straits, having been bled dry by the Germans. The Nazis had made the Vichy administration pay vast sums for the privilege of being under German Occupation. The French had been forced to hand nearly all their foreign currency reserves over to the Germans, but even that was not enough. They found the rest by printing money, which fuelled inflation.

People survived, often by dispensing with the cash economy and returning to a barter system. Goods and services were exchanged and even factory workers were frequently paid in kind. Starvation was commonplace in many towns and cities. Those who lived in the country fared better, and those in better-off areas, unsurprisingly, did best. Rationing was tight. France was no longer occupied, but there were many American soldiers and officials, mainly in Paris, working for Allied agencies. SHAEF received disturbing reports well into the spring of 1946. 'The food position in France continues to be grave. Urban France has never approached the ration of 2,000 calories a head.' Another said the 'imbalance in consumption' was deeply worrying. Most French people were subsisting on 1,350 calories a day, according to SHAEF.

. But of course the black market distorted everything. It was endemic; almost everyone was breaking rules. At one of the smartest schools in Paris, the Lycée Condorcet, a group of schoolboys led by a thirteen-year-old was getting hold of chewing gum in bulk from the Americans and selling it at vast profit. Scams were everywhere; farmers sold produce illegally to diplomats with fuel allowances, who could load their cars with the produce and transport it. Restaurateurs made black-market deals with favoured customers. When firearms were briefly banned after liberation, there was a roaring illegal trade in ammunition. Anyone with access to foreign currency could make a fortune.

Hamilton Fish, the influential editor of *Foreign Affairs*, travelled through France in 1946. He reported: 'There is too little of everything – too few trains, buses, automobiles to transport people to work . . . too little flour to make bread without adulterants . . . and then too little to provide energy for hard labour; too little paper for newspapers to report more than a fraction of the world's news; too little seed for planting and too little fertilizer to nourish; too few houses to live in and not enough glass to supply them with windows; too little leather for shoes, wool for sweaters, gas for heating and cooking, cotton for diapers, sugar for jam, fats for frying, milk for babies, soap for washing . . .'[8]

Some of those who had plenty were shameless, albeit tastefully. Noël Coward recorded a party he held for the Duke and Duchess of Windsor. 'I gave them a delicious dinner: consommé, marrow on toast, grilled langouste, tournedos with sauce béarnaise and chocolate soufflé. Poor starving France.' But there was great resentment. The singer Yves Montand, performing at the Club de Cinq, was furious when he saw a customer order a whole lobster, pick at it, and then stub out a cigar in the half-eaten carcass. He stepped down from the stage and punched him.[9]

*

Around 6,000 people were killed in the first couple of months after the liberation in the so-called *épuration sauvage*, the savage purge, the first wave of revenge carried out by local vigilantes. Known 'collaborators' were lynched or shot, some officials were tortured to death, punished for the offence of 'national degradation' without even the benefit of a kangaroo court. Some women were murdered for horizontal collaboration – sleeping with the enemy – though the usual punishment was to be stripped in public, shorn of their hair, and tarred and feathered. Gradually, though, the law took its course, and in 1945 and 1946 there were 6,763 death sentences of which 791 were carried out by guillotine.

Wartime collaboration had been widespread, and the State had been the main collaborator. De Gaulle tried to unify the country with a narrative in which most French people had 'resisted', but France had been betrayed by the politicians of the pre-war Third Republic and then by a handful of traitors in the Vichy administration. De Gaulle said that throughout the Occupation French men and women had been loyal in their hearts, and usually in their deeds. Once the Vichy Government had gone, France would carry on as normal and forget the last few years.

A problem with this story is that Vichy was actually quite popular and had been installed constitutionally. People working for the regime could legitimately claim that they had done nothing illegal. After the war, around eleven thousand civil servants lost their jobs out of more than six million state employees, a small number compared to the thirty-five thousand who had been fired under the Vichy regime.

Neither had the women who had slept with Germans done anything illegal. A new law was passed governing their offence – 'national unworthiness' – but they were prosecuted retroactively. So were many others (49,723 in all), such as teachers who were overly enthusiastic supporters of Vichy. The punishment was usually the loss of the vote; men had to return their war medals and some were jailed. But most of the judges who sentenced them had sat on the bench during the Vichy administration. Nobody was punished for anything resembling a crime against humanity

– for example, rounding up Jews for transport to the concentration camps in the East. These, like other war crimes, were supposed to have been committed only by the Germans.[10]

*

The Duke and Duchess of Windsor, according to Nancy Mitford in a letter to Evelyn Waugh, 'are telling everyone that France is on the verge of Communism and they must put their jewels in a safe place.' Since the liberation, the communists had been in a series of coalition governments, though always in a minority. But it is true that they won the most votes in the first elections after the war, with 26.5 per cent, though in the poll of June 1946 they fell back to second place behind the Christian Democratic Mouvement Républicain Populaire. In the middle of 1946 the French Communist Party had more members than any other in Europe, outside the USSR. They still claimed a high reputation as the Party of the 75,000 murdered, a vastly exaggerated reference to the number of reprisals against supposed communist resistance fighters.[11]

But the communists would not try to seize power by force, and Stalin would never have allowed it. He was interested in them, supplied them with small amounts of money, and gave them large quantities of moral support, but always told them to stick to a peaceful road. The French Party leader, Maurice Thorez – 'his enemies took his muscular, rubbery face as a mask of deceit' – had spent most of the war in exile in Moscow. He had met Stalin only twice in nearly five years in Russia, and the second time was the day before he returned to Paris when the Soviet leader told him to do nothing 'to upset our alliance with the US'. Thorez, forty-six when the Paris Peace Conference began, a former miner who had educated himself with the help of a formidable memory, was a Stalinist through and through. He obeyed, though many French comrades were disappointed that the Soviets were not encouraging them to seize power.[12]

Thorez repeatedly received messages from the Kremlin

advising him to avoid anything that might result in a break with the West, and 'to continue the path of joining a popular front'. Both Stalin and Thorez believed that in time the French CP could win enough votes to lead a coalition, but Thorez was careful. The CP organised strongly in the trades unions and seduced into the Party or into its orbit as many intellectuals as they could but did nothing unconstitutional.

Nonetheless, the Americans and the British were alarmed precisely *because* Thorez was so correct and apparently sensible. 'It looks as though the communists are having everything their own way everywhere,' said the British Ambassador, Duff Cooper. The American Ambassador, Jefferson Caffery, reported to the State Department: 'Paris is a veritable hive of Communist agents. The Soviet Trojan horse is so well camouflaged that millions of Communist militants, sympathisers and opportunists have been brought to believe that the best way of defending France is to identify French national interests with the aims of the Soviet Union.'[13]

Many French people were equally concerned about the influence of another foreign power on France. Simone de Beauvoir, not long after her evening at the Schehérézade club, went on a lecture tour in the US. 'Their anti-Communism bordered on neurosis; their attitude towards Europe, towards France, was one of arrogant condescension ... I heard students, teachers and journalists seriously wondering whether it wouldn't be better to drop their bombs on Moscow before the USSR was in a position to fight back. It was explained to me that in order to defend freedom it was becoming necessary to suppress it. The witch hunt was getting underway.' Back in Paris, she saw some American soldiers in a restaurant. 'We had loved them, these tall soldiers in khaki, who had looked so peaceful; they were our liberty ... Now they represent our dependence and moral threat.'[14]

The writer Robert Aron seemed to represent the majority. He did not love all that America had to offer. Its economic system was not a 'model of humanity'. But the choice for individuals, as for nations, was 'to be in the universe of the free ... or else in that of lands placed under harsh ... rule.' It was fairly straightforward. 'It is never a struggle between good and evil, but between the preferable and the detestable.'[15]

# 26

## Stalin's Turkish Bluff

Towards the end of his life, the slavishly loyal Molotov admitted that his boss made one big mistake. Stalin had got almost everything right in decades of power, he said, except with regard to Turkey in 1946. There he had miscalculated badly, and the Soviets and Americans nearly stumbled into a war neither of them wanted. It was avoided only by the quick action of a British spy.

During August and September, as we have seen, the Paris Peace Conference became increasingly ill-tempered. At one of their first meetings Ernest Bevin had likened Molotov to Hitler; the Soviet luminary (who had actually met Hitler) first looked shocked, then sneered and turned his back on the British Foreign Secretary. Bevin apologised but the encounter festered. Bevin had loathed communists since they had tried to penetrate his beloved Transport and General Workers' Union and some sections of the Labour Party in the Twenties and Thirties, and seldom hid his feelings. In Paris he said, 'Molotov is like a communist in a local Labour Party. Treat him badly and he makes the most of his grievance and if you treat him well he only puts his price up and abuses you afterwards.'[1]

Behind the scenes, the Soviets were trying to bully the Turkish Government into granting them military bases on the Bosphorus – a key Russian objective since Tsarist times – and free access for warships through the Hellespont. Immediately after the war, Stalin had demanded joint ownership with the Turks of the small towns of Kars and Ardahan in north-eastern Turkey. They had been conquered by Russia in the reign of Catherine the Great, but were ceded back to Turkey by Lenin in 1921, when the Bolsheviks were preoccupied with the Russian Civil War. The Turks refused and at Potsdam the Americans and the British had backed them. The Soviets could have access through the Straits but no bases.

Stalin would not give up. There were 200,000 Soviet troops in Bulgaria and 75,000 in Romania. He calculated that if he exerted enough pressure on the Turks they would give in to Soviet demands and the Western Allies would accept it as a fait accompli.

Molotov for once disagreed with the Soviet leader. 'The West won't accept it. It is a step too far,' he told Stalin; as he said later, 'It was always an ill-timed and unrealistic thing . . . but Stalin insisted and [ordered me] to go ahead and push for joint ownership.'[2]

The Turks approached the Americans for help. Convinced that the Soviets were preparing to invade Turkey, Truman saw this as a major test of his tougher 'containment' policy. In the Oval office on the morning of Thursday 15 August, he met the Joint Chiefs of Staff, the Director of Central Intelligence, and Dean Acheson, standing in for the Secretary of State, Byrnes, who was in Paris. The generals and the intelligence chief reported that there was no obvious sign of Soviet troop movements in the Balkans, but this was far more a political than a military matter. Acheson had not urged a strong line in the Iran crisis six months earlier; instead, he had recommended leaving the Russians a graceful exit route. This time, however, he was unequivocal. 'It is a vital American interest to deter the Soviets,' he told the President. 'And it can only be done if the Soviets are persuaded that the United States is prepared to meet their aggression with force of arms.'[3]

Truman agreed almost at once. He ordered the immediate despatch of a fleet to the Mediterranean. The Pentagon had the previous year begun work on Operation Pincher, a plan for war in the Middle East, but it had been left in abeyance. The President wanted the plan looked at carefully once again.*

He asked Acheson to approach the British and ask them to allow American B-29s, armed with atom bombs, to use bases in England. He also said he would pursue Acheson's policy 'to the end'. Acheson said later that Truman had made his decisions so quickly that one of the generals asked him whether he entirely understood the implications. Truman reached into his desk, pulled out a large and well-worn wall map of the world, and began to lecture the room about the historic importance of the Middle East from ancient times. 'We might as well find out if the Russians are bent on world conquest now as in five or ten years,' he declared.[4]

Four days later, 19 August, the State Department told Molotov emphatically that the 'defence of the Straits is a matter best left to Turkey'. Soviet ships could pass through peacefully, but if there was any threat or attack intended to secure Soviet bases in Turkey it would be 'subject to UN Security Council action'. The implication was that the US would go to Turkey's defence.

Tension was increased the same day when the US heard that the Yugoslavs had shot down an unarmed US Army C-47 transport plane, killing its five-man crew. The plane was just two miles into Yugoslavian air space and the attack came without warning.

---

* The British, too, had worked out a war plan against the Soviets, but in Europe, and the idea was to use German soldiers if necessary. Churchill, two weeks before his defeat in the 1945 election, told his Imperial Chiefs of Staff to plan a 'hypothetical' attack on the USSR. The planners were told they would have the 'full support' of the British and American governments. It was code-named Unthinkable – which, only two months after VE Day, it was. The brief was 'how to impose upon Russia the will of the US and the British Empire' to get a 'square deal' for Eastern Europe. Despite the superior numbers of the Red Army, the plan was to attack with forty-seven divisions and quickly penetrate further inside the Soviet Union than Germany managed in 1941/42. Even using the former enemy's forces the planners reckoned the odds were 'fanciful'. Sir Alan Brooke (later Lord Alanbrooke), Chief of the Imperial General Staff, wrote in his diary: 'The whole idea was fantastic and the chances of success quite impossible.' The scheme was quietly dropped – and Churchill never mentioned its existence in his detailed war memoirs.

It was coincidence, entirely unplanned, and had nothing to do with the Russians, but the President and the State Department were sceptical. Many in the administration saw Tito as a stalking horse for Stalin and did not believe rumours of an imminent split in the communist 'camp'. Immediately the news of the downed plane came through, Eisenhower, Chairman of the Joint Chiefs, cautioned against over-reacting. It wasn't a crisis, he said. He told the Defense Department he didn't think that the shooting down of a transport plane was a cause for war.[5]

Later that night, Acheson summoned the new British Ambassador in Washington, the recently ennobled Lord Inverchapel – who, as Sir Archibald Clark Kerr, had been Ambassador to Moscow until a few weeks previously – to the State Department. He reported Truman's comment that he would see the matter through 'to the end.' The Ambassador asked if the US was prepared to go to war. Acheson looked grave and replied that, 'The President fully realised the seriousness of the issue and was prepared to act accordingly.'[6]

In Washington they waited for the next step. Molotov explained, 'It is good we retreated in time or . . . there would have been joint aggression against us.' The Soviets climbed down two days later and withdrew their demands for bases. Molotov said they had 'over-reached' and intriguingly added, 'Intelligence may have prevented the outbreak of war.'[7]

It was in fact the Soviet agent Donald Maclean, part of the Cambridge spy ring, who had prevented it. Maclean was then First Secretary at the British Embassy in Washington. He knew about the conversation between his boss, Lord Inverchapel, and Acheson, and read the cable the Ambassador had sent back to London highlighting Truman's comment that he would see the matter 'through to the end'. He urgently passed the information to Moscow.

Stalin had never intended to provoke a war. As Molotov said, he was 'probing' to see exactly how far the West would go, in line with

Lenin's dictum: 'You probe with bayonets. When you feel soft flesh, push further. If you meet resistance, feel steel, you withdraw and think again.' Now Stalin had a better understanding of the Americans – or thought he had.

The crisis did not change Molotov's view of spies. He relied on them extensively. As one KGB agent who was seconded from 'the organs' to work with him recalled, 'We were stretched to the limit with the demands he made . . . Molotov flew into rages when he felt he was not sufficiently informed. "Why", he once roared, "why are there no documents?" '[8]

Molotov distrusted everybody; it was a cast of mind among the Soviet chieftains. But he reserved special suspicion for spies. 'One cannot rely on intelligence officers. One can listen to them, but it is necessary to check up on them. Intelligence officers can lead you to a very dangerous position . . . there are . . . [among them] many provocateurs here there and everywhere.'

President Truman saw the Turkey crisis as a bloodless victory, a vindication of the policy of 'containment'. The Russians perceived it differently – they were never intending to attack the Turks anyway. The end result, though, was that Stalin's 'probe' into Turkey used up much of his political capital in the US and in Europe. He was never given the benefit of the doubt again; there would soon be American military bases in Turkey, right along the USSR's southern border – and the hand of cold warriors in Washington who were recommending a firm hand against the Russians was strengthened.

# 27

## The Bloodbath in Calcutta

By eight in the morning of Friday 16 August the temperature in the centre of Calcutta was already thirty-one degrees centigrade, with humidity of 91 per cent. It was the height of the monsoon season. Mohammed Ali Jinnah had called this Direct Action Day, a day of strikes and demonstrations (in Urdu and Hindi a *hartal*) in which Muslims throughout India would pledge their commitment to the creation of Pakistan and their opposition to the Congress. Throughout most of the country, Jinnah's repeated calls for a peaceful day of protest were heeded. But in Calcutta the *hartal* was the start of three days of bloody riots that left more than six thousand people dead, at least fifteen thousand injured and an overpowering stench of decomposing bodies throughout Bengal's main city.

The proximate cause for Direct Action Day was the formation of an interim government of Indians following the spring elections. Jinnah claimed that there were not enough senior positions being offered to Muslims by the British and what he called 'the Fascist Grand Council' of the Congress. He issued a message calling for all League followers 'to conduct themselves peacefully and in a disciplined manner and not to play into the hands . . . of enemies.'

But on the morning of the *hartal*, League supporters opened their newspaper to find a prominent advertisement:

Today is Direct Action Day.

Today Muslims of India dedicate their lives and all they possess
to the cause of freedom

Today let every Muslim swear in the name of Allah to resist
aggression

Direct Action is now their only course

Because they offered peace but peace was spurned

They honoured their word but they were betrayed

They claimed Liberty but were offered Thraldom

Now Might alone can secure their Right.

The Mayor of Calcutta was quoted on a handbill advertising a
rally planned for early in the afternoon: 'We Muslims have had the
crown and have ruled. Do not lose heart, be ready and take
swords. Oh Kafir! [heathen unbelievers] Your doom is not far and
the great massacre will come.'[1]

Throughout the morning, as the day became stickier and
hotter, Muslims headed for the *maidan*, the public open space in
the heart of the city where the demonstration was due to begin.
Calcutta's Hindus had prepared for trouble. Many had barricaded
themselves into their areas of the city. Hindu criminal gangs
(*goondas*) had been arming themselves for a week in advance of the
Muslim Direct Action Day, and that morning they had blocked
two bridges across the Hooghly river to prevent Muslims reaching
the rally.

At around 2 p.m., tens of thousands of men, some armed with
knives, *lathis* and assorted clubs, congregated by the Ochterlony
monument, a famously ugly 165-foot obelisk, topped by a Byzan-
tine-style mini-dome. It was built in 1828 in honour of Sir David
Ochterlony, the Scottish general who won the war to annexe
Nepal. The monument was one of the principal landmarks of
British Calcutta. That afternoon, it was where the corpulent
Chief Minister of Bengal and one of the main leaders of the
Muslim League, Husain Shaheed Suhrawardy – 'one of the most

inefficient, conceited and crooked politicians in India . . . a self-seeking careerist with no principles' according to the Viceroy, Lord Wavell – made an incendiary speech. No reliable record of his exact words exists, but many who were there remembered it as bloodcurdling, especially under the circumstances.

Within a few minutes of the demonstration breaking up, fires were burning throughout Calcutta. Nobody knows precisely how the violence started or who struck the first blow, but Muslims looted Hindu homes and shops, and Hindus brutally retaliated. At 4.15 p.m., the British military headquarters in Calcutta, Fort William, sent out an urgent code-word 'Red', informing the rest of British India that serious violence had broken out in the city.

The British Commander, Lieutenant General Sir Francis Tuker, ordered a curfew. When troops from the Green Howards moved around the city, they saw that the violence had spread from the city centre to the docks and the poor slum areas on the outskirts. Contemporary accounts are harrowing. Jugal Chandra Ghosh, who ran a gymnasium for young Hindu men, admitted he had helped organise a 'retaliation squad' after Muslims had attacked his street. 'I saw . . . four trucks standing, all with dead bodies about three feet high; like molasses in sacks they were stacked on trucks and blood and brain was oozing out . . . the whole sight of it had a tremendous impression on me.' The result was that he went and killed more Muslims. Another Hindu *goonda* remembered that 'a Congress politician took me around in his jeep. I saw many dead bodies. Hindu dead bodies. I told him . . . there would be retaliation.'

'People . . . [were] intoxicated, either with alcohol or enthusiasm,' recalled Sayed Nazim Hashim, a Muslim university student. There was a 'euphoria' among Leaguers he said, as if in battle. Huge portraits of Jinnah riding on a white horse and brandishing a scimitar were carried through the city. Another student remembered the sight of College Street, home to dozens of Muslim booksellers, after the riot. 'When we went there . . . we saw dead bodies piled up on both sides, men, women, children, and all the books on the road, burnt, gutted.'[2]

There was calm for a few hours overnight, but the next day violence erupted again, worse than the previous day. There had been numerous riots between Hindus and Muslims before in India, but none had been on this scale or of this intense ferocity. On the second day, Calcutta's small Sikh community joined in 'charging through the Muslim areas, slaying indiscriminately', according to a witness. Nobody was safe; unbelievers – secularists – had to be identified with one community or another. They took to wearing red crosses on their clothes to indicate they were neither Hindu nor Muslim, but it made no difference.

Neither the police nor the army could bring the city under control. Calcutta looked like a battlefield. General Tuker reported to the Viceroy: 'It was unbridled savagery, with homicidal maniacs let loose to kill and to maim and to burn. The Underworld of Calcutta was taking control of the city . . . the police were not controlling it.'[3]

The Governor of Bengal, Sir Frederick Burrows, was horrified when he went on a heavily guarded tour of Calcutta on the third day. 'I can honestly say that parts of the city are as bad as anything I saw when I was with the Guards on the Somme . . . I actually saw a crowd clubbing three unfortunate individuals to death . . . many corpses were stripped and mutilated.'[4]

The army sent large-scale reinforcements – four British battalions, with another on the way, and two Indian battalions, with two more due within the next few days. By the Monday, 19 August, when the temperature reached nearly forty degrees, there were forty-five thousand troops in Calcutta and some semblance of order was restored. Dead bodies littered the streets. One journalist counted fifty corpses piled high on Upper Chitpore Road, one of the city's main thoroughfares. He reported how vultures enjoyed feeding on them, preferring the human flesh and ignoring dead dogs lying nearby. Tuker wanted to begin burying the dead, fearing an outbreak of cholera, but that offended the religious feelings of both sides. Yet he risked their religious wrath. Soldiers were awarded bonus payments for carrying the dead to the Muslim burial grounds or the Hindi burning *ghats*. It took a day and a night to clear all the rotting corpses from the city streets.[5]

Those who could leave the city took the first available opportunity. More than a hundred thousand fled in three days; the roads out of Calcutta were clogged. Even though at least one train had been stopped and the crew of Sikhs butchered, people tried desperately to leave by train. Howrah railway station looked like a refugee camp. When a rough-and-ready body count was made after the city quieted down, nearly three-quarters of the dead were Muslims.

\*

The Great Calcutta Killings, as they were called, were the first of the wave of massacres that accompanied the Partition of India the following summer. Nobody knows exactly how many people were killed. The best estimate is between 1 million and 1.2 million. Around 15 million people were uprooted in a mass migration. The world had never been so full of refugees.

In the immediate aftermath of the riots, Jinnah was blamed by both the British and the Congress for calling the Direct Action Day, and the Muslim League was blamed for ratcheting up the rhetoric of Islamic nationalism. But all the leaders in India were guilty of playing ethnic politics and then affecting surprise when their harsh words resulted in violent deeds.

Nehru said that 'when the British go there will be no more communal trouble in India'. Nor did Jinnah foresee what would happen when the country was split. The Hindu and Muslim elites occasionally mixed socially, and there were close friendships – but even then they were invariably hedged with caste rules and all kinds of Koranic taboos. The mass of Hindus and Muslims had lived separate lives, usually in separate villages and clearly delineated areas of major towns and cities. They strictly followed their separate customs. It is a comforting myth that the Muslims and Hindus had got on peaceably for centuries before the British arrived. There were periods when the Mughal empire had been relatively tolerant of unbelievers, but others when it was anything but.

The British may have done little to unite them over the centuries, but divide and rule was not a deliberate policy or a conspiracy; rather, it had been a convenience on occasions. But certainly not in 1946. As V. P. Menon, the most senior Indian-born civil servant in the Government, who had watched a succession of colonial administrators come and go, observed: 'The policy [of] the British government in India ... evolved more by the exigencies of the circumstances than as a result of deliberate planning.'[6]

Gandhi understood motivation in a way the more elitist leaders did not. He had fought all his life for a united India and had tried desperately in his unique way to halt the riots. Twice he managed, if only for a short while. Massacres in Bombay stopped when he went on a hunger strike at the end of 1946. He led by example, but fewer people than before were following it. Halting the bloodshed or preventing the breakup of India was beyond him. 'If the vast majority of Muslims regard themselves as a separate nation, no power on earth can compel them to think otherwise. If they want to partition India they must ... unless Hindus want to fight,' he had said as early as 1942.[7]

Besides, he knew a great deal about separateness. When his son Manilal was caught kissing a young married Indian woman, Gandhi had forced her into shaving her head and extracted a pledge of lifelong chastity from him. Manilal kept to the vow for many years, but in 1926 he fell in love with a Muslim girl, Fatima, and announced he would marry her. Gandhi was appalled and insisted the marriage should be called off. He wrote to his son: 'Your desire is against your religion. It would be like putting two swords in one scabbard . . . Your marriage will be a great jolt to Hindu–Moslem relations.' His son obeyed and the marriage was not to be.[8]

*

The riots hastened British withdrawal. The Labour Government had originally planned to hand over power in the middle of 1948, but plans were brought forward, and at the end of 1946 Attlee appointed Lord Louis Mountbatten to be the last Viceroy. Mountbatten was a master of public relations and his task the following year was somehow to present the end of the Raj as a victory for British decency and stewardship of India. Others, Churchill for example, called it an indecent 'scuttle'. Attlee was often reminded that there would probably be a catastrophe in India when the British left, but he would say, at least in private, that the disaster 'won't be on our watch'.

In November 1946 Attlee had brought Nehru, Jinnah and other leaders to London in one last effort to agree a power-sharing arrangement in a united India. The summit started badly. The delegation flew to Britain on the same small plane, but Jinnah arrived late for take-off and did not utter a word to anybody on the flight, except to order a beer before breakfast from the cabin steward. After four days of meandering negotiations in Downing Street, the talks had got nowhere, and the group returned home on an equally unfriendly flight.

Attlee then fired Wavell, who had prepared a plan for Britain to withdraw within a year unless the Government agreed to a 'massive military reinforcement'. Even that could only last a decade or so. He said that already, in most of India, the powers of the Government 'can only be enforced to a limited degree by persuasion and bluff'. The plan, named Operation Madhouse, recommended fairly detailed boundaries for partitioning India.

Attlee rejected it as 'alarmist' – and then brought in Mountbatten to push through an almost identical plan.

It was Attlee who decided the timing of the British withdrawal – by August 1947 – not, as Mountbatten claimed in various misleading accounts, the last Viceroy himself. The Prime Minister had the last word and continually pushed for the hastiest retreat possible.[9]

The boundaries of the new state of Pakistan were decided by a High Court judge, Sir Cyril Radcliffe, who knew very little about India. His Boundary Commission had forty-seven days to decide on complex arrangements to separate people who had lived side by side, or at least tolerated one another, for centuries. Now they could tolerate one another no longer.

It was often said the Hindus got the best out of both Partition and the financial settlement that accompanied it. Most Labour politicians in Britain got on far better with the leftish Congress leaders than with the Muslim Leaguers. Attlee loathed Jinnah, whom he called, misleadingly, 'the only Indian fascist I ever met'. But the Congress lost their main prize: a united, secular India. Jinnah and the Muslims got theirs, even if it was not all that they had dreamed of but, instead, as some Muslims put it, 'a moth-eaten Pakistan'.

The British were blamed for withdrawing so fast. Could they not have stayed for a short while to oversee a peaceful partition – if there had to *be* partition? It seems a fanciful notion. To most Indians, Hindu or Muslim, the British were the Army of Occupation. Having had two hundred years' 'stewardship' of the subcontinent, it is hard to see how a further two years would have made much of a difference. For Indian leaders of both sides the British were the problem, not the solution. They did not want the British there. Nehru made the point plain: 'I would rather have every village in India go up in flames than keep a single British soldier in India a moment longer than necessary,' he said.[10]

European colonialism was no longer sustainable. And it effectively ended when the Union flag was lowered at the Vice-regal Lodge in Delhi. Chakravarti Rajagopalachari, who became Governor-General of India a year after the British left, said that if the British had not transferred power when they did 'there could well have been no power to transfer.'[11]

# 28

## 'Half-Nun, Half-Whore'

On the evening of 16 August, some of the best-known authors in Russia were packed into the lecture hall of the Leningrad Writers' Union, a beautiful building of classical simplicity just off Nevsky Prospekt, the city's main thoroughfare. It was a muggy night and the atmosphere was tense, anticipation mixed with apprehension. Most people in the audience had been primed to expect that the main speaker would say something dramatic and important.

The main speaker was a plump, pasty-faced figure with a neat moustache. Wheezing and sweating profusely, Andrey Zhdanov, then aged fifty and looking the picture of ill health, was among the most powerful and feared Communist Party grandees in the USSR. He launched into his theme immediately, with a vicious attack on a celebrated and much-loved daughter of Leningrad, the poet Anna Akhmatova. Zhdanov could barely contain his sneering bile:

> Her subject matter is thoroughly individualistic. The range of her poetry is pitifully limited, with her petty, narrow private life, her trivial experiences. This is the poetry of a feral lady from the salons, moving between the boudoir and the prayer-stool. It is based on erotic motifs linked with motifs of mourning, melancholy death, mysticism and isolation . . . she is half-nun, half-whore, or rather both whore and nun, fornication and prayer being intermingled in her world.

Zhdanov then turned his attention to another highly respected Leningrad writer, the popular satirist Mikhail Zoschenko – 'a vulgar and trivial petty bourgeois, who oozes anti-Soviet poison, indulges in vile obscenities and political hooliganism.' Russian writers, he said, had been given too much latitude during the war, they had been far too influenced by the decadent West, and it was time to return to Soviet styles in all forms of art, socialist realism and 'morally and politically sound values'.[1]

This infamous speech signalled a new crackdown on artists. It spread quickly from literature to painting, music, film-making and even architecture. The Russians called it the *Zhdanovshchina*, but it was orchestrated by Stalin, who regarded his cultural purge with great seriousness. Zhdanov was the rottweiler, but he was doing his master's bidding.

*

Born in the Sea of Azov port of Mariupol, Andrey Zhdanov came from the minor nobility (as had Lenin and Molotov). His father, like Lenin's, was a nineteenth-century schools inspector, his mother a trained pianist of the highest order who taught her son to play well. He was widely read in the classics, but knew nothing about painting. He fancied himself an intellectual, and Stalin respected his intelligence, though others doubted his depth: 'more a librarian, than an intellectual', according to one fellow Kremlin magnate. An obsessively hard worker, he was a favourite of Stalin's not only for his diligence, but also for his fathomless sycophancy, and he was quickly promoted to senior positions in Stalin's court. Unusually, Stalin addressed him with the familiar *ty* – similar to the French *tu* – rather than the more formal *vy* he used to his other underlings. Stalin persuaded his daughter, Svetlana, to marry Zhdanov's son, Yury, and Zhdanov senior was considered by many Kremlin watchers to be number two in the hierarchy – a dangerous place to be.[2] But however useful and obedient Zhdanov was, Stalin could still turn on him, as he did on everybody at some point or another. At one of the interminable dinners at Stalin's dacha, despite knowing Zhdanov had heart problems, severe asthma and chronic hypertension, the Leader was provoked by Zhdanov's silence at the table. According to Svetlana's account, he pointed to his 'favourite', looked coldly in his direction, 'and said "look at him, sitting there like a little Christ as if nothing was of any concern to him." Zhdanov grew pale and beads of perspiration stood out on his forehead.'[*][3]

For Stalin, who read so much, writers were crucially important, 'the engineers of the soul' as he often put it. Unlike his lick-spittle Zhdanov, who had probably not read the lyrical and haunting poems of Akhmatova, Stalin certainly had. The object of the cultural terror would not be just to revive Marxist–Leninist purity; it was more about Russian nationalism and a paranoid suspicion of the West – which is why the *Zhdanovshchina* mattered to the rest of the world outside the writers' unions or the concert halls in the Soviet Union. 'Some of our literary people . . . have slipped into a tone of servility and cringing before philistine foreign literature,' Stalin said, echoing the tenor of the instructions he was giving to Molotov at international conferences. The ideological purge would soon extend to the sciences, too, resulting in extravagant and inaccurate claims that Russian researchers had made important discoveries in a range of natural sciences.[4]

Stalin was a severe film critic too. He met the great director Sergei Eisenstein after he had watched a preview of the second part of *Ivan the Terrible*. He had broadly approved Part One, released in 1944, and Eisenstein intended to make a trilogy. But Stalin thought Part Two was 'some kind of nightmare', lacking Russian pride, and in places simply inaccurate. 'It does not show historical

---

[*] Two months after launching the cultural purge Zhdanov had a heart attack and had to rest in the Crimea, where he remained for several weeks. He died in 1948 and there were numerous conspiracy theories throughout the Soviet years that he was killed, either on Stalin's orders, or by rogue elements within 'the organs', or rival magnates jealous of his position. None is plausible. He was so ill and weak during the last years of his life, smoked so heavily, and worked so much, that he could have died at any moment.

figures correctly in their period,' Stalin told the film-maker. 'For instance, in the first part, it was wrong that Ivan spent so long kissing his wife. That was not tolerated in those times . . . Your Tsar is indecisive, like Hamlet . . . everyone suggests to him what should be done but he cannot make a decision.'*5

Then Stalin reached the more clearly political points relevant to the present. 'Ivan was prudent, a national Tsar. He did not allow foreign influences into Russia whereas Peter [The Great] opened the gates to Europe and let in too many foreigners. Ivan was very cruel. You can show he was cruel. But you have to show why he *had* to be cruel.'

Stalin took immense time and trouble over the attack on artists. A week before Zhdanov's Leningrad speech, he had summoned Boris Likharev, editor of the obscure, small-circulation literary journal *Leningrad*, to a late-night meeting at the Kremlin. Stalin told Likharev that he had read the latest issue and wondered why it contained pieces translated from foreign writers. 'Is it worthy of Soviet men to walk on tiptoe in front of foreign countries? This is how you cultivate servile feelings. This is a great sin.' The editor was terrified but managed to mumble that it was true his journal every now and then published foreign writers but not very often. Stalin rebuked him. 'By doing this you are instilling the feeling that we are second rate . . . which is wrong. You are the pupils; they are the teacher. In its essence this is wrong.' Some writers were jailed or sent to labour camps in the Arctic wastes – Aleksandr Solzhenitsyn, for example – though it was not on the scale of the purges in the 1930s. But as it was designed to do, the *Zhdanovshchina* enforced self-censorship on writers and other artists. Soviet cultural life went into a deep freeze until Stalin's death.6

---

\* Part Two did not come out until 1958, well after Eisenstein's death (1948) and Stalin's (1953), and, when it finally did appear, there were very few kisses in it.

# 29

## The Return of the King

When King George II of Greece returned from exile on Friday 27 September he found that his royal villa at Tatoi, just outside Athens, had been looted, the trees in the woods cut down for firewood and dozens of corpses buried in shallow graves throughout the grounds. It was his second restoration to the throne; and his father, too, had been forced into exile after the First World War. Asked soon after he came back what a good king needed he replied, 'A suitcase. All Greek kings need a good suitcase.'[1]

In the plebiscite organised by the British at the beginning of the month, a two-thirds majority had favoured the return of the monarchy, but it was not a triumphant return for King George, aged fifty-six and already seriously ill from arteriosclerosis. He looked a decade or more older than he was. Voters may have hoped that the monarchy would be the best chance to unite a country torn apart by civil war, but even many of those who voted for restoration had doubts about the King himself. Famously, he had charm and wit, but he was never loved, and was still identified with the pre-war dictatorship. He disowned the Metaxas regime eventually but far too late – only when it was doomed, had killed hundreds of opponents from right and left, and had descended into brutality – as well as grotesque absurdities. Under Metaxas, the works of Plato and Xenophon were banned, as were any books that contained Pericles' funeral oration as recorded by Thucydides.

Greece was a shambles. Significant parts of the country were controlled by the communist insurgents, the *andartes*; other parts were in the hands of the far-right 'security battalions', death squads. The fragile government was kept in place by the British army and increasing numbers of American advisors, civil servants and large amounts of American money. When Bevin met George II shortly before the King returned to Athens, the Foreign Secretary pleaded with him to go back and act as a constitutional monarch like his cousin, Britain's George VI. 'Kings are pretty cheap these days,' Bevin reminded him. But George II interfered in politics almost immediately. Within a month of his return the American Ambassador to Greece, Lincoln MacVeagh, was reporting back to Washington: 'The King, who has been brought back as a solution for the problems the politicians will not tackle, is the same old, muddled, indecisive figure that he always was.'[2]

The Government's writ ran in half the country, in Athens and in most of the big towns, but there were endless rifts in the majority Party and its supporters. Some leading government figures were well-known former Nazi collaborators, such as the Minister for Public Order, Napoleon Zervas, who according to MacVeagh was running such a brutal security apparatus that he was 'making more communists than he is eliminating'.[3]

The rebels were mostly being supplied and financed by the Yugoslavs, and communist guerrillas were trained by former Partisans who had fought under Tito. There were splits in their ranks, too, which at times blew up into violent conflict between rival *andarte* bands. Some wanted an urban uprising in Athens and other cities; others wanted to wage a peasant war in the countryside. In some villages and towns which the communists controlled, anyone even remotely middle class was beaten up or sometimes killed.

Subhi Sadi, the Chase Bank's Middle East representative and anything but a leftist, went to Greece in the late autumn of 1946 to negotiate a loan. He travelled around the country extensively. Greece, he reported back to his New York headquarters, 'is in a complete state of chaos, and outside the cities in . . . anarchy.

Actually there are two Greece's: the cities such as Athens, Piraeus and Salonica, where the Government is in control, but with the help of strong security – and the rest.'[4]

The Americans, who were now running much of the country's administration, were appalled by the incompetence and corruption they found when they arrived. Paul Potter, wartime head of the Office of Price Administration, was economic advisor to the US Mission in Greece. He told the US Ambassador that Greece was 'virtually bankrupt'. The Government had 'spent half the national income on non-productive uses . . . corruption is rampant and the civil service a farce . . . the wealthy escape taxes and the [Prime Minister] is inept. There really is no state here in the Western concept, only a loose hierarchy of politicians who care only about their own power struggles' and lining their pockets. He said Greece could only be 'saved economically and politically if the US provides day by day guidance'.[5]

The corruption was damaging the military effort against the guerrillas. From a handful of American troops in the country at the start of 1946, their numbers grew throughout the year. By the autumn the American Mission had two representatives on Greece's Supreme Defence Council, which was directing the Civil War against the insurgents: Dwight Griswold and General James van Fleet. They reported to Washington: 'The official assigned to the [Greek] Ministry of National Economy insisted on signing not only the originals of all documents leaving the ministry but the carbon copies too because . . . [he] does not trust any of the Greek officials that the copies made from the original draft will be true copies.'[6]

The British were desperate to pull out of Greece and hand over entirely to the Americans. They couldn't afford to maintain troops there, fighting a guerrilla war, when they had Palestine on their hands and decisions to make about withdrawing from India. Remaining a great power was draining resources. Bevin, in particular, hated showing weakness, but there was little alternative.

The British began to plead with the US to take the lead in the fight against communism in Greece. The Chancellor, Hugh Dalton, said in November 1946 that he wasn't sure 'even if we had the money . . . that we ought to spend it in this way.' He told the Cabinet, 'I am doubtful about this policy of propping up, even with American aid, weak states in the Eastern Mediterranean against Russia . . . We are, I am afraid, drifting in a state of semi-animation towards the rapids.' Eventually, the rest of the British Government, even Bevin, acknowledged the inevitable. It was time, said Dalton, 'to put an end to our endless dribble of British taxpayers' money to the Americans . . . and to present the matter in Washington in a way to incite the Americans to assume responsibility.'[7]

The Truman administration didn't need much incitement. Dean Acheson repeatedly said that if 'Greece went communist, like apples in a barrel . . . the infection would spread to the Middle East, Africa . . . The world faced the greatest polarization of power since Athens and Sparta.' But Truman did need to persuade Americans to bear the cost and the consequences. In November the Republicans won an overwhelming victory in the mid-term elections. They were in control of both houses in Congress for the first time in nearly twenty years, leaving Truman looking like a lame-duck leader. Yet three months later he made the most famous speech of his life, which introduced the 'doctrine' that bore his name. Henceforth, he said, it would be 'the policy of the United States to support free people who are resisting attempted subjugation by armed minorities or by outside pressures.' Congress approved $400 million in military and economic aid to the Greeks.

Stalin changed his mind about helping the Greek communists after the 'Truman Doctrine' speech. He began a generous aid programme, sending weapons and money, though no troops. But it was too late. By the time the aid arrived, the tide had already turned against the rebels and they were near to losing the war, though their final defeat took another two years. More than

108,000 Greeks had died by then and 800,000 more refugees created on a continent filled with refugees.

The wider consequence was, as George Orwell put it, in the first reference to a 'cold war' in the context of the West and the Russians: 'We may be heading not for general breakdown but for an epoch as horribly stable as the slave empires of antiquity. The Soviet Union is a state at once unconquerable and in a permanent state of Cold War with its neighbours.'[*8]

---

[*] But the phrase predates Orwell. Many people ascribe it to the Marxist German historian of the late nineteenth century, Edward Bernstein: 'This continual arming, compelling the others to keep up with Germany, is itself a kind of warfare. I do not know if this expression has been used previously. But one could say it is a "cold war." There is no shooting, but there is bleeding.' In fact an idea like it had been much used. The first use I can find is by a Castilian knight, Don Juan Manuel (1282–1348), in the fourteenth century. 'War that is very strong and very hot ends either with death or peace, whereas cold war brings neither peace nor gives honour to . . . [those who make it].'

# 30

## 'Sand Down a Rat-Hole'

In Taiwan, then still known as Formosa, the people were preparing for a special visitor. On the afternoon of Monday 21 October, the Chinese President, Generalissimo Chiang Kai-shek, set foot on the island for the first time. It was a custom for Chinese leaders to 'shun' official birthday fanfares in their honour and hold private celebrations amongst family. So to avoid fuss for his sixtieth birthday in ten days' time, Chiang left his Kuomintang stronghold and capital in Nanjing, and with his wife, Mei-ling, he flew to the small provincial town of Taihoku (later Taipei). It was not an entirely quiet or low-key arrival. The streets were lined with well-wishers as the President's entourage drove to the newly repaired mansion where he was to stay – a birthday gift from the people of the island to Chiang for his role in liberating them from the Japanese and reuniting them with mainland China.

For the last fifty years, the Taiwanese had suffered terribly under Japanese occupation, particularly so in the past decade of warfare in Asia. The island was a major producer of rice and vegetables, but thousands of local people a year starved to death while food was exported to Japan. Young girls had been picked at random from the streets and despatched to Japan or the Imperial Army's bases as 'comfort women' for Japanese troops. Japan's colonial administrators and a few commercial traders lived luxuriously while the Taiwanese were viciously exploited. The grandiose villa given to Chiang had originally been built for the Japanese

Governor General. Work started in 1912, cost nearly 10 per cent of that year's annual budget, and took six years to complete.*

There was another important reason why Chiang went to Taiwan, and was joined for his week-long stay by a group of his most loyal KMT cronies and senior army officers. It was a reconnaissance trip. He still believed he would win the Civil War against the communists. But he was preparing a line of retreat in case things went wrong, a strategic place from which to regroup if it became necessary, and chose Taiwan. Now he needed to test the loyalty of the Taiwanese as well as to check tactical military positions. He was not entirely satisfied: there was a small minority who wanted independence from the mainland. He ordered the Governor, Chen-Yi, to crack down on troublemakers. The ringleaders of a fledgling independence movement were arrested; hundreds of people were jailed, tortured, and killed in the following weeks. Chiang returned to Nanjing after his birthday celebrations to continue his war to the finish with Mao Zedong.

*

The American peace envoy's optimism had vanished. The ceasefire George Marshall had brokered soon after he had arrived in China at the beginning of the year lasted a bare few weeks, as with a series of similar ceasefires throughout 1946. By now he realised his China Mission would be a failure. He blamed both sides as neither wanted an agreement and each was prepared to accept only outright victory over the other.

Marshall had tried persuasion and quiet diplomacy which at first seemed to be working. He negotiated a deal that would have established a parliament with some assured authority for the opposition, including both liberals and communists, and a coalition

---

* The mansion had been seriously damaged by American bombing raids in the war. The public, even schoolchildren, chipped in to pay for repairs, ready for Chiang's visit and it was renamed in his honour. It has been the President's office since then.

government. But Chiang's own party rejected the plan, as did Mao. The Communist People's Liberation Army broke the cease-fire first and launched a major offensive in Manchuria in the spring. Initially they took a few big cities, but the KMT fought back. The Americans gave Chiang vital assistance by using their C-46 transport planes to move thousands of Nationalist troops north from their strongholds in the south of the country. They recaptured some of the territory the communists had taken and took some important communist bases along the Yangtze River.

But then Marshall had insisted on a ceasefire and, as he put it, 'used a big stick' to get one. He did not believe the KMT could deliver a knockout blow against the communists and, at that point, continued war was 'hindering the aspirations of the Chinese people'. He told Chiang the Americans would no longer help him with money or equipment and would halt the transport of Nation-alist troops.

On 31 May he wrote to Chiang: 'Under the circumstances of the continued advance of government troops in Manchuria . . . I must repeat that a point is being reached where the integrity of my position is open to serious question . . . Therefore I request again that you immediately issue an order terminating advances, attacks or pursuits by government forces.'[1]

Chiang had no choice. America was funding him to the tune of $3 billion and a further $850 million in gifts of arms, fighter planes and ships. He accepted a ceasefire, saying it was 'a grievous error' and he was doing so reluctantly. 'If you want to fight com-munism, fight it to the end . . . no good to fire and ceasefire, ceasefire and fire,' he told one of his entourage, Chen Li-Fu.[2] He loathed Marshall from that point on, and the feeling was mutual.

Chiang wrote to Truman begging to be allowed freedom of action, but the President backed his envoy. A poll conducted in the late summer in the US showed that, however strong the China lobby was in Congress and in the press, only 15 per cent of Amer-icans favoured supporting Chiang, while 50 per cent wanted to 'stay out of China' altogether. Truman now told Chiang that the American people 'viewed with repugnance events in China . . . [we] might have to re-define America's position in China if there is no peaceful settlement.' Mei-ling went on an American speaking tour to drum up support for her husband. Three years earlier, in 1943, she had become the first Chinese national to address both houses of Congress. This time she was not asked to speak in Washington, though she was a great draw and attracted huge crowds in venues that included Madison Square Garden in New York and at her old college, Wellesley. Truman had told aides that he did not want to continue throwing 'sand down a rat-hole in China'.[3]

Chiang thought Marshall naïve. 'Can it be that Marshall has not yet understood the deceptive nature of the communists? More and more he is being taken in by them. The Americans tend to be . . . trusting. This is true even of a man as experienced as Marshall.'[4]

The ceasefire helped Mao and gave the communists breathing space and valuable time; it was 'a bad mistake by Chiang' to have agreed to it, according to the PLA's top commander Lin Biao. But it was not the cause of the KMT's defeat. They were already doomed. The only way Chiang could have won would have been with a huge influx of American troops on his side, something that, at the time, was both politically and diplomatically impossible.[5]

*

Marshall was not taken in by Mao, whom he described as a 'dyed-in-the-wool Communist', and definitely on the side of the Soviets. Mao and his henchmen continually tried to woo the Americans and persuade them that what he really meant by 'revolution' was democratic reform, agrarian socialism. When the charming and urbane Zhou Enlai, one of Mao's leading officials, met Marshall, he told him that the values of the Chinese Communist Party had a lot in common with America's. They 'desired a democracy of the American style'. He said that Mao 'preferred Americans to Russians' and had told him that 'if he ever went abroad he would rather go to the US than the Soviet Union'. Marshall listened, but he was not fooled. He knew from intercepts, and other intelligence sources, that there was constant contact between Mao's Yen'an base and the Kremlin. Mao told his key advisors that whatever he might say in public his approaches to the Americans were 'only tactics of expedience in our struggle against Chiang'.[6]

At one point the future communist dictator of China toyed with the idea of renaming his Party, but only for show. He told the chief Russian advisor to his court, Vladimirov, 'We have been thinking of calling our Party not Communist but something else. Then the situation with the Americans may be more favourable.' The Soviets, for their part, attempted to distance themselves from their Chinese comrades, at least in public. Molotov told Hurley, Marshall's predecessor as American envoy in China, 'The CCP is not really a Communist Party . . . in China some people call themselves "communist" but they bear no relation to Communists. They were merely expressing their dissatisfaction at their economic conditions by calling themselves communists. However, once their economic conditions have improved they'll forget this political inclination.'[7]

The Russians had recognised Chiang as President of China, but they were aiding the Chinese Reds with vast amounts of arms and supplies. This was easy enough to do via the train link from the area of Manchuria that the Soviets controlled as part of the Yalta agreements, along a safe corridor to the communist-held sectors of southern Manchuria.

Whatever the relations between Mao and Stalin, the Soviets would inevitably support the communists, not only out of ideology, but because they wanted to back the side most likely to win. In 1946 and 1947, the Soviets sent the Chinese communists between 700,000 and 900,000 rifles, 14,000 heavy guns, anti-aircraft weapons, tanks and other military equipment. In Manchuria they captured at least fifty thousand Japanese prisoners of war, including many experienced officers. The Russians ordered them to train the communist army and they sent talented military advisors, including one of their most senior Marshals, Rodion Malinovsky, one of the heroes of Stalingrad, to aid the CCP. The PLA was never the peasant army it claimed to be.

*

The Civil War was brutal on both sides, fought often by press-ganged troops. Mass defections reduced the size of both armies. The Nationalists resorted to increasing repression, and the corruption within their ranks was destroying the KMT from the inside. Soldiers hijacked medical supplies sent from the US and pilfered blood plasma was being sold on the black market in Shanghai for $25 (US currency) a pint. Famine gripped Henan province, where more than forty thousand people died of hunger in 1946; Nationalist soldiers were discovered stealing food aid sent by the West to feed China's orphans and then selling it on the black market.

All opposition groups were being harassed by the KMT, including the Democratic League, an independent liberal party that opposed the communists. A police colonel explained his orders: 'If we think that a man is a communist agent we grab him and it is up to him to prove that he's not. The Chinese masses are used to . . . cruelty. They understand it. They have always understood it.' In Beijing, troops fired on a protest demonstration supporting the liberals, killing scores of students.[8]

Truman received a report on the scale of the embezzlement of American aid amongst KMT officials, particularly by Chiang's circle of cronies. 'Grafters and crooks' in the Chinese Government had stolen a billion dollars from the US in loans over the previous ten years, he was told by the State Department. 'They're all thieves, every damned one of them,' he recorded in his diary. Chief among them were, of course, Chiang's relatives. The Generalissimo did little about it, though he did order an inquiry into the foreign currency scam that had netted the First Lady's family around $300 million.

The report was strictly confidential but was leaked to a newspaper. It caused an immense scandal, though Chiang did little more than temporarily demote his brother-in-law and Foreign Minister, T. V. Soong; within a few months Soong returned to high office. Mei-ling made a series of angry phone calls to the editor of the offending newspaper. Two days after printing the original story the paper, under considerable pressure, published a 'clarification' claiming it had made a mistake by putting the decimal point in the wrong place. The amount taken by the Soongs was not $300 million but 'only' $3 million.

The communists brutalised the people in areas under their control. Mao's personality cult grew, and a huge square was created in Yen'an for mass rallies during which the Chairman was glorified. Purges wiped out all opposition. Troops were threatened into joining the PLA and intimidated into remaining in the ranks. Even then, according to the PLA's own figures, in one month alone during 1946, forty thousand troops deserted. As Zhan Zhenlong, a PLA officer during the Manchurian campaign in the autumn of 1946, reported:

> The thing that gave us the worst headaches was desertion. Generally . . . all of us Party members, squad commanders, combat team leaders had our own 'wobblies' to watch. We would do everything together – sentry duty, our chores . . . When the wobblies wanted to take a leak, we'd say 'I want to have a piss too.' Signs of depression, homesickness, complaints – all had to be dealt with instantly. After fighting, particularly [after] defeats, we kept our eyes peeled. Most of those who ran away did so after camp was pitched. So as well as normal sentries we placed 'secret' sentries . . . some of us tied ourselves to our wobblies at night . . . some were so desperate we adopted a method the Japanese used with their forced labourers – collected the men's trousers and stowed them in the company HQ for the night.[9]

At the end of the year Marshall finally gave up, admitted that his China Mission had failed, and cursed both sides. At his last meeting just before returning to Washington on 7 January 1947, he told Chiang plainly that he was going to lose the war. The Generalissimo looked unconcerned, replying that Marshall was wrong and he would claim victory 'within ten months.'[10]

# 31

## The General Orders – Democracy

The Emperor was seldom seen by the people, and rarely set foot outside his royal palace. He had declared himself human at the beginning of 1946, but on the morning of Sunday 3 November a vast crowd thronged the streets of Tokyo to catch a glimpse of the former living God, descendant of the Sun deity Amaterasu Omikami. Hirohito appeared as a bashful, rather weedy man, seated stiffly in his carriage as it travelled the short distance to the National Diet or parliament. There, in a sombre ceremony, he officially promulgated Japan's new, ground-breaking, constitution.

Until Japan's catastrophic defeat, Hirohito had shown little enthusiasm for democracy, pacifism, votes for women, or Western-style civil rights in general; he was a stickler for imperial absolutism, hierarchy, aristocratic titles, and feudal forms of land ownership. Now he – or his ministers – proclaimed a constitutional monarchy, women's suffrage, the removal of the peerage, an independent judiciary, wholesale land reform, and – most revolutionary of all – the abolition of Japan's armed forces. 'The Japanese people renounce forever war ... or the use of force as a means of settling international disputes.' The government ministers, mostly from the nobility, looked miserable throughout the ceremony. The Emperor appeared uncomfortable, as he often did, but relatively unconcerned; after all, he was still on the throne, and he had evaded all possibility of death by hanging.

At the SCAP headquarters nearby, the real ruler of Japan, General Douglas MacArthur, professed himself well satisfied. The economist J. K. Galbraith, then a State Department official visiting Japan, said that the Supreme Commander always showed 'the arrogant certainty of high purpose'. He had displayed it in abundance when he high-handedly forced through the new constitution. In fact, it was one of the best things MacArthur did, a crucial step towards turning Japan into a model democratic state, but he did it through threats and intimidation, using methods that, as one of his officials said, 'were reminiscent of Al Capone'.[1]

The document had been written in only ten days by American lawyers and a few legal academics who, according to the man who drafted most of it, Colonel Charles Kades, an attorney from Brooklyn before the war, knew next to nothing about Japan: 'I had no knowledge about the history of Japan or its culture,' he said. 'I was a blank on Japan . . . other than what one could glean from a daily newspaper.'[2]

At the end of 1945 MacArthur had ordered the Japanese to come up with a new 'modern, democratic framework guaranteeing freedom for all'. As the US Constitution was so central to the American way of life, he told the Japanese to prepare a comparable document. Many weeks later, the deeply conservative ministers and courtiers of the Royal Household produced a draft in which the Emperor was 'supreme' and sovereign, offered no votes for women and no universal suffrage, and kept power in the hands of the nobility. MacArthur rejected it, along with a not-so-veiled threat in saying that there were Allied nations, and many people in Washington, who wanted to remove the Emperor and put him on trial. He himself, he said 'was not omnipotent' – a rare admission for MacArthur – and if the Japanese politicians were not 'more cooperative', the other Allies might get their way, even against SCAP's wishes. They had ten days to make up their minds or he would produce a 'radical' new constitution. At the same time he ordered his second in command, General Courtney Whitney, to prepare a team of Americans to write a new document under which the Emperor would become a constitutional monarch, and American-style individual freedoms would be enshrined in law.

The Japanese Government thought MacArthur was bluffing. At 10 a.m. on the day of the deadline, 13 February, accompanied by his senior officers, General Whitney went to the home of the Foreign Minister, Shigeru Yoshida, who was waiting with his own aides and the man who had written the preferred Japanese version of the constitution, the Professor of Jurisprudence, Juji Matsumoto. According to Whitney's own vivid account, the Japanese delegation began to explain why they wouldn't change their draft. Whitney interrupted, pushed aside the Matsumoto document, and said: 'The draft . . . you submitted to us the other day is wholly unacceptable to the Supreme Commander as a document of freedom and democracy.' He drew out fifteen copies of the American draft and left them on a table. Then at ten past ten he left the room and walked 'into the sunshine of the garden . . . fortuitously, just at that moment an American plane passed overhead.' Fifteen minutes later, Jiro Shirasu, one of the Professor's aides, went outside to ask Whitney a question. The Colonel observed that 'we are here enjoying the warmth of atomic energy'. It was a deliberately unsubtle comment and resulted in 'an important psychological shift'.

At 11 a.m. Whitney went back inside the house and told the Japanese clearly what would happen next if they did not immediately accept SCAP's terms. The position of the Emperor 'would be reviewed' and the Americans would put their draft constitution to a referendum. As MacArthur was at that time far more popular in Japan than the governing class that had taken the people into a disastrous war – the very people in the room – the people were bound to vote yes. It was a brutal tactic but it worked. The Japanese delegation accepted, but not before asking 'if they were about to be taken outside and shot'.[3]

Shortly after that dramatic meeting, the Japanese Prime Minister, Kijuro Shidehara, was introduced to Colonel Kades, who he had been told was the author of much of the constitution. 'So,

Colonel, you think you can make Japan a democratic country?'
Kades replied, 'Sir, we can try.'[4]

MacArthur said later that establishing the new constitution
was the most important thing he did in his five years as US Proconsul in Japan. He also explained that it was often necessary to
treat the Japanese as errant children because they were not mature,
'as for example the Germans were'. In a paper he sent to a Con-
gressional Committee in Washington he wrote: 'If the Anglo-Saxon
was, say 45 years of age in his development in the sciences, the arts,
in culture, the Germans were as mature. The Japanese, however, in
spite of their antiquity . . . were in a very tuitionary condition.
Measured by the standards of modern civilization they would be
like a boy of 12, as compared with our 45 . . . they were suscep-
tible to following new models, new ideas . . . they were still close
enough to their origin to be elastic and . . . [willing to] accept new
concepts.'*[5]

*

A few weeks before Hirohito decreed the new constitution, an editorial appeared in *Jiji Shimpo*, a highly respected monthly political
and cultural magazine. A new biography of MacArthur had just
been published that was way too gushing and sycophantic for the
magazine's liking. It described the General in terms formerly
reserved for the Emperor – a 'living God' and 'the sun coming from
dark clouds.' The magazine was on the whole a great supporter of
MacArthur and the Occupation but was critical of sycophantic
hagiography, and made an entirely reasonable argument: 'If the conception that government is something imposed upon the people by

---

* MacArthur could be a wonderfully eloquent speaker and off-the-cuff was witty
and, at times, sparkling. But he was a hopeless writer. He insisted on writing his
memoirs himself, which was a mistake. They are almost unreadably awful. As his
friend, the author John Gunther, remarked, 'It is astonishing that anyone who talks
as well as MacArthur could write so badly . . . it is not merely that his style is
pompous. It is worse than that.'

an outstanding God, great man or leader is not restricted, democratic government is likely to be wrecked. We fear the day after General MacArthur's withdrawal that some living God might be searched out to bring the sort of dictatorship that made the Pacific War ... the way to express gratitude towards General MacArthur, for the wisdom with which he is managing post-War Japan and for his efforts to democratise the nation is not to worship him as a God, but to cast away the servile spirit and gain the self-respect that would not bow down its head to anybody.' The piece was pulled, and banned in translation for the mostly American readers of the *Nippon Times*. It was considered in poor taste and liable to diminish the reputation of the Occupying force.[6]

The media had been tightly controlled both before and during the war. No criticism of the regime was permitted. The much-feared 'Thought Police' – the Tokubetsu Koto Keisatsu (they predated Orwell, although they actually were called the 'thought department' of the police) – treated any dissidents or trouble-making journalists with extreme brutality. But the Tokko, as they were known, seldom lectured anyone about democracy or the right to dissent.

The Americans created a vast bureaucracy of censorship, which grew out of all proportion to any imagined threats. Japan was a highly literate society. By the end of 1946 there were six thousand American censors who, every month, would examine and translate 26,000 issues of newspapers, 3,800 news agency reports, 23,000 radio scripts, 4,000 issues of various magazines and periodicals, and 1,800 books and pamphlets. Censors are almost all ignorant and obtuse, as they have been throughout history, and the more of them there are the pettier their task becomes. Nobody was tortured, beaten up, or killed for publishing material the US did not like, as had happened to many writers in the past, but there were absurdities in the four years of American control, some humorous, others just sinister. Censorship caused deep resentment among educated Japanese, especially as they were paying for the

Occupation – vast amounts of money, the details of which were kept secret for many years.

The censors were warned to look out for anything that smacked of 'militarism', so for a while they banned *War and Peace* (it is unlikely that whoever issued the ban had read Tolstoy). No criticism was permitted of any of the Allies – even, rather oddly, of Russia, in the early stages of the Cold War – so an obscure piece in an academic journal about Columbus, which simply stated the fact that European powers like Britain, Spain, France and Holland had colonised many lands throughout the world, was banned.

At the beginning of the Occupation, a Freedom of Speech Directive from SCAP declared that there 'should be the absolute minimum of restrictions' so long as the press stuck to 'the truth' and did nothing 'to disturb public tranquility', but the elaborate system grew and grew. A long list of banned subjects was sent to editors and publishers, and the first rule was that there should be no mention that censorship existed. 'All publishers [must] understand fully that no publicity regarding censorship procedure is desired ... it is assumed that all publishers understand that no physical indications of censorship (such as blackened out print, blank spaces, pasted over areas etc) may appear ... nothing such as "passed by censorship" or "publication permitted by Occupation forces" or any other mention or implication of censorship must be made.'[7]

The banned list was exhaustive and sometimes confusing. There were to be no film or newsreel pictures of GIs; no pictures anywhere of American soldiers and Japanese women. No pictures were permitted of soldiers in jeeps: no reports were allowed of any criminal offences by GIs (there were very few cases to report anyway; generally the troops behaved well). The conflict had to be called the Pacific War, not as the Japanese had been used to refer to it, the Great East Asia War. No mention was allowed of black market activities; references to hunger and rationing should not be 'overplayed'; there was to be no militaristic propaganda; no criticism of SCAP and especially of General MacArthur.

One of the biggest taboos was mention of Hiroshima and Nagasaki. No pictures could be published of the devastation of the cities caused by the atom bombs. John Hersey's superb book *Hiroshima*, which originally appeared on 31 August as a long article in the *New Yorker*, was published in the US in November. A Japanese publisher wanted to translate it into Japanese. SCAP refused point blank and the book was banned in Japan until late 1948. In well-educated circles of Tokyo a few people who read English passed round smuggled copies of the US edition, like *samizdat* manuscripts behind the Iron Curtain.

*

MacArthur started out with an ambitious and radical plan to transform the Japanese economy as thoroughly as he was changing its form of government. He wanted to remove the huge monopoly corporations that ran Japan's industry and introduce free-market competition. MacArthur is often portrayed as a simplistic reactionary who believed in God, the white man, and big business. He did have many right-wing views which he tried, and usually failed, to hide from the New Deal Democrats whom he loathed. When they were his commanders-in chief, however, he usually obeyed them. But he was far more sophisticated, sincere and imaginative than most of his critics claim.[8] One of his first acts as SCAP was to free all political prisoners of the previous regime. Hundreds of communists were let out of jail. Many who knew MacArthur's views were amused by the gushing praise of the General as 'a great liberator' from Tokuda Kyuichi, the ultra-orthodox Marxist leader of Japan's Communist Party. The day he was released, after eighteen years in prison, Kyuichi said: 'We express our deepest gratitude that the Occupation of Japan by the Allied forces, dedicated to liberating the world from fascism and militarism, has opened the way for democratic revolution in Japan.' The relationship did not remain as friendly after the Cold War set in, but MacArthur always maintained that freeing the communists was the correct thing to do – unless they disobeyed *his* laws.[9]

*

MacArthur's orders were to root out those who had made Japan's wars possible. To him, that meant destroying the Zaibatsu, the huge monopoly industrialists who owned and ran the Japanese economy. During the war, ten companies had controlled more than three-quarters of Japan's industry and finance and of these, four – Mitsubishi, Mitsui, Sumitomo and Yasuda – controlled half. They were now ordered to produce plans for their own dissolution. MacArthur said in his memoirs later: 'The world has never seen a counterpart to so abnormal an economic system. It permitted the exploitation of the many for the sole benefit of the few. The integration of these few . . . [companies] with the Government was complete and their influence upon government inordinate . . . [they] set the course which ultimately led to war.'[10]

The SCAP economist Eleanor Hadley reported to MacArthur that the Mitsubishi family holdings alone were, in relative terms, 'the equivalent of a single American conglomerate comprising US Steel, General Motors, Standard Oil of New Jersey, Douglas Aircraft, Dupont, Sun Shipbuilding, Westinghouse, AT&T, IBM, US Rubber, Sea Island Sugar, Dole Pineapple, US Lines, National City Bank, Metropolitan Life Insurance and Woolworth stores.'[11]

The Zaibatsu believed they were untouchable and went back to MacArthur, proposing a few cosmetic changes that would have removed some of the senior management and dissolved a few subsidiaries, but kept their family holdings intact and allowed them to retain ownership and control of the companies through a smoke-screen of exemptions and legal loopholes. MacArthur rejected the proposal and, as he had done with the politicians, told the industrialists to come up with a better plan or he would impose one that would be considerably more painful for them.

The economist Corwin D. Edwards had prepared a 'trust busting' plan to break up the cartels, share ownership more widely, crack down on monopolies, and encourage the development of active trades unions. It was entirely in keeping with MacArthur's views of fair competition in an open market – the American Way, as he saw it. It was the kind of vigorous, pro-capitalist policy pursued by the Republican President Theodore Roosevelt when he wanted to break up monopolistic US corporations at the turn of the century.

The Zaibatsu, according to Edwards, 'were the guys principally responsible for the war and the principal factor in Japan's war potential ... they enforced semi-feudal relations between employer and employee, held down wages ... they had retarded the rise of a Japanese middle class ... as a counterweight to military despotism.'[12]

MacArthur was all set to fight the cartels with his usual vigour, but was warned to back off by Washington. The Zaibatsu companies had contacted their business friends in America, who in turn put pressure on the Truman administration. Nor did the Japanese politicians have much interest in challenging big business which was often their paymaster. MacArthur was told that his plan was too risky and that he must let the Japanese run their economy the way they wished, as long as it was broadly a free enterprise system. This time he made a tactical retreat and, by the end of 1946, his campaign against the most powerful business leaders was over. But the supposedly rabid Right-winger had more success with the farmers. He stripped the absentee landlords and owners of the huge estates of their holdings, ensuring millions of peasants owned their own farms. He thought – rightly as it turned out, judging by future Japanese elections – that small landowners would be naturally conservative. MacArthur's land reforms were more radical than anything then happening behind the Iron Curtain.

*

In Nuremberg on 16 October 1946, nine of the leading Nazi war criminals were hanged one after the other at the gymnasium of the city's Palace of Justice. In Tokyo, similar trials would continue for another two years and lead to far more serious questions about what the point of the hearings really was. The main trial of twenty-five defendants had begun in May, but the public soon lost interest, not only in Japan but also in the Allied countries, and the press, too, ceased to report on the proceedings.

In the Asian countries that Japan had occupied during the war, 984 Japanese had already been executed, many without proper trials, including 236 by the Dutch, 223 by the British, 153 by the Australians, 140 by the Americans. Nearly all were Japanese soldiers who had mistreated and killed prisoners of war. The trials of the Japanese leaders charged with 'waging a war of aggression' were an altogether more complex matter. The primary issue, as two of the judges noted, was that the greatest war criminal was not in the dock. The Australian judge Sir William Webb said: 'The leader of the crime, though available for trial, was granted immunity. The Emperor's authority was required for war. If he did not want war, he should have withheld his authority.'

The French judge Henri Bernard stated that the entire proceedings were flawed and he couldn't pass judgement at all. The absence of the Emperor in court was 'a glaring inequity . . . Japan's crimes against peace had a principal author who escaped all prosecution. Measuring the Emperor by different standards undermines the cause of justice.'[13]

Many of the Americans who organised the trial later said that it backfired. MacArthur was doubtful about the hearings in the first place. He told Truman that it was 'comparatively simple' where the Nazis were concerned to prove genocidal intent and apportion guilt, but in Japan 'no such line of demarcation has been fixed.' One of the officers who interrogated the defendants to decide who should face trial, Brigadier-General Elliot Thorpe, told MacArthur that the entire proceedings were 'mumbo-jumbo . . .

we made up the rules as we went along.' Later, Thorpe wrote that 'we wanted blood and by God we got blood'.[14]

For many others, the trials were not only victor's justice; they were white man's justice. People in the occupied Asian countries had suffered the most, but not one was represented on the panel of judges. A British judge represented the Malays, a French judge acted for the Vietnamese and the Cambodians. Korea had been colonised with brute rapacity by Japan for nearly fifty years; there was no Korean judge. Among the charges faced by the two dozen defendants was that they 'engaged in a plan or conspiracy to secure military, naval and political domination over East Asia, the Pacific and the Indian Ocean'. During the thirty-one months that the trial lasted, the French were waging a war to regain their colony in Vietnam against an independence movement led by Ho Chi Minh; the Dutch fought the nationalists in an attempt to repossess their Indonesian territories, and the British fought guerrillas seeking independence in Malaya.

Only one of the judges, the Indian Radhabinod Pal, pointed out the double standard involved. He agreed that the Japanese had committed vile crimes during their invasion and occupation of various countries but, he argued, they were neither unique nor without precedent. 'It would be pertinent to recall ... that the majority of the interests claimed by the Western prosecuting powers in the Eastern hemisphere were acquired by such aggressive methods.' They claimed 'national honour' or 'the protection of vital interests' or concepts of 'manifest destiny' similar to the Japanese. The Japanese conquerors were guilty of crimes, but those crimes should be set in context.[15] For much of Asia, the end of the Pacific War was only the beginning of the process of liberation, not the end. The trials opened up the entire question of how long the old European powers could maintain their empires. This was not the message the Allies wanted to hear – or to send to the world – when, in 1948, they executed seven military chiefs of the former Japanese empire, including the Prime Minister, Hideki Tojo, who had earlier tried, and failed, to commit suicide.

As in Germany, some leading Japanese war criminals were hunted down and punished, but several got away – and later prospered – principally because in the Cold War they were seen as friends and allies against the Soviets. Several squadrons of Japanese pilots took themselves and their planes to China to fight with Chiang Kai-shek's forces – and joined him in Taiwan when the KMT lost the Chinese Civil War.

The best-known fugitive (though there were scores of others) was Tsuji Masanobu, a ruthless and vicious officer who had ordered massacres of both soldiers and civilians in Singapore and the Philippines. He was a master of disguise, and a senior intelligence agent who had rooted out 'subversives' in Japan and its colonies. He escaped capture by the British and reached Chiang's capital, Nanjing, but returned to Japan two years after the war finished, living quietly in hiding concealed as a professor of Chinese. Like some Nazi suspects, he had useful information with which to barter and was soon working for American military intelligence, which he did until the end of the Occupation, after which he worked for Japan's counter-intelligence service, planning operations against communists. He wrote a massively popular book about his wartime exploits and secret life, and despite the ban on 'militarists and ultra-nationalists' returning to politics, spent years as a member of the lower House in the Japanese Diet.

Since the Second World War, Japan has been a model pacifist nation.* It disarmed, but not completely. Throughout 1946 there were accidents in hidden arms and ammunition dumps that had simply been overlooked. Dozens of people were killed. A small defence force of ten divisions was established, and towards the end

---

* Although as a reaction to the increasing power and wealth of China the Japanese have quietly increased the strength of their army, which supposedly existed to help with humanitarian relief work at home and abroad. There has been debate in Japan since 2012 about abandoning the 'pacifist' clause in the MacArthur-inspired constitution.

of 1946 a group of a hundred and ninety generals set up a 'historical research' institute as a cover for a military intelligence unit run by Seizo Arisue, the notoriously violent head of the Imperial Army's intelligence service during the war. Arisue and Tojo's former private secretary – both of whom were lucky to escape prosecution as war criminals – also set up a 'shadow' general staff of fifty senior officers, working alongside SCAP.[16]

\*

On 8 November 1946, five days after the Emperor's decree on the constitution, the Government banned 162,915 civil servants, local administrators, politicians, and even some high-school principals from holding public office. They were being punished for excessive militarism or extreme nationalism. Membership in organisations with bizarre names such as the White Corpuscle League, the Black Dragon Society, the Anti-Foreign Spirits Society, and the Bayonet Practice Society was deemed enough for expulsion. Within a year, 10 per cent of those banned had been reinstated, including some members of the former 'Thought Police'. The ban dated from August 1945, which meant that by the summer of 1946 the state was once again permitted to employ them; by the end of 1948 more than a third had been reinstated and only 9,000 had not by 1949. As in Germany, the Japanese wanted to forget and seemed to have been successful. Kishi Nobusuke was a senior official in the brutal Japanese occupation of Manchuria and organised the system of slave labour under which thousands of Chinese died. He was Minister of Munitions during the war and a Class A war crimes suspect (the highest category), incarcerated with Tojo in Sugamo Prison, Tokyo, for two years. But he was never charged or tried. Just over ten years after Hiroshima, in January 1957, Nobusuke was elected Prime Minister. Reordering Japan was a huge undertaking and one of America's greatest post-war achievements. But it was not a seamless or unalloyed triumph for justice and democracy.[17]

# 32

## The Big Freeze

In Britain, Sunday 29 December was the coldest day for fifty years; in France, the weather bureau said that the entire month had been the coldest since they began keeping records in the previous century. The whole of Europe was gripped by a long winter that some people would remember almost as vividly as they recalled the war. 'Friends said "this is worse than the War" ... [and] I understood. This couldn't be viewed as a challenge to self-sacrifice and patriotism; it was merely hell,' said the writer Christopher Isherwood, who had returned to London from California. Even the perennially optimistic Winston Churchill found it hard to be cheerful towards the end of 1946. 'What is the plight to which Europe has been reduced? Over wide areas a vast quivering mass of tormented, hungry, careworn and bewildered human beings gape at the ruins of their cities and homes and scan the dark horizons for the approach of some new peril, tyranny or terror. Among the victors there is a Babel of jarring voices; among the vanquished a sullen silence of despair.'[1]

In London and much of Britain, power cuts began a few days after Christmas and the lights went out for long periods until the following April. The gas supply was down to a quarter of its normal pressure, leaving fires to run on flickering flames. Transport ground to a near-halt, so coal couldn't be moved around the country. People made grim puns on the name of the unfortunate Minister of Fuel and Power– 'Shiver with [Emmanuel] Shinwell.' Things were just as bad in Paris. Schools and offices were left unheated; many children were so afflicted by chilblains that they couldn't hold a pen. There were cases of surgeons halting operations when the electricity supply was cut without warning.

Throughout Europe everyone was obsessed with the cold. Diaries and letters by those who lived through it invariably began with a weather report. 'Snow assumed the aspect of an invading enemy,' wrote Isherwood, perhaps dreaming of his home on America's sunny West Coast. 'Soldiers turned out to fight it . . . (in some areas) with flame-throwers. The newspapers spoke about it with quasi-military language "Scotland isolated", or "England cut in half".' One night he went to the theatre; the actors played to an empty house and 'heroically stripped down to their indoor clothes, while we (few) in the audience were huddled together in a tight clump, muffled to the chin in overcoats, sweaters, scarves.'[2]

James Lees-Milne wrote in his diary on 4 January 1947, 'Wearing my snow boots and fur-lined coat, I was not once warm. All my pipes, including WC pipes are frozen so a bath or wash is out of the question. The WC at the office is frozen likewise. And we live in the twentieth century. Even the basic elements of civilisation are denied us.'[3]

Nancy Mitford who in the spring of 1946 moved to Paris, where she would remain until she died in 1973, said that it was simply impossible to work at home as her hands were too cold, even wearing mittens. 'Every breath is like a sword,' she wrote to her sister Diana. Pipes were bursting throughout the city, she said; water poured out and then re-froze on to the streets: 'I never saw anything like the burst pipes in this town. Every house a waterfall.' *The New Yorker*'s Janet Flanner described a 'sense of helplessness, impending disaster . . . a climate of malaise in Paris and perhaps all over Europe . . . where people expected something to happen or, worse, nothing to happen. The . . . whole continent is slowly entering a new ice age.'[4]

Along with the meagre rations and general austerity, that winter stuck in the memory of the future Rolling Stone Bill

Wyman, who was then a ten-year-old called William Perks, living in Penge, south-east London. His father, a bricklayer, was laid off because of the weather; things were tough, and he was one of five children. 'There wasn't enough food to go round', Wyman recalled, 'so he would hit a couple of us and send us to bed with no dinner.' It was a cruel punishment, not only because of the beating and the hunger but 'in the house we lived in you didn't want to go to bed. It was freezing . . . with ice on the inside of the windows.'[5]

*

For many people in Europe, the temperature, the power cuts, the hunger, the chaos, were a physical expression of something deeper: a general decline, a further descent into chaos. 'Morally and economically Europe . . . lost the war,' said Cyril Connolly. 'The great marquee of European civilisation in whose light we all grew up, and read, and wrote, or loved, or travelled has fallen down; the side ropes are frayed; the centre pole is broken, the chairs and tables are all in pieces, the tent is empty, the roses are withered on their stands.'[6]

Very few people at the end of 1946 believed that recovery was around the corner, or even that it was possible. Some were apocalyptic in their gloom: 'There is a situation in the world, very clearly illustrated in Europe, but true also in the Far East, which threatens the very foundations, the whole fabric of world organisation, which we have known in our lifetimes and which our fathers and grandfathers knew,' Dean Acheson told President Truman.[7]

Yet recovery was in fact far speedier than anyone predicted – thanks, principally, to the United States and to people such as Dean Acheson and, especially, George Marshall, who saw how it could be achieved. The post-war priority for America was to keep Western Europe from falling to the communists. The Marshall Plan, launched the next summer, was a product of the Cold War.

The US provided more aid in the following four years – $13 billion – than in the rest of its history combined to kick-start economies destroyed by the war. The Plan was visionary, and self-interested, and would transform the post-war world. But, as so often, it is in apparently small things that first signs can be spotted. Janet Flanner made an interesting observation midway through the year: in Paris department stores frequented by women, the biggest selling goods were, unsurprisingly, underwear. But the second item they were ordering was prams, a biological vote of confidence in the future.

# Epilogue

Alexis de Tocqueville, writing in the 1830s, foresaw that 'one day the United States of America and Russia will each hold in its hand the destinies of half the world.' That day arrived after the Second World War. The war had dramatically shifted the balance of global power, and how the two sides in the so-called 'bipolar world' saw each other.[1]

America abandoned isolationism after Pearl Harbor. Following the victories over Nazi Germany and Japan there were surprisingly few demands within the US for a retreat to Fortress America, as there had been after the First World War. In the words of the American President, 1946 was 'the year of decisions', a year in which the US resolved to extend its influence, its ideology – and its military muscle throughout the world. 'We were forced to take over the leadership of the free peoples,' Dean Acheson proclaimed. 'The British were no longer able to do it. We could.'[2]

The Soviets found themselves the second power (though not yet a superpower) courtesy of Adolf Hitler, and, paradoxically, the United States. If the Nazis had not invaded the USSR, the Soviets would not have ended the Second World War occupying most of Eastern and Central Europe, with an empire and a swaggering purpose of victory that seemed to pose a challenge to the West's ideals of liberal democracy. During the war, it had been the Americans who had given the Soviets the arms, the food and, to a significant degree, the industrial capability to do so. The

Bolsheviks had always possessed the will to export 'Revolution'. The US had provided them with the means.

From 1941 to 1945, while the Russians did most of the fighting and dying against the Nazis, it had seemed a price worth paying to defeat the Germans and the Japanese. In 1946 the full cost became clearer.

Stalin was essentially right when he said that whoever occupies a country imposes his own system on its territory. There is no moral equivalence between Stalin's brutal control of Hungary, Romania, Bulgaria and elsewhere behind the 'Iron Curtain', and America's six-and-a-half-year-long Occupation of Japan. But America remade Japan in its own image, and ensured it remained in the Western orbit. The Americans spent vast amounts of money to keep Western Europe free and democratic and, in later years, prosperous. The Soviet empire was built and maintained on coercion; the post-war pax Americana – an empire in its way – was built on choice, but circumscribed choice. This was becoming apparent in 1946.

*

There were misunderstandings and misjudgements by various leaders as world war turned swiftly into Cold War. But the differences became so sharp so quickly between West and East, and the aims and ambitions of the two sides were so divergent, that it is unlikely they could simply have rubbed along together without conflict. The more power and influence Stalin wielded, the more frustrating and difficult other leaders found it to deal with him but the more mistakes he was making from the USSR's point of view.

Most of Stalin's gains were made before the war ended, in Central and Eastern Europe; and some of those were a mirage. If he had been more flexible there, his 'outer empire' might have had a more popular base. He failed to get what he wanted elsewhere. In Iran he did not acquire the oilfield he coveted; and he used up political capital in the West by making demands that even a man as servile as Molotov knew were so outrageous they would never be accepted in Washington and London. Stalin unintentionally brought America and Britain together in a strengthened 'special relationship' at a time when they were beginning to have differences. Even communist victory in China in 1949 had less to do with the help the Soviets were giving Mao Zedong than with the reluctance of the Americans to give open-ended aid to the Chinese Nationalists under Chiang Kai-shek. That was the result of a decision made by Harry Truman and George Marshall in 1946.

The logical thing in the East–West conflict would perhaps have been for both sides to agree to let the other do what they wanted in their own 'sphere of interest'. This, after all, was a traditional Big Powers arrangement and, in reality, is what happened, though the public in the West, and more particularly their leaders, would never acknowledge it openly. Perhaps it was too cynical to advocate such a deal so soon after a war against dictatorship. The alternative – to try to force the Soviets to withdraw from Eastern Europe – was even more unpalatable and impractical. An aggressive war against the USSR was not going to happen, even with the atomic monopoly which the Americans possessed until 1949. The result, for many years, was a curious blend of overblown rhetoric and relatively cautious and cool action from both sides, which characterised most of the Cold War era.

In the 'bipolar world', decision makers on all sides seemed to see everything from a Cold War perspective, through the prism of Soviet–Western rivalry. This was a distortion that continued until the collapse of the Soviet Union in 1991, but began within months of the end of the Second World War. When at the end of 1947 the Soviet Union enthusiastically backed the Partition of Palestine and the creation of Israel, the Americans grew jittery. Stalin was a rabid anti-Semite and was about to launch his last big purge – against Jews in the USSR. But at this time he thought that the socialist Jews, who in those days were the principal leaders of the Zionist movement, might be persuaded to show support for the Soviets and Russia would gain some influence in the Middle East. His other main aim was simply to cause mischief and discomfort for the Americans, which he did. In 1948, when Israel came into being, the US State Department advised President Truman not to recognise the new country – partly because the Soviets would. One of the most influential of Washington insiders, the Assistant Secretary of State Robert Lovett, told Truman that Israel would most likely turn into an enemy, a client of the Russians 'which we must not allow'. Truman rejected their advice, but for the first few years of Israel's existence, until the Soviets saw they were getting nowhere, Cold War warriors in the US were wary of Israel.[3]

Another obvious example was the anti-imperialist, and anti-French, President Truman supporting the return to France of colonies such as Vietnam and Cambodia, though it was clear the French were too weak and incompetent to beat popular nationalist rebellions in South East Asia, or, indeed, anywhere else. That decision led soon afterwards, with bloody consequences, to America's own disaster in Vietnam, the biggest of the proxy wars between East and West fought over the next forty years. One of the most interesting 'what if?' questions in modern history is what if the Americans had, instead, backed the Vietnamese nationalists in 1946, albeit that they professed themselves communists? Asia might have looked very different in the twenty-first century, as might America's view of when to use its military power.

Elsewhere, the European retreat from empire might have happened in a different way, though it certainly *would* have happened. Some notions of imperial glory lingered on for a while, as did ideas of racial superiority, but the reins of power did not. In 1946 the British could see no way of leaving behind a united India, and neither could the Indians. For some years afterwards, many Britons agonised over whether the departure was a humiliating 'scuttle', whether they could have prevented the inter-communal slaughter between Hindus and Muslims. The story afterwards – the three wars between Pakistan and India over the next twenty-five years, the uneasy, uncomfortable nuclear standoff between them – should perhaps prompt deeper questions from philosophers about the nature of human conflict, rather than deeper analysis of the fine details of the Partition. In Western Europe, much of the new thinking was about forms of unity rather than division. The first seeds of what became the European Union were planted by economists, politicians, and business leaders in order to bind economies and markets so closely together that another war of the kind that had all but destroyed the continent could not happen again. Nothing practical would start to happen for nearly a decade, but the hope, the plans and the resolution were seen for the first time in 1946 – as were so many of the ideas that shaped the modern world.

# Acknowledgements

The action in this book takes place on four continents, mostly in one year. But the finished product is the work of dozens of trips throughout many parts of the world spread over many years as a journalist and, later, as an author. Often when covering one event of immediate news interest, I would end up talking to people about their memories. Frequently their clearest, most powerful reminiscences were of the period immediately post-war; some have since died but I have liberally used their insights and stories here. I don't claim that when I was talking with them about the past in this general way, I was subconsciously thinking about eventually working on this book. It might not have been written but for a chance conversation with the wise Anthony Cheetham, which gave me the seedling of the idea; a subsequent re-reading of Margaret MacMillan's brilliant *Peacemakers*, about the post-World War One settlement, convinced me that something along similar lines – though by no means an imitation – could be done on the aftermath of the Second World War.

I am vastly indebted to a great number of people and organisations for the time and effort they spent in helping me with ideas, support, advice on new avenues of research and contacts. In the UK, I am grateful to Richard Addis, Anne Applebaum, Bryan and Christena Appleyard, Don Berry, Patrick Bishop, Professor Archie Brown, Richard Burge, Sir Bryan Cartledge, Jung Chang, Anthony Curtis, Mitro Dimitrov, Hugo Dixon, Mark Dixon, April Edwards, Jonathan Fenby, Iain Fergusson, Serena Fokschaner, Jonathan Ford, Professor Maurice Fraser, Timothy Garton Ash, Adela Gooch, Lord and Lady

Goodhart, Sophie Graham, John Hamilton, Sir Max Hastings, Susannah Herbert, Andrew Holgate, Mark Jones, Barbara Kiss, Ben Lewis, Keith Lowe, Edward Lucas, Anne McElvoy, Bronwen Maddox, Andrew Martin, Annabel Markova, Philippa Norris, Debbie Owen, Julia Pearie, Lord Powell, Anna Reid, Richard Sachs, Matyas Sarkozi, Dr Simon Sebag Montefiore, Amanda Sebestyen and George Szirtes. A big thank you to Piers Dixon, who gave me access to some private papers of his father, Sir Pierson Dixon. The staff at the London Library, at Chatham House, the Bodleian Library and St Antony's College Oxford, the National Archives in Kew, and the library at King's College London, with its invaluable Liddell Hart Centre for Military Archives, were hugely helpful and efficient. I am indebted to the staff and other trustees of Wilton Park for their encouragement and assistance.

I was helped by many people in the United States: Carol Blue, John Lewis Gaddis, Charles Gati, Kati Marton, Jack Matlock, Rebecca Mead, Helen Moynihan, Christian Osterman, Frank Robertson, Condoleezza Rice, Professor Ronald Radosh, Bob Simms, Joan Stein, Vladimir Tismaneanu and Martin Walker among them. I want to thank the staff at the Cold War International History Project at the Wilson Centre in Washington, DC, the Library of Congress in Washington, the Hoover Institution at Stanford University, and the library at Columbia University in New York City for their courtesy and unfailing efficiency. The staff at the George Marshall Foundation in Lexington, Virginia were helpful as was, some time ago, the Harry S. Truman Presidential Library in Independence, Missouri.

In the Middle East and Asia I wish to thank old friends Sanjev and Mukti Bulchandani, who helped to find a scholar of modern Indian history who could translate Hindi for me, Amit Chilabaj. And for their guidance and patience I am grateful to Mira Bar Hillel, Alex Chang, Minderat Chaudhuri, Nimrad Chaudhuri, Len Chi, William Dalrymple, Hu Daneng for Mandarin translation, David Eppel, Laxmal Erpidu, Tom Gross, Norio Kuboi, Yushiro Kuroda, His

Excellency Shimon Peres, Mariel Schneider, and Kindera Sinjei for Japanese translations.

I have space here to thank only a handful of the many people in Europe who, during dozens of visits over two and a half decades, have helped me in myriad ways. I shall mention Dasa Antelova, Csaba Békes, Phillippe Boneuve, Peta Brod, Anna Bryson, Pavel Campeanu, Sergiu Çelac, Rumen Danov, Claire Defors, Gábor Demszky, Jiri Dienstbier, Blaga Dimitrova, László Eörsi, Danuta Galecka, Miklos Haraszti, János Kis, Ferenc Köszeg, Carsten Krenz, Adam LeBor, Jean Longines, Vera Lengsfeld, Károly Makk, Tadeusz Mazowiecki, Anne-Elisabeth Moutet, Dr Matthias Müller, Imre Poszgay, Aram Radomski, Laszlo Rajk, Günther Schabowski, Rheinhard Schult, Professor Timothy Snyder, Krassen Stanchev, Nick Thorpe, Peter Uhl, Jerzy Urban and Dr Maria Vásarhelyi. Many individuals in Russia helped me enormously in tracking down documents in archives, approaching contacts and finding people to interview. It is one of the tragedies of modern Russia that not a single one wanted to be mentioned in these acknowledgements. But I am vastly grateful to them nonetheless.

The archives of the Gorbachev Foundation in Moscow were helpful, as were the archive of the Russian President, the Foreign Ministry and the Russian State Archive of Social and Political History. In Germany I would like to thank the German Federal Archive for their unfailing efforts to help me find just the right documents and the staff in charge of the Stasi files, the Commission for Records of the State Security, Berlin and the State Archive of Political Parties. In the Czech Republic I want to thank the staff of the Archive of the President's Office, and the Interior Ministry archive which houses the documents of the State Security Department, the StB. In Poland the Central Military Archives, the central Archive of Parliament and the Interior Ministry Archive were enormously useful. So was the Institute of National Remembrance in Moscow. In Bucharest I wish to thank the Romanian Ministry of Home Affairs

Archive, and in particular, the Institute for the Investigation of Communist Crimes.

The support of my brother and sister, John Walko and Judith Maynard, my niece, Andrea Walko-Roberts, and Jayne Diggory and Adil Ali, was of supreme importance.

I would like to thank my editor at Macmillan, George Morley, for her cool judgement, reassuring common sense and wisdom through the sometimes tricky editing process. Nicholas Blake and Zennor Compton, also at Macmillan, have been tremendously helpful.

George Capel's optimism, calm and uncanny ability to lift her authors' spirits is astonishing. I am lucky to have her as my agent.

There is no way I can adequately thank Jessica Pulay for all her work on this book. She read the manuscript tirelessly, found countless ways to improve the text and lovingly encouraged me to strive harder. Without the clarity of her mind as a support and a foil, and the generosity of her spirit, this book would never have been finished. I will forever be in her debt.

# Bibliography

## Archives

APRF – Arkhiv Presidenta Rossiisskoi Federatsii (Archive of the
   President of the Russian Federation), Moscow
Archive of the Gorbachev Foundation, Moscow
Archive of the Polish Government-in-exile, Hoover Institution,
   Stanford University, California
AVPRF – Arkhiv Vneshnei Politiki Rossiisskoi Federatsii (Archive of
   Foreign Policy of the Russian Federation), Moscow
Bundesarchiv (German Federal Archives), Berlin
Central Archive of Modern Records, Warsaw
Central Military Archive, Warsaw
Charles Bohlen Papers, Averell Harriman Collection, Library of
   Congress Manuscripts, Washington, DC
CNN Cold War Series Archive, Liddell Hart Centre for Military
   Archives, King's College London
Cold War International History Project, George Washington
   University, Washington, DC
Columbia University Oral History Project, New York
Federal Commission for the State Archives of the GDR (Stasi
   Archives), Berlin
FRUS (Foreign Relations of the United States), National Archives,
   Washington, DC
Harry Hopkins Papers, Georgetown University, Washington, DC
Harry S. Truman Library, Independence, Missouri

Hoover Institution, Stanford University, California
Hungarian National Archives, Budapest
Imperial War Museum Archive, London
Institute for the History of the 1956 Hungarian Revolution Archive,
    Budapest
Institute of National Remembrance, SB Secret Police Archive, Warsaw
Jewish Historical Institute, Warsaw
Jewish History Museum and Archive, Budapest
Liddell Hart Centre for Military Archives, King's College London
Memorial Library of the Victims of Commission, The National
    Archives of the UK, London
OMGUS – Office of the Military Government of the United States,
    National Archives, Washington, DC
Oral History Program, Hoover Institution, Stanford, California
RGASPI – Rossiiskii Gosudarvstestvennyi Arkhiv Sotsialno-
    politicheskoi Istorii (Russian State Archive of Social and Political
    History), Moscow

## Published Documents

*Anglo-American Commission Report on Palestine.* Cmd 6808. HMSO,
    London, 1946
*DDR: Dokumente zur Geschichte der Deutschen Demokratischen
    Republik.* Herman Weber, Munich, 1986
*Documents on Germany 1944–1945.* US Department of State, Office of
    the Historian, Washington, DC
Iratok a Magyar-Szoviet, Kapcsolatok történetéhez 1944–1948 1945–
    1985 ed. Isztván Buda, Budapest, 2005
Marshall, George, *Mission to China.* Foreign Relations of the United
    States. Washington, DC
Pirzada, Syed Sharifuddin, *Foundations of Pakistan.* Muslim League
    Documents 1906–1948. Karachi, 1990

## Books and Periodicals

Abdullah, King of Jordan, *My Memoirs Completed: 'Al-Takmilah'*. Longman, London, 1978

Acheson, Dean, *Present at the Creation: My Years in the State Department*. Norton, New York, 1969

Alanbrooke, Field Marshal Lord, *War Diaries, 1939–1945*. Weidenfeld and Nicolson, London, 2001

Aldrich, Richard, *The Hidden Hand, Britain: America and Cold War Secret Intelligence*. John Murray, London, 2001

Alexander, G. M., *The Prelude to the Truman Doctrine: British Policy in Greece 1944–1947*. Clarendon Press, Oxford, 1982

Alliluyeva, Svetlana, *Twenty Letters to a Friend*. HarperCollins, London, 1967

Alperovitz, Gar, *Atomic Diplomacy: Hiroshima and Potsdam*. Penguin, New York, 1985

Ambrose, Stephen, *Eisenhower: Soldier and President*. Simon and Schuster, New York, 1990

Andreas-Friedrich, Ruth, *Battleground Berlin: Diaries 1945–1948* (trans. Anna Boerreson). Paragon House, New York, 1990

Annan, Noel, *Changing Enemies: The Defeat and Regeneration of Germany*. HarperCollins, London, 1995

Anonymous, *A Woman in Berlin* (trans. Philip Boehm). London, 2005

Applebaum, Anne, *Iron Curtain*. Allen Lane, London, 2012

Arendt, Hannah, *The Origins of Totalitarianism*. Allen & Unwin, London, 1958

Attlee, Clement, *As it Happened*. Heinemann, London, 1954

Azad, Abdul Kalam, *India Wins Freedom*. Sangam Books, Delhi, 1998

Bauer, Yehuda, *Flight and Rescue: Brichah*. Random House, New York, 1970

Beevor, Antony, *Berlin: The Downfall 1945*. Penguin, London, 2003

——, and Artemis Cooper, *Paris After the Liberation*. Penguin, London, 1995

Begin, Menachem, *The Revolt*. Futura, London, 1980

Ben Gurion, David, *Israel: A Personal History*. Funk and Wagnalls, New York, 1971

——, *Recollections*. Macdonald, London, 1970

Berezhkov, Valentin (trans. Sergei M. Mikheyev), *At Stalin's Side: His Interpreter's Memoirs*. Birch Lane Press, Secaucus, NJ, 1994

Beria, Sergo, *My Father: Inside Stalin's Kremlin*. Duckworth, London, 2001

Bessel, Richard, *Germany 1945: From War to Peace*. Harper Perennial, London, 2009

Biddiscombe, Perry, *The Denazification of Germany: A History 1945–1950*. Tempus, Stroud, 2007

Bohlen, Charles, *Witness to History*. Norton, New York, 1973

Bourdrel, Philippe, *L'Épuration Sauvage*. Perrin, Paris, 2002

Bower, Tom, *Blind Eye to Murder*. Deutsch, London, 1982

Brown, Judith, *Nehru: A Political Life*. Yale University Press, 2003

Bullock, Alan, *Ernest Bevin: Foreign Secretary 1945–1951*. Heinemann, London, 2002

Buruma, Ian, *Year Zero: A History of 1945*. Atlantic Books, London, 2013

Cadogan, Sir Alexander, *The Diaries of Sir Alexander Cadogan, OM, 1938–1945* (ed. David Dilks). Faber and Faber, London, 2010

Cameron, James, *Points of Departure*. Oriel Press, London, 1978

Chandra, Bipan, *Essays on Colonialism*. Longman, Delhi, 1999

——, *India's Struggle for Independence*. Penguin, Delhi, 1988

Charters, David, *The British Army and the Jewish Insurgency in Palestine 1945–1947*. Macmillan, London, 1989

Chaudhuri, Nirad, *Autobiography of an Unknown Indian*. Macmillan, London, 1951

——, *Thy Hand, Great Anarch!* Chatto and Windus, London, 1987

Chen, Jian, *Mao's China and the Cold War*. North Carolina University Press, 2001

Chuev, Feliks, *Molotov Remembers: Inside Kremlin Politics: Conversations with Felix Chuev* (ed. Albert Resis). I.R. Dee, Chicago, IL, 1993. (Russian edition: *Molotov: Poluderzhavnyi vlastelin*. OLMA-Press, Moscow, 1999)

Churchill, Winston S., *Triumph and Tragedy*. Mariner, New York, 1986

Clare, George, *Berlin Days: 1946–1947*. Macmillan, London, 1989

Clay, Lucius, *Decisions in Germany*. Heinemann, London, 1950

Clifford, Clark, *Counsel to the President: A Memoir*. Random House, New York, 1991

Colville, Sir John, *The Fringes of Power: Downing Street Diaries 1939–1945*. Weidenfeld and Nicolson, London, 2004

Conot, Robert E., *Justice at Nuremberg*. Basic Books, New York, 1993

Cooper, Duff, *The Duff Cooper Diaries* (ed. John Julius Norwich). Weidenfeld and Nicolson, London, 2005

Crossman, Richard, *A Nation Reborn*. Hamish Hamilton, London, 1960

——, *Palestine Mission*. Hamish Hamilton, London, 1947

Cunningham, Alan, 'The Last Days of the Mandate', *International Affairs* 24. London, 1948


Dallas, Gregor, *Poisoned Peace: 1945 – The War that Never Ended*. John Murray, London, 2006

Dallek, Robert, *Franklin D. Roosevelt and American Foreign Policy 1932–1945*. Oxford University Press, New York, 1995

——, 'Franklin Roosevelt as World Leader', *American Historical Review* 76, 1971

——, *Harry S. Truman*. Times Books. New York, 2008

——, *The Lost Peace: Leadership in a Time of Horror and Hope, 1945–1953*. HarperCollins, New York, 2010

Dalton, Hugh, *Memoirs*: vol. 3, *High Tide and After, 1945–1960*. Muller, London, 1953

Davies, Norman, *God's Playground: A History of Poland*. Oxford University Press, London, 2005

——, *Rising '44: the Battle for Warsaw*. Macmillan, London, 2004

Deák, István, Jan T. Gross, and Tony Judt (eds.), *The Politics of Retribution in Europe*. Princeton University Press, Princeton, NJ, 2000

Dimitrov, George (ed. Ivo Branac; trans. Jane T. Hedges, Timothy D. Sergay, Irina Faion), *The Diary of George Dimitrov*. Yale University Press, New Haven, CT, 2012

Djilas, Milovan, *Conversations with Stalin* (trans. Michael B. Petrovich). Harcourt Brace Jovanovich, New York, 1962

Dobbs, Michael, *Six Months in 1945*. Knopf, New York, 2012

Dönhoff, Gräfin Marion, *Namen, die keiner mehr nennt: Ostpreussen, Menschen und Geschichte*. Diederichs, Munich, 2005

Dos Passos, John, *Tour of Duty*. Praeger, New York, 1946

Douglas, R. M., *Orderly and Humane, The Expulsion of the Germans after the Second World War*. Yale University Press, New Haven, CT, 2012

Dower, John, *Embracing Defeat: Japan in the Wake of World War Two*. Allen Lane, London, 1999

——, *Empire and Aftermath: Yoshida Shigeru and the Japanese Experience, 1878–1954*. Harvard University Press, Cambridge, MA, 1979

——, *Japan in War and Peace: Selected Essays*. New Press, New York, 1993

Drakulić, Slavenka, *Balkan Express*. Hutchinson, London, 1993

Dwarkadas, Kanji, *Ten Years to Freedom*. Popular Prakashan, Bombay, 1968

Faludy, György, *My Happy Days in Hell*. Andre Deutsch, London, 1962

Fawcett, Louise L'Estrange, *Iran and the Cold War: The Azerbaijan Crisis of 1946*. Cambridge University Press, New York, 1992

Fehér, István, *Az utolsó percben: Magyarország nemzetiségei 1945–1990*. Kossuth, Budapest, 1993

Fenby, Jonathan, *The General: General de Gaulle and the France He Saved*. Simon and Schuster, London, 2011

——, *Generalissimo: Chiang Kai-Shek and the China He Lost*. Free Press, London, 2003

——, *The Penguin History of Modern China*. Allen Lane, London, 2008

French, Patrick, *Liberty or Death: India's Journey to Independence and Division*. Flamingo, London, 1998

Furet, François (trans. Deborah Furet), *The Passing of an Illusion: The Idea of Communism in the Twentieth Century*. Chicago University Press, Chicago, IL, 1999


Gaddis, John, *The Cold War*. Allen Lane, London, 2006

——, *George Kennan: An American Life*. Penguin, New York, 2011

——, *The Long Peace: Inquiries into the History of the Cold War*. Oxford University Press, New York, 1984

——, *We Now Know: Rethinking Cold War History*. Oxford University Press, London, 1997

Gellately, Robert, *Stalin's Curse: Battling for Communism in War and Cold War*. Oxford University Press, Oxford, 2013

Gieseke, Jens (trans. Mary Carlene Forszt), *The GDR State Security: Sword and Shield of the Party*. Federal Commissioner, Berlin, 2002

Gleason, Abbot, *Totalitarianism: The Inner History of the Cold War*. Oxford University Press, New York, 1995

Gollancz, Victor, *Leaving Them to Their Fate: The Ethics of Starvation in Germany*. Gollancz, London, 1947

Gomułka, Władysław, *Pamiętniki (Memoirs)*. Polska Oficyna Wydawnicza BGW, Warsaw, 1994

Gopal, Sarvepalli, *Jawaharlal Nehru: A Biography*, 3 vols. Jonathan Cape, London, 1976–84

Gromyko, Andrei (trans. Harold Shukman), *Memoirs*. Doubleday, New York, 1989

Grose, Peter, *Gentleman Spy, The Life of Allen Dulles.* Houghton Mifflin, Boston, MA, 1994

Gross, Jan, *Fear: Anti-Semitism in Poland after Auschwitz.* Random House, New York, 2006

Hamby, Alonzo, *Man of the People, A Life of Harry S. Truman.* Oxford University Press, New York, 1995

Harbutt, Fraser J., *The Iron Curtain: Churchill, America, and the Origins of the Cold War.* Oxford University Press, New York and Oxford, 1986

Harriman, W. Averell, and Elie Abel, *Special Envoy to Churchill and Stalin, 1941–1946.* Random House, New York, 1975

Harris, Kenneth, *Attlee.* Weidenfeld & Nicolson, London, 1982

Harvey, Robert, *American Shogun: MacArthur, Hirohito and the American Duel with Japan.* John Murray, London, 2006

Hasan, Mushirul (ed.), *India Partitioned: The Other Face of Freedom.* Roli Books, New Delhi, 2013

Haslam, Jonathan, *Russia's Cold War: From the October Revolution to the Fall of the Wall.* Yale University Press, New Haven, CT, and London, 2011

Hay, Julius (trans. and abridged by J. A. Underwood), *Born 1900: Memoirs.* Hutchinson, London, 1974

Hitchcock, William, *The Bitter Road to Freedom: A New History of the Liberation of Europe.* Free Press, New York, 2008

——, *France Restored: Cold War Diplomacy and the Quest for Leadership in Europe, 1944–1954.* University of North Carolina Press, Chapel Hill, NC, 1998

——, *The Struggle for Europe.* Doubleday, New York, 2003

Hixson, William, *Parting the Curtain: Propaganda, Culture and the Cold War, 1945–1961.* Macmillan, London, 1997

Hobsbawm, Eric, *The Age of Extremes: A History of the World, 1914–1991.* Pantheon, New York, 1994

Holloway, David, *Stalin and the Bomb: The Soviet Union and*

*Atomic Energy, 1939–1956.* Yale University Press, New Haven, CT, 1994

Hoxha, Enver, *With Stalin: Memoirs.* 8 Nëntori, Tirana, 1979

Iatrides, John O. (ed.), *Ambassador MacVeagh Reports: Greece, 1933–1947.* Princeton University Press, Princeton, NJ, 1980

——, *Greece in the 1940s: A Bibliographic Companion.* University Press of New England, Hanover, NH, 1981

——, and Linda Wrigley (eds.), *Greece at the Crossroads: The Civil War and its Legacy.* Pennsylvania State University Press, University Park, PA, 1995

Ionesco, Ghita, *Communism in Romania, 1944–1962.* Oxford University Press, London, 1964

Isaacson, Walter, and Evan Thomas, *The Wise Men: Six Friends and the World They Made.* Faber and Faber, London, 1986

Judt, Tony, *Postwar: a History of Europe since 1945.* Heinemann, London, 2005

Jung Chang and Jon Halliday, *Mao: The Untold Story.* Jonathan Cape, London, 2005

Kaplan, Karel, *The Short March: The Communist Takeover in Czechoslovakia, 1945–1948.* St Martin's Press, New York, 1987

Katz, Barry, 'The Criticism of Arms: The Frankfurt School Goes to War', *Journal of Modern History*, vol. 59, No. 3 (September 1987)

Kawai, Kazuo, *Japan's American Interlude.* University of Chicago Press, Chicago, IL, 1979

Kennan, George F., *Memoirs, 1925–1950.* Little Brown, Boston, MA, 1967

Kersten, Krystyna, *The Establishment of Communist Rule in Poland, 1943–1948.* University of California Press, Berkeley, CA, 1991

Khan, Yasmin, *The Great Partition: The Making of India and Pakistan.* Yale University Press, 2007

Khlevniuk, Oleg V., and Yoram Gorlizki, *Cold Peace: Stalin and the*

*Soviet Ruling Circle 1945–1953*. Oxford University Press, Oxford, 2004

Khrushchev, Nikita (trans. and ed. Jerrold L. Schecter with Vyacheslav V. Luchkov), *Khrushchev Remembers: The Glasnost Tapes*. Little Brown, Boston, MA, 1990

Kimball, Warren, *The Juggler: Franklin Roosevelt as Wartime Statesman*. Princeton University Press, 1991

Kissinger, Henry. *Diplomacy*. Simon and Schuster, New York, 1994

——, 'Reflections on Containment', *Foreign Affairs 73*, No. 3, 1994

Klemperer, Victor (ed. and abridged by Martin Chalmers), *To the Bitter End: The Diaries of Victor Klemperer, 1942–1945*. Weidenfeld and Nicolson, London, 1999

——, *The Lesser Evil: The Diaries of Victor Klemperer, 1945–1959*. Weidenfeld and Nicolson, 2003

Kovály, Heda Margolius, *Prague Farewell* (trans. Franci Epstein and Helen Epstein). Victor Gollancz, London, 1988

Krämer, Gudrun (trans. Graham Harman), *A History of Palestine: From the Ottoman Conquest to the Founding of the State of Israel*. Princeton University Press, Princeton, NJ, 2008

Kynaston, David, *Austerity Britain, 1945–1951: Tales of a New Jerusalem*. Bloomsbury, London, 2008

Larina, Anna, *This I Cannot Forget: The Memoirs of Nikolai Bukharin's Widow*. Norton, New York, 1995

Leffler, Melvyn, *For the Soul of Mankind*. Hill and Wang, New York, 2007

Leonhard, Wolfgang, *Child of the Revolution*. Collins, London, 1957

Lowe, Keith, *Savage Continent: Europe in the Aftermath of World War II*. Viking, London, 2012

MacArthur, Douglas, *Reminiscences*. McGraw-Hill, New York, 1964

McCullough, David, *Truman*. Simon and Schuster, New York, 1993

McDonogh, Giles, *After the Reich: from the Liberation of Vienna to the Berlin Airlift*. John Murray, London, 2007

Mastny, Vojtech, *The Cold War and Soviet Insecurity: the Stalin Years.*
Oxford University Press, New York, 1996

Mazower, Mark, *The Balkans.* Weidenfeld and Nicolson, London, 2000

——, *Inside Hitler's Greece: the Experience of Occupation, 1941–1944.*
Yale University Press, New Haven, CT, 1995

——, (ed.), *After the War Was Over: Reconstructing the Family,
Nation, and State in Greece, 1943–1960.* Princeton University
Press, Princeton, NJ, 2000

Mehta, Ved, *Mahatma Gandhi and his Apostles.* Yale University Press,
New Haven, CT, 1977

Menand, Louis, 'Getting Real: George Kennan's Cold War', *New
Yorker*, 14 November 2011

Menon, V. P., *The Story of the Integration of the Indian States.*
Longmans, Green, London, 1956

——, *The Transfer of Power in India.* Longmans, Green, London,
1957

Mikołajczyk, Stanisław, *The Rape of Poland: Pattern of Soviet
Aggression.* Whittlesey House, New York, 1948

Miscamble, Wilson, *From Roosevelt to Truman: Potsdam, Hiroshima,
and the Cold War.* Cambridge University Press, New York, 2007

Mitrokhin, Vassily, and Christopher Andrew, *The Mitrokhin Archive:
The KGB in Europe and the West.* Allen Lane, London, 1999

Moon, Sir Penderel, *Divide and Quit: An Eyewitness Account of the
Partition of India.* Oxford University Press, Delhi, 1998

Moran, Lord, *Winston Churchill: The Struggle for Survival, 1940–1965.*
Sphere, London, 1968

Morris, Benny, *Righteous Victims.* Vintage, New York, 2001

Murphy, Robert, *Diplomat Among Warriors.* Doubleday, New York,
1964

Naimark, Norman, *The Fires of Hatred.* Harvard University Press,
Cambridge, MA, 2002

——, *The Russians in Germany, 1945–1949.* Harvard University Press,
Cambridge, MA, 2001

Nehru, Jawaharlal, *An Autobiography.* Bodley Head, London, 1955
——, *The Discovery of India.* Meridian, Delhi, 1956
——, *Jawaharlal Nehru's Speeches.* Indian Ministry of Information, Delhi, 1968
Nicolson, Harold, *Diaries and Letters, 1930–1964* (ed. and condensed by Stanley Olson). Collins, London, 1980

Offner, Arnold, *Another Such Victory: President Truman and the Cold War, 1945–1953.* Stanford University Press, Stanford, CA, 2002
Oz, Amos (trans. Nicholas de Lange), *A Tale of Love and Darkness.* Vintage, London, 2005

Padover, Saul, *Psychologist in Germany: The Story of an American Intelligence Officer.* Phoenix House, London, 1946
Plokhy, Sergei, *Yalta: The Price of Peace.* Viking, New York, 2010

Rákosi, Mátyás, *Visszaemlékezések 1944–1956* [Memoirs 1944–1956]. Napvilág, Kiadó, Budapest, 1991
Reynolds, David, *The Origins of the Cold War in Europe.* Yale University Press, New Haven, CT, 1994
Rioux, Jean-Pierre (trans. Geoffrey Rogers), *The Fourth Republic, 1944–1958.* Cambridge University Press, Cambridge, 1987
Roberts, Andrew, *Eminent Churchillians.* Weidenfeld and Nicolson, London, 1994
——, *Masters and Commanders: How Roosevelt, Churchill, Marshall and Alanbrooke Won the War in the West.* Allen Lane, London, 2008
Rose, Norman, *A Senseless, Squalid War: Voices from Palestine, 1890s–1948.* Pimlico, London, 2010

Sakharov, Andrei, *Memoirs* (trans. Richard Lourie). Hutchinson, London, 1990
Salomon, Ernst von, *The Answers of Ernst von Salomon to the 131 Questions in the Allied Military Government*

'*Fragebogen*' (trans. Constantine FitzGibbon). Putnam, London, 1954

Saunders, Frances Stonor, *Who Paid the Piper? The CIA and the Cultural Cold War*. Granta, London, 1999

Schlesinger, Arthur, Jr., 'The Origins of the Cold War', *Foreign Affairs*, No. 46, October 1967

Sebag Montefiore, Simon, *Jerusalem: The Biography*. Weidenfeld and Nicolson, London, 2011

——, *Stalin: The Court of the Red Tsar*. Weidenfeld and Nicolson, London, 2003

Sebestyen, Victor, *Revolution 1989: The Fall of the Soviet Empire*. Weidenfeld and Nicolson, 2009

——, *Twelve Days: The Story of the 1956 Hungarian Revolution*. Weidenfeld and Nicolson, London, 2006

Segev, Tom, *One Palestine, Complete: Jews and Arabs Under the British Mandate*. Abacus, London, 2001

Service, Robert, *Comrades: Communism: A World History*. Pan Books, London, 2008

——, *A History of Twentieth-Century Russia*. Harvard University Press, Cambridge, MA, 1997

——, *Stalin: A Biography*. Macmillan, London, 2004

Shephard, Ben, *The Long Road Home: The Aftermath of the Second World War*. The Bodley Head, London, 2010

Shilon, Avi, *Menachem Begin: A Life*. Yale University Press, New Haven, CT, 2012

Shore, Marci, *Caviar and Ashes: A Warsaw Generation's Life and Death in Marxism, 1918–1968*. Yale University Press, New Haven, CT, 2006

Singh, Anita Inder, *The Origins of the Partition of India*. Oxford University Press, Delhi, 1981

Sissons, Michael, and Philip French (eds.), *Age of Austerity*. Hodder and Stoughton, London, 1963

Slatoff, Walter J., 'GI Morals in Germany', *New Republic*, vol. 114, issue 19, 3 May 1946.

# Bibliography

Snyder, Tim, *Bloodlands*. Vintage, London, 2011
——, *The Reconstruction of Nations: Poland, Ukraine, Lithuania, Belarus 1569–1999*. Yale University Press, New Haven, CT, 2003
Stern, Carola (trans. Abe Farbstein), *Ulbricht: A Political Biography*. Praeger, New York, 1965
Strunk, Peter, *Zensur und Zensoren*. Wiley, Berlin, 1996
Sudoplatov, Pavel, *Special Tasks: The Memoirs of an Unwanted Witness – a Soviet Spymaster*. Little Brown, London, 1994
Szabó, Robert Győri, *A Kummunizmus és a zsidóság az 1945 utáni Magyarországon*. Budapest, 2009

Taubman, William, *Khrushchev: The Man and His Era*. Free Press, London, 2005
Taylor, Frederick, *Exorcising Hitler: The Occupation and Denazification of Germany*. Bloomsbury, London, 2011
Thomas, Hugh, *Armed Truce: The Beginning of the Cold War*. Hamish Hamilton, London, 1986
Tismăneanu, Vladimir, *Reinventing Politics: Eastern Europe from Stalin to Havel*. Free Press, New York, 1992
——, (ed.), *Stalinism Revisited: The Establishment of Communist Regimes in Eastern Europe*. CEU, New York and Budapest, 2009
Truman, Harry, *Dear Bess: The Letters from Harry to Bess Truman, 1910–1959*. University of Missouri Press, Columbia, MO, 1998
——, *Memoirs*. Vol. 2: *Years of Trial and Hope*. Hodder and Stoughton, London, 1956
Tunzelmann, Alex von, *Indian Summer: The Secret History of the End of an Empire*. Pocket Books, London, 2008

Wasserstein, Bernard, *Britain and the Jews of Europe, 1939–1945*. Institute of Jewish Affairs, Clarendon Press, Oxford, 1979
——, *The British in Palestine: The Mandatory Government and the Arab–Jewish Conflict 1917–1929*. Oxford University Press, Oxford, 1974

Wavell, Archibald Lord, *The Viceroy's Journal* (ed. Penderel Moon). Oxford University Press, Dhaka, 1998

Westad, Odd Arne, *The Global Cold War: Third World Interventions and the Making of Our Times.* Cambridge, New York, 2005

Willoughby, John, 'The Sexual Behaviour of American GIs during the Early Years of the Occupation of Germany', *Journal of Military History*, vol. 62, January 1998

Wilson, Francesca, *Aftermath: France, Germany, Austria, Yugoslavia, 1945 and 1946.* Penguin, London, 1947

Wolff-Mönckeberg, Mathilde, *On the Other Side: To My Children: From Germany, 1940–1945.* Persephone Books, London, 2007

Wolpert, Stanley, *Gandhi's Passion: The Life and Legacy of Mahatma Gandhi.* Oxford University Press, New York, 2001

——, *Jinnah of Pakistan.* Oxford University Press, New York, 1984

——, *Nehru: A Tryst with Destiny.* Oxford University Press, New York, 1996

Yergin, Daniel, *Shattered Peace: The Origins of the Cold War and the National Security State.* André Deutsch, London, 1978

Zhukov, Georgi, *The Memoirs of Marshal Zhukov.* Jonathan Cape, London, 1971

Zubok, Vladislav, '"To Hell with Yalta": The Soviet Union Opts for the Status Quo', *Cold War International History Project*, Bulletin Nos. 6 and 7, Winter 1995/6

——, *A Failed Empire: The Soviet Union in the Cold War from Stalin to Gorbachev.* University of North Carolina Press, Chapel Hill, NC, 2007

Zuckmayer, Carl, *A Part of Myself: Portrait of an Epoch* (trans. Richard and Clara Winston). Secker and Warburg, London, 1970

# Notes

## Introduction

1. Arthur Schlesinger Jr., 'The Origins of the Cold War', *Foreign Affairs*, no. 46, October 1967.

## 1. 'I'm Tired of Babying the Soviets'

1. The best general sources for the Iran crisis of 1946 are Bruce Kuniholm, *The Origins of the Cold War in the Near East*, Princeton University Press, 1980; Michael Dobbs, *Six Months in 1945*, Knopf, 2013; Louise L'Estrange Fawcett, *Iran and the Cold War: The Azerbaijan Crisis of 1946*, Cambridge University Press, 1992; Natalia Egorova, *The Iran Crisis of 1945–1946: A View From the Russian Archives*, Cold War International History Project, Working Paper 15, Woodrow Wilson International Center, George Washington University, 1996.
2. Robert Rossow to US Department of State, 30 January 1946, FRUS, vol. 8, p. 322, and quoted in Dobbs, *Six Months in 1945*, p. 190.
3. Archive of the Russian Federation, Foreign Policy, f. 094, op. 30, p. 357 and in Egorova, *The Iran Crisis of 1945–1946*, pp. 8–9.
4. AVPRF, f. 094, op. 31, p. 246.
5. Quoted in Dobbs, *Six Months in 1945*, p. 197.
6. Leo Amery to Anthony Eden, 13 February 1941.

7. Murray to Stettinius, 20 April 1944, FRUS, vol. 6, p. 346; and quoted in Kuniholm, *The Origins of the Cold War in the Near East*.

8. Beria to Stalin, 23 November 1944, AVPRF, f. 06, op. 7, p. 133; and quoted in Egorova, *The Iran Crisis of 1945–1946*, p. 13.

9. S. Kavtaradze to Molotov, 7 June 1945, AVPRF, f. 06, op. 7, p. 7.

10. Molotov to Averell Harriman, 29 November 1945, AVPRF, f. 94, op. 31, p. 351.

11. Truman, *Memoirs*, p. 379.

## 2. The American Century

1. In conversation with Dean Acheson, as reported in the *New Republic*, 14 January 1946.

2. Quote from Roosevelt in Dallek, *The Lost Peace*, p. 225.

3. Harry Hopkins Papers, Box 9.

4. Ibid., diary entry, 24 March 1943.

5. Truman's diaries, 25 October 1944, Harry S. Truman Library. The best biography of Truman is David McCullough's Pulitzer Prize-winning *Truman*, but *Dear Bess*, his correspondence with his wife, is a mine of useful information and anecdote. Roy Jenkins's excellent *Truman*, Collins, 1986, is a brief and elegant biography by a practising politician that shows a subtle understanding of his subject which others lack.

6. Bohlen, *Witness to History*, p. 379.

7. Truman's diaries, 19 January 1942.

8. Truman, *Dear Bess*, p. 96.

9. To Joseph Davies, former Ambassador to Moscow, as quoted in Isaacson and Thomas, *The Wise Men*.

## 3. The Russians: 'A Tsarist People'

1. In Vladislav Zubok, *Inside the Kremlin*, pp. 142–7, Sebag Montefiore, *Stalin*, pp. 436–9, and Holloway, *Stalin and the Bomb*, pp. 138–42.
2. Holloway, *Stalin and the Bomb*, p. 86.
3. Gromyko, *Memoirs*, p. 319; Sudoplatov, *Special Tasks*; Beria, *My Father*.
4. Clark Kerr to Eden, 23 December 1945.
5. Holloway, *Stalin and the Bomb*, p. 127.
6. Sakharov, *Memoirs*, p. 146.
7. Zubok, *Inside the Kremlin*, p. 141, and Holloway, *Stalin and the Bomb*, p. 144.
8. Chuev, *Molotov Remembers*, p. 214.
9. Holloway, *Stalin and the Bomb*, p. 145, and Sebag Montefiore, *Stalin*, p. 438.
10. Sebag Montefiore, *Stalin*, p. 422.
11. Cadogan, *Diaries*, p. 476.
12. Khrushchev, *Khrushchev Remembers*, p. 365.
13. Beria, *My Father*, p. 260.
14. Khrushchev, *Khrushchev Remembers*, p. 343.
15. Sebag Montefiore, *Stalin*, pp. 435–8, and Khlevniuk and Gorlizki, *Cold Peace*, pp. 223–7. Also in RGASPI 538.12. 744.
16. Gellately, *Stalin's Curse*, p. 247.

## 4. Stunde Null – Zero Hour

1. Andrew Murray, *Coal Dust Covered Decisions*, monograph, University College Dublin, 2010, p. 19.
2. Ibid., p. 22.
3. Clare, *Berlin Days*, p. 43.

4. Klemperer, *To The Bitter End*, p. 298; Anne O'Hare McCormick, *New York Times*, 30 May 1945.

5. Cabinet Office to Ernest Bevin, 30 October 1945. TNA: FO 370/800/514 Europe/34.

6. Kennan, *Memoirs*, p. 369.

7. Cadogan to Churchill, 23 May 1945, TNA: FO 370/14/219.

8. Montgomery to War Department, 30 January 1946, National Archive; Clay to State Department, FRUS, 1945, vol. 4, p. 354.

9. Konrad Adenauer, quoted in McDonogh, *After the Reich*, p. 236; Ernst Jünger, quoted in Julien Hervier (trans. Joachim Neugroschel), *The Details of Time: Conversations with Ernst Jünger*, Marsilio, New York, 1995, p. 144.

10. Murphy, *Diplomat Among Warriors*, p. 112.

11. Quotes from McDonogh, *After the Reich*, p. 180.

12. Wolff-Mönckeberg, *On the Other Side*, p. 136.

13. Stephen Hermlin, in *Ulenspiegel*, 30 October 1946.

14. Quoted in Lewis Joachim Edinger, *Kurt Schumacher: A Study in Personality and Behaviour*, Stanford University Press, 1965, p. 143, and in Taylor, *Exorcising Hitler*, p. 217.

15. FRUS 1945, vol. 5, p. 236.

16. Clare, *Berlin Days*, p. 167.

17. Captain Walter Gerrard, Welsh Guards, in conversation with the author, September 1995.

18. Gunther Neumann, *Ulenspiegel*, 17 February 1946.

19. Arthur Moon quoted in Hitchcock, *The Bitter Road to Freedom*, p. 127; Zuckmayer, *A Part of Myself*, p. 168.

20. Clare, *Berlin Days*; Walter Slatoff, *New Republic*, 19 July 1946.

21. Bessel, *Germany 1945*, p. 245.

22. TNA: WO 32/10790. 18.

23. EN2. 32 Imperial War Museum Archive, London.

24. European War Papers, National Archives, Washington, DC, 1945/740/ 100767.

25. OMGUS, vol. 5, 3005.

26. Anonymous, *A Woman in Berlin*, p. 86; Andreas-Friedrich, *Battleground Berlin*, 13 March 1946.
27. TNA: FO 371/2055/8; OMGUS, vol. 5, 2091.
28. *Time* magazine, 22 February 1946.
29. Frank Howley to State Department, 13 November 1945, FRUS, vol. 4, p. 647; Botting, quoted in Taylor, *Exorcising Hitler*, p. 263.
30. Morgan to Foreign Office, 13 June 1946, TNA: WO 32/ 1163. 12.

## 5. Austria Forgets Its Past

1. Clare, *Berlin Days*, p. 275.
2. *Chicago Tribune*, 30 October 1945.
3. John Dos Passos, *Tour of Duty*, p. 93.

## 6. The Spy Comes In from the Cold

1. The best account of the Gouzenko affair is in Amy Knight, *How the Cold War Began: The Gouzenko Affair and the Hunt for Soviet Spies*, McClelland and Stewart, 2005. There is also good background in Mitrokhin and Andrew, *The Mitrokhin Archive*.
2. Jack Anderson, *Confessions of a Muckraker*, Random House, 1979.
3. Haynes Johnson, *The Age of Anxiety*, Mariner Books, 2006, is an excellent account of McCarthyism and its effect on America.
4. Pamela Hansford Johnson, *Important to Me*, Macmillan, 2012.
5. Zubok, *A Failed Empire*, p. 358.

## 7. Austerity Britain

1. 'Snoek Piquante', essay in Sissons and French, *Age of Austerity*.
2. Ibid.; Smith quote, *Daily Mirror*, 20 February 1946.
3. Gollancz, *Leaving Them to Their Fate*, p. 12.

4. Hugh Dalton quoted in Bullock, *Ernest Bevin*, p. 488; *Daily Mirror*, 29 May 1946; *Sunday Pictorial*, 28 April 1946.

5. Lord Keynes Papers, TNA: T 247/40, Reel 6.

6. Acheson, *Present at the Creation*, p. 377.

7. Quoted in Philip Ziegler, *Wilson*, Weidenfeld and Nicolson, 1993, p. 247.

8. *The Economist*, 14 December 1945; *New Statesman*, 13 December 1945.

9. Both Pierson Dixon and Attlee quoted in Bullock, *Ernest Bevin*, pp. 567–8.

10. Clark Clifford, in CNN Cold War series interviews, Liddell Hart Centre for Military Archives.

11. Lord Keynes Papers, TNA: T 247/40, Reel 6; Tony Judt, *Postwar*, p. 119.

12. Clayton to State Department, 28 January 1946, FRUS, vol. 4, p. 277.

13. Nicolson, *Diaries and Letters*, 10 November 1947.

14. Harris, *Attlee*, p. 365.

15. Anthony Howard, essay 'The Labour Victory', in Sissons and French, *Age of Austerity*. Footnote: Sir Henry Channon, 21 January 1946, in *Chips: The Diaries of Sir Henry Channon* (ed. Robert Rhodes James), Phoenix, 1996.

## 8. A Performance at the Bolshoi

1. *Pravda*, 10 February 1946.

2. Alliluyeva, *Twenty Letters to a Friend*, p. 138.

3. Alexander N. Yakovlev (trans. Anthony Austin), *A Century of Violence in Soviet Russia*, Yale University Press, 2002.

4. RGASPI 671. 53. 376.

5. Harry Hopkins Papers, Box 18.

6. Quoted in *Time* magazine, 11 March 1946.

### 9. The Declaration of Cold War

1. Roosevelt to Stalin, FRUS, 1945, vol. 4, p. 537; Roosevelt to Churchill, ibid., p. 546; comment to McCormick quoted in Jon Meacham, *Franklin and Winston: An Intimate Portrait of an Epic Friendship*, Random House, 2003, p. 268.
2. Quoted in Dallek, *The Lost Peace*, p. 89; Harriman and Abel, *Special Envoy to Churchill and Stalin*, p. 346.
3. Harriman and Abel, *Special Envoy to Churchill and Stalin*, p. 374.
4. Kennan, *Memoirs*, p. 423.
5. The Long Telegram, FRUS, 1946, vol. 5, pp. 356–90.
6. Vandenberg to Truman, 24 March 1946, War Department Papers, Military Intelligence Division, 165.4.7, National Archives, Washington, DC.
7. Military Intelligence Division to Joint Chiefs of Staff, February 1946, 165.4.9, ibid.
8. Eisenhower to Truman, 19 January 1946, National Archives, Washington, DC, and Truman Library; Joint Chiefs to Secretary for War, War Department Papers, Military Intelligence Division, 165.2.8, National Archives, Washington, DC.
9. Acheson, *Present at the Creation*, p. 362; Vandenberg to Truman, 24 March 1946, War Department Papers, Military Intelligence Division, 165.4.7, National Archives, Washington, DC.

### 10. The Abdication Crisis

1. 'The Emperor Should Abdicate Quickly', in June 1946 issue of the news magazine *Shinchō*.
2. Michio Kinoshita, *Shorthand Diary*, Bungei Shunjū, 1990; text of the Imperial Rescript in English translation, FRUS, 1946, vol. 8, pp. 134–5; Matsumoto quote in Dower, *Embracing Defeat*, p. 353.
3. FRUS, 1946, vol. 8, p. 98.

4. The Bonner Fellers Memorandum: 'Basic Military Plan for Psychological Warfare Against Japan', Fellers Papers, Hoover Institution, Stanford University, California.

5. MacArthur to Joint Chiefs, FRUS, vol. 8, pp. 395–7.

6. FRUS, vol. 8, p. 416.

7. Dower, *Embracing Defeat*, p. 363.

8. FRUS, vol. 8, p. 242.

9. US Department of the Army Reports to General MacArthur, a multi-volume series of papers with supplements to MacArthur in Japan, The Occupation, The Military Phase. A fascinating insight from the SCAP's intelligence services and officers reporting back home to the US. US Army records, National Archives, Washington, DC, 1966.

10. FRUS, vol. 8, p. 412; *Shinchō*, January 1946.

11. Army Reports to MacArthur, vol. 2, p. 359.

12. *Kyōryoku Shimbun*, 18 March 1946.

13. Winston Churchill, *Triumph and Tragedy*, Mariner Books, 1986, p. 542; Kazuo Kawai, *Japan's American Interlude*, p. 135.

14. Harvey, *American Shogun*, pp. 68–71.

15. Quoted in Dallek, *The Lost Peace*, p. 94.

16. Truman, *Diaries*, 16 March 1946.

17. Harvey, *American Shogun*, p. 158.

18. MacArthur, *Reminiscences*, p. 233.

19. Faubion Bowers, 'The Day the General Blinked', *New York Times*, 30 September 1988.

20. Army Reports to MacArthur, vol. 2, pp. 399–402.

21. *Time* magazine, 20 March 1955.

22. Bowers, 'The Day the General Blinked'.

23. *Saturday Evening Post*, 15 December 1945; quoted in Dower, *Embracing Defeat*, p. 97.

24. Kawai, *Japan's American Interlude*, p 143.

25. Bowers, 'The Day the General Blinked'; Kennan, *Memoirs*, pp. 376–7.

26. Dower, *Embracing Defeat*, p. 73.

## 11. Rape and Pillage

1. Djilas, *Conversations with Stalin*, p. 142.
2. Naimark, *The Russians in Germany*, p. 289.
3. FRUS, 1945, vol. 4, p. 366.
4. Annan, *Changing Enemies*, p. 228.
5. Andreas-Friedrich, *Battleground Berlin*, 30 May 1945.
6. Gustav Regler, *The Owl of Minerva*, Hart Davis, 1959; Leonhard, *Child of the Revolution*, p. 369.
7. Leonhard, *Child of the Revolution*, p. 378.
8. APRF, 162. f. 43. 87.
9. Applebaum, *Iron Curtain*, p. 162.
10. *Tägliche Rundschau*, 20 June 1945.
11. *Tägliche Rundschau*, 18 April 1946.
12. *Ulenspiegel*, 2 January 1946.
13. FRUS, 1945, vol. 4, p. 477.
14. Naimark, *The Russians in Germany*, p. 198.
15. FRUS, 1945, vol. 5, p. 227.
16. Quoted in Dobbs, *Six Months in 1945*, p. 278.
17. Pauley to Truman, 26 October 1945, Harry S. Truman Library.
18. Leonhard, *Child of the Revolution*, p. 308.
19. RGASPI 688. 53. 277.
20. Zubok, *Inside the Kremlin*, p. 365.
21. Colin MacInnes, *To the Victors the Spoils*, Faber (reprint), London, 1991, p. 196.

## 12. 'Woe, Woe to the Germans'

1. Beneš, message to Czechs, BBC, 20 April 1943. From 1939 Beneš made weekly, sometimes daily, BBC talks to the Czech underground.
2. Beneš, speech on return to Prague at the Old Town Hall, 16 March

1945; Churchill to House of Commons, 12 December 1944; Stalin to Beneš in Moscow, 12 December 1943, APRF, 232 f. 60. 133.

3. Drtina and Svoboda quotes in Judt, *Postwar*, p. 122; Mgr Stašek sermon 25 June 1945, quoted later in Czech newspaper *Rude Pravo*, 19 October 1946.

4. Prague Radio 'news' broadcast, 20 February 1946; McCormick, *New York Times*, 26 October 1945.

5. Lowe, *Savage Continent*, p. 134. The best accounts of the ethnic cleansing of the Germans are in Lowe; Shephard, *The Long Road Home*; Douglas, *Orderly and Humane*; Alfred de Zayas, *A Terrible Revenge*; Naimark, *The Fires of Hatred*, and McDonogh, *After the Reich*.

6. Radio Praha, *Reminiscences of the Brno March*, programme 12 May 2010, presented by Jan Richter.

7. APRF, 422, f. 35. 346; Zhukov comment in his *Memoirs*, p. 399.

8. Radio Praha, *Reminiscences*.

9. Stalin, letter to Gomułka, Polish Communist Party Papers, Central Archive of Modern Records, Warsaw, 1945, 300. 25; Bishop quoted in Judt, *Postwar*, p. 139.

10. Cche 21, 22, Archive of the Polish Government-in-exile.

11. Box 17, Stanisław Mikołajczyk Collection, ibid.

12. Polish Communist Party Papers 1945, 303. 44, Central Archive of Modern Records, Warsaw.

13. McDonogh, *After the Reich*, pp. 296–7 and Douglas, *Orderly and Humane*, pp. 188–9.

14. Report to OMG Bavaria, Welfare Section, RG 260/390/40, National Archives, Washington, DC.

15. Bogusław Kopka has compiled the most comprehensive database of the Polish labour camps from 1944 to 1950: *Obozy pracy w Polsce 1944–1950: przewodnik encyklopedyczny*, Ośrodek Karta, Warsaw, 2002.

16. OMGUS Welfare Department, RG 260/287/32, and McDonogh, *After the Reich*, p. 259.

## 13. 'Anywhere but Home'

1. Sebag Montefiore, *Stalin*, p. 524, and Khlevniuk and Gorlizki, *Cold Peace*, p. 257.
2. Stalin to Zhukov, Sebag Montefiore, *Stalin*, p. 525; Military Council statement, *Izvestia*, 26 June 1946.
3. APRF, 437. f. 28. 424.
4. Harriman and Abel, *Special Envoy*, p. 286.
5. Eden to Churchill, TNA: FO 371 2097/304; Dean quoted in Lowe, *Savage Continent*, p. 256; Selborne to Churchill, Cabinet papers TNA: PREM 4/109.113.
6. Chuev, *Molotov*, p. 127.
7. Churchill, *Triumph and Tragedy*, Mariner Books, 1986, p. 477; Alexandra Kollontai, *The Autobiography of a Sexually Emancipated Woman*, Createspace, 2011, p. 166.
8. Harriman and Abel, *Special Envoy*, p. 335.
9. FRUS, 1946, vol. 5, p. 688.
10. FRUS, 1946, vol. 5, p. 135.
11. Repatriation quote by officer, in Lowe, *Savage Continent*, p. 297; Susan Crosland, *Tony Crosland*, Jonathan Cape, 1982, p. 128.
12. Lowe, *Savage Continent*, p. 302.
13. Ibid., p. 306.
14. Milovan Djilas, *The Story from the Inside*, Phoenix, 2001.

## 14. 'This Chinese Cesspit'

1. Marshall to Truman, 6 March 1946, FRUS, vol. 3, p. 288.
2. Quoted in Fenby, *The Penguin History of Modern China*, p. 266.
3. *Time* magazine, 18 April 1943.
4. Stilwell to War Department, 28 May 1943, FRUS, vol. 3, p. 298; Stilwell to State Department, 25 July 1943, FRUS, vol. 3, p. 485; Chiang quoted in Fenby, *Generalissimo*, p. 325, and Theodore H.

White and Annalee Jacoby, *Thunder Out of China*, Da Capo, 1975, p. 156.

5. Chiang's diaries, 24 March 1940, at the Hoover Institution.
6. Dobbs, *Six Months in 1945*, p. 275; Roosevelt quote from Dallek, *The Lost Peace*, p. 137, Willkie anecdote from Fenby, *The Penguin History of Modern China*, p. 288.
7. Lin Biao quote in Li Cheng, *China's Leaders: The New Generation*, Rowman and Littlefield, 2001; Vladimorov to Molotov, APRF 304 f. 56. 67.
8. White and Jacoby, *Thunder Out of China*, p. 198.
9. Dun J. Li, *Modern China: From Mandarin to Commissar*, Charles Scribner, New York, 1978.
10. Jung Chang and Jon Halliday, *Mao*, p. 239.
11. APRF 301 f. 67. 45.
12. Hurley resignation, *New York Times*, 27 November 1945; Truman, *Dear Bess*, 28 November 1945.
13. Truman's diaries, 15 July 1945, Truman Library.

## 15. Iron Curtain

1. Beria, *My Father*.
2. Full text of Churchill's Fulton speech in *Churchill Speaks, The Collected Speeches of Winston Churchill 1897–1963*, Atheneum, 1981.
3. Djilas, *Conversations with Stalin*, p. 163.
4. Polish Communist Party Papers, Warsaw, 1945, 525. 41. 65; Institute for the History of the 1956 Hungarian Revolution Archive, Budapest, Box 30, 303; Sebestyen, *Twelve Days*, p. 86.
5. Sebestyen, *Twelve Days*, p. 82.
6. Tibor Meray and Tamas Aczel, *Revolt of the Mind: A Case History of Intellectual Resistance Behind the Iron Curtain*, Praeger, 1975.
7. After Beneš and Stalin meeting in Moscow, December 1943, RGASPI 438. 72. 755.

8. Full record of the Yalta Conference in English is at the National Archives, Washington, DC, 43.4.1 and in Russian at the APRF 533 f. 45. 248; Chuev, *Molotov Remembers*, p. 235.

9. Mikołajczyk Papers, Box 15, Hoover Institution.

10. Harriman and Abel, *Special Envoy to Churchill and Stalin*, p. 237; FRUS, 1943, vol. 4, p. 733.

11. Moran, *Winston Churchill*, p. 176.

12. Harbutt, *The Iron Curtain*, p. 254.

13. APRF 533 f. 45. 248.

14. Quoted in Applebaum, *Iron Curtain*, p. 215.

15. FRUS, 1945, vol. 4, p. 488.

16. Susan Butler (ed.), *My Dear Mr Stalin: The Complete Correspondence between Franklin D. Roosevelt and Joseph V. Stalin*, Yale University Press, 2008.

17. FRUS, 1944, vol. 5, p. 749.

18. Mikołajczyk and Anders quoted in Dallek, *The Lost Peace*, p. 127.

19. Arthur Bliss Lane, *I Saw Poland Betrayed*, Regency, 1949, p. 186; Truman's diaries, 28 September 1945, Truman Library.

20. Sir Frank Roberts, in review in CNN Cold War Series, Episode 1, full interview transcript at Liddell Hart Centre for Military Archives.

21. Chuev, *Molotov Remembers*, p. 216.

22. I am grateful to Michael Dobbs's *Six Months in 1945*, p. 185, for drawing my attention to Stalin's operatic tastes.

23. Applebaum, *Iron Curtain*, pp. 237–9.

24. Sebestyen, *Revolution 1989*, p. 85.

25. David Reynolds, *From World War to Cold War: Churchill, Roosevelt, and the International History of the 1940s*, Oxford University Press, 2006, p. 215.

26. Truman–Churchill correspondence, Truman Library.

27. Ibid.

28. Reynolds, *From World War to Cold War*, p. 286.

29. *Pravda*, 11 March 1946.

30. Wallace quote in the *New York Times*, 9 March 1946; Pearl Buck

quoted in *Chicago Tribune*, 8 March 1946; Eleanor Roosevelt in the *New York Times*, 9 March 1946.

31. Eden and Salisbury quoted in Reynolds, *From World War to Cold War*, p. 223.
32. TNA: PREM 4, 135. 46; TNA: PREM 4, 124. 86.
33. Churchill, *Triumph and Tragedy*, p. 554.
34. Mary Soames (ed.), *Speaking for Themselves: The Personal Letters of Winston and Clementine Churchill*, Black Swan, 1999; quote about Neville Chamberlain in TNA: CAB 128.12. 44.
35. Roy Jenkins, *Churchill*, Pan Books, 2002, p. 785.
36. Moran, *Winston Churchill*, p. 227.

## 16. The Fog of War

1. FRUS, 1946, vol. 7, p. 466.
2. Ibid., p. 470.
3. Ibid., p. 477.
4. Ibid., p. 513; Harriman and Abel, *Special Envoy to Churchill and Stalin*, p. 313.
5. Acheson, *Present at the Creation*, p. 126.
6. Bevin quote in Hugh Dalton, *Diaries*, 2 March 1946; Alia quoted in Fawcett, *Iran and the Cold War*, p. 263.
7. AVPRF, f. 194. op. 37, p. 277.
8. Fawcett, *Iran and the Cold War*, p. 177.
9. Qavam to Ambassador Murray, FRUS, 1946, vol. 7, p. 529.
10. Ibid., p. 482.
11. Schwarzkopf and Eisenhower comments, FRUS, 1946, vol. 7, p. 156; Kennan to State Department, FRUS, 1946, vol. 4, p. 376; Halifax quote in Bullock, *Ernest Bevin*, p. 455.
12. FRUS, 1946, vol. 7, p. 558; Acheson, *Present at the Creation*, p. 129.
13. *Pravda*, 9 March 1946; Qavam quote in Bullock, *Ernest Bevin*, p. 456.

14. *New York Times*, 27 March 1946.

15. Robert Rossow, 'The Battle for Azerbaijan', *Middle East Journal* 10, 1956.

16. APRF, Moscow, 45 f. 73. 457.


17. Sunset on the Raj


1. Woodrow Wyatt, *Confessions of an Optimist*, HarperCollins, 1987, p. 256.

2. India Office Records, British Library, London R/3/1945. 299/

3. Wavell, *The Viceroy's Journal* (ed. Penderel Moon), 29 April 1946.

4. Azad, *India Wins Freedom*, p. 224.

5. Khan, *The Great Partition*, pp. 67–8. One of the best books on the subject, but among general books for this chapter I have drawn also from French, *Liberty or Death*; Brown, *Nehru: A Political Life*; Wolpert, *Jinnah of Pakistan*; Moon, *Divide and Quit*.

6. Anthony Read and David Fisher, *The Proudest Day: India's Long Road to Independence*, Norton, New York, 1999.

7. TNA: CAB 129.5. 21; Moon, *Divide and Quit*, p. 288.

8. Quoted in Khan, *The Great Partition*, p. 149.

9. Desmond Young, *Lucknow Pioneer*, 15 June 1946, and quoted in Khan, *The Great Partition*, p. 76

10. *Modern Times*, 20 October 1938. The story is well told in Brown, *Nehru*.

11. Nehru, *An Autobiography*, p. 225; Pamela Hicks quote in Tunzelmann, *Indian Summer*.

12. Chaudhuri, *Autobiography of an Unknown Indian*, p. 266.

13. Quoted in Brown, *Nehru*, p. 338.

14. In French, *Liberty or Death*, p. 173.

15. Wolpert, *Jinnah of Pakistan*, p. 144.

16. Dwarkadas, *Ten Years to Freedom*.

17. Mahomed Ali Jinnah, *Speeches and Statements 1947–1948*, Oxford University Press, Karachi, 2000.

18. Wavell, *Journal*, entries 13 May and 18 May; Wavell to Cabinet, TNA: CAB 129/17/29.

19. Jawaharlal Nehru, speech at Congress Rally, Calcutta, 2 October 1939, quoted in Nehru, *An Autobiography*.

20. TNA: CAB 129. 5. 34.

21. Leo Amery, *The Empire at Bay: The Leo Amery Diaries, 1929–1945* (eds. John Barnes and David Nicholson), Hutchinson, London, 1988, 16 April 1941.

22. Martin Gilbert, *Churchill: A Life*, Pimlico, London, 2000, p. 680.

23. Amery, *The Empire at Bay*, 13 June 1943.

24. Cadogan, *Diaries*, 20 August 1943; Alanbrooke, *War Diaries*, 2 December 1943.

25. Dalton, *Memoirs*, 27 November 1946.

## 18. Refugees

1. *New York Times*, 13 April 1946.

2. Quoted in Shephard, *The Long Road Home*, p. 148, and also in Miscamble, *From Roosevelt to Truman*, p. 189.

3. TNA: FO 371 5732; Acheson quote in *Present at the Creation*, p. 399, and quoted in Isaacson and Thomas, *The Wise Men*.

4. Robert Caro, *The Power Broker: Robert Moses and the Fall of New York*, Vintage, 1975.

5. *New York Times*, 13 April 1946.

6. Quoted in Lowe, *Savage Continent*, p. 97.

7. Iris Murdoch, *A Writer at War, Letters and Diaries 1939–1945* (ed. Peter Conradi), Oxford University Press, 2010.

8. Control Commission for Germany Records, TNA: FO 371/310/217.

9. Kathryn Hulme, *The Wild Place*, Pocket Books, 1960, p. 126.

10. FRUS, 1945, vol. 4, p. 767 and quoted in Judt, *Postwar*.

11. Wilson, *Aftermath*, p. 117.

12. Shephard, *The Long Road Home*, p. 237.

13. *Time* magazine, 12 February 1946.

14. Shephard, *The Long Road Home*, p. 197.

15. Tadeusz Nowakowski, *Camp of All Saints* (trans. Norbert Guterman), St Martin's Press, 1962, p. 138.

16. Shephard, *The Long Road Home*, p. 188.

17. Wilson, *Aftermath*, p. 166.

18. Buruma, *Year Zero*, p. 116.

## 19. Trials and Errors

1. Clay, *Decisions in Germany*, p. 113; O'Neill quote in Buruma, *Year Zero*, p. 128.

2. Clay, *Decisions in Germany*, p. 85.

3. Kay Summersby Morgan, *Past Forgetting: My Love Affair with Dwight D. Eisenhower*, Simon and Schuster, 1976.

4. Attlee, *As it Happened*, p. 299; and Victor Gollancz, *In Darkest Germany*, Gollancz, 1947.

5. McDonogh, *After the Reich*, p. 276.

6. Interview transcripts in CNN Cold War Series, Liddell Hart Centre for Military Archives.

7. CDU Founding Conference, Cologne, 23 March 1946, and quoted in Judt, *Postwar*, p. 176.

8. Karl Jaspers, *The Question of German Guilt*, Fordham University Press, 2000, Lecture 2.

9. Ibid., Lecture 3.

10. Hannah Arendt, *Eichmann in Jerusalem*, Viking, 1964.

11. TNA: FO 371. 8773. 302.

12. Quoted in Buruma, *Year Zero*, p. 179.

13. OMGUS, RG 197/105/66.

14. OMGUS Military Intelligence Division, RG 103/377/28.

15. OMGUS Military Intelligence Department to Clay, 23 July 1946, RG 103/325/68.

16. Annan, *Changing Enemies*, p. 187.

17. Cordell Hull, *The Memoirs of Cordell Hull*, Macmillan, 1948;

Churchill quoted by Moran, *Winston Churchill*, p. 399; Cadogan memo, TNA: CAB 122. 65. 53.

18. Kennan, *Memoirs*, p. 465.

19. TNA: PREM 4. 109. 102. 28.

20. Shawcross to Attlee, 20 January 1946, TNA: PREM 4 108. 203. 34; Attlee to Shawcross, 22 January 1946, TNA: PREM 4 108. 203. 63.

21. Report about Operation Paperclip, FRUS, 1945, vol. 4, p. 455; quote about Rudolph, OMGUS Intelligence Department, RG 19.357.

22. OMGUS Intelligence Department, RG 16. 454.

23. Applebaum, *Iron Curtain*, p. 279.

24. Ibid., p. 242.

25. Andreas-Friedrich, *Battleground Berlin*, 26 April 1946.

26. Zubok, *Inside the Kremlin*, p. 312.

## 20. A Greek Tragedy

1. André Gerolymatos, *Red Acropolis, Black Terror: the Greek Civil War and the Origins of Soviet–American Rivalry, 1943–1949*, Basic Books, 2004, p. 114.

2. AVPRF 191 f. 46. 335; Grigory Popov quote in Haslam, *Russia's Cold War*, p. 233.

3. Gerolymatos, *Red Acropolis, Black Terror*, p. 78, and also in Lowe, *Savage Continent*, p. 247.

4. Iatrides and Wrigley, *Greece at the Crossroads*, p. 168.

5. Djilas, *Conversations with Stalin*, p. 177.

6. Gerolymatos, *Red Acropolis, Black Terror*, p. 144.

7. Dimitrov, *The Diary of George Dimitrov*, p. 396.

8. Quoted in Lowe, *Savage Continent*, p. 249.

9. Bevin in speech to the Labour Party Conference, 28 September 1945.

10. AVPRF 192. f. 44. 277; Dimitrov, *The Diary of George Dimitrov*, p. 366.

11. Churchill, *Triumph and Tragedy*, Mariner Books, 1986, p. 533; quote to Mackenzie King in Gilbert, *Churchill: A Life*, Pimlico, London, 2000, p. 646.
12. Djilas, *Conversations with Stalin*, p. 197.

## 21. She'erit ha-pleta: The Surviving Remnant

1. FRUS, 1945, vol. 5, p. 455.
2. Ibid.
3. Acheson, *Present at the Creation*, p. 288.
4. Truman to Saudi King Ib'n Saud, FRUS, 1945, vol. 5, p. 488; on midterm elections and domestic politics Truman's Diaries, 24 October 1945, Harry S. Truman Library.
5. On Jewish immigration into Palestine see Segev, *One Palestine Complete*; Krämer, *A History of Palestine*; Ben Gurion, *Israel, A Personal History*; Sebag Montefiore, *Jerusalem: the Biography*.
6. Crossman, *Palestine Mission*, p. 68.
7. Quoted in Bullock, *Ernest Bevin*, p. 498.
8. Truman to Attlee, 24 August 1945, Harry S. Truman Library.
9. TNA: PREM 4 105.57; and Truman and Attlee arguments in Wasserstein, *The British in Palestine*, pp. 307–10.
10. For immigration routes, see Morris, *Righteous Victims*, and Ben Gurion, *Israel, A Personal History*.
11. Ben Gurion description, Oz, *A Tale of Love and Darkness*, p. 112; Ben Gurion on anti-Semitism, *Recollections*, pp. 157–9.
12. Ben Gurion quotes from Segev, *One Palestine Complete*, p. 364, and on his political views, Shimon Peres, *Ben Gurion: A Political Life*, Shocken, 2011.
13. Ben Gurion, *Recollections*, p. 214.
14. Ibid., p. 230.
15. Segev, *One Palestine Complete*, p. 388.
16. Ibid., p. 396.
17. The best biography of Weizmann is Norman Rose, *Weizmann: A*

*Biography*, Viking, 1986; his autobiography, *Trial and Error*, Hamish Hamilton, 1949, is an indispensable source as are his *Papers and Letters* (eds. Barnet Litvinov and Bernard Wasserstein), Rutgers University Press, 1968–80.

18. Ben Gurion, *Recollections*, pp. 108 and 231; Weizmann, *Papers*, vol. 3, p. 708.

19. Montgomery letter to K. C. O'Connor, quoted in Segev, *One Palestine Complete*, p. 332.

20. On land ownership, Sebag Montefiore, *Jerusalem*, pp. 440–6; Segev, *One Palestine Complete*, pp. 330–36; George Antonius, *The Arab Awakening: The Story of the Arab National Movement*, Kegan Paul, 2000; Rashid Khalidi, *The Iron Cage, The Story of the Palestinian Struggle for Statehood*, Beacon Press, 2007, and *Palestinian Identity*, Columbia University Press, 1998; and Morris, *Righteous Victims*, pp. 126–34, are excellent.

21. MacDonald quote in Wasserstein, *The British in Palestine*, p. 248.

22. Report of the Anglo-American Committee of Enquiry Regarding the Problems of European Jewry and Palestine, Cmd 6808.

23. Koestler quote, Arthur Koestler, *Promise and Fulfilment: Palestine 1917–1949*, Ramage Press, 2007; Weizmann, *Papers*, vol. 3, p. 469.

24. Segev, *One Palestine Complete*, p. 213.

25. Quoted in Bullock, *Ernest Bevin*, p. 715.

26. Morris, *Righteous Victims*, p. 186.

27. From Bullock, *Ernest Bevin*, pp. 668–88.

28. Weizmann, *Papers*, vol. 3, p. 378.

29. Bullock, *Ernest Bevin*, pp. 695–6.

30. Cavendish-Bentinck to Bevin, 30 September 1945, TNA: FO 371/1027. 305.

31. Bullock, *Ernest Bevin*, pp. 537–8, and Wasserstein, *The British in Palestine*, p. 301.

32. Begin, *The Revolt*, p. 103.

33. Sebag Montefiore, *Jerusalem*, p. 462.

34. Segev, *One Palestine Complete*, p. 436.

35. Bernard Montgomery, *The Memoirs of Field Marshal Montgomery of Alamein*, Collins, 1958.

## 22. 'A Jewish–Bolshevik Plot' – Blood Libels

1. The story of the Kielce 'pogrom' is told best in Jan Gross, *Fear: Anti-Semitism in Poland after Auschwitz*, Random House, New York, 2006. Also Anne Applebaum, *Iron Curtain*; Anita Prazmowska, *A History of Modern Poland*, IB Tauris, 2010 and Keith Lowe, *Savage Continent*.
2. Quoted in Applebaum, p. 312.
3. Quoted in Lowe, p. 336.
4. Kovály, *Prague Farewell*, p. 114.
5. Rachel Auerbach, *On the Fields of Treblinka*, Report of Historical Commission of Polish Jews, Warsaw, 1947.
6. *Odrodzenie*, 25 September 1946.
7. Cardinal Hlond press conference, 11 July 1946, in *New York Times*, 13 July.
8. Gross, *Fear*, pp. 218–27.
9. Cavendish-Bentinck to Foreign Office, 18 July 1946, TNA: FO 371/1027.412.
10. Teresa Toranska, *Oni: Stalin's Polish Puppets*, Collins/Harvill, 1987, p. 135.
11. Gross, *Fear*, p. 286; Prazmowska and Applebaum are enlightening on Żydokomuna.
12. Victor Sebestyen, *Twelve Days*, pp. 83–5.

## 23. The War Against Terror

1. Account of King David Hotel bombing from David Leitch's essay in Sissons and French, *Age of Austerity*, pp. 203–30; Begin, *The*

*Revolt*, pp. 235–40; *Times* reports 23–26 July 1946; *New York Times*, 25 and 26 July 1946; Segev, *One Palestine Complete*, pp. 467–8, and Norman Rose, *A Senseless, Squalid War*, pp. 158–69.

2. Segev, *One Palestine Complete*, p. 475.
3. Bernard Montgomery, *The Memoirs of Field Marshal Montgomery of Alamein*, Collins, 1958, pp. 466–70; Barker letter in *New York Times*, 6 August 1946.
4. Crossman, *Palestine Mission*, p. 137.
5. Scores of the Barker–Katy Antonius letters are in the Israeli State Archives in Jerusalem. He wrote to her every day during the affair, and often more – they make a pathetic, rather squalid read.
6. Clifford, *Counsel to The President*; Truman's diaries, Harry S. Truman Library.
7. Ben Gurion, *Recollections*, p. 355.
8. Martin Gilbert, *Churchill and the Jews*, Henry Holt, 2007.
9. Dalton in Cabinet, TNA: CAB 128/10.321.
10. Bullock, *Ernest Bevin*, pp. 688–93.

## 24. 'Listen World. This Is Crossroads.'

1. Cameron, *Points of Departure*, pp. 93–5.
2. Lincoln quote, letter to Truman, 1 September 1945, WO 165.8. 1. 233, National Archives, Washington, DC; Forrestal quote, Clifford, *Counsel to the President*, p. 396; Ambrose, *Eisenhower*.
3. Yergin, *Shattered Peace*, p. 238.
4. Holloway, *Stalin and the Bomb*, p. 322.
5. Dallek, *The Lost Peace*, p. 165, and Yergin, *Shattered Peace*, p. 228.
6. Acheson, *Present at the Creation*, p. 277.
7. Ibid., p. 280.
8. Ray Monk, *Robert Oppenheimer: A Life at the Centre*, Doubleday, 2013.
9. Harris, *Attlee*, p. 383.

10. Yergin, *Shattered Peace*, p. 355; Miscamble, *From Roosevelt to Truman*, p. 244.
11. Stimson to Truman, Correspondence, 46, Truman Library.
12. Bullock, *Ernest Bevin*, p. 525.
13. Ibid., p. 530.
14. Yergin, *Shattered Peace*, p. 366.
15. Ibid., p. 368.


### 25. The Glory of France: 'Resistance in the Heart'

1. The Koestler–Sartre story is told in Beevor and Cooper, *Paris After the Liberation*, pp. 300–2, and in Celia Goodman (ed.), *Living with Koestler, Mamaine Koestler's Letters 1945–1951*, St Martin's Press, 1985.
2. George Orwell, 'Politics and the English Language', *Horizon*, March 1946.
3. Quoted in Bullock, *Ernest Bevin*, p. 535.
4. Quoted in Offner, *Another Such Victory*, p. 276.
5. On Charles de Gaulle and the rebuilding of France see Fenby, *The General*, pp. 277–340; Beevor and Cooper, *The Liberation of Paris*; Robert Aron, *L'Histoire de la Libération de La France*, Fayard, 1959; Charles de Galut, *Le Salut, 1944–1946*, Plon, 1962; André Malraux, *Antimémoires*, Gallimard, 1967; and Hitchcock, *France Restored*.
6. Kennan letter to Charles Bohlen, 20 July 1945, quoted in Isaacson and Thomas, *The Wise Men*, p. 306, and in Yergin, *Shattered Peace*, p. 288.
7. Letter to Diana Mosley, 9 August 1946, in Beevor and Cooper, *The Liberation of Paris*, p. 296, and Charlotte Mosley (ed.), *The Mitfords: Letters Between Six Sisters*, Harper Perennial, 2008.
8. Quoted in Judt, *Postwar*, p. 132.
9. Quoted in Beevor and Cooper, *The Liberation of Paris*, p. 325.

10. For the post-liberation 'purge' in France see Judt, *Postwar*,
    pp. 112–16, Hitchcock, *France Restored*, and Aron, *L'Histoire de la
    Libération de La France*, pp. 235–45.
11. Mitford to Waugh, 21 October 1946, in Charlotte Mosley (ed.),
    *The Letters of Nancy Mitford and Evelyn Waugh*, Penguin,
    London, 2010.
12. Beevor and Cooper, *The Liberation of Paris*, pp. 243–5.
13. Ambassador Caffery to the State Department, 30 September 1946,
    FRUS, vol. 5, p. 776.
14. Simone de Beauvoir, *Force of Circumstance* (trans. Richard
    Howard), Penguin, 1968, p. 455.
15. Quoted in Judt, *Postwar*, p. 184.

## 26. Stalin's Turkish Bluff

1. In Thomas, *Armed Truce*, p. 163.
2. Chuev, *Molotov Remembers*, p. 194.
3. Acheson, *Present at the Creation*, p. 306.
4. Ibid., p. 308.
5. Dallek, *The Lost Peace*, p. 216.
6. Acheson, *Present at the Creation*, p. 309.
7. Chuev, *Molotov Remembers*, p. 196.
8. Sudoplatov, *Special Tasks*, p. 353.

## 27. The Bloodbath in Calcutta

1. Khan, *The Great Partition*, pp. 114–18, and French, *Liberty or
   Death*, pp. 288–92.
2. Khan, *The Great Partition*, p. 120.
3. Wavell, *The Viscount's Journal*, entry 19 August 1946.
4. In French, *Liberty or Death*, p. 293.
5. *The Times*, 20 August 1946.

6. In Moon, *Divide and Quit*, p. 133.
7. In Joseph Lelyveld, *Great Soul: Mahatma Gandhi and his Struggle with India*, Knopf, 2011.
8. In Wolpert, *Gandhi's Passion*, p. 266, and Tunzelmann, *An Indian Summer*, p. 194.
9. Harris, *Attlee*, p. 345 and also a point made by Patrick French, Penderel Moon and Lord Wavell in their accounts.
10. Brown, *Nehru*, p. 396.
11. French, *Liberty or Death*, p. 397.

## 28. 'Half-Nun, Half-Whore'

1. A version of Zhdanov's speech appeared in *Pravda* on 20 August 1946.
2. The 'Librarian' remark ascribed to Beria by his son Sergo in *My Father*, p. 144.
3. Alliluyeva, *Twenty Letters to a Friend*, p. 157.
4. Sebag Montefiore, *Stalin*, p. 488.
5. Ibid., p. 496.
6. Gellately, *Stalin's Curse*, p. 297.

## 29. The Return of the King

1. Sissons and French, *Age of Austerity*, p. 119.
2. Bevin quote in Hugh Thomas, *Armed Truce*, p. 338; Ambassador MacVeagh quotes, FRUS, vol. 5, p. 674, and in Iatrides, *Ambassador MacVeagh Reports*, p. 64.
3. Iatrides, *Ambassador MacVeagh Reports*, p. 53.
4. In Melvyn Leffler and David Paynter (eds.), *The Origins of the Cold War*, Routledge, 2005, p. 135.
5. Ibid., p. 136. The corruption of the Greek Government is also described well in Offner, *Another Such Victory*, and André

Gerolymatos, *Red Acropolis, Black Terror: the Greek Civil War and the Origins of Soviet–American Rivalry, 1943–1949*, Basic Books, 2004.

6. Leffler and Paynter, *The Origins of the Cold War*, p. 137.
7. TNA: FO 371/634/47 and in Yergin, *Shattered Peace*, p. 334.
8. George Orwell, 'You and the Atomic bomb', *Tribune*, 19 October 1945.

## 30. 'Sand Down a Rat-Hole'

1. FRUS, vol. 10, p. 656 and Marshall, *Mission to China*.
2. Fenby, *The Penguin History of Modern China*, p. 384.
3. Truman letter to Chiang, 18 August 1946, FRUS, vol. 10, p. 778; 'Sand down a rat-hole' comment to Clifford, in *Counsel to the President*, p. 487.
4. Dun J. Li, *Modern China: From Mandarin to Commissar*, Scribner, 1978.
5. Jung Chang and Jon Halliday, *Mao*, p. 253.
6. Fenby, *The Penguin History of Modern China*, p. 304 and Chang and Halliday, *Mao*, p. 277.
7. Vladislav Zubok, *Inside the Kremlin*, p. 368.
8. Fenby, *The Penguin History of Modern China*, p. 307 and Li, *Modern China*, p. 399.
9. Chang and Halliday, *Mao*, p. 356.
10. Marshall, *Mission to China*, vol. 2, p. 498.

## 31. The General Orders – Democracy

1. J. K. Galbraith, *A Life in Our Times: Memoirs*, André Deutsch, 1981; Colonel Charles Kades interview with Professor Jonathan Hapey, George Washington University, recorded 23 May 1989, on YouTube.

2. Charles Kades, 'The American Role in Revising Japan's Imperial Constitution', *Political Science Quarterly*, 1989, vol. 104, no. 2.

3. Courtney Whitney, *MacArthur: His Rendezvous With History*, Knopf, 1956, pp. 249–55; a Japanese account of the meeting is in Soseki Soichi, *The Birth of Japan's Postwar Constitution* (trans. Ray Moore), Westview Press, 1997.

4. Kades, 'The American Role'.

5. MacArthur, *Reminiscences*, p. 376.

6. *Jiji Shimpo*, 25 September 1946.

7. Dower, *Embracing Defeat*, pp. 410–40, provides an overview of SCAP's censorship procedures. The scholar Eizaburo Okuizumi compiled an almost complete list of the thousands of items censored by the SCAP authorities, on microfilm at the University of Maryland East Asia Collection, College Park. The short list is on pp. 41–2.

8. Harvey, *American Shogun*, p. 215.

9. Dower, *Embracing Defeat*, p. 186.

10. Army Reports to MacArthur, vol. 3, p. 290, National Archives, Washington, DC.

11. Ibid., vol. 2, p. 128.

12. Ibid., vol. 3, pp. 409–11.

13. Dower, *Embracing Defeat*, pp. 435–75, provides an excellent account of the Tokyo trials. There is a full transcript of the conclusions of the proceedings in *The Tokyo Judgment: The International Military Tribunal for the Far East*, Amsterdam University Press, 1977, available at the Library of Congress, Washington, DC.

14. Interview with General Elliott Thorpe on 29 May 1977, at MacArthur Memorial, Norfolk, Virginia, Box 6.

15. *The Tokyo Judgment*, vol. 2, p. 235.

16. Dower is excellent on the war criminals that got away; *Embracing Defeat*, pp. 520–53.

17. Ibid., pp. 540–2.

## 32. The Big Freeze

1. Christopher Isherwood, *The Lost Years 1945–51: A Memoir*, HarperCollins, 2000; Churchill's famous speech at Zurich University, 19 September 1946, taken to be for or against a united states of Europe, depending on one's attitude to the EU.

2. Isherwood, *The Lost Years*, p. 176.

3. James Lees Milne, *Diaries, 1942–1954*, John Murray, 2007.

4. Nancy Mitford to Diana Mosley, 25 January 1947, quoted in Beevor and Cooper, *Paris After the Liberation*, p. 287; Janet Flanner, *Paris Journal: 1944–1955*, Mariner Books, 1988. Selection of *New Yorker* pieces, column 29, January 1946.

5. Bill Wyman quote in Kynaston, *Austerity Britain*, p. 194.

6. Quoted in Judt, *Postwar*, p. 131.

7. Acheson, *Present at the Creation*, p. 144.

## Epilogue

1. Alexis de Tocqueville, *Democracy in America*, Penguin Classics, 1998, p. 266.

2. Acheson, *Present at the Creation*, p. 109.

3. Lovett quote, FRUS, 1947, vol. 5, p. 567.

# Index

# Index

MacVeagh, Lincoln 342
Maisky, Ivan 126
Malenkov, Georgi 31
Malinovsky, Rodion 351
Manhattan Project 25, 26, 64, 306, 309
Mao Zedong 152, 154, 157–9, 160–1, 348, 349–50
Marcuse, Herbert 235*n*
Marshall, General George 152–3, 161–2, 347, 349–50, 352–3, 369
Marshall Plan 369–70
Marxism 91
Masanobu, Tsuji 365
May, Alan Nunn 65
Menon, V. P. 333
Metaxas, Ioannis 252, 253, 341
Michael, King 167
Mikołajczyk, Stanisław 174, 175, 176, 179
Mikoyan, Anastas 27
Ministry of Food 67
Misaka, Prince 96
*Missouri*, USS 192
Mitford, Nancy 317, 320, 368
Mitsubishi 361
*Modern Times* 205
Molotov, Vyacheslav 23, 25, 28, 193, 198, 304, 350
  and Greece 257
  humiliation of by Stalin 32–3
  and Poland 173, 175, 181
  on Stalin 30
  and Turkey 323, 324
  view of by Churchill 156
Monopol-Grimberg mine accident (Germany) 36–7
Monroe Doctrine 177
Montand, Yves 318
Montgomery, Field Marshal Bernard 35, 36, 42, 223, 230, 271, 273, 281, 297
Moon, Major Arthur 50
Moon, Sir Penderel 204
Morgan, Lieutenant-General Sir Frederick 58

Morgenthau, Henry 39, 40
Morrison, Herbert 275–6, 299
Mountbatten, Edwina 207
Mountbatten, Lord Louis 334, 335
Mournier, Emmanuel 290
Moyne, Lord (Walter Guinness) 280
Munich 38–9
Munich Conference (1938) 171
Murdoch, Iris 221
Murphy, Robert 44, 229
Murray, Wallace 8, 194, 195, 196
Muslim League 202–3, 204, 210, 332

Nagasaki 25, 360
Naidu, Padmaja 207
al-Nashashibi, Ragheb 272
National Liberation Front *see* EAM
National Republican League (EDES) 252
Nazis 6, 37, 38, 45, 59, 119, 125, 129, 132–3, 139, 166, 183, 225, 261, 263, 276, 278, 296, 317, 371 *see also* de-Nazification
Nehru, Jawaharlal 205–8, 212, 213, 332, 334
Neumann, Gunther 50
*New Statesman* 75
Nicolson, Harold 78
NKVD 23, 63, 120, 125, 127, 182
Nobusuke, Kishi 366
Novikov, Air Marshal Aleksandr 141–2
Nowakowski, Tadeusz
  *Camp of All Saints* 224
nuclear weapons *see* atomic bomb
Nuremberg trials (1946) 241–4, 363

*Odrodzenie* (magazine) 287
OGPI 258
Okulicki, General Leopold 181
O'Neill, Con 229
Operation Paperclip 244
Operation Pincher 324–5
opium trade (China) 158–9
Oppenheimer, J. Robert 306
Orwell, George 313, 345